CARING FOR THE MILITARY

With overseas military deployment scaling down in recent years, helping professionals need practical tools for working with servicemen and women returning from deployment. *Caring for the Military*, with its case studies and clinical discussions, is indispensable for social workers and other behavioral health professionals working with these populations. Leading experts contribute chapters on the challenges faced by reintegrating members of the military, including returning to a family, entering the workforce, and caring for those with PTSD, TBI, and moral injury. This text also features unique chapters on telemental health, multidisciplinary settings, and caregiver resiliency.

Joan Beder DSW is a professor in the Wurzweiler School of Social Work at Yeshiva University in New York. She has been a clinical social worker for over 30 years and maintains a private clinical practice in Long Island, NY. She has published extensively on issues related to the military, bereavement, and medical social work and presented at numerous national and international conferences on a variety of topics.

CARING FOR THE MILITARY

A Guide for Helping Professionals

Edited by Joan Beder DSW

Routledge
Taylor & Francis Group

NEW YORK AND LONDON

First published 2017
by Routledge
711 Third Avenue, New York, NY 10017

and by Routledge
2 Park Square, Milton Park, Abingdon, Oxon OX14 4RN

Routledge is an imprint of the Taylor & Francis Group, an informa business

Library of Congress Cataloging in Publication Data
Names: Beder, Joan, 1944- editor of compilation.
Title: Caring for the military : a guide for helping professionals / edited by Joan Beder, DSW.
Description: New York, NY : Routledge, [2016] | Includes bibliographical references and index.
Identifiers: LCCN 2016001142| ISBN 9781138119512 (alk. paper) | ISBN 9781138119529 (alk. paper) | ISBN 9781315652276 (alk. paper)Subjects: LCSH: Soldiers--Mental health services--United States. | Veterans--Mental health--United States. | Veterans--Mental health services--United States. | Families of military personnel--Services for--United States. | Veteran reintegration--United States.
Classification: LCC UH629.3 .C39 2016
DDC 362.860973--dc23
LC record available at http://lccn.loc.gov/2016001142

ISBN: 978-1-138-11951-2 (hbk)
ISBN: 978-1-138-11952-9 (pbk)
ISBN: 978-1-315-65227-6 (ebk)

Typeset in Bembo
by Taylor & Francis Books

Printed and bound in the United States of America by Publishers Graphics, LLC on sustainably sourced paper.

This volume is dedicated to those who serve in our military and to the devoted professionals who care for them. We have been engaged in active warfare for over a decade and for those who have given tirelessly in this endeavor, we are deeply grateful. It is hoped that this volume will enable a broader understanding of needed care for our military, and that it will both inspire and educate helping professionals to best serve our military. I wish to thank family, friends, and colleagues who have encouraged my efforts to complete this work and have always been supportive and appreciative of all I have accomplished. And, of course, to Matthew who has found the most special place in my heart.

CONTENTS

FIGURES

TABLES

PREFACE

In 2007 I watched the James Gandolfini HBO documentary *Alive Day*. In the film, Mr. Gandolfini interviewed ten service members who had returned from Iraq. All had sustained serious wounding of both body and mind. Gandolfini had no presence in the film as he served as the interviewer. Alive Day refers to the day each person realized that they had survived their injuries, that they were in fact alive and the day was to be celebrated. Each service member's story was presented with film footage prior to the service member having been injured and some footage showing explosions and details of their actual injury. During the final part of each interview, Gandolfini asked what their plans were for their future. It is/ was impossible to not be deeply moved by the stories, courage, resilience, and grit of each of those interviewed. I was profoundly impacted by what I saw in the film and made the decision to endeavor to learn as much as I could about the experience of military service and, as a social work educator, to learn what service providers needed to know to help our military.

Up until this point in my life, I had no knowledge or understanding of military life or military care. In 2007, I began a journey of travel across the United States, visiting military bases and Department of Veterans Affairs (VA) and Department of Defense hospitals. I interviewed hundreds of behavioral health practitioners and many active duty and Veteran status service members. It was a very rich, inspiring, and somewhat daunting experience. What I have learned has helped me to appreciate the complexity of military life and care.

In my first book, *Advances in Social Work Practice with the Military* (Routledge, 2012), I asked many of the professionals I met throughout my travels to contribute to the book with a focus on deployment and issues related to areas of care for our returnees. This book has a slightly different focus: the United States has begun to reduce troop strength in Iraq and Afghanistan which has resulted in many more of our service members returning home and facing reintegration issues. As such, authors were asked to keep the focus on what it means to be returning home and dealing with the emotional and physical changes to them and within their families.

Caring for the Military: A Guide for Helping Professions is divided into three parts: Military Culture and Transitions, Special Populations, and Clinical Challenges and Perspectives.

I have learned that it is impossible to understand most things military without a full understanding of the unique culture of the military. This opening part explains the culture and transitions, exploring the challenges faced by the returnee after military service. The part on special populations looks at a number of groupings within the military that present with needs that do not often get acknowledged. The authors have offered a rich collection of observations of their population and have provided guidance in management and care of these often overlooked groups. The third part, on clinical challenges and perspectives, focuses on service providers and some of their needs. It takes a step back and looks at more broad-based needs of the military.

Each author has expertise and experience that has proved invaluable in furthering our understanding of the routes to caring for those injured in both body and mind through their military service. The final chapter in the volume makes a strong assertion that 'carers' have to be cared for in order to do their best work.

It has been an honor and a privilege to work with so many gifted and dedicated professionals who wrote the various chapters. Each is an expert in their field and each has given generously of their time, and put up with the back and forth of editing, to further the knowledge base of those who will care for our military. For this generosity and expertise, I am grateful. What each has contributed to the understanding of the issues faced by our service members will enable a level of care earned and deserved by our military men and women.

ABOUT THE EDITOR

Joan Beder DSW is Professor at Yeshiva University's Wurzweiler School of Social Work in New York City. She has been teaching social work students for over 25 years in both clinical and generalist practice tracks. Her research interests have focused on medical social work as well as issues related to death and dying and grief and bereavement. Over the last several years she has been deeply immersed in issues related to the care of the US military with particular focus on how social work can address the needs of the military. She has presented at numerous national and international conferences on issues related to the military and other areas of social work practice. Her work has been published in numerous peer-reviewed journals and in several social work texts. Her books include *Voices of Bereavement: A Casebook for Grief Counselors* (2004); *Medical Social Work: The Interface of Medicine and Caring* (2006). Dr. Beder was co-editor of *Community Health Care in Cuba* (2010) and editor of *Advances in Social Work Practice with the Military* (2012).

CONTRIBUTORS

David L. Albright (PhD, MSW) is Associate Professor and the Hill Crest Foundation Endowed Chair in Mental Health Research at the University of Alabama. He is a military Veteran and former research fellow with both the DVA and the RAND Corporation's Center for Military Health Policy Research. His scholarship primarily focuses on health promotion and behavioral change among military personnel, Veterans, their families and communities, and the organizations that support them. Dr. Albright has a particular interest in understanding the consequences and correlates of military service that include social determinants and related conditions that influence the health and mental health of Veterans and their dependents, as well as the services that would best meet their needs, across service delivery systems, including criminal justice, medical, and postsecondary institutions.

Joan Beder (DSW, MSW, LCSW) is Professor at the Yeshiva University's Wurzweiler School of Social Work in New York City. She has written extensively on issues related to the military and is the editor of *Advances in Social Work Practice with the Military*. She has spoken at dozens of international and national conferences and has an extensive publication record in military social work and other areas of social work practice. In 2011, Dr. Beder was awarded a Fulbright scholarship to teach military social work in Israel at the Hebrew University. She has been teaching at Wurzweiler for over 20 years, specializing in clinical social work practice.

Yvette Branson (PhD, ME) is Coordinator of Veterans Integration to Academic Leadership and a VA New York Harbor Healthcare System clinical psychologist, working with student Veterans on college campuses. As a psychologist, Dr. Branson's expertise is supportive of those who need guidance in reestablishing a footing in civilian life. Dr. Branson also has a personal interest in the issue of stigma and barriers within our community to seeking help. She is a daughter of an Army Air Corp Tail Gunner and is particularly grateful to the Tuskgee Airmen who protected her father on his 52 missions.

Gabrielle N. Bryen, LTC (LCSW) is a graduate of the University of Pennsylvania School of Social Work. She served a career as an active-duty Army Social Work officer. She has co-authored several behavioral health articles for military publications and written articles about clinical social work for the popular press, including *More* magazine and the *Baltimore Sun*.

Julie Canfield (PhD, CSW) is a clinical social worker specializing in providing treatment and behavioral health services to Veterans and military families in her community. Dr. Canfield is also an adjunct faculty member at Boston College School for Social Work where she developed and teaches two related courses titled "Families Impacted by Military Service" and "Veterans' Health and Mental Health." She is also the spouse of a Veteran who served in two combat-related deployments to Afghanistan during their marriage.

Cory Chen (PhD) is a clinical psychologist and psychotherapy researcher at the VA New York Harbor Healthcare System – Manhattan Campus and an Assistant Clinical Professor in the Department of Psychiatry at NYU. He specializes in the testing and development of psychotherapeutic interventions with a particular interest in family caregiving, depression, and anxiety disorders. Dr. Chen received a PhD from UNC-Chapel Hill and completed his psychoanalytic training at the William Alanson White Institute.

Jose E. Coll (PhD) was born in Havana, Cuba and migrated to the US in the 1980s. After serving as a noncommissioned officer in the US Marine Corps, he completed a bachelor's and master's degree in social work and a PhD in counseling education and supervision from the University of South Florida. Dr. Coll has held various administrative positions including Chair of Military Social Work at the University of Southern California, founder of the USC San Diego Academic Center, Chair of the Department of Social Work at Saint Leo University, and founder and director of the office of Veteran student services at Saint Leo University. He is the author and co-editor of numerous publications, including: *The Counselors Primer for Counseling Veterans*; co-editor of *The Handbook of Military Social Work*, and *Student Veterans in Higher Education: A Primer for Administrators, Faculty, and Advisors*. He is a graduate of the University of California, Berkeley, Executive Leadership Academy, Harvard University Institute for Management Development Program, and an American Council on Education Fellow.

George M. Cuesta (PhD) is a graduate of the US Military Academy at West Point, NY. He served as a captain in the US Army on active duty (1978–1985). He completed an M.Ed. in counseling from Boston University and a PhD in clinical psychology from the California School of Professional Psychology, San Francisco. He completed a postdoctoral residency in clinical neuropsychology at the San Francisco General Hospital and Medical Center. He served as a clinical psychologist in the Active Army Reserves (1999–2004) and was deployed for six months in 2003 with the 883rd Medical Company (Combat & Operational Stress Control) to Iraq. Dr. Cuesta currently works as a neuropsychologist with the VHA in Manhattan.

Tara DeBraber (M.Ed., MSW, LCSW, C-ASWCM, AFC) currently works for the US Navy as a social work case manager in the primary care department of a naval branch health clinic. She primarily provides supportive counseling and assistance with navigating the military health system for active-duty service members engaged with mental health services until they return to full duty, or separate from military service. She also assists Tricare Prime beneficiaries with complex medical needs in navigating the healthcare system. This includes assistance with referral management and coordination of care to ensure cost-effective and timely access to care. She has previously worked for the San Diego VA as part of a homeless outreach demonstration program and as the outpatient social worker for a primary care clinic. Tara is also a military spouse.

Charles R. Figley (PhD) is the Tulane University Paul Henry Kurzweg, MD Distinguished Chair in Disaster Mental Health and Associate Dean for Research, Co-Founder of Disaster Resilience Leadership Academy in the School of Social Work, and Director of the award-winning Traumatology Institute. He is a former professor at both Purdue University (1974–1989) and then at Florida State University (1989–2008) and former Fulbright Fellow and Visiting Distinguished Professor at the Kuwait University (2003–2004). In 2014 Dr. Figley received the John Jay College of Criminal Justice honorary degree of doctor of letters, honoris causa. He has published more than 160 refereed journal articles and 25 books. He is founding editor of the *Journal of Traumatic Stress, Journal of Family Psychotherapy*, and the international journal, *Traumatology*. He is also founding editor of the Book Series Death and Trauma (Taylor & Francis), Innovations in Psychology (CRC Press), and continues to work as editor of the Psychosocial Stress Book Series (Routledge).

Kari L. Fletcher (PhD, MSW, LICSW) is Assistant Professor and Coordinator of Area of Emphasis in Military Practice at the St. Catherine University-University of St. Thomas School of Social Work. Dr. Fletcher received her PhD in social work from Smith College and her MSW from Widener University. Her direct practice experience with military-connected population across age cohorts spans 16 years and includes affiliations with the VA (as a clinical social worker, 2000–2010), Vet Center (as an external consultant in Brooklyn Park, MN, 2014–present), and Military OneSource (as a psychotherapist in private practice, 2015–present). Her scholarship focuses on support systems for military-connected populations, including clinical practice, higher education, and outside of military-supported settings.

Sarah S. Fraley (PhD) is a staff psychologist in the Spinal Cord Injury/Disorders Service at the Long Beach VA Healthcare System and director of the Spinal Cord Injury Peer Mentor Program. Her clinical and research interests include psychological correlates of physical health problems, women's mental health, positive sexuality, and living with disability. Her professional publications have focused on women's health issues, positive sexual expression across the lifespan, and various issues affecting individuals with disabilities.

Eric S. Graybill, Captain (RN, CMSRN) is an eight-year active-duty Army Nurse Corps Officer. Captain Graybill currently serves as the Clinical Nursing Officer in charge of a Medical–Surgical–Pediatric unit at Blanchfield Army Community Hospital and has previously held diverse clinical and administrative positions. He recently returned from a ten-month deployment to the Middle East. Captain Graybill was accepted to the Army-Baylor MHA/MBA program and will begin his studies in May 2016.

Deborah Hino (MSW, BA) received her BA in psychology from the University of California, Irvine and MSW from the University of Southern California. Her focus of work and research is in the mental health community. She has worked as a therapist with military personnel and in the mental health field.

Christie Jackson (PhD) is a clinical psychologist and PTSD Team Lead at the Honolulu VA Medical Center. Dr. Jackson previously served as the Director of the PTSD Clinic at the Manhattan VA Medical Center. She is also a Clinical Assistant Professor of Psychiatry at the NYU School of Medicine. She obtained her PhD in clinical psychology from the University of North Dakota, and completed a postdoctoral fellowship in trauma and dissociative disorders at McLean Hospital. Dr. Jackson also maintains a private psychotherapy practice with specializations in complex trauma, personality disorders, and various forms of CBT, including STAIR and DBT.

Julie M. Landry-Poole (Psy.D, ABPP) is a board-certified clinical psychologist at the Warrior Resiliency Program, Regional Health Command-Central (Provisional), US Army. Dr. Landry-Poole is a former active-duty psychologist and Army Veteran. She has extensive experience consulting with behavioral health organizations to develop and implement process improvements for managing suicidal patients.

Sandra (Sandi) Laski (MSW, LICSW, M.Ed., LADC, DSW candidate) is a clinical social worker at the Minneapolis VA Health Care System. She has been an active advocate for sexual and gender minorities for over a decade. Ms. Laski serves as a consultant and educator on sexual and gender minority issues at the VA nationally, regionally, and locally. Through virtual technology, she is a member of the small team of VA providers who conduct national training under the direction of the National VHA Transgender Workgroup, Patient Care Services. Ms. Laski developed and published a nationwide VA Lesbian, Gay, Bisexual and Transgender Patient Support Group Directory for which she received national recognition through the VHA Diversity and Inclusion Office. Ms. Laski is currently working on her doctoral dissertation with a focus on mitigating health disparities for gender minorities.

Alexandria M. Lewis (MSW, LCSW) is a clinical instructor involved with teaching on the Military Social Work Graduate Certificate Program at the University of Missouri-Columbia. She received her MSW from the University of Missouri-Columbia. Ms. Lewis is a Veteran of the US Army, serving six years on active duty. She has research and practice experience in the field of gerontology; and research and volunteer experience in hospice care.

Kristen Leigh Maisano (OTD, OTR/L) graduated with a B.Sc. in psychology and an M.Sc. in occupational therapy in 2005. Kristen received her post-professional doctorate in occupational therapy at Boston University in May 2010. Dr. Maisano's work with the active-duty and Veteran populations included a focus on mild traumatic brain injury and PTSD. In addition, Kristen has assisted multiple organizations as a subject matter expert related to traumatic brain injury. Organizations include Brainline.org, Defense and Veterans Brain Injury Center, and Defense Centers of Excellence. Kristen is currently the Director of the Occupational Therapy Assistant Program at Trinity Washington University in Washington, DC and is an adjunct faculty member at the University of Scranton.

Brittany D. Martin (MA, M.Litt.) holds an MA from Boston University in psychology as well as an M.Litt. in international security from the University of St. Andrews. Currently, she works as a research health science specialist in the Center for Comprehensive Access & Delivery Research and Evaluation at the Iowa City VA Healthcare System. Her research areas include military families, psychosocial care, trauma, resilience, and child development and health in the national and international context.

Michelle A. Mengeling (PhD) is an affiliate investigator, VA Office of Rural Health, Veterans Rural Health Resource Center-Central Region and the Center for Comprehensive Access & Delivery Research and Evaluation; research scientist, University of Iowa, Carver College of Medicine. Her areas of expertise include survey development, measurement, and statistics. Her primary research interests are access to care, women's health, and measurement.

Ilysa R. Michelson (PhD) is a clinical psychologist at the DVA, NY/NJ region, who manages programs related to caregiver support, women's health, primary care, and patient-centered care. She specializes in treating Veterans in crisis and in primary care settings. Dr. Michelson received her doctorate from George Washington University in Washington, DC.

Don Moncrief is a Marine corps combat Veteran, having served in Iraq. He is pursuing an MSW degree at the University of Southern California, graduating in the spring of 2016. As a two-year board member of the University of Southern California's Military and Veteran Social Work Caucus, Mr. Moncrief is heavily involved in various philanthropies supporting active-duty military, the Veteran population, and their children and families. Mr. Moncrief is also a member of the Omicron Epsilon Chapter of the Phi Alpha Honor Society.

Bret A. Moore (Psy.D., ABPP) is a prescribing psychologist and board-certified clinical psychologist with the Warrior Resiliency Program, Regional Health Command-Central (Provisional), US Army. Dr. Moore is a former active-duty Army psychologist and veteran of Iraq. He has written extensively on topics relevant to military personnel and Veterans including PTSD and sleep disorders.

Kristi L. Mueller (Psy.D.) is a licensed psychologist and captain in the US Army, currently serving overseas in Afghanistan. She received her master's and doctoral degrees in clinical psychology from Argosy University, Hawaii campus and completed her internship and post-doctoral residency at Tripler Army Medical Center. As a military psychologist, Dr. Mueller has been stationed around the world including Hawaii, South Korea, Texas, and Afghanistan. She is supported by her husband Peter and children Chloe and Julian.

Lynette Pujol (PhD) is a clinical psychologist who performs regional tele-behavioral health services for active-duty military members. Dr. Pujol is a fellowship-trained health psychologist and has published in the area of chronic pain, including online self-management of chronic pain. She has presented at national conferences on the implementation of and satisfaction with tele-behavioral health services.

Kimberly A. Rorie (BS) is currently finishing her MSW at St. Catherine University-University of St. Thomas School Social Work. She has been a research assistant in military social work for two years. Prior to work on her MSW, Kim earned a master's degree in women's history from the University of Illinois at Chicago.

Anne G. Sadler (PhD) is a core researcher in the Center for Comprehensive Access & Delivery Research and Evaluation and an associate professor in the Department of Psychiatry, University of Iowa, Carver College of Medicine. She is a marital and family therapist in the mental health service line at the Iowa City VA Healthcare system. Her funded research has focused on risk factors for and prevention of sexual violence in military populations, health impact of deployment and assault related exposures, and eHealth interventions to improve Veterans' access to care.

Hannah Stryker-Thomas, CPT (MSW) is the Behavioral Health Officer for the 1st Sustainment Brigade, 1st Cavalry Division and Graduate of the University of Southern California School of Social Work.

Pauline A. Swiger (MSN, CNL, CMSRN) is a 15-year active-duty Army Nurse Corps Officer. Major Swiger has held diverse clinical, administrative, and educational positions within military nursing and has been deployed twice. Currently, Pauline is a doctoral student at the University of Alabama at Birmingham with research interests in nursing work environments, nursing care quality, patient outcomes, and nursing workload.

Diane L. Vaccarell (MS, LMFT) earned an M.Sc. from the University of New Hampshire in family studies: marriage and family therapy in 1999. She is a level II certified EMDR therapist and areas of specialty include anxiety, trauma, and medical family therapy. She is a clinical fellow in the American Association for Marriage and Family Therapy and has been a licensed marriage and family therapist in the State of New Hampshire since 2002. Prior to founding a private group practice in 2004, Diane was a regional director at a statewide non-profit counseling agency. She has been a professional conduct investigator and in 2014 was appointed by the Governor of NH to the New Hampshire Board of Mental Health Practice.

Carissa van den Berk-Clark (Pd.D., MSW) is currently an assistant professor of family and community medicine at Saint Louis University. Dr. van den Berk-Clark has extensive clinical and research expertise in homeless populations, including a four-year evaluation study of permanent supportive housing programs in the Los Angeles, California neighborhood referred to as "Skid Row." She has also gained extensive experience working with the Los Angeles DVA where she evaluated a number of different emerging homeless programs for integrated health, temporary housing and justice services. Her postdoctoral training via an NIDA T32 grant focused specifically on the implementation of aftercare programs for graduates of substance-abuse treatment centers and on implementation of motivational interviewing and harm reduction interventions.

Eugenia L. Weiss (Psy.D., LCSW) is an educator and a California licensed clinical social worker and licensed psychologist. She is clinical associate professor at the University of Southern California, School of Social Work and is currently serving as the Director of the Orange County Academic Center. She maintained a private practice for 18 years working with military personnel and their families. She is the author and co-author of multiple peer-reviewed journal publications and is co-author of a book titled *A Civilian Counselor's Primer to Counseling Veterans* and co-editor of several books; *Handbook of Military Social Work, Supporting Veterans in Higher Education: A Primer for Administrators, Faculty and Academic Advisors; Transformative Social Work Practice.* Weiss is currently working on co-editing *The Civilian Lives of US Veterans: Issues and Identities.* Her research interests include military/Veteran behavioral health, diversity in social work practice and higher education.

Grace W. Yan (PhD, ABPP) is a board-certified, licensed psychologist working in the New Jersey VA Health Care System. Dr. Yan completed her doctoral education at Rutgers, the State of University, and has been working in the VHA since 2010. She has published articles on Veterans' health and is currently a primary care mental health integration psychologist at the East Orange VA. She specializes in evidence-based, time-limited therapy for Veterans using an integrated health approach. She is also the program evaluation lead at the Center For Health & Wellness in East Orange, and leads a team in the examination of processes and outcomes of new innovative programs at the center.

Jeffrey S. Yarvis (PhD, LCSW, BCD, ACSW) is a published social work and military scholar in the field of psychological trauma and has practiced internationally with disaster, domestic violence, child abuse, sexual abuse, accident, and war-induced trauma across many different cultures and populations. Dr. Yaris received numerous honors for his humanitarian efforts, including the 2008 Uniformed Services Social Worker of the Year, 2008 US Army Social Worker of the Year, 1997 ISTSS/TX Mental Health Professional of the Year, Randolph High School (NJ) Hall of Fame, and numerous decorations including the Bronze Star Medal, Combat Action Badge, induction into the Order of Military Medical Merit. He received the US Army's Alpha proficiency designator as a full professor and military scholar in social work. COL Yarvis is adjunct faculty for University of Southern California military social work program – Virtual Academic Center and visiting professor for the Institute for Clinical Social Work. He is currently the Deputy Commander of one of the Army's premier medical centers.

PART I

The World of the Military: Culture and Transitions

1

MILITARY CULTURAL COMPETENCY

Yvette Branson

"No one understands," they say, "nobody cares about us."

"They make too many assumptions about who we are!"

"When I'm angry and they know I am a Vet, they think it's PTSD. My anger has more to do with my childhood than the military."

These are some of the comments we hear when we press OIF/OEF Veterans to tell us what they are experiencing while transitioning to civilian life. (OIF/OEF = Operation Iraqi Freedom and Operation Enduring Freedom, terms used by the military to refer to recent military campaigns in Iraq and Afghanistan.) Perhaps the biggest desire of US returning Veterans is to feel like everyone else, to blend in. The eventual realization that they are different can be helpful and disturbing. While in combat, they may have an idealized longing for the comforts of home. Once they separate from the service and return home, it inevitably looks very different from those daydreams.

It is our job as civilian practitioners and citizens to help support the returnees as best we can. This requires effort on our part, though small compared with the risk and danger they face while serving this nation. We must do everything possible to understand the trials they dealt with emotionally, physically, and spiritually that will forever change them. The attention we give to become informed about military culture, enough to have even minimal competence when addressing Veterans, will go a long way.

This chapter will focus on the military culture and how it impacts our returnees. Nuances of the culture will be explored and certain areas of concern highlighted as we attempt to embrace our service members and honor their efforts.

Understanding Military Culture

To achieve military cultural competency, it may be useful to review the basics starting with the five branches of the armed services. Each branch of the service is unique in its combat role; likewise, a warrior's self-identity and group identity will vary according to the branch in which they have served. A seemingly innocuous reference to a sailor or marine as "soldier" has surprising consequences. Though Veterans are used to being mislabeled by civilians, an easy expression of our interest in who they are can be facilitated by knowing a few simple facts: the Army is the oldest service branch; founded in 1775, they operate under the Department of the Army and are referred to as Soldiers. The Navy and Marines were also founded in 1775, and they both operate under the Department of the Navy. Members of the Navy are referred to as Sailors, while members of the Marines are simply called Marines. (You may have heard the line "*Semper fidelis* – Always Faithful," which is the motto of the Marines specifically.) The Coast Guard was founded later, in 1790, and operates under the Department of the Navy or sometimes the Department of Defense (depending on federal mandate). Its members are referred to as Guardians or Coasties. The Air Force was founded in 1947 and was originally known as the Army Air Corps; they operate under the Department of the Air Force, and its personnel of any gender are referred to as Airmen.

There are benign prejudices that members of each branch tend to hold toward the other branches. Spend enough time with Veterans and you begin to learn the partisanships. Beyond the rivalry between branches, the distinctions within the rank and structure of the military hierarchy are important to grasp. There are three rank types: Commissioned Officers, Warrant Officers, and Enlisted. Commissioned Officers are among the highest ranks; similar to managers and executives of a corporation, they comprise 14% of the military. Warrant Officers are highly specialized subject matter experts and are 2% of the military. Enlisted personnel include noncommissioned officers, making up 84% of the military. There is a clear hierarchy and bureaucratic structure in the military; social status is clear as officers hold a higher status than enlisted personnel. Duties, responsibilities, pay, living arrangements, and social interactions are all determined by rank (Coll, Weiss, & Metal, 2013).

Commissioned Officers are appointed a rank after they complete Officer's Training School. There are several ways to become an Officer: to attend a Military Academy; to enroll at a college with a Reserve Officer Training Corps (ROTC) program; to attend Officer Candidate School (OCS) after graduating from college; or to receive a direct commission after earning a professional degree, for example an MD or PhD.[1]

All individuals who serve in the military are required to complete basic training, also called "boot camp" (slang used by the Navy and Marines, now commonly appropriated by fitness-crazed civilians). The boot camp experience is intense, demanding and has as a goal to transform the individual into a warrior. There is also the goal of creating cohesion within a unit between the trainees. This sense of cohesion often endures far beyond their military service. The interpersonal bonds that begin at boot camp are a central factor in the military culture.[2]

At boot camp the enlistees are introduced to the values, beliefs, traditions, norms, perceptions, and behaviors that govern how members of the armed forces think, communicate, and interact. It does not matter which branch one serves, the shared threads of all Veterans are reflected in the indoctrination and socialization of the military core values: honor, courage, loyalty, integrity, and commitment. These values serve as the standard of conduct for military personnel, regardless of whether the service member is in uniform (Coll et al., 2013).

Within the boot camp experience, unlike civilian culture, individuality is downplayed and the unit has central importance. From the point of arrival at boot camp, depersonalization occurs as apparent in the homogeneous uniforms and haircuts. The military environment is such that there is a clear understanding that an individual's purpose is to support the mission; individual achievement is important to the degree that it supports efficient and effective completion of the assigned task/mission and that in so doing, they put their life at risk (Exum, Coll, & Weiss, 2011).

Military recruits, or people who enlist, represent racially and socioeconomically diverse communities across the nation. In order to enlist, recruits must hold a high school diploma, the equivalent, or have scored above 50% on the Armed Forces Qualifying Test (AFQT). Those who join have many reasons for doing so. A good number seek the educational benefits offered through the GI Bill.[3]

In addition, many join because of patriotism, family tradition, and/or job scarcity in the US economy. Enlistment has supported many with the opportunities to gain employment and attend college, which may not previously have been possible.

All military personnel have a job specialty for which they go to training school after "basic." If you ask a Vet, "What was your MOS while you were active duty?," they will know you mean "Military Occupational Specialty," even though this is technically the term used only by the Army and Marine Corps. The Air Force goes by Air Force Specialty Code and the Navy's job designation is called Rating. This career training in the military is known as Advanced Individual Training (AIT), or "A" school by some of the branches. Examples of AIT training include Medic, Infantry, and Logistics. The author's nephew, for example, went to "A" school to become a linguist for the Navy, and is now fully employed as a professional translator.

Military training is dedicated to building professionalism and mastery while teaching its members basic skills as warriors. The training is physically and mentally challenging in order to create a disciplined corps, a corps that is warrior ready, and that "meets the challenges of combat and the mastery of fear."[4]

Houppert (2005) explains that basic training is not designed to move an adolescent into independence but rather to shift the recruit from independence on his/her family to dependence on the team: "the soldier must learn that he can trust no one but his buddies" (p. 84). This powerful commitment to the unit often creates difficulty at home with family members, especially when the family may be secondary to the unit/mission. Segal (1986) eloquently described this potential conflict in her article "The Military and the Family as Greedy Institutions." She discusses the 'military' and the 'family' as social institutions, noting that each institution depends on the loyalty and commitment of its members. But, all too often in military life, with its emphasis on the primacy of unit cohesion, the family becomes less valued/important or at a minimum the service member can predictably experience a conflict of loyalty. Once training is complete, the service member moves on to active duty placed within a unit. The demands of a total commitment to the military – typically a commitment to one's unit, the unit's mission, and its members – are the very essence of military unit cohesion (Martin & McClure, 2000).

While on active duty, a service member is considered a full-time employee who may be required to work 24/7. This active duty may be stateside or on a deployment. Before or after a deployment, the service member is stationed at their home installation. Not every service member you meet will have been deployed, but it is common to meet Veterans who have been on multiple deployments – three, four, or even five. A deployment is six to 15 months during which a service member will move from a home installation to a designated theater of operation, which may or may not be an active combat zone. If one's military service is part of the Reserve or National Guard, the service member is considered a part-time employee. They train one weekend a month and two weeks annually thus invoking the pejorative, "weekend warrior." Stresses on these personnel include the possibility of being called suddenly for active-duty deployments, leaving jobs, family, and community often on short notice. Some military personnel will continue to serve in the Reserve after finishing their active-duty contracts.

As with any culture the Military has its own "language" which often takes the form of an acronym. Military acronyms can be bland or colorful depending on their usage. The acronyms included here are meant to give a sense of what you may hear when in the vicinity of service members. An attempt to explain and provide an example will follow: BAH: Basic Allowance for Housing; FOB: Forward Operating Base (used in combat theater); GI: General Issue (belief that they are interchangeable); IED: improvised explosive device; JAG: Judge Advocate General (legal branch of military); MEDEVAC: MEDical EVACuation (air ambulance); MIA: Missing in Action (unknown whether alive or dead); MP: Military Police; PSYOP: Psychological Operations.

The IEDs we hear about in the news can best be explained as guerrilla warfare, small-scale actions against orthodox military, the US Armed Forces, in this case.[5] The IEDs are surprise hits that are devastating on morale and mortality rates. Highly stressful situations, such as an IED exploding randomly on a convoy, might not be interpreted by a service member as "combat." If the Vet was fired upon or targeted while on a convoy there may be serious damage inflicted on the unit yet if the Vet did not "discharge" his/her weapon they may not consider this experience combat! Regardless of personal acknowledgement of the dangers in which they served, civilians need to understand the traumatic potential of such a situation. The tendency to downplay traumatic experience is emblematic of these warriors.

Another example: if a service member's MOS is to provide support service to the mission, they may not leave the FOB and will sometimes be referred to as a FOBBIT (person who rarely leaves the FOB while deployed or has not "seen" combat). This term may sound derogatory, and it is meant to insult those who did work considered less important than a "Grunt" (general term for Infantry). While a Grunt may be in actual combat, kicking in doors while on "search and clear" missions, anyone other than a Grunt, or "Pogue" (Personnel Other than Grunt) might be on the FOB working on combat vehicles or computers, in support of the mission. Awareness of this hierarchy within enlisted circles is important as a service member may also underplay their role in the military by denigrating its significance. It may also breed arrogance and create distance between those who served. We can address this issue by reassuring any service member of the importance of service to their country, regardless.

The emphasis on group cohesion and bonding in all branches of the military can have a lasting effect on Veterans. Some may feel an acute loss of connection upon leaving the military leading to isolation and depression. Survival in the theater of war depends not only on the discipline and organization of the ranks but the intense relationships that develop during training. Trainings rely on teamwork, encapsulated in: "I got your back." This topic will be revisited when we discuss the Veteran upon transition out of the military.

Common military stressors and experiences while in the service include the wear and tear of the mission when one may become physically and mentally worn down. Lack of control of one's coming and going, exposure to combat or life-threatening situations, loss of a close friend or team member, limited access to food and water on deployment, the operational stress as a result of lack of sleep or rest, high expectations at all times, military sexual trauma, and harassment. These stressors when compounded by multiple and lengthy deployments can create a very onerous load to carry once expected to return to the civilian world.

One stressor to consider more thoroughly is that of the inner conflict and self-doubt that may arise at the onset of acculturation into the Armed Forces. This stress may be related to developmental considerations of late adolescence. Reflect for a moment upon the age group of those who are generally joining the military. The average age of those who enlist in the Army is 20.[6]

This latter part of adolescence, when there is an expectation that the change from childhood to adulthood will solidify, can also be a time of continued disorientation affecting one's sense of independence and self-identity.[7] Combine this with the demands of military training and the mix can be combustible.

The phenomenon of suicide among those recruits who have not seen combat is startling. We may equate suicides in the military to combat but statistics show that only 15% of the suicides were among those who were in combat (Reger et al., 2015). Who are the others and what accounts for the remainder of deaths? This information is very difficult to gather although the branches of the military and VA are continuing to improve their reporting methods. Each institution understands that in order to reduce the number of suicides, an accurate picture of who is dying is crucial (Joiner et al., 2009; Kemp, 2014; Kemp & Bossarte, 2012).

Data shows that those with less time in the service, and having legal or relationship problems tend to be among the highest numbers with completed suicides (Reger et al., 2015). This information can be helpful for providers to understand so that adequate support is offered to those with these particular issues. Those with less time in the service may be the same people who are asked to leave the military before their contracted commitments are completed due to injury, illness (emotional or physical), or disciplinary concerns. If this separation also leads to a less than honorable discharge on a member's DD214 (document of service and separation), then they would also be denied care at VA, no healthcare or educational benefits offered. This becomes complicated because these members would still be considered Veterans yet would be unable to access many of the benefits extended to those with an honorable discharge. These are the same people who would be seeking care in the community; they may also have higher rates of homelessness or prison time.

On the other hand, for the multitudes who leave the service honorably, access to the VA for healthcare (Veterans Health Administration (VHA)) has shown decreases in suicide rates in male VHA users relative to Veterans who do not utilize the VA for healthcare (Hoffmire, Kemp, & Bossarte et al., 2015). This statistic is critical for anyone in the civilian population to comprehend. Even if a Veteran prefers to regularly use non-VA providers, enrolling in the VA is an important protective factor. One significant service provided by VA that can be used anonymously by any Veteran, regardless of discharge status, is the Veterans Crisis Line (800-273-8255). Any service member, Veteran, family, friend, or member of the general public can use this line if they have questions or concerns about a Veteran.

Transitioning to the Civilian World

This section confronts how combat tour stressors can affect the transition back to civilian conventions. Transitioning individuals have reported that they could use a Civilian 101 class to help them understand nonmilitary individuals (reported to the author by student Veterans at a CUNY college, 2014). Veterans leave for battle at a tender age and become deeply embedded in military culture, etiquette, and ceremony. Upon return, ordinary civilian discourse can become confusing and even burdensome.

This may lead Veterans to feeling "lost" or "alone," like no one understands them. Many Veterans will say, "I want to go back to the war zone (Iraq or Afghanistan), being a civilian is too hard." We are talking about fearless warriors facing the challenges of ordinary life! The theater of war became their new "home," the place where they knew the rules and the comfort that brings. Lost or alone at "home" also relates to the comradery while in the military that has now dematerialized. This estrangement needs to be addressed by communities and families of our Veterans. College campuses, where many Veterans are transitioning and using their educational benefits, are prime places where these issues can be addressed.

Campuses, workplaces, and communities want to be considered Veteran friendly, because it seems like the right thing to do and cynically may also mean tuition dollars and tax incentives. But how aware are we of the myriad of transition issues that may arise at any given moment? Some questions we might ask, moving forward: Are there limitations in the functional capacity among some Veterans? How severe are they, how should they be handled? Are institutions creating cultures and policies that foster Veterans' resilience? Do we have adequate support services in place? Have we been trained sufficiently to work with the unique psychological problems associated with combat-related trauma? If not, who do we refer to? (800-273-8255 Veterans Crisis Line, is always a good start) (Rudd et al., 2011; Thiede & Vinatieri, 2014).

While not wanting to propagate the many negative stereotypes surrounding Veterans in transition, it is favorable and appropriate that we seek to understand the seriousness of the issues many Veterans face when they are readjusting to civilian life. We can readily deal with diagnoses but must also regard how the individual is grappling with the moral injuries inflicted by war. The inevitable transgressions and betrayals of bloody war: moral, spiritual, and religious, that lead to unpronounceable shame and guilt (Maguen et al., 2010; Shay, 1994, 2002).

An additional factor in caring for US service members is the reluctance many feel about seeking mental health services. It is not part of the warrior mindset to be weak, and, sadly, many still think of mental health issues as a sign of weakness. Returnees face numerous challenges post-active service including reintegration issues at home (settling back with family, children, etc., and the exigencies of home life), finding employment (many military skills are not necessarily utilized in civilian settings), potential issues related to service (PTSD, wounding), and other demands made during wartime. By allowing the stigma associated with accessing behavioral health services, many returnees will suffer in silence to the detriment of themselves and others.

In conclusion, while the Veterans are taught to be deeply loyal to their country and their fellow countrymen, they are often misunderstood. The more we can reassure them that we honor and respect them for their service, for which they take pride to the core of their being, even while agreeing about how hateful war is, the more they will be able to trust that we really care about their well-being. In addition, the strengths they carry from their time in service, their motivation, leadership, timeliness, preparedness, attention to detail, organization, and discipline are ultimately valuable for our society to grow and prosper. We, as professionals, need to familiarize ourselves with the nuances of military culture to best understand and serve our war heroes.

Notes

I would like to extend a special thank you to colleagues in the VA VITAL Initiative: Celina Dugas and Damien Bramlette.
1   http://todaysmilitary.com/joining/becomingamilitaryofficer
2   http://dictionary.reference.com/browse/boot+camp
3   www.heritage.org/research/reports/2006/10/who-are-the-recruits-the-demographic-characteristics-of-us-military-enlistment-2003-2005
4   www.hqmc.marines.mil/hrom/NewEmployees/AbouttheMarineCorps/Values.aspx
5   www.britannica.com/EBchecked/topic/248353/guerrillawarfare
6   www.usarec.army.mil/support/faqs.htm#age
7   www.psychologytoday.com/basics/adolescence

References

Coll, J., Weiss, E., & Metal, M. (2013). Military culture and diversity. In A. Rubin, E. Weiss, & J. Coll, (Eds.), *Handbook of military social work* (pp. 21–36). New York: Wiley.

Exum, H., Coll, J., & Weiss, E. L. (2011). *A civilian counselor's primer for counseling Veterans* (2nd ed.). Deerpark, NY: Linus.

Hoffmire, C. A., Kemp, J. E., & Bossarte (2015). Changes in suicide mortality for Veterans and non-Veterans by gender and history of VHA service use, 2000–2010. *Psychiatric Services*, 959–965.

Houppert, K. (2005). *Home fires burning: Married to the military for better or worse*. New York: Ballantine Books.

Joiner Jr, T. E., Van Orden, K., Witte, T., & Rudd, M. D. (2009). *The interpersonal theory of suicide, guidance for working with suicidal clients*. Washington, DC: US American Psychological Association. x246 dx. doi.org/10.1037/11869000

Kemp, J. (2014). *Suicide Rates in VHA patients through 2011 with comparisons with other Americans and other Veterans through 2010*. US Department of Veterans Affairs Mental Health Services Suicide Prevention Program.

Kemp, J. & Bossarte, M. (2012). Surveillance of suicide and suicide attempts among Veterans: addressing a national imperative. *American Journal of Public Health*, 102 Suppl., 4–5.

Maguen, S., Lucenko, B., Reger, M., Gahm, A., Litz, B., Seal, K. et al. (2010). The impact of reported direct and indirect killing on mental health symptoms in Iraq war Veterans. *Journal of Traumatic Stress*, 23(1), 86–93. doi: 10.10002/jts.20434

Martin, J. A. & McClure, P. (2000). Today's active duty military family: The evolving challenges of military life. In J. A., Martin, L. N. Rosen, & I. R. Sparacino (Eds.), *The military family: A practice guide for human service providers* (pp. 3–24). Westport CT: Praeger.

Reger, M. A., Smolenski, D. J., Skopp, N. A., & Metzger-Abamukang, M. J. (2015). Risk of suicide among US Military Service Members following Operation Enduring Freedom or Operation Iraqi Freedom Deployment and Separation from the US Military. *JAMA Psychiatry*, 72(6), 561–569. doi: 10.1001/jamapsychiatry.2014.3195

Rudd, D., Goulding, J., & Bryan, C. (2011). Student Veterans: A national survey exploring psychological symptoms and suicide risk. *Professional Psychology: Research and Practice*, 42(5), 354–360.

Segal, M. (1986). The military and the family as greedy institutions. *Armed Forces and Society*, 13(1), 19–38.

Shay, J. (1994). *Achilles in Vietnam*. New York: Scribner.

Shay, J. (2002). *Odysseus in America*. New York: Scribner.

Thiede, J. & Vinatieri, T. (2014). Veterans' Integration to Academic Leadership. Presentation at VA Psychology leadership conference.

2

MILITARY CULTURE AND VETERAN TRANSITION

Jose E. Coll and Eugenia L. Weiss

Transition is the process by which during a period of time something changes from one state or condition to another. The difficulty of transitioning for military personnel is when a desire to return to the more familiar stage (i.e. military service) is stronger than that of entering the new stage and joining the ranks of civilian society. By the end of 2015 it is expected that the total force for the US military will consist of 1,355,571 strong which is a mere representation of the force in 2010 which consisted of 3,017,414 (Defense Manpower Data Center, 2015). In 2015 the Army alone expected approximately 140,000 soldiers to attend the Army transition course which is intended to help soldiers transition out of the military and into civilian roles.

Veterans are by the nature of their training a homogeneous group made up of common values and a military culture which guides their daily interactions (Exum, Coll, & Weiss, 2011). While we speak of homogeneity, it should be noted that the military remains one of the most heterogeneous and diverse workplace environments in the country but remains skewed with a leadership profile that comprises predominantly white males.

A significant number of Veterans do well in their transition, particularly when they have a supportive social network, are able to secure employment, and have access to healthcare (Hoge, Auchterloine, & Milliken, 2006). However, in the metamorphosis that must occur from service member to civilian we must not lose sight or dismiss the possibilities of psychological invisibility or conceptual identity redevelopment as a result of readjustment challenges (Coll & Weiss, 2013).

For many Veterans, the transition to civilian society creates a psychological invisibility which can be defined as a sensation of depersonalization and a feeling of being overshadowed by stereotypical assumptions and prejudices. These assumptions are created by the media and society regarding postwar Veterans (Gross & Weiss, 2014). This psychological phenomenon can negatively impact our Veteran population with regard to stigmatization, particularly regarding post-traumatic stress disorder (PTSD). Unfortunately, most Veterans, whether disabled or not, will typically be viewed under the lens of negative stereotypes by their civilian counterparts possibly causing a sense of invisibility. Often these negative stereotypes are based in feelings about the war effort in general and are articulated against a returnee. This may be more damaging than we think and this *psychological invisibility*, as originally applied to racial minority groups in the US (Cho, Crenshaw, & McCall, 2013; Franklin & Boyd-Franklin, 2000), may be the catalyst for isolation, loss of self, depression, lack of trust, lack of attachment, and loneliness on the part of the military person. The invisibility is added to the already difficult act of separating from the military. We will propose addressing identity reformation and development through Chickering's (1969) model as applied to Veterans in a manner that may mitigate the potential effects of this invisibility.

It should be noted that there are more serious challenges that some Veterans face, including severe mental illness, substance abuse, suicide, and other problems often associated with wartime deployments that can compound the transition process (Hoge et al., 2004). This chapter will focus on what we consider to be the more "typical" transition processes from active-duty status, regardless of type of service (i.e. enlisted military, career military, National Guard, or Reserve forces) and will not focus on behavioral or health-related factors (nor are we addressing the specific challenges faced by those Veterans that are not eligible for Department of Veterans Affairs (VA) services and benefits as a result of a less than honorable discharge). This chapter will address common elements of transition and how culture, identity, education, and re-entry into the workforce play a role in the success of service member transition from the military into the civilian sector.

Military Culture

As a result of military downsizing, Veterans are currently transitioning into their communities by attending college and beginning a new career as part of the civilian workforce. Many of these Veterans participated in combat or in combat support positions in Iraq (OIF – Operation Iraqi Freedom), Operation New Dawn (OND – Iraq post-September 2010); and Afghanistan (OEF – Operation Enduring Freedom). And, as previously alluded to, the majority have not returned with pervasive mental health disorders (i.e. PTSD, depressive disorders, and other anxiety disorders); medical issues (i.e. traumatic brain injury and physical injuries) (Coll, Weiss, Draves, & Dyer, 2012; Tanielian & Jaycox, 2008). However, all Veterans, disabled and non-disabled, will need to learn how to navigate within their new environment (civilian society) and effectively utilize their military experience and culture in non-military settings (Hoge, 2010).

As human service providers, if we are to assist Veterans who are separating from active duty and seek to develop programs that help create a seamless transition, recognition should be placed first and foremost on establishing culturally responsive programs and services. Although there has been an increased interest in military culture and its implication to assisting service members with successful transition (Coll & Weiss, 2013), a gap remains in the skill and knowledge of service providers understanding military culture and their ability to effectively support military personnel and Veterans' adjustment issues (Coll, Weiss, Draves, & Dyer, 2012). This gap is particularly problematic today, given the increasing reliance on civilian and community-based practitioners to provide the needed behavioral health and other adjustment-related services to military personnel who are returning to their civilian lives. Estimates suggest that approximately 60% of Veterans do not turn to the VA for assistance (Seal et al., 2009), and, as such, they will turn to and will be turning to civilian practitioners for care.

Military culture, as all other types of subcultures in American society, comprises the values, beliefs, traditions, norms, perceptions, and behaviors that govern how members of a group think, communicate, and interact with one another as well as with the outside world (Exum et al., 2011; Hall, 2011). Developing a warrior identity and immersing into the military culture is critical for new soldiers who depend on each other during times of war or conflict (Grossman, 1995). Wertsch (2006), in her study of adults who grew up in military families post-World War II, described the military culture metaphorically as a "fortress" symbolizing the kind of separateness that military life entails from the rest of society. Culture also determines how military personnel view their functioning in life, their status, and the role of the military in US society (Hall, 2011).

No matter the branch of service or era of service, the common threads shared by Veterans are reflected in the indoctrination or socialization of the military core values, which include honor, courage, loyalty, integrity, and commitment. These core values guide service members in the highest ethical principles through creeds such as "I will bear true faith and allegiance," "I will obey my orders," "Semper Fidelis," ("Always Faithful") (US Marine Corps values, as cited in Exum et al., 2011).

Also the notion of culture and stigma with regard to mental health determines how members of the military view their life and seek help; this may have a direct impact on their ability to ask for help when transitioning (Hoge et al., 2004). It is imperative for human service providers to understand the implications of this indoctrination where military cultural values determine the behaviors, standards, and code of conduct, for service members, in or out of uniform. The military as a socializing institution holds that this pervasive application of standards of conduct is necessary because members of the armed forces must be "combat ready" (Exum et al., 2011). The challenge for the service member transitioning is how does he or she "turn off" or diminish the rigidity associated with military culture and immerse in what is typically a more pronounced laissez-faire environment (i.e. civilian society)? Hoge (2010) recommends that successful reintegration for combat Veterans entails not necessarily giving up being a warrior, but learning how to modulate warrior responses depending on the situation.

Providers need to examine the military population on a continuum, from active involvement in the military lifestyle to the wounded warriors to the Veterans transitioning into civilian society. We need to consider as many facets of the military experience as possible and take into account the ethnic, personal, and familial predispositions toward worldviews and the evolution of the belief systems post combat in the life span of the military service member (Weiss, Coll, & Metal, 2011). Additionally, there is an intersectionality that must be considered: the intersection between military culture and other aspects of diversity, such as ethnicity, race, socioeconomic status, gender, and sexual orientation (Yamada, Atuel, & Weiss, 2013).

Military Transition Programs

In an effort to meet the needs of service members prior to separating from the military, The Department of Defense (DOD), VA, Department of Transportation, and the Labor Department's Veterans' Employment and Training Service (VETS) established a partnership known as the Transition Assistance Program (TAP) and the Disabled Transition Assistant Program (DTAP) to assist service members separating from active duty (Coll & Weiss, 2013). These transition assistance programs were established to meet the needs of service members prior to their separation. The evaluation of the program showed that, on average, those who participated in TAPs have a higher success rate of finding employment post separation.

Service members who attend TAPs learn how to conduct job searches, explore education benefits, and receive assistance with regard to career decision-making (Coll & Weiss, 2013). For example, information is provided about current occupational and labor market conditions and services are rendered in resume writing and interview techniques. Furthermore, information is provided on Veteran benefits such as: burial in military cemeteries; home loan guarantees; Veterans' employment; and healthcare benefits.

Civilian Transition

Tice (2015) suggests that those who have the highest level of success transitioning into the civilian sector are those individuals who take advantage of or are permitted to begin TAPs early and follow up with VA or state agencies once separated. A successful transition can be measured by the clarity of professional goals established by the Veteran and the ability of the service member to establish a healthy means of coping with various stressors associated with transition such as: loss, anxiety, fear, anger, and at times a sense of grandiosity (Coll & Weiss, 2013).

A means of addressing these difficult feelings is by exploring resources such as education and workforce transferable skills. Information on how to find adequate housing and ways to get back into a civilian lifestyle can also assist the service member in their transition. With the current Post-9/11 GI Bill, qualified Veterans have access to funding to support a college degree as well as funding for housing through Basic Housing Allowance (BHA). For those who are not interested in personally taking advantage of the educational benefits, as of August 1, 2009 the benefits can be transferred to a spouse or to an eligible dependent (US Department of Veterans Affairs, 2016). Additionally, in 2011, a stipend for living expenses was included in the Post-9/11 GI Bill of 2008, so that those who do not seek a college education could use the stipend if they were engaged in on-the-job training opportunities or in an apprenticeship. Unfortunately, a recent report from the Government Accountability Office (GAO) noted that only 2% of eligible Veterans were using this benefit (Tilghman, 2015). Various reasons for this lack of utilization were cited, including Veterans not being aware of this benefit through the VA-run TAP and employer reluctance in having to fill out forms.

Transitioning: Aspects to Consider

Whether or not to separate from active duty is a difficult process even when the service member is being involuntarily separated due to a Department of Defense downsize or he or she is being medically discharged. For those who are fortunate enough to plan ahead and have the opportunity to make a decision with regard to transitioning there are several things they must keep in mind when determining their post-service lifestyle. One of the most stressful aspects of transitioning prior to achieving retirement or separation is access to healthcare. While in the service, military personnel and their families have a unilateral form of health coverage which includes medical, dental, vision, pharmacy, life insurance, and overseas provisions (Coll & Weiss, 2013). Unfortunately, what many Veterans will find is that a large proportion of civilian sector companies have had to drastically increase healthcare coverage cost and other benefits, or have eliminated their covered portion completely in recent years forcing the workforce to purchase care directly. Unlike the military health insurance, the civilian sector has limitations for pre-existing medical conditions, forcing the Veteran to make a choice between primary care physicians for his/her service-connected disability through the VA and a physician through their employers' healthcare plan. Another factor to consider is employment security as one of the major issues that separated service members will have to face as the guaranteed paycheck is no longer available and now most of their income is based on hours worked (Coll & Weiss, 2013).

Housing, specifically when an individual is separating with dependents, becomes one of the most daunting and stressful issues faced by Veterans and their families during the transition (Caplin & Kranz Lewis, 2011). It is of course one of the most obvious financial and structural difficulties of separation, and, at the extreme, if not adequately addressed, can put one at risk of becoming homeless. While on active duty, service members who are married have an option to live in a military dwelling (i.e. on a military installation); while those who prefer to live off-base receive a Basic Allowance for Housing (as of 2011, 63% of military families are living outside of base housing [DoD, 2011]). The expected life on a military base is fairly uniform with homes built to appear similar to the service members' rank. There are strict housing rules, many of the yards are maintained alike and the homes should be kept clean while the family is limited in terms of what types of pets they can own, as well as how many pets they can have and even parking is designated in most areas, based on rank. Civilian life is not always so clear-cut and as a civilian an individual must find his or her own schools, home, provide its expensive maintenance, and adhere to standards set forth by the homeowners' association (if there is one) or by city or community standards.

Another consideration when separating from the military involves the prior access to support systems that the military community provides. This is similar to Guard and Reserve families who often live at lengthy distances from military installations (Harnett, 2013). Support systems can be very strong within the military community and the perception is that military families have been through similar situations and therefore other military families within the military community will understand what a family is going through. Unfortunately, the bond that is created within the military community can also lead to military families cutting themselves off from civilian families and lead to social isolation. In contrast, civilian families tend to be self-reliant and typically turn to their extended families and friendship networks for support. Although military families can also be close to their own extended family, geographic distances may get in the way of maintaining the bonds between extended family members and the military family (Hall, 2011).

Transitioning into Higher Education and Civilian Employment

Since the end of World War II many Veterans have utilized their education benefits (e.g. through the GI Bill and its many iterations) to attain a college degree or gain technical skills. It goes without saying that learning within a traditional format can be difficult after years of being outside of a formal educational setting. Veterans that attend colleges with younger peers may have more difficulty integrating into campus life than if they attend colleges with a demographically diverse student body (Coll & Weiss, 2015). As the number of Veterans attending college increases, more colleges and universities are beginning to realize the difficulties associated with Veteran reintegration and are hiring Veteran liaisons to assist in this transition among many other campus initiatives (for more information, see Coll & Weiss, 2015).

As a means of providing institutions of higher learning assistance with the increase of student Veterans, the American Council on Education (ACE) developed several working groups that have identified key areas and programs of service that colleges can institute in order to support these students. Many schools appear to be already doing many of the things that ACE has suggested, such as acknowledging the importance of serving military and Veteran students and incorporating their needs into the institutional strategic plans. More specifically, it is recommended that colleges develop programs designed especially for student Veterans, such as offering credits for prior service experience, training, and occupational education, which some colleges have implemented (ACE, 2009). Although many Veterans will seek counseling through the VA or local Vet Centers, ACE recommends that schools become aware of their students' psychosocial needs and community resources in order to assist in finding appropriate counseling services. This is a critical need for schools in rural America (where there is less access to military and Veteran resources).

As far as employment is concerned, in order to improve the transition process from active-duty military service to civilian employment, there are several recommendations that military personnel should consider. For instance, the service member should not wait until 30 days from separation or retirement before starting the military to civilian transition process, instead service members should start as early as possible (Griffin, 2011). Seeking out the services of agencies such as the VA, county-operated Veteran services, and traditional Veteran service organizations can be extremely helpful to those Veterans who are seeking to transition from the military. The service member should make certain prior to separation to research key certifications and go after them while they are still in the service. Also, getting assistance from a sponsor, mentor, or a job coach on how to translate the military skills into civilian language and terminology would be useful. Attending career fairs for military Veterans and seeking out recruiting firms that specialize in placing military Veterans is also recommended. Additionally, exploring all employment options, such as federal, state, and civilian opportunities is a good idea; this includes not settling for the first job that comes along that may not be a good fit. A workplace transition model proposed by Chari (2008), and promoted by Harnett and DeSimone (2011), can be applied to helping Veterans with the transition to the civilian workforce. For example, the Veteran increasing his or her self-awareness; investing in specific learning opportunities that are job related; managing key relationships (workwise and socially); building coalitions; and developing short-term and long-term goals.

In terms of understanding the impact of military worldviews and the Veteran navigating through the civilian workplace, Weiss et al. (2011) suggest that Veterans can follow orders very well. However, there needs to be a clear chain of command. Therefore, it would be helpful for employers to provide Veteran employees with an organizational chart explaining who are in command and who they need to turn to if they are having any challenges. Veterans also work best in teams, as they are combat trained to function as part of a unit (e.g. unit cohesion) (Grossman, 1995). Military group cohesion (Siebold, 2006) has also been associated with an increase in morale (Britt & Dickinson, 2006). Service members are very loyal to their team and loyal to the organization as long as they understand their function in the team (by having clear direction). This way they can avoid feeling frustrated. In fact, the sense of loyalty to the team is so strong that oftentimes military personnel will volunteer to go on deployments in order to "be there" for their battle buddies. This aspect of group cohesion, in terms of belonging to a military unit, can be a strong pull toward re-enlisting or remaining in the military. Thus, employers can utilize the strengths of military culture (i.e. cohesion & mission), rather than responding to these as workplace barriers or limitations.

Lafferty et al. (2008) offer tips for employers and educators regarding engaging Veteran employees or students. For example, employers/educators should learn to curb their own anxiety about working with a Veteran, in that, although military service trains individuals for combat and in the use of weapons, there is no empirical evidence that a Veteran will be more likely to resort to violence than a civilian employee or student. They (and human service professionals as well) should not engage in political discussions with the Veterans around anti-war sentiments. They should curb their curiosity and not ask insensitive questions such as "Did you shoot anyone?" (Lafferty et al., 2008). Canfield and Weiss (2015) also offer tips for educators in managing a college classroom. There should be an awareness of signs of emotional stress in Veterans (such as trouble with extended concentration, uneasiness in large gatherings, an increase in absenteeism, and disturbances in peer relationships). Consequently, they should be familiar with community and Veteran resources. Finally, in light of post-traumatic stress symptoms among Veterans (as discussed in chapters of this book), employers may want to take a proactive and preventative stance toward all of their employees (not to single out Veterans), and provide wellness seminars focusing on stress management, sleep hygiene, health, and diet as well as seminars on interpersonal and communication skill building (to help manage or prevent potentially conflict ridden relationships at the workplace).

Post-Service Identity Development

As Veterans transition, they find themselves seeking to develop a new identity which enables successful coping mechanisms within their new environment. The following discussion will address an adoption of identity development theories to explore and further ascertain the challenges faced by Veterans transitioning.

Psychosocial theories state that an individual's life span is characterized by predictable stages and tasks through which he or she develops. Each developmental task or issue must be completed in order for the next stage to occur. Central to psychosocial theories is the belief that the social context and environment surrounding the individual influences and shapes the way in which development occurs. Therefore, a critical aspect of understanding a Veteran's behavior through transition and separation is to understand the person within his/her environment or social context (Coll, 2012).

Building upon Erikson's psychosocial theory of development (1963) and understanding the person within his/her environment, Tick (2005) made the connection between Erikson's theory and how it applies to Veterans. "According to Erikson, one of the most important achievements of development is a sound identity, formulated during adolescence and culminating at the ages at which we typically send young people off to war" (Tick, 2005, p. 104). He further noted that Erikson, in working with Veteran clients, observed that what impressed him the most was the loss of identity and that a "Veteran must rebuild a coherent identity" (Tick, 2005, p. 105). Chickering (1969), in his application of identity theory to college students, emphasized that an individual's development and growth occurs along seven vectors and will vary accordingly, depending on the person and his or her environment. In this case, while Chickering was referring to college students, we believe his model can best inform our understanding of Veterans' transitioning. In the subsequent paragraphs we will briefly outline Chickering's theoretical model and apply it to Veterans, noting how this model can be applied to comprehending Veterans in their transition.

The first stage or vector, *developing competence*, comprises the following components: intellectual, physical and manual skills, and social and interpersonal competence. The ability to perceive a sense of self-competence by the individual appears to be the most important aspect of this stage. Confidence in this vector is described as the individual's ability to cope with crisis and successfully attain his/her goals (Chickering & Reisser, 1993). Veterans develop specific competencies related to their job in the military (i.e. military occupational specialty) and must learn to transfer mastered competencies to civilian settings.

The second vector, *managing emotions*, encompasses an individual's ability to learn and understand how to control emotions. A particular concern for Veteran identity development is the ability to control aggression while being able to express softer emotions. This vector provides an opportunity for growth, self-reflection, and an increase in an individual's awareness, while developing more effective means of emotional expression. In the military, the expression of emotions is not promoted; anger tends to be more acceptable than soft emotions, such as sadness, hurt and disappointment. This is an area that Veterans often struggle with in their transition to civilian settings and relationships that are outside of the military.

The third vector, *developing autonomy*, is composed of three components: emotional independence, instrumental independence, and interdependence. An emotionally independent individual is free from the need for continued reassurance. Instrumental independence is the ability to achieve specific activities and resolve problems with little or no assistance. Service members function as part of a unit and thus this sense of autonomous functioning may present challenges for Veterans as they transition. The third component, interdependence, represents an individual who is "attuned to the whole, and aware" of his/her environment and responsibilities, which Veterans have been accustomed to as part of their military service and this can be viewed as a strength.

The fourth vector, *establishing identity*, was identified in Chickering's (1969) earlier work as dependent on the development and successful completion of the first three vectors. Identity development requires an individual to reflect on his/her sense of self. Part of this involves the Veteran being honest with him or herself and developing a self-acceptance of who they are and who they are becoming.

The fifth vector, *interpersonal relationships*, is defined as an increase of tolerance for others (i.e. diverse populations). Service members operate in diverse work environments, however, they may have little understanding or patience with civilians who may be regarded as lazy or unmotivated by Veterans who tend to adhere to the strict discipline of military lifestyle even when they are no longer in the military.

Developing purpose, the sixth vector, is attributed to an individual's ability to develop direction in his/her life. The Veteran can develop a sense of renewed purpose through the use of goal setting and by outlining priorities that will allow the individual to pursue or look into vocational interests, or a new sense of mission, post-military life.

The seventh vector, which is the last vector in Chickering's theory, encompasses *developing integrity*, the culmination of all of the other vectors, whereby an individual develops a set of beliefs and values that influence behavior. Veterans bring a unique identity encompassing military core values that need to be balanced with non-military values and thus will need to re-evaluate values and develop new ones that will more closely align with civilian or societally based values.

The utility of Chickering's model is that it alerts civilian practitioners to the struggles many returnees/Veterans will face and encourages the practitioner to be proactive in identifying these areas and offering needed guidance.

Conclusion

This chapter offers community-based human services providers an opportunity to begin to understand cultural aspects with regard to the strengths and challenges that transitioning from the military to a civilian lifestyle can entail for Veterans. Transitioning was explored from the point of view of Veterans entering the civilian workplace and higher education as well as the importance of identity development in understanding successful Veteran reintegration. Chickering's (1969) identity development model was suggested as a theoretical tool that could be applied to Veterans as a way of further defining what is entailed in the shift from military culture to civilian culture and the impact on identity formation. Further research and empirical studies would strengthen the theoretical connections that we are proposing. However, at this juncture, the literature is sparse on how to assist Veterans with what can be a difficult transition from a cultural perspective, and thus we offer our insights with the hopes that these will assist our readers working in community settings in order to facilitate more effective engagement of Veterans in navigating reintegration challenges.

References

American Council on Education (2009). Serving those who serve: Higher education and America's Veterans (Issue Brief). Washinton DC. Retrieved from www.accent.edu/news-room/Documents/Serving-Those-Who-Serve-Making-Your-Institution-Veteran-Friendly.pdf

Britt, T. W. & Dickinson, J. M. (2006). Morale during military operations: A positive psychology approach. In T. W. Britt, C. A. Castro, & A. B. Adler (Eds.), *Military life: The psychology of serving in peace and combat. Vol 1: Military performance* (pp. 157–184). Westport, CT: Praeger Security International.

Canfield, J. & Weiss, E. L. (2015). Student Veterans and mental health: Posttraumatic stress in the classroom. In J. E. Coll & E. L. Weiss (Eds.), *Supporting Veterans in higher education: A primer for administrators, faculty and academic advisors* (pp. 260–287). Chicago, IL: Lyceum Books.

Caplin, D. & Kranz Lewis, K. (2011). Coming home: Examining the homecoming experiences of young Veterans. In D. C. Kelly, S. Howe-Barksdale, & D. Gitelson (Eds.), *Treating young Veterans: Promoting resilience through practice and advocacy* (pp. 101–124). New York: Springer.

Chari, S. (2008). Handling career role transitions with confidence. *International Journal of Clinical Leadership*, 16, 109–114.

Chickering, A. W. (1969). *Education and identity.* San Francisco, CA: Jossey-Bass.

Chickering, A. & Reisser, L. (1993). The seven vectors: An overview (pp. 43–52). *Education and identity.* San Francisco, CA: Jossey-Bass.

Cho, S., Crenshaw, K. W., & McCall, L. (2013). Toward a field of intersectionality studies: Theory, applications, and praxis. *Signs*, 38(4), 785–810.

Coll, J. E. (2012). How universities can better support military students. *Journal of Defense Management*, 2(3), 114. doi:10.4172/2167-0374.1000e114.

Coll, J. E. & Weiss, E. L. (2013). Transitioning Veterans into civilian life. In A. Rubin, J. E. Coll, & E. L. Weiss (Eds.), *Handbook of military social work* (pp. 281–297). Hoboken, NJ: Wiley.

Coll, J. E. & Weiss, E. L. (2015). Preface: The call to higher education. In J. E. Coll & E. L. Weiss (Eds.), *Supporting Veterans in higher education: A primer for administrators, faculty and academic advisors* (pp. xi–xxi). Chicago, IL: Lyceum Books.

Coll, J. E., Weiss, E. L., Draves, P., & Dyer, D. (2012).The impact of military cultural awareness, experience, attitudes, and education on clinician self efficacy in treatment of Veterans. *Journal of International Continuing Social Work Education*, 15(1), 39–48.

Defense Manpower Data Center (2015). Strength change historical reports. Department of Defense. Retrieved from: www.dmdc.osd.mil/appj/dwp/dwp_reports.jsp

Erikson, E. H. (1963). *Childhood and society.* New York: Norton.

Exum, H. A., Coll, J. E., & Weiss, E. L. (2011). *A civilian counselor's primer to counseling veterans* (2nd ed.). Deer Park, NY: Linus Publications.

Franklin, A. J. & Boyd-Franklin, N. (2000). Invisibility syndrome: A clinical model of the effects of racism on African-American males. *American Journal of Orthopsychiatry*, 70(1), 33.

Griffin, S. (2011). Iraq, Afghanistan and the future of British military doctrine: from counterinsurgency to stabilization. *International Affairs*, 87(2), 317–333.

Gross, G. & Weiss, E. L. (2014). The vanishing military Veteran: A postmodern disappearance of the hero. *Social Work in Mental Health*, 12(6), 575–590.

Grossman, D. (1995). *On killing: The psychological cost of learning to kill in war and society.* Boston, MA: Little, Brown & Co.

Hall, L. K. (2011). The importance of understanding military culture. *Social Work in Health Care*, 50(1), 4–18.

Harnett, C. (2013). Supporting National Guard and Reserve members and their families. In A. Rubin, E. L. Weiss, & J. E. Coll (Eds.), *Handbook of military social work* (pp. 335–357). Hoboken, NJ: Wiley.

Harnett, C. & DeSimone, J. (2011). Managing the return to the workplace: Reservists navigating the stormy seas of the homeland. In D. C. Kelly, S. Howe-Barksdale, & D. Gitelson (Eds.), *Treating young Veterans: Promoting resilience through practice and advocacy* (pp. 219–255). New York: Springer.

Hoge, C. W. (2010). *Once a warrior, always a warrior: Navigating the transition from combat to home including combat stress, PTSD and mTBI.* Guilford, CT: Globe Pequot Press.

Hoge, C. W., Auchterloine, J. L., & Milliken, C.S. (2006). Mental health problems, use of mental health services and attrition from military service after returning from deployment to Iraq and Afghanistan. *Journal of the American Medical Association*, 295, 1023–1032.

Hoge, C. W., Castro, C. A., Messer, S. C., McGurk, D., Cotting, D. I., & Koffman, R. L. (2004). Combat duty in Iraq and Afghanistan, mental health problems, and barriers to care. *New England Journal of Medicine*, 351(1), 13–22.

Lafferty, C. L., Alford, K. L., Davis, M. K., O'Connor, R. (2008). "Did you shoot anyone?": A practitioner's guide to combat Veteran workplace and classroom integration. *Advanced Management Journal*, 73(4), 4–11.

Seal, K. H., Metzler, T. J., Gima, K. S.Berenthal, D., Maguen, S., & Marmar, C. R. (2009). Trends and risk factors for mental health diagnosis among Iraq and Afghanistan Veterans using Department of Veterans Affairs Health Care 2002–2008. *American Journal of Public Health*, 99, 1651–1658.

Siebold, G. L. (2006). Military group cohesion. In T. W. Britt, C. A. Castro, & A. B. Adler (Eds.), *Military life: The psychology of serving in peace and combat. Vol 1: Military performance* (pp. 185–201). Westport, CT: Praeger Security International.

Tanielian, T. & Jaycox, L. (Eds.) (2008). *Invisible wounds of war: Psychological and cognitive injuries, their consequences, and services to assist recovery*. Santa Monica, CA: RAND Corp.

Tice, J. (2015, November 3). Army: Young soldiers over estimate likely civilian pay. *Army Times*. Retrieved from: www.armytimes.com/story/military/careers/army/2015/11/03/army-young-soldiers-overestimate-likely-civilian-pay/73644254

Tick, E. (2005). *War and the soul: Healing our nation's Veterans from post-traumatic stress disorder*. Wheaton, IL: Quest Books.

Tilghman, A. (2015, November 15). Report: GI Bills on-the-job training benefit not being used. *Military Times*. Retrieved from: http://militari.ly/1NQRNZc

US Department of Defense (2011). Strengthening our military families: Meeting America's commitment. Retrieved from: www.defense.gov/home/features/2011/0111_initiative/strengthening_our_military_january_2011.pdf

US Department of Veteran Affairs (2016). The Post-9/11 GI Bill. Retrieved from: www.benefits.va.gov/GIBILL/resources/benefits_resources/rates/ch33/ch33rates080115.asp#HOUSING

Weiss, E. L., & Coll, J. E., & Metal, M. (2011). The influence of military culture and Veteran worldviews on mental health treatment: Implications for Veteran help seeking and wellness. *International Journal of Health, Wellness & Society*, 1(2), 75–86.

Wertsch, M. E. (2006). *Military brats: Legacies of childhood inside the fortress*. St. Louis, MO: Brightwell Publishing.

Yamada, A., Atuel, H. R., & Weiss, E. L. (2013). Military culture and multicultural diversity among military service members: Implications for mental health providers. In F. A. Paniagua & A. Yamada (Eds.), *Handbook of multicultural mental health* (2nd ed.) (pp. 389–410). New York: Academic Press.

PART II
Special Populations

3

HOMELESS VETERANS

Carissa van den Berk-Clark and David L. Albright

According to the US Department of Housing and Urban Development (HUD), 442,723 Americans were homeless in 2014. Homelessness, according to the Homeless Emergency Assistance and Rapid Transition to Housing (HEARTH) Act, is defined as not having a "fixed, regular and adequate residence" (McKinney–Vento Homeless Assistance Act as amended by S.896). Individuals who are homeless commonly stay in homeless shelters, abandoned buildings, vehicles, or other accommodation unfit for human habitation. Homelessness is a significant problem because it is associated with a large number of negative outcomes, including higher chronic health conditions and mortality, more frequent emergency room utilization and more frequent incarceration (see Tsai & Rosenheck, 2014 for review).

Homelessness began to be regarded as a social problem in the 1980s and coincided with cuts to social services and welfare, deinstitutionalization, increasing problems with housing affordability and the failure of community mental health facilities (Marcuse & Keating, 2006). The policy response to homelessness (i.e. the Stewart B. McKinney Assistance Act of 1987) was the only significant piece of legislation proposing a federal response to affordable housing and mental health treatment shortages since the Carter Administration. This policy provided emergency shelter and six-month transitional housing to individuals who were able to maintain a drug-free lifestyle and take psychiatric medication via HUD funding. Later, in 1992 and 2009, "housing first" permanent supportive housing programs dominated funding streams for homeless populations (Culhane & Metraux, 2008). These programs provided homeless individuals permanent housing directly from the street without requirements for sobriety or psychiatric medication usage. They often provide homeless individuals with case managers who manage referrals to psychiatric, substance abuse, medical, and other types of social services (van den Berk-Clark, 2015). However, even though such programs are often less expensive to run than prisons, emergency shelters, or psychiatric wards (Culhane & Metraux, 2008), the demand for housing among the homeless often far outstrips supply, which leads to large waiting lists (van den Berk-Clark, 2015). Also, in order to access permanent housing, individuals need to be "chronically homeless," meaning they have been consecutively homeless for at least one year or have been homeless three times in the past year and have a physician-verified disability.

Homelessness among Veterans

Over 10% of homeless individuals are Veterans. Within the past 20 years, a number of studies have shown that there is a higher rate of homelessness among Veterans (Rosenheck, Frisman, & Chung, 1994; Tessler, Rosenheck, & Gamache, 2002; Tsai, Mares, & Rosenheck, 2012). This is partially the result of high inflation and economic recession during the 1980s, which increased the rate of homelessness in general.

Homeless Veterans are also very different from non-Veterans because they have access to a range of additional benefits through the US Department of Veteran Affairs (VA) system. Studies show that Veterans tend to be older, have higher levels of education, have higher income, have more and better health insurance, and are more likely to be married than the general population (Tsai, Mares, & Rosenheck, 2012; Tsai & Rosenheck, 2014). All these characteristics decrease the risk of homelessness among this population. However, their risk increases because they are exposed to higher levels of trauma than the general population and because they are often isolated due to deployment-related geographic displacement (Perl, 2011).

As Table 3.1 shows, specific demographic factors (age, gender, race, education, and marital status) increase risk across Veteran and non-Veteran populations (Khadduri et al., 2009; Tsai

TABLE 3.1 Differences between Homeless Veterans and Non-Veterans When It Comes to Risk for Homelessness

	Vietnam Veterans	*Iraq/Afghanistan Veterans*	*Non-Veterans*
Age	Year of birth	18–35	Over age 24
Gender	Male	Male	Male
Race		African American	African American
Education		High school education or lower	High school education or lower
Marital status	Unmarried	Unmarried	Never married
Military status		Low military rank; problematic military discharges	
Physical health	Chronic medical conditions; Hepatitis/cirrhosis; High emergency room use	Traumatic brain injury; high emergency room use	Traumatic brain injury; higher mortality, high emergency room use
Mental health	Psychiatric disorder; PTSD	Psychotic disorder (diagnosed while in military service); PTSD	Psychiatric disorders; developmental disability
Substance use	Substance abuse	Substance use disorder	Substance use disorder
Childhood	Physical and sexual abuse, foster care		Physical and sexual abuse, foster care
Service utilization	Outpatient mental health service use higher	Outpatient mental health service use higher	
Other	Low levels of social support 1 year after military discharge	Urban location; VA service connection; criminal history; income level; military sexual trauma	Low levels of social support; criminal history; income level; unemployment

et al., 2012; van den Berk-Clark & McGuire, 2013). Chronic health problems, traumatic brain injury, psychiatric disorders, and substance abuse further increase risk across Veteran and non-Veteran populations. Differences tend to occur in the context of war-related events and as a result of military policies, especially those related to access to VA benefits and services. For example, among Vietnam Veterans there were certain birth years which were associated with an increased risk of homelessness. Veterans were also at higher risk if they had a lower rank, received a non-honorable discharge, or experienced military sexual trauma.

Services Available for Homeless Veterans

The high rate of homelessness among Veterans has, for a long time, been considered a national embarrassment. Given the shortage of permanent housing available via HUD, civilian providers could not effectively serve homeless Veteran populations. By 2009, then Secretary of the VA, General Erin Shinseki, made a pledge that the VA would end Veteran homelessness within five years. Single night estimates by HUD show drastic reductions in homelessness – by almost 33% from 2009 to 2014 (see Table 3.2).

Although Veteran homelessness has not been eliminated, increased funding has led to the creation and expansion of a number of innovative services for homeless Veterans. Two such programs focus specifically on the provision of permanent supportive housing: HUD–VASH and the Supportive Housing Program. Both programs involved partnerships between the VA, HUD and the US Department of Health and Human Services, and both programs utilized the housing first model, a model which has shown significant successes in civilian homeless populations (Montgomery et al., 2013). Housing first programs provide housing directly from the street (so there is no need for a homeless person to graduate from substance abuse treatment or become stable in his/her medication). They also provide on-site (or home visit), enriched supports – such as case management, and psychiatric, medical, and substance abuse counseling.

The service-rich model, which is essential to housing first, has also been adapted to provide health services to homeless Veterans. VA hospitals were some of the first US hospitals to adapt European models of integrated care (O'Toole et al., 2013; van den Berk-Clark & McGuire, 2014). In other words, VA hospitals utilize teams to deliver both health and mental health services to Veterans. A growing movement in primary care, now referred to as the Primary Care Medical Home (PCMH), has shown to improve health outcomes by utilizing a combination of teams composed of both health and mental health workers and by implementing self-management programs (Jackson et al., 2013). PCMH also have extended hours, next day appointments or allow for web, email, and phone correspondence between patients and their primary care providers, which makes access easier for at-risk populations who tend to over-utilize emergency room services because of greater convenience. The Commonwealth Fund and now more recently, the Affordable Care Act, provide incentives

TABLE 3.2 Change in Number of Homeless Veterans from HUD 2014 Homeless Count

	2009–2014	
	Number	%
Homeless Veterans	−24,117	−32.6
Sheltered	−11,361	−26.2
Unsheltered	−12,756	−41.6

Source: Adapted from US Department of Housing and Urban Development (2014: Part 1, 45).

for the use of PCMHs, especially at Federally Qualified Medical Centers and via the Medicaid program. Following these trends in medical care, the HCHV program utilizes a primary care medical home model, which is tailor-made for homeless Veterans. This model utilizes a service-rich/team-based approach which integrates healthcare with mental healthcare and social service delivery systems, via the use of case workers who focus specifically on facilitating housing and VA services to homeless Veterans with health issues. It must be noted that these specialized homeless programs exist alongside already existing VA programs. All such programming is listed in Table 3.3 which stratifies VA programing by VA homeless, and VA non-homeless status.

Case Vignettes

The following five cases show the different pre-military, military, and post-military factors which can influence risk for homelessness and how VA services are constructed to intervene. Within these vignettes, we use references to the scientific evidence base, to clarify the existence of these problems in homeless Veterans and the effectiveness of VA interventions.

TABLE 3.3 VA Programs and Initiatives for Homeless Veterans

Program	Homeless Veterans	All Veterans
Housing	HUD–VASH vouchers; Grant and Per Diem Program; supported housing	VA Community Living Centers (nursing homes); Home and community-based services (long-term care); housing grants for disabled veterans; home loan guaranty
Cash	VBA–VHA special outreach and benefits assistance	Disability compensation; VA pension; unemployment
Employment	Compensated Work Therapy/ Transitional Residence (CWT/TR), Homeless Veterans Supported Employment Program (HVSEP)	Therapeutic & Supported Employment Services (TSES) Program; CWT/Transitional Work (CWT/TW); CWT/Supported Employment (CWT/SE); vocational assistance; compensated work therapy/ sheltered workshop; incentive therapy (IT); Veterans Retraining Assistance Program (VRAP)
Mental Health	Domiciliary Care for Homeless Veterans (DCHV)	VA healthcare benefits package
Physical Health	Healthcare for Homeless Veterans (HCHV)	VA healthcare benefits package
Crisis Intervention	National Call Center for Homeless Veterans; VA Assistance Stand Downs; Community Homelessness Assessment, Local Education and Networking Groups (CHALENG); Drop-in centers	Veterans Crisis Line; Veterans Chat;
Case Management	Supportive housing	Veterans Justice Outreach (VJO); VetSuccess on Campus
Other	VBA's Acquired Property Sales for Homeless Providers; VA Excess Property for Homeless Veterans Initiative; program monitoring and evaluation	GI Bill

JACK, VIETNAM VETERAN, AGE 68

Jack is a 68-year-old African American male who had been admitted to psychiatric hospitals approximately 20 times. He has currently been referred to the VA hospital through the Salvation Army shelter. The case worker at the Salvation Army reported that he was becoming increasingly agitated, repeatedly getting into fights with residents and staff. After being admitted, Jack had left abruptly and was later found outside the Veteran Health Administration (VHA) smoking cigarettes by another staff member. When asked to explain, he told the staff person that he had trouble controlling his emotions. He told the attending physician that he often becomes suspicious of his surroundings, and becomes afraid of garbage trucks and other large vehicles. He is often distressed and preoccupied with these delusional ideas. He was extremely resistant and argumentative with staff members. The next day, he was admitted to the VHA hospital in the city, and then transferred to another VHA close by, which had inpatient psychiatric beds. At that point, he was administered Haldol, and the nurses reported that he was coherent and his irritability vanished. At that time, he explained that he has been hearing voices pretty regularly since he was in his late twenties. Although he does find that medication improves these symptoms, he has problems with side effects and often discontinues use when his psychiatric stability improves.

When Jack entered the military, he thought he would make a career out of being in the Air Force but was later disbanded for "speaking up" about the treatment of fellow African Americans in the South. Jack spoke about racially motivated incidences, including a Black man being hanged by the Ku Klux Klan, which have traumatized him and stayed with him his whole life. Although he had been in and out of psychiatric hospitals through most of his life, he still expressed a desire to work. The ability to work, however, had been interrupted by paranoia and suspicion which made it difficult for him to maintain a stable job and retain housing. Jack had worked as an aircraft mechanic for 15 years but he never got married. He had generally been isolated and had few friends.

Jack explained that he first became homeless when his landlady sold the apartment building he was living in. Currently, he spends his nights sleeping on the bus, though he occasionally stays in shelters. He typically accesses healthcare through the emergency room and uses his Medicaid benefits because he gets frustrated dealing with the VA's bureaucratic system and finds that staff are usually rude and unhelpful.

Jack appears to have significant problems with aggressive, agitated, and disruptive behavior. He also has cognitive problems and problems with hallucinations and delusions. Like many other homeless people with severe mental illnesses (Wenzel et al., 1995), he has a history of psychiatric hospitalization but until recently had been able to retain stable housing. However, because his psychiatric issues do not overtly appear to be "service connected," he may have difficulties attaining VA disability benefits.

Treatment Options

Jack would benefit from Domiciliary Care for Homeless Veterans or Long Term Care through the VA. Because he has interest in working, he could participate in a work therapy program through the VA's CWT/TR (Rosenheck & Mares, 2007). In addition, a medical home which provides integrated mental health and physical health services through the VA's HCHV program or even through a local Federally Qualified Health Center (FQHC; depending on availability) could improve Jack's mental health stability, and help determine better medication options (O'Toole et al., 2003). Participation in medical home programs also reduces emergency department utilization and leads to better health outcomes. If it is determined that Jack is able to live independently, then he should be referred to supportive housing. Supportive housing will be a better choice for Jack because he has access to a range of "in-house" social services, including case management, medical, and psychiatric. Supportive housing can be accessed through the traditional HUD system (usually via nonprofits who have contracts to provide permanent housing via HUD or through Section 8 vouchers) or through the VA's HUD–VASH program.

RICHARD, VIETNAM VETERAN, AFRICAN AMERICAN, AGE 57[1]

Richard encountered extreme trauma from being raped at gunpoint when he was young. He also served in Vietnam and reported witnessing many members of his platoon die or receive extensive injuries. His resulting PTSD (see: Stehberg, Albright, & Weiss, 2012) has led to the breakup of his marriage and to drug use which originally led him to go to the VA for treatment. At the time, Richard had been living on the streets or on the beach, in his car or with his daughter or friend. He explained to the case manager, "You know, you might think you have something going for you while drinking that beer," but after a cop noticed that he not only was publicly intoxicated but already had an existing warrant, he ended up having to spend 30 days in jail to clear that warrant. After the one-month incarceration, Richard's Supplemental Security Income (SSI) check was cut off and he had to go through the process of getting it back. A month later, he was picked up at the subway for not paying the fare and the system had not cleared the previous warrant, so he was required to do the whole sentence all over again.

It is common for many service members to take their trauma into military service. Individuals who have been exposed to multiple forms of trauma have an increased risk of developing PTSD (Bremner, Southwick, Darnell, & Charney, 1996). Richard's experience also relates to that of many chronically homeless who have high arrest rates due to petty violations and substance use, which often lead to homelessness (Tsai et al., 2012).

Treatment Options

Richard can access a case manager while incarcerated through the VA's Justice Outreach and Veterans Treatment Courts initiatives (Canada & Albright, 2014). In addition, Richard would benefit from a residential treatment program at the VA (Montgomery et al., 2013). Transitional housing through the Per Diem Program would also help him work through substance use issues while he begins to save money for permanent housing and possibly apply for VA disability benefits. If securing housing is still not feasible, HUD–VASH, civilian Shelter Plus Care programs, or even HUD Section 8 vouchers are another option. Richard also has the potential to be helped by prolonged exposure therapy, a well-known cognitive therapy used by the VA to treat PTSD (Institute of Medicine, 2007).

TOM, OIF/OEF VETERAN, AGE 28[2]

Tom has completed several tours of duty in Iraq and Afghanistan while he was on active duty. Tom joined the military after being in foster care for much of his life. When he reached 18, his foster care case manager recommended the military as a way for him to transition into adulthood and potentially go to college. Although Tom had suffered no injuries while overseas, he had been exposed to repeated blast explosions which were left untreated because he felt uneasy asking for help. The leadership in his unit were not very supportive and were often outright hostile to individuals who expressed any problems coping with military life. At the time, Tom wanted a career in the military and worried he would harm his career if he told his commanding officer about his cognitive issues. Tom reports consistent problems with headaches, blurred vision, and dizziness throughout his deployment. He had serious problems with sleeping, flashbacks, and emotional detachment. In a violent rage, he had yelled at his commanding officer and took off in the army issued Humvee. Afterwards, he was given an "other than honorable" discharge from the military (see Seamone et al., 2014, for additional information on military discharge proceedings). Since returning from military service, he has been drinking heavily and has found it difficult to find employment. He currently resides in a one-bedroom apartment with a roommate and is late on his rent.

Tom has co-morbid PTSD and TBI which causes a mixture of confusion and problems with anger, sleeping, and other symptoms (Zatzick et al., 2010). He also, like many homeless Veterans, has limited access to VA services due to his military discharge status (Tsai, Pietrzak, & Rosenheck, 2012; Tsai & Rosenheck, 2014).

Treatment Options

Unfortunately, because he has an "other than honorable discharge," it is up to the VA to determine the circumstances of his discharge to determine whether he is eligible for benefits. Some Veteran service organizations, like the Homeless Advocacy Project's Veterans program, work with these Veterans. Also, the military, through their different branches, also maintains discharge review boards who will review discharges and sometimes upgrade discharge records. When it comes to getting money to pay his rent, there are several civilian HUD programs with limited funds, which are typically implemented through local nonprofits, like the Salvation Army, which can help individuals at risk of becoming homeless pay utility bills or rent.

EDDY, AFGHANISTAN, NATIONAL GUARD, AGE 30

Eddy had enrolled in National Guard service in order for his wife to also stay employed. She currently has a job as a preschool teacher. He was reluctant to enroll in active duty because it required him to move around and his wife would have to quit her well-paying job. Eddy also enrolled in the National Guard because he thought it would help him finish college, learn some job skills, and would allow him to make some extra money to help out his wife, their daughter, and a son from a previous marriage. He did not expect, however, that the National Guard would send him overseas to Afghanistan. The deployment put enormous stress on his new marriage and when he left for Afghanistan, his wife did not have many people to help her cope with the dual responsibilities of employment and motherhood. She eventually lost her job and the bank is foreclosing on their house.

Meanwhile, Eddy got severely injured while involved in combat operations. The injuries required significant surgery and aftercare so Eddy was sent back to Walter Reed hospital to recover. After he was stabilized, his doctor prescribed pain medication and he moved into his stepmother's house. It wasn't long before Eddy began to crave medication and took higher dosages than the recommended prescription. By the time he started engaging in doctor shopping (that is, he "shopped" around for doctors willing to give him a prescription for pain medication), his wife kicked him out of the house. Eddy currently works as a manager of a pizza restaurant and has managed to keep his job despite his substance abuse issues. He is currently waiting to hear whether he will receive any Veteran disability benefits for his ongoing issues with chronic pain.

Rates of pain medication misuse have escalated both among the general population and Veterans (Seal et al., 2012). Substance misuse puts Veterans at significant risk for homelessness (Tsai, Kasprow, & Rosenheck, 2014). Military service puts enormous strains on military families, with National Guard families particularly at risk because they are not located on a military base and have less access to military supportive services (Griffith, 2010). Additionally, exiting the military can be a trying time for military families and can deplete relational resilience (Cox & Albright, 2014).

Treatment Options

Eddy is eligible for substance abuse treatment either through the Department of Defense's Tricare Program or through the VA Health Care Benefits Package. Family therapy and counseling for his wife is available through the Military Family Consultant Program and Military One Source (Beardslee et al., 2011). Eddy is eligible for legal relief under the Servicemembers Civil Relief Act (SCRA), which is for military personnel at risk of foreclosure. As a disabled Veteran, he is also eligible for housing grants through the VA. Outside of the VA system, Eddy could also seek relief through the Making Home Affordable Program which can lower his monthly mortgage payment to 31% of his gross monthly income. Eddy may also have a redemption period available for his house where he can still pay the outstanding mortgage balance plus fees to avoid foreclosure.

CINDY, AFGHANISTAN, NAVY, AGE 25[3]

Cindy was seen at the VA emergency room after attempting to commit suicide with over-the-counter sleeping pills. Cindy joined the Navy because she was not really going anywhere with her life and wanted something to do. She also had an older brother who joined and was beginning what seemed like a very promising military career. Cindy essentially just wanted to be part of something that she felt "meant something." However, when she entered the military she was consistently harassed, sexually and non-sexually. She did not feel like she was part of the group or that she did meaningful work. She remembers clearly crying when she told another female service member about her experience with an officer who had raped her. The service member told Cindy not to tell anyone but Cindy still believed that when she did say something to a commanding officer, her situation would change. Unfortunately, once the incident was recorded, she was subsequently diagnosed as having borderline personality disorder and was sent back to her base in South Carolina. Even though Cindy had a few friends among the male service members, and was even friendly with some of the officers, she quickly found that after this incident, the men stuck together and remained on the side of the perpetrator.

After the rape, Cindy sank into a deep depression and became even more isolated. By this time, she was back at the naval base in the US and had easy access to alcohol. The military commissary also had deeply discounted rum which she used to cope with the rape (see Ames, Cunradi, Moore, & Stern, 2007). Her commanding officer eventually got her a general discharge under honorable conditions because of minor discipline problems and her failure to progress in training. After returning from the military, Cindy's employment situation, as well as her relationships with men, were extremely unstable. She also began using cocaine in addition to alcohol to help cope with her stressful life. Her family disapproved of her behavior and became estranged from her. The drug use eventually led to homelessness.

Almost 40% of homeless female Veterans and 3% of homeless male Veterans who utilize VHA services, have experienced military sexual assault. Military sexual assault is associated with a range of negative outcomes, including depression, PTSD, substance abuse, and suicide (Pavao et al., 2013). One problem with many VA programs for the homeless, is that they tend to focus on male homeless populations. This is also of concern among female Veterans who have been sexually assaulted.

Treatment Options

Cindy can receive information about mental health programs for military sexual trauma through her local Vet Center. Even though Cindy may not be eligible for many services through the VA due to her discharge status, she can get access to Military Sexual Trauma (MST) related care which includes inpatient services (Institute of Medicine, 2007). She also has the option to work with the Homeless Advocacy Project to determine whether she can get access to other VA programs. On the civilian side, there are counseling programs for women who have experienced domestic violence or sexual assault that are funded as part of the Violence Against Women Act of 1994. In addition, Cindy could also seek out a residential substance abuse treatment center which is women only because many of these programs also provide trauma services (Ashley, Marsden, & Brady, 2003).

Conclusion

As the cases illustrate, there are many reasons for and challenges for the homeless Veteran. In general, it is suggested that civilian practitioners partner with local VA programs to address the multiplicity of needs faced by the homeless Vet. In addition, it behooves practitioners to be aware of local resources and organizations that help the homeless in their community.

Notes

1 Quotations and descriptions provided by original draft (unpublished) (van den Berk–Clark & McGuire 2013).

2 Characteristics of OIF/OEF populations were acquired from: Denneson et al. (2014); Liu et al. (2009); Watts (2012).
3 Quotations and descriptions from: Gutierrez et al. (2013); Hamilton, Poza, and Washington (2011); Hamilton, Washington, and Zuchowski (2014).

References

Ames, G., Cunradi, C., Moore, R., & Stern, P. (2007). Military culture and drinking behavior among US Navy careerists. *Journal of Studies of Alcohol and Drugs*, 68(3), 336–344.

Ashley, O. S., Marsden, M. E., & Brady, T. M. (2003). Effectiveness of substance abuse treatment programming for women: A review. *American Journal of Drug and Alcohol Abuse*, 29(1), 19–53.

Beardslee, W., Lester, P., Kosinski, L., Saltzman, W., Woodward, K., Nash, W., & Mogi et al. (2011). Family-centered preventive intervention for military sciences: Implication for implementation science. *Prevention Science*, 12(4), 339–348.

Bremner, J., Southwick, S., Darnell, A., & Charney, D. (1996). Chronic PTSD in Vietnam combat Veterans: Course of illness and substance abuse. *American Journal of Psychiatry*, 153(3), 369–375.

Canada, K. E. & Albright, D. L. (2014). Veterans in the criminal justice system and the role of social work. *Journal of Forensic Social Work*, 4, 48–62.

Cox, J. & Albright, D.L. (2014). The road to recovery: Addressing the challenges and resilience of military couples in the scope of Veterans' mental health. *Social Work in Mental Health*, 12, 560–574.

Culhane, D. P. & Metraux, S. (2008). Rearranging the deck chairs or reallocating the lifeboats? Homelessness assistance and its alternatives. *Journal of the American Planning Association*, 74(1), 111–121.

Denneson, L. M., Teo, A. R., Ganzini, L., Helmer, D. A., Bair, M. J., & Dorscha, S. K. (2014). Military Veterans' experiences with suicidal ideation: Implications for intervention and prevention. *Suicide and Life Threatening Behavior*. doi: 10.1111/sltb.12136

Griffith, J. (2010). Citizens coping as soldiers: A review of deployment stress symptoms among reservists. *Military Psychology*, 22, 176–206.

Gutierrez, P. M., Brenner, L. A., Rings, J. A., Evore, M. D., Kelly, P. J., Staves, P. J., & Kelly, C. et al. (2013). A qualitative description of female Veterans' deployment-related experiences and potential suicide risk factors. *Journal of Clinical Psychology*, 69(9), 923–935.

Hamilton, A. B., Poza, I., & Washington, D. L. (2011). Homelessness and trauma go hand-in-hand: Pathways to homelessness among women Veterans. *Women's Health Issues*, 21(4S), S203–S209.

Hamilton, A. B., Washington, D. L., & Zuchowski, J. L. (2014). Gendered social roots of homelessness among women Veterans. *Annals of Anthropological Practice*, 37(2), 92–107.

Institute of Medicine (2007). *Treatment of PTSD: An assessment of the evidence*. Washington, DC: National Academies Press.

Jackson, G. L., Powers, B. J., Chatterjee, R., Bettger, J., Kemper, A. R., Hasselblad, V., & Dolor et al. (2013). The patient-centered medical home: A systematic review. *Annals of Internal Medicine*, 158, 169–178.

Khadduri, J., Culhane, D., & Cortes, A. (2009). *The Veteran homelessness: A supplemental report to the 2009 annual homeless assessment*. Washington, DC: Veterans Administration.

Liu, W. M., Stinson, R., Hernandez, J., Shepard, S., & Haag, S. (2009). A qualitative examination of masculinity, homelessness and social class among men in a transitional shelter. *Psychology of Men & Masculinity*, 10(2), 131–148.

McKinney–Vento Homeless Assistance Act as amended by S.896. The Homeless Emergency Assistance and Rapid Transition to Housing (HEARTH) Act of 2009 (2009).

Marcuse, P. & Keating, W. D. (2006). The permanent housing crisis: The failures of conservatism and the limitations of liberalism. *A right to housing: Foundation for a new social agenda*, 142.

Montgomery, A. E., Hill, L. L., Kane, V., & Culhane, D. P. (2013). Housing chronically homeless Veterans: Evaluating the efficacy of a housing first approach to HUD–VASH. *Journal of Community Psychology*, 41(4), 505–514.

O'Toole, T. P., Bourgault, C., Johnson, E. E., Redihan, S. G., Borgia, M., Aiello, R., & Kane, V. (2013). New to Care: Demands on a Health System When Homeless Veterans Are Enrolled in a Medical Home Model. *American Journal of Public Health*, 103, S374–S379. doi: 10.2105/ajph.2013.301632

O'Toole, T. P., Conde-Martel, A., Gibbon, J. L., Hanusa, B. H., & Fine, M. J. (2003). Health care of homeless Veterans. *Journal of General Internal Medicine*, 18, 929–933.

Pavao, J., Turchik, J. A., Hyun, J. K., Karpenko, J., Saweikis, M., McCutcheon, & Kane, V. et al. (2013). Military sexual trauma among homeless Veterans. *Journal of General Internal Medicine*, 28, 1–17.

Perl, L. (2011). *Veterans and homelessness.* Washington, DC: Congressional Research Service.

Rosenheck, R., Frisman, L., & Chung, An-me. (1994). The proportion of Veterans among homeless men. *American Journal of Public Health*, 84, 466–469.

Rosenheck, R. A. & Mares, A. S. (2007). Implementation of supported employment for homeless Veterans with psychiatric and addiction disorders: Two-year outcomes. *Psychiatric Services*, 58, 325–333.

Seal, K. H., Shi, Y., Cohen, G., Maguen, B. E., Krebs, E. E., & Neylan, T. C. (2012). Associations of mental health disorders with prescription opioids and high-risk opioid use in US Veterans of Iraq and Afghanistan. *JAMA*, 307(9), 940–947.

Seamone, E. R., McGuire, J., Sreenivasan, S., Clark, S., Smee, D., & Dow, D. (2014). Moving upstream: Why rehabilitative justice in military discharge proceedings serves a public health interest. *American Journal of Public Health*, 104(10), 1805–1811.

Stehberg, J., Albright, D. L., & Weiss, E. L. (2012). The neurobiology of PTSD and cognitive processing therapy (CPT). In A. Rubin, E. L. Weiss, & J. E. Coll (Eds.), *Handbook of military social work* (pp. 99–111). Hoboken: Wiley.

Tessler, R., Rosenheck, R., & Gamache, G. (2002). Comparison of homeless Veterans with other homeless men in a large clinical outreach program. *Psychiatric Quarterly*, 73(2), 109–120.

Tsai, J., Kasprow, W. J., & Rosenheck, R. A. (2014). Alcohol and drug use disorders among homeless Veterans: Prevalence and association with supported housing outcomes. *Addictive Behaviors*, 39, 455–460.

Tsai, J., Mares, A. S., & Rosenheck, R. A. (2012). Do homeless Veterans have the same needs and outcomes as non-Veterans? *Military Medicine*, 177(1), 27–33.

Tsai, J., Pietrzak, R. H., & Rosenheck, R. A. (2012). Homeless Veterans who served in Iraq and Afghanistan: Gender differences, combat exposure, and comparisons with previous cohorts of homeless Veterans. *Administrative Policy Mental Health*, 40, 400–405.

Tsai, J. & Rosenheck, R. A. (2014). Risk factors for homelessness among US Veterans. *Epidemiologic Reviews*. doi: 10.1093/epirev/mxu004

US Department of Housing and Urban Development (2014). *Annual Homeless Assessment Report (AHAR) to Congress.* Link: www.hudexchange.info/resources/documents/2014-AHAR-Part1.pdf

van den Berk-Clark, C. (2015). The Dilemmas of frontline staff working with the homeless: Housing first, discretion, and the task environment. *Housing Policy Debate*, 1–18.

van den Berk-Clark, C., & McGuire, J. (2013). Elderly homeless Veterans in Los Angeles: Chronicity and precipitants of homelessness. *American Journal of Public Health*, 103, S232–S238.

van den Berk-Clark, C., & McGuire, J. (2014). Trust in health care providers: factors predicting trust among homeless Veterans over time. *Journal of Health Care for the Poor and Underserved*, 25(3), 1278–1290.

Watts, M. (2012). A qualitative exploration of the lived experience of being homeless. PhD dissertation, University of Southampton, Southampton, UK.

Wenzel, S. L., Bakhtiar, L., Caskey, N. H., Hardie, E., Redford, C., Sadler, N., & Gelberg, L. (1995). Homeless Veterans' utilization of medical, psychiatric, and substance abuse services. *Medical Care*, 33(11), 1132–1144.

Zatzick, D., Rivara, F., Jurkovich, G., Hoge, C., Wang, F., & Fan, M. (2010). Multisite investigation of traumatic brain injuries, PTSD and self-reported health and cognitive impairments. *Archives of General Psychiatry*, 67, 1291–1300.

4

WOMEN SERVICE MEMBERS AND VETERANS

Anne G. Sadler, Michelle A. Mengeling, Sarah S. Fraley and Brittany D. Martin

Military Women's Increasing Roles and Numbers

Women have served this country for decades, sometimes disguised as male soldiers, often as nurses, and now in combat (National Center for Veterans Analysis and Statistics, 2011). In 2013, the repeal of the military ban on women in combat at last acknowledged women's service in war, although they have carried arms or been at risk from the enemy in every US war conflict since the American Revolution (Murdoch et al., 2006). Prior to officially allowing women in direct combat roles, the military was the only major social institution in the nation that could legally discriminate in employment on the basis of gender (Kelty, Kleykamp, & Segal, 2010).

Recent wars in the Middle East have called attention not only to the courage and sacrifice of those serving in the US Armed Forces but to the emerging numbers and roles of military women. The number of women serving on active duty has risen dramatically since the US military ended conscription and established an all-volunteer force in 1973. Women currently are a greater proportion of active-duty military than ever before (Patten & Parker, 2011) and the number of females serving is expected to expand to 20% by 2020 (Department of Defense, 2014). Specifically, women comprise 15% (N = 203,895) of the Department of Defense (DoD) active-duty force and 19% (N = 155,589) of the Selected Reserve Force (the Reserve and National Guard) (Department of Defense, 2013).

Women Veterans are the fastest growing group of Veterans Health Administration (VHA) users and are estimated to make up 15% of VHA users by 2020. Unfortunately, most women seek their healthcare outside of the VHA (Washington, Yano, Simon, & Sun, 2006) where their Veteran status is rarely recognized (Murdoch et al., 2006). Recently the Veterans Access, Choice, and Accountability Act of 2014 (VACAA) authorized Veterans who reside more than 40 miles from their nearest VHA facility to access healthcare closer to home through VHA-approved non-VHA community healthcare facilities. While VACAA is a temporary program that enables the VHA to meet the healthcare demand among enrolled Veterans in the short term, this too has resulted in an influx of Veterans treated in community settings. These factors have vital implications for providers who may be unaware that the women who serve our country have substantial health risks often resulting in complex care needs. In order to provide optimal care, all health organizations and providers should become familiar with and consider the unique healthcare needs of women Veterans, and become familiar with Department of Veterans Affairs (VA) resources to best serve them (Committee on Health Care for Underserved Women,

2012). This chapter will provide an overview to address this need. In addition, we will provide an overview of sexual health, social support, and family issues associated with military service that are just now emerging as important considerations in providing care for military women.

Service Options: Active Duty versus Selected Reserve Service

Individuals interested in serving our country may choose to pursue a full-time role as an active-duty service member, or a part-time role within the Reserves or National Guard (RNG). Active-duty military and selected Reserves component service is distinctly different and can influence military women's occupational health exposures, support networks, and access to care. Active-duty service is full-time and women may live on a military base and can be deployed at any time. RNG are not full-time, although they can be deployed at any time should the need arise (US Department of Veterans Affairs, 2012).

There are also important differences between Reserve and National Guard service roles. The US military is composed of five service branches with unique responsibilities (Army, Navy, Air Force, Marines, Coast Guard). Each military branch has a Reserve component under the command of their respective military branch. The purpose of the Reserves is to maintain qualified individuals and trained units to be available for active-duty service should the need arise (e.g. war, national emergency, threats to national security). The Reserves are essential to filling gaps in stateside service when active-duty forces are overseas. In contrast, the National Guard (consisting of the Army National Guard and Air Force Air National Guard) is federally funded but organized and controlled by each state. The services of the National Guard (NG) are diverse and NG service women can also become federalized and deployed during times of war and may see combat. They are given Veteran status only if they serve for 30 consecutive days in a war zone. They assist stateside, e.g. with communities endangered by natural disasters. Both Reserve and NG requires training drills one weekend a month and two weeks per year (US Department of Veterans Affairs, 2012).

These distinctions in service are important to note not only with regard to women Veterans' access to VA and other care but because recent studies indicate that current eras of RNG may have higher rates of post-deployment mental health problems than active-duty peers (Thomas et al., 2010). Widespread readjustment problems have been found in NG service members with almost half experiencing post-deployment financial or family concerns (Kline, Ciccone, Falca-Dodson, Black, & Losonczy, 2011). Clinicians must be aware that, in contrast to active-duty service members who return from deployment to military environments familiar with the activities and consequences of war, RNG service members return to civilian communities, workplaces, and local care providers likely unfamiliar with post-deployment readjustment needs and concerns. An additional consequence of RNG service compared with active duty is that of returning home and being disbanded from their military unit. RNG service women will likely have decreased interface with military peers; peers who might note and respond to post-deployment functioning or readjustment concerns observable in daily work and living environments, which is significantly different from active-duty settings.

Who Are Military Women?

Age

The US military differs substantially from the civilian workforce as it relies heavily on the young. This younger age distribution is due to the military up-or-out promotion system, lack of lateral transfers, and high demand for physical fitness (Kelty et al., 2010). Almost three-quarters (72%) of active duty enlisted are 30 years of age or younger relative to 60% of RNG peers. The smallest group of enlisted service men and women (6%) are age 41 and older, whereas the largest group of officers fall within this age (26%) (Department of Defense, 2013). Those men and women serving in the Selected Reserve (RNG) are also a young workforce, with 59% of enlisted service members 30 years of age or younger, relative to 18% of officers. Over two-thirds (68%) of active-duty women are 30 and under as are over one-third of officers (36%). Relatively, around half (53%) of RNG military women are 30 years of age or younger as are almost one-fifth (19%) of officers (Department of Defense, 2013). More men than women are found in the older age ranges and this may be attributable to attrition because of sexual violence experiences (Sadler, Booth, Cook, & Doebbeling, 2003), family reasons (Kelty et al., 2010), or a military environment that retains and promotes men more than women given prior access to combat roles that enhance promotion opportunities.

Rank and Service Branch

Women represent 15% of enlisted service members and 16% of commissioned officers. Notably, the number of female commissioned officers is proportional to the number of female enlisted service members (1 female officer to 4.2 female enlisted; 1 male officer to 4.8 male enlisted). The Air Force has the largest percentage of female enlisted Service members (19%), followed by Navy (18%), Army (14%) with the US Marine Corps having the smallest percentage (7%). Proportions of women officers by branch follow this same trend with Air Force (20%) having the highest percentage of female officers followed by Navy 17%, Army 16% and following last, the Marine Corps at 7% (Department of Defense, 2013).

Race

Women serving in active duty are more racially diverse than male peers. The majority of active-duty men are white (71%) relative to approximately half of active-duty women (53%) (Patten & Parker, 2011).

Marriage

Around half of male and female active duty and RNG service members are married (55%, 45%, respectively). However, the percentages for service women only is lower: 46% for active-duty service women and 36% for RNG service women. In both active duty and RNG branches, a higher percentage of female military members are married to another military member (i.e. in dual-military marriages) than males (21% vs. 4% in active duty and 24% vs. 3% in RNG).

Parenthood

Over 40% of active-duty women are mothers (Mulhall, 2009). When compared with men, women are more frequently single parents (12%) (Patten & Parker, 2011).

Reasons Women Join the Military

Women have integrated into what were traditionally male occupations in both civilian and military sectors of our society. Yet research exploring why women join the armed forces is sparse. Early research considering high school seniors' propensity to enlist in the military found that most female senior high school students do not expect or desire to serve in the military (Segal, Segal, Bachman, Freedman-Doan, & O'Malley, 1998). Women from intact families, who have parents with higher educational achievement, and who have children were found to be less likely to join the military (Segal et al., 1998). Research in VA-enrolled women Veterans found that women report joining the military to leave abusive or distressing home lives (Sadler et al., 2003). This possibility is corroborated by the rates of childhood sexual victimization in active military women (25–49%) that are markedly higher than that found among civilians (Blosnich, Dichter, Cerulli, Batten, & Bossarte, 2014; Merrill et al., 1998; Rosen & Martin, 1996; Sadler, Booth, & Doebbeling, 2005; Sadler, Booth, Mengeling, & Doebbeling, 2004). A recent study of post 9/11 female Veterans found that women's reasons for joining the armed forces were similar to men's. Most women (83%) joined to serve their country, with 70% wanting to see more of the world (Patten & Parker, 2011). Other reasons for enlisting were a means for future vocational security, including the desire to receive educational benefits (82%), learning skills for civilian jobs (67%) and almost half (42%) joined because jobs were hard to find (Patten & Parker, 2011). Women's enlistment has been found to be higher in regions and communities where there is a greater military visibility (Segal et al., 1998). However, subsequent research found that civilian women living in areas with a high military presence experience higher rates of unemployment and lower earnings than peers in non-military locations (Kleykamp, 2006). Consequently, service may be viewed as the most viable job option given these environments.

Post-Military Gender Differences: Vocational and Educational

Military service can serve as a bridge between high school and post-service careers, yet there is limited research in this area with respect to women (Cooney, Segal, Segal, & Falk, 2003). Earlier work found that although women Veterans are able to transfer their military skills to civilian employments at higher rates than men, they benefit less from their service than men with regard to wages. This was speculated to be because of the concentration of women in traditionally female roles within the military in the early 1990s (Firestone, 1992). Yet, a more recent Census Bureau survey (2011) confirmed this wage discrepancy may persist as women Veterans have lower median personal incomes than male Veterans ($30,378 vs. $35,814) when comparisons are made among individuals who work year-round and full-time. However, Veterans had higher incomes in both genders than non-Veterans (US Department of Veterans Affairs, 2013).

Conversely, women Veterans are more likely to complete higher education than male peers. In comparison with male peers, a higher percentage of female Veterans have completed a bachelor's or advanced degree (20% vs. 15% and 12% vs. 10%, respectively). And, almost half of women Veterans had completed some college (47%) compared with approximately one-third (36%) of male Veterans.

CASE EXAMPLE

Mary is a 35-year-old married white female seeking care in a primary care clinic. She returned from her first deployment to Iraq as a commissioned officer with her Reserve unit approximately six months ago. She is single-parenting 11- and 13-year-old sons while her husband is now deployed to Iraq with his Reserve unit. They had a two-month overlap together prior to his deployment. She reports she is concerned about being labeled as unfit for duty if she seeks mental healthcare but her nightmares and pacing the house to check for safety is exhausting. In addition, she sustained a back injury when an IED (improvised explosive device) exploded near her truck and turned it over. The chronic discomfort also impairs her quality of life. She reports she doesn't have family in the area and has distanced herself from her peers in her unit as she doesn't want to talk about her war experiences. She doesn't want to be any more specific about her deployment than indicating the origins of her pain. She doesn't know whether she has any VA eligibility and she is concerned members of her unit will see her if she seeks care there. She reports she cannot talk with her husband about what happened during her deployment as he is already under too much stress and she has concern for his safety during deployment. She states their relationship has become distant ever since she knew she was going to be deployed. She may be redeployed. Time with her sons is her primary pleasure and she wants medication to help her be less anxious and to be able to sleep so that she can be the best mother possible. The material following describes what is important in conceptualizing help for Mary.

Military Women's Experiences with and Health Consequences of War and Sexual Assault

Combat and sexual assault are the most common traumatic exposures experienced by military women. In recent wars, service women have experienced a substantial increase in combat exposures, with approximately one-quarter (24%) of service women who have served since 1990 reporting these experiences relative to 7% of service women serving previously (Patten & Parker, 2011). While 18% to 25% of American women experience an attempted or completed sexual assault (SA) in their lifetime (Fisher, Cullen, & Turner, 2000; Tjaden & Thoennes, 2000), rates of sexual assault in military (SAIM) are equal or higher during military women's relatively shorter duration of service (Surís & Lind, 2008; Turchik & Wilson, 2010) where rates have been found to range from approximately one-quarter to one-third of women (Surís & Lind, 2008). The 2014 RAND Military Workplace Study of more than a million service members estimated that the rate of sexual assault in the past year was approximately 1 in 20 service women (Morral, Gore, & Schell, 2014). Furthermore, many military women who experience sexual assault experience more than one sexual assault during military service (Sadler et al., 2004).

Among the outcomes of SAIM are severe and chronic physical and mental health burdens as well as the adverse impacts on military force morale, readiness, and retention (Booth, Mengeling, Torner, & Sadler, 2011; Frayne et al., 1999; Sadler, Booth, Nielson, & Doebbeling, 2000; Sadler, Mengeling, Fraley, Torner, & Booth, 2012; Surís & Lind, 2008). The degree of risk of post-traumatic stress disorder (PTSD) associated with SAIM has been found to be similar to that associated with "high" combat exposure in a community sample of female Persian Gulf War Veterans (Kang, Dalager, Mahan, & Ishii, 2005).

Sexual Health and Military Women

Despite known challenges for service women returning to civilian life in terms of reintegration into family and romantic relationships, especially among Operation Iraqi Freedom or Operation Enduring Freedom (OIF/OEF) service members (Sayers, Farrow, Ross, & Oslin, 2009), particular attention to sexual intimacy – including sexual health and functioning – has been under-discussed in literature focused on women Veterans. Sexual health is defined as "a state of physical, emotional, mental and social well-being in relation to sexuality; it is not merely the absence of disease, dysfunction or infirmity" (World Health Organization, 2002) and has generally been linked to emotional health and quality of life (Bridges, Lease, & Ellison, 2004; Lauman, Pail, & Rosen, 1999). While data on women Veterans in this area of functioning may be minimal, we can augment this with research on active-duty service women as well as on civilian women with various health issues similar to women Veterans for important considerations.

Women Veteran patients may experience shame, shyness, or anxiety in seeking care for sexual health issues and may perceive various barriers to receiving this care, including confusion about who to consult and whether care will be effective (Kedde, Van de Wiel, Schultz, Vanwesenbeeck, & Bender, 2012). As a result, these women appear to be more satisfied with specialized women's clinics where issues are addressed more sensitively, than with traditional primary care clinics (Bean-Mayberry et al., 2003). General treatment approaches should aim to achieve a balance between prevention/harm-reduction with regard to risky sexual behaviors and a sex-positive approach (Cameron et al., 2011). The PLISSIT (permission, limited information, specific suggestions, intensive therapy; Annon, 1976) model may also be useful in providing sexuality education and treatment. This model has four components: P, permission; L, limited information; SS, specific suggestions; and IT, intensive therapy. Initially, it is important for a provider to give permission (P) to discuss the topic by asking a general question such as "Do you have any concerns about sexual intimacy or sexual satisfaction in your life right now?" The provider can then move to providing limited information (LI) about any concerns, then offer (if appropriate) specific suggestions (SS) or intensive therapy (IT). Alternately, a provider can refer the individual to someone with specific expertise in treating sexual problems. Providing permission in itself allows a woman to recognize that the provider is comfortable discussing sexuality (at least on some level) and will be open if and when she wishes to discuss it further.

Sexual Violence Impact on Sexual Health

As noted previously, sexual trauma histories are common among women Veterans – with sexual violence occurrences both during military service as well as throughout the Veteran's life span (Sadler et al., 2004). Other forms of sexual victimization, such as sexual harassment and coerced sexual activity, are also potentially distressing and even more prevalent (Sadler et al., 2012). While immediate attention post-trauma is usually paid to identifying and treating sexually transmitted infections (STIs) or physical injuries, other issues causing changes in sexual functioning can create challenges in future consensual sexual intimacy. Substantial reproductive health consequences associated with sexual violence have been found in women Veterans, including higher rates of abnormal cervical cytology (Sadler, Mengeling, Syrop, Torner, & Booth, 2011), urinary incontinence (Bradley et al., 2012, 2014), infertility (Ryan et al., 2014), and hysterectomy (Ryan et al., 2015).

Weaver (2009) notes that sexual trauma for women is not only associated with physical issues such as painful menstruation and other problems associated with reproductive functioning, but that sexual functioning is also often impaired as a unique experience from medically explained problems. These impairments can include low sexual satisfaction, inhibited arousal and desire dysfunctions, painful intercourse, and impaired ability to achieve orgasm. Many women are reluctant to seek help for these problems in functioning due to prior hurtful or insensitive contact with medical professionals and feelings of depression, anxiety, mistrust, or blame from others regarding their sexual trauma (Campbell & Raja, 2005). Again, giving permission and recognizing that this area of functioning is important can help encourage women to seek additional help. It is also helpful to be familiar with local providers who can assist with these issues so that one can be assured of making referrals to caring and sensitive professionals.

PTSD and Sexual Health

Another issue that is closely related to sexual functioning is PTSD, which may or may not be the result of a sexual trauma. Lifetime prevalence of PTSD for women is estimated at 12.8% (Kilpatrick et al., 2013) and PTSD is the most prevalent mental health diagnosis for Veterans enrolled in Department of Veterans Affairs hospitals (Seal, Bertenthal, Miner, Sen, & Marmar, 2007). While not part of the clinical criteria for a PTSD diagnosis, sexual dysfunction is extremely common among those with PTSD (Yehuda, Lehmer, & Rosenbaum, 2015). Not all individuals who experience sexual trauma develop PTSD; however, there is some indication that women with a PTSD diagnosis are more prone to several reproductive and sexual health problems, including chronic pelvic pain, STIs, painful intercourse, and endometriosis (Weaver, 2009). Other sexual functioning problems noted in men and women with PTSD include impairments in desire, arousal, and satisfaction. There are several theories as to the mechanism by which PTSD affects sexual functioning, including disruptions in body physiology/arousal, emotional numbing, intrusive symptoms that occur during sexual activity (and subsequent avoidance of sexual activity), and poor relationship functioning (Tran, Dunckel, & Teng, 2015). Yehuda et al. (2015) note also that psychotropic medications commonly prescribed for PTSD and co-occurring depression are known to have a high rate of associated sexual side effects – and that simply having co-occurring depression may itself cause dysfunction. These authors also stress the importance of including intimate partners in treatment of PTSD if possible and propose that effective assessment and treatment of PTSD should include attention to sexual functioning. Providers who prescribe medications for PTSD and depression should regularly assess for sexual side effects – and those who collaborate with these types of providers can encourage women to communicate to their providers if these side effects occur. In terms of psychotherapy, any empirically supported treatment for PTSD can also incorporate attention to sexual health, at least in terms of assessment and recognition of this area of functioning.

Health Problems, Disability, and Sexual Health

Women Veterans with chronic health problems or disabling physical conditions (e.g. traumatic brain injury, spinal cord injury, multiple sclerosis) are yet another sector of this population who have unique sexual functioning concerns. In addition to more traditional sexual functioning issues such as desire and arousal disorders, many women with disabilities struggle with chronic pain, limited mobility, fatigue, body image concerns, and low sexual self-esteem (Clemency Cordes, Mona, Syme, Cameron, & Smith, 2013). Nosek, Howland, Rintala, Young, and Chanpong (2001) also report that women with disabilities as a whole express lower satisfaction with dating and relationships compared with non-disabled women. When women with disabilities seek treatment around sexual expression issues, they often perceive negative attitudes from providers surrounding disability and sexuality, which can cause some women to postpone needed care and experience worsening symptoms or secondary conditions (Parish & Huh, 2006). Piotrowski and Snell (2007) outline several attitudinal, informational, environmental, and geographic barriers for women with disabilities seeking healthcare in general. They also acknowledge that women with disabilities are more at risk from various types of abuse (partner, caregiver, medical provider) and need access to information on STIs and pregnancy prevention (despite the pervasive belief that people with disabilities do not engage in sexual activity). Simply asking women with disabilities about sexual functioning and intimacy issues can be affirming and encouraging of further discussion. As with many sensitive clinical issues, it can be useful for providers to examine their own personal beliefs about sexuality in general and sexuality and disability in particular in order to provide more objective patient-centered care (Tran, Dunckel, & Teng, 2015). It is also important to be aware of community resources for further information and treatment, such as physical rehabilitation providers who could offer assistance with pain management, safe sexual positioning, or use of sexual aids to assist in adapted sexual pleasure (Fraley, Mona, & Theodore, 2007).

Social Support and Military Women

Social support is a vital aspect of resilience and recovery for individuals exposed to stressful experiences, and for the service member, the cycles of deployment exert substantial stress. Social support is affected by the time/era when women Veterans have served deployments. The proportions of women serving in the most recent eras of service are comparable: 27% from the end of Vietnam to the Persian Gulf; 26% from the Persian Gulf to 9/11; and 23% since 9/11 (Patten & Parker, 2011) but with changes in warfare come changes in women's post-deployment needs. As OEF/OIF-era service women have experienced more combat deployments, the separations create higher levels of stress on the family system including spouses and children (Department of Defense, 2010; Chandra et al., 2008). Gender comparison studies have found that women have less interpersonal support during OEF/OIF conflicts compared with men (Fontana, Rosenheck, & Desai, 2010; Frayne et al., 2006) although when compared with other eras, Vietnam women had the least social support (Fontana et al., 2010; Cotten, Skinner, & Sullivan, 2000). Consequently, the nature of combat, deployment, and time of service should always be considered an important part of understanding how best to address the specific needs of a woman Veteran. Military women can be deployed in support of combat but be stationed outside of war zones (e.g. military healthcare workers, pilots, body handlers); deployed elsewhere (e.g. in or outside of the continental United States but not in a combat-related area or in support of it); or to combat-related areas (e.g. direct combat roles, healthcare workers). Era of service provides a picture of wartime versus peacetime service; gender ratios, with regard to the number of fellow women serving at that time; differences in combat roles or exposures (officially or unofficially); and perceptions of male service members' and society's views of women serving in the military.

Social support and the development of PTSD or its symptoms are interconnected. If the Veteran has PTSD or its symptomatology, their positive coping resources are lowered, which affects their responses to others and may hinder access to positive social support, and in turn leads to exacerbation of the stress system (Benotsch et al., 2000). However, social support is also able to serve as a protective source during the adjustment process after high stress (Benotsch et al. 2000; Guay, Billette, & Marchand, 2006; Park, Wachen, Kaiser, & Mager Stellman, 2015). For women, social support is a common form of coping with stress (Groer & Burns, 2009) and through it, positive coping can be enhanced by interrupting negative patterns that lead to PTSD and depression (Pietrzak et al., 2010). Research on Veterans has revealed that social support has particular value for women Veterans in juxtaposition to men when recovering from the effects of combat (Benda, 2005, 2006; King, King, Fairbank, Keane, & Adams 1998; King, King, Foy, Keane, & Fairbank, 1999; Park et al., 2015; Yan et al., 2013). Of especial importance is functional social support, which is related to the type of support received from the friend and family network as it relates to emotional availability and quality of the interpersonal relationships.

An important time when social support is most needed is during the post-deployment period. Post-deployment reintegration produces multiple stressors (Chandra, Burns, Tanielian, Jaycox, & Scott, 2008; Finley et al., 2010; Mattocks et al., 2012; Vogt et al., 2011; Wooten, 2012) that can overwhelm the returning Veteran who is still coping from living under high stress. Research has found that women who report less post-deployment social support have greater relational problems which in turn affect the trajectory of their mental health (Nayback-Beebe & Yoder, 2011; Vogt et al., 2011) since women Veterans appear to be more vulnerable for mental health problems if they experience interpersonal stress (Vogt, Pless, King, & King, 2005; Vogt et al., 2011). When homecoming support is low and stressors high, there is a greater risk for mental health disorders to develop (Fontana et al., 1997; Wooten, 2012). Thus, the level and type of interpersonal support or strain is essential to understand and address in female Veterans.

Although about one-third of newly returning war Veterans have been found to have consequent mental health problems, most men and women do not seek needed mental healthcare (Seal et al., 2007). This failure to engage in needed treatment may be due to predisposing factors, such as younger age; features of PTSD (e.g. avoidance), and other priorities that compete, such as employment (Seal et al., 2007). Widespread post-deployment financial and family problems have also been found (Kline et al., 2011). Practitioners must be cognizant that women Veterans may not be aware that they have treatable mental health conditions and are concerned about the stigma of mental health treatment or possible adverse consequences of treatment on their military or civilian careers. They may also have concerns about time or cost of care. Consequently, the need for routine screening, normalizing that experiences in military and war can impact mental health and quality of life, and that treatment can help, are important. Veterans should be made aware that the VA provides services to returning war Veterans as a priority population and, as a provider, collaboration with their local VA is encouraged. Veterans should be educated that treatment helps and that treatment options are diverse, as will be seen in subsequent chapters. Counseling can be focused on symptom management (e.g. sleep disturbances); or overall programs of care (e.g. evidence-based treatment for PTSD). Many VAs offer complementary alternative treatments found to be helpful (e.g. mindfulness-based meditation). Most importantly, providers must engage the returning female Veteran in shared decision-making about what treatment options are available and what her next steps in getting help are according to her unique needs, priorities, and preferences.

Family and Military Women

Post-Deployment Readjustment and Family

For women Veterans, main areas of stress are often family related (Cotten et al., 2000; Mattocks et al., 2012; Polusny et al., 2014; Vogt et al., 2005; Yan et al., 2013). Yet, dependent on their relational and career status (e.g. active duty, Reserve/NG, married, single, with or without children), military women also have different familial and social support needs (Blow et al., 2012; Kelley et al., 2002; Werber Castaneda et al., 2008). Bringing to awareness such important factors will aid in providing the best care to women Veterans. Women Veterans may feel the needs of their children and other family members should take priority over their personal physical and mental care (Mattocks et al., 2012). However, if the service woman is not receiving proper care, then the natural demands of life exacerbate her own personal stress. Research has demonstrated that without addressing Veterans' social supports and family situations, successful provision of care is compromised. Therefore more needs to be done with family-centered services, as treating the Veteran is not enough (Dekel & Monson, 2010; Galovski & Lyons, 2004; Lester et al., 2013). Importantly, Veterans themselves desire more family-focused assistance over individualized therapy (Khaylis, Polusny, Erbes, Gewirtz, & Rath, 2011). What is still lacking is literature about what is most helpful in assisting women Veterans during their post-deployment reintegration into their roles as mothers and partners. Practitioners must be aware that family issues may be a key concern for returning women Veterans and query them about this directly. The DVA now includes licensed marital and family therapists integrally within their mental health service lines and these clinicians are experienced in addressing such concerns and working collaboratively with local providers.

Post-Deployment Family Readjustment

Returning women are demonstrating a higher risk for family readjustment problems (Mattocks et al., 2012; Sayers et al., 2009; Vogt et al., 2011) with women Veterans having divorce rates three times higher than their male counterparts (Boyd, Bradshaw, & Robinson, 2013; Mulhall, 2009), and spousal abuse/aggression being prevalent (Fonseca, Schmaling, Stoever, & Gutierrez, 2006; Gibbs, Clinton-Sherrod, & Johnson, 2012; McCarroll et al., 2010; Rabenhorst et al., 2012, 2013; Sayers et al., 2009). Due to the value of interpersonal relationships for women (Yan et al., 2013), the quality of social support received from partners is important to keep in mind. Although research is still growing regarding social support and its role in Veterans' post-deployment adjustment, some work has highlighted the dichotomy of partners as sources of stress and support (Benotsch et al., 2000; Laffaye, Cavella, Drescher, & Rosen, 2008). Spouses of Veterans also have higher rates of mental health needs (Blow et al., 2012) which need to be acknowledged and treated since their relationship with the service member will influence their adjustment and well-being. If interpersonal and partner relationships exert strain, one form of negative coping women Veterans adopt is social isolation that can entail involvement with such problematic behaviors as excessive exercise, prescription drug use, or overeating (Mattocks et al., 2012). With the stress of role reintegration and the avoidance or numbing that accompanies PTSD or the response to traumatic exposure (Galovski & Lyons, 2004), women Veterans who feel they lack support often have less effective social functioning and greater interpersonal problems with their family and friends (Cotten et al., 2000), which contributes to isolation. Intimate partner violence and aggression are other factors that can affect women Veterans in the reintegration process, and prevalence rates span from 13.5% to 58% (Jones, 2012; Marshall, Panuzio, & Taft, 2005). Not only do they experience it from their partners but they are just as likely to be the perpetrators, since some studies have found that women Veterans are more likely to perpetrate aggression in the family environment (Dutra, de Blank, Scheiderer, & Taft, 2012; Foran, Slep, & Heyman, 2011; Gierisch et al., 2013; Jones, 2012; Sullivan & Elbogen, 2014).

Motherhood, Deployment and Military Retention

While children are significantly affected by parental deployment, not much is known about how mothers are affected by their dual roles. A study that considered the duality of work and family stress for Air Force active and reserve military women (Vinokur, Pierce, & Buck, 1999) highlighted that the role of motherhood is the main factor that affects the stress experienced between career and family responsibilities, which contributes to their level of functioning and mental health, specifically depression.

For single mothers, at least 30,000 have experienced OEF/OIF deployments (Mulhall, 2009). Single parents have less access to social support systems (Barker & Berry, 2009; Goodman et al., 2013; Kelley et al., 2002), so it is important to verify the relational status of the female Veteran when providing care since her unique position and responsibilities will influence her readjustment.

The role of motherhood also has a strong influence on whether women stay in the military or not. Retention or separation from the military for women Veterans largely depends on their family situation (Kelley et al., 2001; Pierce, 1998) since the time away from spouse and children has been cited as a top reason for why some women leave the military before retirement (Mulhall, 2009).

What Practitioners Should Know about the Department of Veterans Affairs

Accessing Veterans Health Administration (VHA) Care

Not all Veterans are eligible for VHA care. Access to VA healthcare is managed through an annual enrollment system that ensures certain groups of Veterans are given priority. All Veterans who meet the basic requirements are encouraged to enroll. Additional information about Veteran Eligibility can be found on the www.va.gov website (www.va.gov/healthbe nefits/apply/Veterans.asp). Enrollment can be done online, by phone, by mail, or in person at a VA Medical Center or clinic.

Women who have served in the most recent conflicts during Operation Enduring Freedom (OEF), Operation Iraqi Freedom (OIF), and Operation New Dawn (OND), are enrolling in VA in historically high rates. Forty-four percent of all women who were deployed and served in Iraq or Afghanistan have enrolled in VA's healthcare system (US Department of Veterans Affairs, 2015). And among all women VHA patients, nearly one in five served in OEF/OIF/ OND. OEF/OIF/OND Veterans have access to enhanced VA healthcare benefits. These Combat Veterans are provided with five years of healthcare eligibility post-discharge. Combat service can be demonstrated by military service in a combat theater, receipt of combat tax exemption, imminent danger or hostile fire pay, or receipt of combat service medals.

VHA Women's Health Care

Women Veterans comprise one of the fastest growing groups of Veterans and VA healthcare users and are estimated to make up 15% of VA users by 2020. VHA has historically provided care to a predominantly male population, but as the numbers of women Veterans have increased, so have concerns about the availability and delivery of women's gender-specific healthcare. In response, Congress has passed multiple legislative acts that have profoundly changed the array of services offered to women Veterans by VHA. The Veterans Health Act of 1992 (P.L. 102-585) expanded gender-specific care (e.g. Pap smears, breast examinations, management of menopause, mammography) for eligible women Veterans seeking care within VHA. Additionally, the law authorized VA to provide women Veterans counseling services for conditions related to military sexual trauma (MST). In 1994, VA was authorized to expand services for MST beyond counseling to include "appropriate care and services for conditions related to sexual trauma" (P.L. 103-452). Notably, the law also authorized VA authority to treat women *and men* for MST-related conditions. In 1995, maternity and infertility services were added to VA's Uniform Medical Benefits package. These included pregnancy and delivery services and certain medically necessary infertility services. Abortions, abortion counseling, and in-vitro fertilization were expressly excluded from the medical benefits package. Research has shown that women Veterans who do not use VA healthcare are less likely to know about the availability of VA women's health services (Washington et al., 2006).

Every VHA medical facility has a full-time Women Veterans Program Manager (WVPM) who assists and coordinates women Veterans' healthcare within VHA. In addition, the VA has established the Women Veterans Call Center (WVCC) to provide women Veterans with information about benefits, eligibility and services specifically for women Veterans (phone number: 1.855.VA.WOMEN). All WVCC representatives are women and many are Veterans. WVCC representatives may refer women Veterans to a WVPM. Because VA knows that women Veterans under-utilize VA basic care a lack of knowledge regarding eligibility, benefits, and services, WVCC also reaches out to women Veterans to educate them about their benefits and connect them to the services for which they are eligible.

VHA Women Veteran Users

Approximately 32% of women Veterans are VA enrolled and of those, approximately 60% are VHA care users (Frayne et al., 2014; National Center for Veterans Analysis and Statistics, 2011). The age distribution of VHA women Veteran users are 18–44 (42%), 45–64 (46%), and 65 or older (12%). Within each age range the peaks in occur at 29, 50, and 88. The top five domains of health conditions among VHA women Veteran users include endocrine/metabolic/nutritional (51%), mental health and substance use disorders (45%), cardiovascular (37%), and reproductive health (31%) and are ranked differently for each age cohort. Women, across all age groups, use VHA outpatient services more heavily than men. The proportion of women Veteran patients with a service-connected (SC) disability rating has been increasing and now more than half of women Veteran patients have an SC disability rating, which makes them eligible for lifelong VHA care for their SC conditions (Frayne et al., 2006). Women Veterans who use VA services have poorer physical and mental health than women in the general population (Frayne et al., 2006; Lehavot, Hoerster, Nelson, Jakupcak, & Simpson, 2012).

VHA and Rural Women Veterans

Among VHA healthcare users, approximately one-quarter (28%) of women Veterans reside in rural areas (Frayne et al., 2014). Compared with urban VHA users, rural women Veterans tend to be older, married, and more likely to have served in eras prior to OEF/OIF/OND (Brooks, Dailey, Bair, & Shore, 2014). Rates of PTSD, mood disorders, eating disorders, hypertension, and diabetes were similar for rural and urban women Veterans. With regard to healthcare preferences, rural women Veterans are less likely to endorse specific care preferences than urban women Veterans, such as a need for separate waiting areas just for women, to want a female chaperone in the room during a physical examination (Mengeling, Sadler, Torner, & Booth, 2011), or the option of being treated by a male or female healthcare provider. Perceptions of VHA care are similar for rural and urban women Veterans.

VHA has a mission to provide care to all Veterans eligible for services, regardless of where the Veteran resides. Therefore, VHA has pursued initiatives that support rural Veterans' care access. Community Based Outpatient Clinics (CBOCs) were designed to accomplish multiple goals such as improving access to care for historically underserved Veteran populations, reducing travel burdens, and by providing primary care in a community ambulatory care setting rather than a hospital-based clinic (Chapko et al., 2002). CBOCs have been shown to provide the same level of care quality as their affiliated parent VA Medical Center (Hedeen, Chapko, Fortney, & Borowsky, 2000).

Implications for Behavioral Health Practitioners

In conclusion, there are several considerations in providing competent care for women in the military and Veterans:

1. Be aware that military women and Veterans are at high risk of trauma exposure, which can have a long-lasting impact throughout their lifetime; these experiences can result in adverse reproductive, physical, emotional, and sexual health consequences that are both severe and chronic.
2. Ask women in your care "Have you ever or are you currently serving in US Armed Forces, Reserves or National Guard?" Women do not routinely volunteer this information (Committee on Health Care for Underserved Women, 2012).
3. Assess for histories of sexual violence. The VA screening questions used to address this are: "While you were in the military: (a) Did you receive uninvited and unwanted sexual attention, such as touching, cornering, pressure for sexual favors, or verbal remarks?" (b) "Did someone ever use force or threat of force to have sexual contact with you against your will?" Given the high rates of violence women experience over their lifetimes, these questions can also be framed to also address lifespan violence. The number of and identification of the most recent violent event experienced is also important information influencing care needs.
4. Be knowledgeable that the type of service has different impacts on military service roles and exposures, access to services, and post-deployment readjustment. Era of service also can inform the clinician about women's possible experiences (e.g. combat and roles as a female in a male dominant occupation). Ask military women and Veterans to tell you their history and experiences in military.
5. Assess sexual health variables for women of all ages (not only those of childbearing age). This allows for detection of issues that may be long-term sexual health consequences of sexual trauma or mental health consequences of both combat and sexual violence (Sadler et al., 2012). It is important to present a positive attitude toward sexuality and to engage in sensitive communication on this topic (Westgren & Levi, 1999). Taking a neutral stance toward various types of sexual activities, avoidance of an assumption of heterosexuality, and recognition of single individuals (who may have interest in solitary sexual activity) is also helpful for inclusive care (Cameron et al., 2011).
6. Be aware of the effects of military service on the female client's couple and family relationships and the partner and families well-being in general. Recognize that it is important to assess how these relationships impact her well-being. Screening for intimate partner violence with respect to both victimization and perpetration is key. Women Veterans have been found to desire more family-focused interventions over individual treatment (Khaylis et al., 2011) and this too may have implications for services rendered. Recognize that trauma exposures may adversely impact women's reproductive health and family planning
7. Recognize that social support is an important concern for military women and Veterans. Women may face challenges with unit support as a gender minority in the military.

Following military discharge and return from deployment, women may experience social isolation as they reintegrate. Furthermore, mental health consequences of trauma exposures (e.g. PTSD, depression, and substance abuse) can also exacerbate isolation.

8. Inform Veterans that VA provides services specific to military women's healthcare and to deployment-related concerns. Let them know that VA resources provide services for both their physical and mental healthcare. If possible, meet with local VA providers in women's health to gain knowledge regarding services available and to increase provider comfort in making referrals for more sensitive issues (e.g. sexual trauma, sexual dysfunction). According to Veteran care preference, refer to and/or partner with VA care providers to collaborate so that the female Veteran receives optimal care and benefits that they are entitled to because of their service. Benefit information is accessible online (www.va.gov/healthbenefits/access/medical_benefits_package.asp).

References

Annon, C. J. (1976). The PLISSIT model: A proposed conceptual scheme for the behavioral treatment of sexual problems. *Journal of Sex Education and Therapy*, 2, 1–15.

Barker, L. H. & Berry, K. D. (2009). Developmental issues impacting military families with young children during single and multiple deployments. *Military Medicine*, 174(10), 1033–1040. doi: 10.7205/MILMED-D-04-1108

Bean-Mayberry, B. A., Chang, C.-C. H. McNeil, M. A., Whittle, J., Hayes, P. M., & Scholle, S. H. (2003). Patient satisfaction in women's clinics versus traditional primary care clinics in the Veterans Administration. *Journal of General Internal Medicine*, 18, 175–181.

Benda, B. B. (2005). A study of substance abuse, traumata, and social support systems among homeless Veterans. *Journal of Human Behavior in the Social Environment*, 12(1), 59–82. doi: 10.1300/J137v12n01_04

Benda, B. B. (2006). Survival analyses of social support and trauma among homeless male and female Veterans who abuse substances. *American Journal of Orthopsychiatry*, 76(1), 70–79. doi: 10.1037/0002-9432.76.1.70

Benotsch, E. G., Brailey, K., Vasterling, J. J., Uddo, M., Constans, J. I., & Sutker, P. B. (2000). War zone stress, personal and environmental resources, and PTSD symptoms in Gulf War Veterans: A longitudinal perspective. *Journal of Abnormal Psychology*, 109(2), 205–213. doi: 10.1037//0021-0843X.109.2.205

Blosnich, J. R., Dichter, M. E., Cerulli, C., Batten, S. V., & Bossarte, R. M. (2014). Disparities in adverse childhood experiences among individuals with a history of military service. *JAMA Psychiatry*, 71(9), 1041–1048. doi: 10.1001/jamapsychiatry.2014.724

Blow, A., MacInnes, M. D., Hamel, J., Ames, B., Onaga, E., Holtrop, K., & Smith, S. (2012). National Guard service members returning home after deployment: The case for increased community support. *Administration and Policy in Mental Health and Mental Health Services Research*, 39(5), 383–393. doi: 10.1007/s10488-10011-0356-x

Booth, B. M., Mengeling, M., Torner, J., & Sadler, A. G. (2011). Rape, sex partnership, and substance use consequences in women Veterans. *Journal of Traumatic Stress*, 24(3), 287–294. doi: 10.1002/jts.20643

Boyd, M. A., Bradshaw, W., & Robinson, M. (2013). Mental health issues of women deployed to Iraq and Afghanistan. *Archives of Psychiatric Nursing*, 27(1), 10–22. doi: 10.1016/j.apnu.2012.10.005

Bradley, C. S., Nygaard, I. E., Mengeling, M. A., Torner, J. C., Stockdale, C. K., Booth, B. M., & Sadler, A. G. (2012). Urinary incontinence, depression and posttraumatic stress disorder in women Veterans. *American Journal of Obstetrics and Gynecology*, 206(6), 502.e1–502.e8. doi: 10.1016/j.ajog.2012.04.016

Bradley, C. S., Nygaard, I. E., Torner, J. C., Hillis, S. L., Johnson, S., & Sadler, A. G. (2014). Overactive bladder and mental health symptoms in recently deployed female Veterans. *Journal of Urology*, 191(5), 1327–1332. doi: 10.1016/j.juro.2013.11.100

Bridges, S. K., Lease, S. H., & Ellison, C. R. (2004). Predicting sexual satisfaction in women: Implications for counselor education and training. *Journal of Counseling and Development: JCD*, 82(2), 158.

Brooks, E., Dailey, N., Bair, B., & Shore, J. (2014). Rural women Veterans demographic report: Defining VA users' health and health care access in rural areas. *Journal of Rural Health*, 30(2), 146–152. doi: 10.1111/jrh.12037

Cameron, R. P., Mona, L. R., Syme, M. L., Clemency Cordes, C., Fraley, S. S., Chen, S. S., Klein, L. S. et al. (2011). Sexuality among wounded Veterans of Operation Enduring Freedom (OEF), Operation Iraqi Freedom (OIF), and Operation New Dawn (OND): Implications for rehabilitation psychologists. *Rehabilitation Psychology*, 56(4), 289–301.

Campbell, R. & Raja, S. (2005). The sexual assault and secondary victimization of female Veterans: Help-seeking experiences with military and civilian social systems. *Psychology of Women Quarterly*, 29, 97–106.

Chandra, A., Burns, R. M., Tanielian, T., Jaycox, L. H., & Scott, M. M. (2008). Understanding the impact of deployment on children and families: Findings from a pilot study of operation purple camp participants. Santa Monica, CA: RAND. Retrieved from www.rand.org/content/dam/rand/pubs/working_papers/2008/RAND_WR566.pdf

Clemency Cordes, C., Mona, L. R., Syme, M. L., Cameron, R. P., & Smith, K. (2013). Sexuality and sexual health among women with physical disabilities. In D. Castaneda (Ed.), *An essential handbook of women's sexuality: Diversity, health, and violence introduction* (Vol. 2, pp. 71–92). Santa Barbara, CA: Praeger.

Committee on Health Care for Underserved Women, American College of Obstetricians and Gynecologists (2012). Committee Opinion No. 547: Health care for women in the military and women Veterans. *Obstetrics and Gynecology, 120*(6), 1538–1542. doi: 10.1097/01.AOG.0000423821.70036.5a

Cooney, R. T., Segal, M. W., Segal, D. R., & Falk, W. W. (2003). Racial differences in the impact of military service on the socioeconomic status of women Veterans. *Armed Forces & Society, 30*(1), 53–85. doi: 10.1177/0095327X0303000103

Cotten, S. R., Skinner, K. M., & Sullivan, L. M. (2000). Social support among women Veterans. *Journal of Women & Aging*, 12(1–2), 39–62.

Dekel, R. & Monson, C. M. (2010). Military-related post-traumatic stress disorder and family relations: Current knowledge and future directions. *Aggression and Violent Behavior*, 15(4), 303–309. doi: 10.1016/j.avb.2010.03.001

Department of Defense (2010). *Report on the impact of deployment of members of the armed forces on their dependent children.* Retrieved from http://download.militaryonesource.mil/12038/MOS/Reports/Report_to_Congress_on_Impact_of_Deployment_on_Military_Children.pdf

Department of Defense (2011). *America's women Veterans: Military service history and VA benefit utilization statistics.* Washington, DC: National Center for Veterans Analysis and Statistics, Department of Veterans Affairs. Retrieved from www.va.gov/vetdata/docs/SpecialReports/Final_Womens_Report_3_2_12_v_7.pdf

Department of Defense (2013). *2013 Demographics: Profile of the Military Community.* Retrieved from http://download.militaryonesource.mil/12038/MOS/Reports/2013-Demographics-Report.pdf

Department of Defense (2014). *DACOWITS: Defense Advisory Committee on Women in the Services, 2014 Report.* Retrieved from http://dacowits.defense.gov/Portals/48/Documents/Reports/2014/Annual%20Report/2014%20DACOWITS%20Annual%20Report_Final.pdf

Dutra, L., de Blank, G., Scheiderer, E., & Taft, C. (2012). Correlates of female Veterans' perpetration of relationship aggression. *Psychological Trauma: Theory, Research, Practice, and Policy*, 4(3), 323–329. doi: 10.1037/a0026849

Finley, E. P., Zeber, J. E., Pugh, M. J. V., Cantu, G., Copeland, L. A., Parchman, M. L., & Noel, P. H. (2010). Postdeployment health care for returning OEF/OIF military personnel and their social networks: A qualitative approach. *Military Medicine*, 175(12), 953–957. doi: 10.7205/MILMED-D-10-00040

Firestone, J. M. (1992). Occupational Segregation: Comparing the Civilian and Military Work Force. *Armed Forces & Society*, 18(3), 363–381. doi: 10.1177/0095327X9201800304

Fisher, B. S., Cullen, F. T., & Turner, M. G. (2000). *The sexual victimization of college women. Research report.* Washington DC: US Department of Justice. Retrieved from www.ncjrs.gov/pdffiles1/nij/182369.pdf

Fonseca, C. A., Schmaling, K. B., Stoever, C., & Gutierrez, C. (2006). Variables associated with intimate partner violence in a deploying military sample. *Military Medicine*, 171(7), 627–631.

Fontana, A., Rosenheck, R., & Horvath, T. (1997). Social support and psychopathology in the war zone. *Journal of Nervous and Mental Disease*, 185(11), 675–681. doi: 10.1097/00005053–199711000–00004

Fontana, A., Rosenheck, R., & Desai, R. (2010). Female Veterans of Iraq and Afghanistan seeking care from VA specialized PTSD programs: Comparison with male Veterans and female war zone Veterans of previous eras. *Journal of Women's Health*, 19(4), 751–757. doi: 10.1089/jwh.2009.1389

Foran, H. M., Slep, A. M. S., & Heyman, R. E. (2011). Prevalences of intimate partner violence in a representative US Air Force sample. *Journal of Consulting and Clinical Psychology*, 79(3), 391–397. doi: 10.1037/a0022962

Fraley, S. S., Mona, L. R., & Theodore, P. S. (2007). The sexual lives of lesbian, gay, and bisexual people with disabilities: Psychological perspectives. *Sexuality Research & Social Policy*, 4(1), 15–26.

Frayne, S. M., Parker, V. A., Christiansen, C. L., Loveland, S., Seaver, M. R., Kazis, L. E., & Skinner, K. M. (2006). Health status among 28,000 women Veterans. *Journal of General Internal Medicine*, 21(S3), S40–S46. doi: 10.1111/j.1525-1497.2006.00373.x

Frayne, S. M., Phibbs, C. S., Saechao, F., Maisel, N. C., Friedman, S. A., Finlay, A., & Berg, E. (2014). *Sourcebook: Women Veterans in the Veterans Health Administration. Volume 3. Sociodemographics, utilization, costs of care, and health profile.* Washington DC: Women's Health Evaluation Initiative, Women's Health Services, Veterans Health Administration, Department of Veterans Affairs.

Frayne, S. M., Skinner, K. M., Sullivan, L. M., Tripp, T. J., Hankin, C. S., Kressin, N. R., & Miller, D. R. (1999). Medical profile of women Veterans Administration outpatients who report a history of sexual assault occurring while in the military. *Journal of Women's Health & Gender-Based Medicine*, 8(6), 835–845.

Galovski, T. & Lyons, J. A. (2004). Psychological sequelae of combat violence: A review of the impact of PTSD on the Veteran's family and possible interventions. *Aggression and Violent Behavior*, 9(5), 477–501. doi: 10.1016/S1359-1789(03)00045-00044

Gibbs, D. A., Clinton-Sherrod, A. M., & Johnson, R. E. (2012). Interpersonal conflict and referrals to counseling among married soldiers following return from deployment. *Military Medicine*, 177(10), 1178–1183. doi: 10.7205/MILMED-D-12-00008

Gierisch, J. M., Shapiro, A., Grant, N. N., King, H. A., McDuffie, J. R., & Williams, J. W. (2013). *Intimate partner violence: Prevalence among US Military Veterans and Active Duty Servicemembers and a review of intervention approaches.* VA-ESP Project 09-010. Washington, DC: Department of Veterans Affairs.

Goodman, P., Turner, A., Agazio, J., Throop, M., Padden, D., Greiner, S., & Hillier, S. L. (2013). Deployment of military mothers: Supportive and nonsupportive military programs, processes, and policies. *Military Medicine*, 178(7), 729–734. doi: 10.7205/MILMED-D-12-00460

Goyal, V., Mengeling, M. A., Booth, B. M., Torner, J. C., Syrop, C. H., & Sadler, A. G. (in press). Lifetime sexual assault and sexually transmitted infections among women Veterans.

Groer, M. W. & Burns, C. (2009). Stress response in female Veterans: An allostatic perspective. *Rehabilitation Nursing*, 34(3), 96–104. doi: 10.1002/j.2048-7940.2009.tb00263.x

Guay, S., Billette, V., & Marchand, A. (2006). Exploring the links between posttraumatic stress disorder and social support: Processes and potential research avenues. *Journal of Traumatic Stress*, 19(3), 327–338. doi: 10.1002/jts.20124

Hedeen, A., Chapko, M. K., Fortney, J., & Borowsky, S. (2000). CBOC performance evaluation. Performance report 3: Quality of care measures based on medical record review. Washington DC: Management Decision and Research Center, Health Services Research and Development Service, Department of Veterans Affairs. Retrieved from www.research.va.gov/resources/pubs/docs/cboc_3.pdf

Jones, A. D. (2012). Intimate partner violence in military couples: A review of the literature. *Aggression and Violent Behavior*, 17(2), 147–157. doi: 10.1016/j.avb.2011.12.002

Kang, H., Dalager, N., Mahan, C., & Ishii, E. (2005). The role of sexual assault on the risk of PTSD among Gulf War Veterans. *Annals of Epidemiology*, 15(3), 191–195. doi: 10.1016/j.annepidem.2004.05.009

Kedde, H., Van de Wiel, H., Schultz, W. W., Vanwesenbeeck, I. & Bender, J. (2012). Sexual health problems and associated help-seeking behavior of people with physical disabilities and chronic diseases. *Journal of Sex & Marital Therapy*, 38, 63–78.

Kelley, M. L., Hock, E., Bonney, J. F., Jarvis, M. S., Smith, K. M., & Gaffney, M. A. (2001). Navy mothers experiencing and not experiencing deployment: Reasons for staying in or leaving the military. *Military Psychology*, 13(1), 55–71. doi: 10.1207/S15327876MP1301_04

Kelley, M. L., Hock, E., Jarvis, M. S., Smith, K. M., Gaffney, M. A., & Bonney, J. F. (2002). Psychological adjustment of Navy mothers experiencing deployment. *Military Psychology*, 14(3), 199–216. doi: 10.1207/S15327876MP1403_2

Kelty, R., Kleykamp, M., & Segal, D. R. (2010). The military and the transition to adulthood. *Future of Children*, 20(1), 181–207.

Khaylis, A., Polusny, M. A., Erbes, C. R., Gewirtz, A., & Rath, M. (2011). Posttraumatic stress, family adjustment, and treatment preferences among National Guard soldiers deployed to OEF/OIF. *Military Medicine*, 176(2), 126–131. doi: 10.7205/MILMED-D-10-00094

Kilpatrick, D. G., Resnick, H. S., Milanak, M. E., Miller, M. W., Keyes, K. M. & Friedman, M. J. (2013). National estimates of exposure to traumatic events and PTSD prevalence using DSM-IV and DSM-5 criteria. *Journal of Traumatic Stress*, 26, 537–547.

King, L. A., King, D. W., Fairbank, J. A., Keane, T. M., & Adams, G. A. (1998). Resilience–recovery factors in post-traumatic stress disorder among female and male Vietnam Veterans: Hardiness, post-war social support, and additional stressful life events. *Journal of Personality and Social Psychology*, 74(2), 420–434. doi: 10.1037/0022-3514.74.2.420

King, D. W., King, L. A., Foy, D. W., Keane, T. M., & Fairbank, J. A. (1999). Posttraumatic stress disorder in a national sample of female and male Vietnam Veterans: Risk factors, war-zone stressors, and resilience-recovery variables. *Journal of Abnormal Psychology*, 108(1), 164–170. doi: 10.1037/0021-843X.108.1.164

Kleykamp, M. A. (2006). College, jobs, or the military? Enlistment during a time of war. *Social Science Quarterly*, 87(2), 272–290. doi: 10.1111/j.1540-6237.2006.00380.x

Kline, A., Ciccone, D. S., Falca-Dodson, M., Black, C. M., & Losonczy, M. (2011). Suicidal ideation among National Guard troops deployed to Iraq: The association with postdeployment readjustment problems. *Journal of Nervous and Mental Disease*, 199(12), 914–920. doi: 10.1097/NMD.0b013e 3182392917

Laffaye, C., Cavella, S., Drescher, K., & Rosen, C. (2008). Relationships among PTSD symptoms, social support, and support source in Veterans with chronic PTSD. *Journal of Traumatic Stress*, 21(4), 394–401. doi: 10.1002/jts.20348

Lauman, E. O., Pail, A., & Rosen, R.C. (1999). Sexual dysfunction in the United States: Prevalence and predictors. *JAMA*, 281, 537–544.

Lehavot, K., Hoerster, K. D., Nelson, K. M., Jakupcak, M., & Simpson, T. L. (2012). Health indicators for military, Veteran, and civilian women. *American Journal of Preventive Medicine*, 42(5), 473–480. doi: 10.1016/j.amepre.2012.01.006

Lester, P., Stein, J. A., Saltzman, W., Woodward, K., MacDermid, S. W., Milburn, N. et al. (2013). Psychological health of military children: Longitudinal evaluation of a family-centered prevention program to enhance family resilience. *Military Medicine*, 178(8), 838–845. doi: 10.7205/MILMED-D-12-00502

McCarroll, J. E., Ursano, R. J., Liu, X., Thayer, L. E., Newby, J. H., Norwood, A. E., & Fullerton, C. S. (2010). Deployment and the probability of spousal aggression by US Army soldiers. *Military Medicine*, 175(5), 352–356.

Marshall, A. D., Panuzio, J., & Taft, C. T. (2005). Intimate partner violence among military Veterans and active duty servicemen. *Clinical Psychology Review*, 25(7), 862–876. doi: 10.1016/j.cpr. 2005.05.009

Mattocks, K. M., Haskell, S. G., Krebs, E. E., Justice, A. C., Yano, E. M., & Brandt, C. (2012). Women at war: Understanding how women Veterans cope with combat and military sexual trauma. *Social Science & Medicine*, 74(4), 537–545. doi: 10.1016/j.socscimed.2011.10.039

Mengeling, M. A., Sadler, A. G., Torner, J., & Booth, B. M. (2011). Evolving comprehensive VA women's health care: Patient characteristics, needs, and preferences. *Women's Health Issues*, 21(4), S120–S129. doi: 10.1016/j.whi.2011.04.021

Merrill, L. L., Hervig, L. K., Newell, C. E., Gold, S. R., Milner, J. S., Rosswork, S. G. et al. (1998). Prevalence of premilitary adult sexual victimization and aggression in a Navy recruit sample. *Military Medicine*, 163(4), 209–212.

Morral, A. R., Gore, K. L., & Schell, T. L. (2014). *Sexual assault and sexual harassment in the US Military. Volume 1. Design of the 2014 RAND military workplace study.* Santa Monica, CA: RAND National Defense Research Institute.

Mulhall, E. (2009). *Women warriors: Supporting she 'who has borne the battle.'* Washington DC: IAVA. Retrieved from http://media.iava.org/IAVA_WomenWarriors_2009.pdf

Murdoch, M., Bradley, A., Mather, S. H., Klein, R. E., Turner, C. L., & Yano, E. M. (2006). Women and war. *Journal of General Internal Medicine,* 21(S3), S5–S10. doi: 10.1111/j.1525-1497.2006.00368.x

National Center for Veterans Analysis and Statistics (2011). *America's women Veterans: Military service history and VA benefit utilization statistics.* Washington, DC: National Center for Veterans Analysis and Statistics, Department of Veterans Affairs. Retrieved from www.va.gov/vetdata/docs/SpecialRep orts/Final_Womens_Report_3_2_12_v_7.pdf

Nayback-Beebe, A. M., & Yoder, L. H. (2011). Social conflict versus social support: What is more influential in mental health symptom severity for female service members? *Archives of Psychiatric Nursing,* 25(6), 469–478. doi: 10.1016/j.apnu.2011.02.005

Nosek, M. A., Howland, C., Rintala, D.H., Young, M. E., & Chanpong, G. F. (2001) National study of women with physical disabilities: Final report. *Sexuality and Disability,* 19, 5–39.

Parish, S. L. & Huh, J. (2006). Health care for women with disabilities: Population-based evidence of disparities. *Health & Social Work,* 31(1): 7–15.

Park, C. L., Wachen, J. S., Kaiser, A. P., & Mager Stellman, J. (2015). Cumulative trauma and midlife well-being in American women who served in Vietnam: Effects of combat exposure and post-deployment social support. *Anxiety, Stress, & Coping,* 28(2), 144–161. doi: 10.1080/10615806. 2014.944905

Patten, E. & Parker, K. (2011). *Women in the US military: Growing share, distinctive profile.* Washington, DC: Pew Research Center. Retrieved from www.pewsocialtrends.org/2011/12/22/women-in-the-u-s-military-growing-share-distinctive-profile

Pierce, P. F. (1998). Retention of Air Force women serving during Desert Shield and Desert Storm. *Military Psychology,* 10(3), 195–213. doi: 10.1207/s15327876mp1003_4

Pietrzak, R. H., Johnson, D. C., Goldstein, M. B., Malley, J. C., Rivers, A. J., Morgan, C. A., & Southwick, S. M. (2010). Psychosocial buffers of traumatic stress, depressive symptoms, and psychosocial difficulties in Veterans of Operations Enduring Freedom and Iraqi Freedom: The role of resilience, unit support, and postdeployment social support. *Journal of Affective Disorders,* 120(1), 188–192. doi: 10.1016/j.jad.2009.04.015

Piotrowski, K. & Snell, L. (2007). Health needs of women with disabilities across the lifespan. *Journal of Obstetric, Gynecological, & Neonatal Nursing,* 36(1), 79–87.

Polusny, M. A., Kumpula, M. J., Meis, L. A., Erbes, C. R., Arbisi, P. A., Murdoch, M. et al. (2014). Gender differences in the effects of deployment-related stressors and pre-deployment risk factors on the development of PTSD symptoms in National Guard Soldiers deployed to Iraq and Afghanistan. *Journal of Psychiatric Research,* 49, 1–9. doi: 10.1016/j.jpsychires.2013.09.016

Rabenhorst, M. M., McCarthy, R. J., Thomsen, C. J., Milner, J. S., Travis, W. J., Foster, R. E., & Copeland, C. W. (2013). Spouse abuse among United States Air Force personnel who deployed in support of Operation Iraqi Freedom/Operation Enduring Freedom. *Journal of Family Psychology,* 27(5), 754–761. doi: 10.1037/a0034283

Rabenhorst, M. M., Thomsen, C. J., Milner, J. S., Foster, R. E., Linkh, D. J., & Copeland, C. W. (2012). Spouse abuse and combat-related deployments in active duty Air Force couples. *Psychology of Violence,* 2(3), 273–284. doi: 10.1037/a0027094

Rosen, L. N., & Martin, L. (1996). Impact of childhood abuse history on psychological symptoms among male and female soldiers in the US Army. *Child Abuse & Neglect,* 20(12), 1149–1160. doi: 10.1016/S0145-2134(96)00112-00113

Ryan, G. L., Mengeling, M. A., Booth, B. M., Torner, J. C., Syrop, C. H., & Sadler, A. G. (2014). Voluntary and involuntary childlessness in female Veterans: Associations with sexual assault. *Fertility and Sterility,* 102(2), 539–547. doi: 10.1016/j.fertnstert.2014.04.042

Ryan, G. L., Mengeling, M. A., Summers, K., Booth, B. M., Torner, J. C., Syrop, C. H., & Sadler, A. G. (2015). Hysterectomy risk in premenopausal-aged military Veterans- associations with sexual assault and gynecologic symptoms. *American Journal of Obstetrics & Gynecology,* 49, 573–582.

Sadler, A. G., Booth, B. M., Cook, B. L., & Doebbeling, B. N. (2003). Factors associated with women's risk of rape in the military environment. *American Journal of Industrial Medicine*, 43(3), 262–273. doi: 10.1002/ajim.10202

Sadler, A. G., Booth, B. M., & Doebbeling, B. N. (2005). Gang and multiple rapes during military service: Health consequences and health care. *Journal of the American Medical Women's Association (1972)*, 60(1), 33–41.

Sadler, A. G., Booth, B. M., Mengeling, M. A., & Doebbeling, B. N. (2004). Life span and repeated violence against women during military service: Effects on health status and outpatient utilization. *Journal of Women's Health*, 13(7), 799–811. doi: 10.1089/jwh.2004.13.799

Sadler, A. G., Booth, B. M., Nielson, D., & Doebbeling, B. N. (2000). Health-related consequences of physical and sexual violence: Women in the military. *Obstetrics & Gynecology*, 96(3), 473–480. doi: 10.1016/S0029–7844(00)00919–00914

Sadler, A. G., Mengeling, M. A., Fraley, S. S., Torner, J. C., & Booth, B. M. (2012). Correlates of sexual functioning in women Veterans: Mental health, gynecologic health, health status, and sexual assault history. *International Journal of Sexual Health*, 24(1), 60–77. doi: 10.1080/19317611. 2011.640388

Sadler, A. G., Mengeling, M. A., Syrop, C. H., Torner, J. C., & Booth, B. M. (2011). Lifetime sexual assault and cervical cytologic abnormalities among military women. *Journal of Women's Health*, 20(11), 1693–1701. doi: 10.1089/jwh.2010.2399

Sayers, S. L., Farrow, V. A., Ross, J., & Oslin, D. W. (2009). Family problems among recently returned military Veterans referred for a mental health evaluation. *Journal of Clinical Psychiatry*, 70(2), 163–170. doi: 10.4088/JCP.07m03863

Seal, K. H., Bertenthal, D., Miner, C. R., Sen, S., & Marmar, C. (2007). Bringing the war back home: Mental health disorders among 103,788 US Veterans returning from Iraq and Afghanistan seen at Department of Veterans Affairs facilities. *Archives of Internal Medicine*, 167, 476–482.

Segal, M. W., Segal, D. R., Bachman, J. G., Freedman-Doan, P., & O'Malley, P. M. (1998). Gender and the propensity to enlist in the US Military. *Gender Issues*, 16(3), 65–87. doi: 10.1007/s12147-12998-0022-0

Sullivan, C. P., & Elbogen, E. B. (2014). PTSD symptoms and family versus stranger violence in Iraq and Afghanistan Veterans. *Law and Human Behavior*, 38(1), 1–9. doi: 10.1037/lhb0000035

Surís, A. & Lind, L. (2008). Military sexual trauma: A review of prevalence and associated health consequences in Veterans. *Trauma, Violence, & Abuse*, 9(4), 250–269. doi: 10.1177/1524838008324419

Thomas, J. L., Wilk, J. E., Riviere, L. A., McGurk, D., Castro, C. A., & Hoge, C. W. (2010). Prevalence of mental health problems and functional impairment among active component and National Guard soldiers 3 and 12 months following combat in Iraq. *Archives of General Psychiatry*, 67(6), 614–623. doi: 10.1001/archgenpsychiatry.2010.54

Tjaden, P. & Thoennes, N. (2000). *Full report of the prevalence, incidence, and consequences of violence against women (NCJ 183781)*. Washington, DC: US Department of Justice, National Institute of Justice, Office of Justice Programs. Retrieved from www.ncjrs.gov/pdffiles1/nij/183781.pdf

Tran, J. K., Dunckel, M. A., & Teng, E. J. (2015). Sexual dysfunction in Veterans with post-traumatic stress disorder. *Journal of Sexual Medicine*, 12: 847–855.

Turchik, J. A. & Wilson, S. M. (2010). Sexual assault in the US military: A review of the literature and recommendations for the future. *Aggression and Violent Behavior*, 15(4), 267–277. doi: 10.1016/j. avb.2010.01.005

US Department of Veterans Affairs (2012). Veterans' employment toolkit. Active duty vs. Reserve or National Guard. Retrieved from www.va.gov/vetsinworkplace/docs/em_activeReserve.html

US Department of Veterans Affairs (2013). Women veteran profile. Retrieved from www.va.gov/VETDATA/docs/SpecialReports/Women_Veteran_Profile5.pdf

US Department of Veterans Affairs (2015). *White House Interagency Council on Women and Girls, Department of Veterans Affairs (VA), Women Veterans and Women VA Employees*. Retrieved from www.va.gov/WOMENVET/docs/VA_Summary_Report_Final_Revised_022210.pdf

Vinokur, A. D., Pierce, P. F., & Buck, C. L. (1999). Work–family conflicts of women in the Air Force: Their influence on mental health and functioning. *Journal of Organizational Behavior*, 20, 865–878.

Vogt, D. S., Pless, A. P., King, L. A., & King, D. W. (2005). Deployment stressors, gender, and mental health outcomes among Gulf War I Veterans. *Journal of Traumatic Stress*, 18(2), 115–127. doi: 10.1002/jts.20018

Vogt, D., Smith, B., Elwy, R., Martin, J., Schultz, M., Drainoni, M. L., & Eisen, S. (2011). Predeployment, deployment, and postdeployment risk factors for posttraumatic stress symptomatology in female and male OEF/OIF Veterans. *Journal of Abnormal Psychology*, 120(4), 819–831. doi: 10.1037/a0024457

Washington, D. L., Yano, E. M., Simon, B., & Sun, S. (2006). To use or not to use. *Journal of General Internal Medicine*, 21(S3), S11–S18. doi: 10.1111/j.1525-1497.2006.00369.x

Weaver, T. L. (2009). Impact of rape on female sexuality: Review of selected literature. *Clinical Obstetrics and Gynecology*, 52(4), 702–711.

Werber Castaneda, L., Harrell, M. C., Varda, D. M., Curry Hall, K., Beckett, M. K., & Howard, S. (2008). *Deployment experiences of Guard and Reserve families: Implications for support and retention.* Santa Monica, CA: RAND. Retrieved from www.dtic.mil/dtic/tr/fulltext/u2/a492576.pdf

Westgren, N. & Levi, R. (1999). Sexuality after injury: Interviews with women after traumatic spinal cord injury. *Sexuality and Disability*, 17(4), 309–319.

Wooten, N. R. (2012). Deployment cycle stressors and post-traumatic stress symptoms in Army National Guard women: The mediating effect of resilience. *Social Work in Health Care*, 51(9), 828–849. doi: 10.1080/00981389.2012.692353

World Health Organization (2002). *Defining sexual health: Report of a technical consultation on sexual health.* Available at: www.who.int/reproductivehealth/publications/sexual_health/defining_sexual_health.pdf (accessed September 28, 2015).

Yan, G. W., McAndrew, L., D'Andrea, E. A., Lange, G., Santos, S. L., Engel, C. C., & Quigley, K. S. (2013). Self-reported stressors of National Guard women Veterans before and after deployment: The relevance of interpersonal relationships. *Journal of General Internal Medicine*, 28(2), 549–555. doi: 10.1007/s11606-11012-2247-2246

Yehuda, R., Lehmer, A., & Rosenbaum, T. Y. (2015). PTSD and sexual dysfunction in men and women. *International Society for Sexual Medicine*, 12, 1107–1119.

5

OLDER VETERANS

Kari L. Fletcher, David L. Albright, Kimberly A. Rorie and Alexandria M. Lewis

In the United States, adults aged 65 and over are a fast-growing segment of the population (Pietrzak & Cook, 2013). "Graying" is particularly evident among Veterans, who are aging at nearly "three times (34%) that of the general population" (Damron-Rodriguez, 2011). According to the US Census Bureau, the median age of Veterans is 57.4 years, which is significantly older than the general population's national average of 36.8 years (US Department of Veterans Affairs [VA], 2013b).

In 2010, older Veterans – who had both "served in the active military, naval, or air service" and been "discharged or released therefrom under conditions other than dishonorable" (VA, 2011) – were estimated to be 23% of Americans 65 and older (VA, 2015d). Despite their sizeable contribution to the overall older population in the United States, the effect of military service over time and how to provide support for older Veterans as a cohort are not well understood. Few, if any, clinical resources are available outlining essential elements of support for providers will invariably work with aging Veterans. The aim of this chapter is to help providers gain a sense of who older Veterans are, what their health concerns are, and how these healthcare needs may be addressed. This chapter is divided into four sections: (a) an overview of older Veterans; (b) considerations relevant to older Veterans over time; (c) healthcare for older Veterans; and (d) implications for clinical practice with older Veterans. A case vignette is provided to help illustrate and support the application of information to clinical work with older Veterans.

An Overview of Older Veterans

Today in the United States, Veterans are a sizeable proportion of the older adult population: 12.8% (US Census Bureau, 2012a, VA, 2014a). The large majority of older Veterans are male (97%) versus female (3%; US Census Bureau, 2012a, 2012b; VA, 2014a; and see Table 5.1), which varies from the general population in which women live longer. Men 65 and older vary widely in age by distribution among Veterans versus non-Veterans in the US population: among 65- to 74-year-olds it is 21.7% versus 6.4%; among 75- to 84-year-olds it is 16.8% versus 2.3%; and among those 85 and older it is 6.6% versus 0.6% (VA, 2009a). Overwhelmingly, older Veterans are White (91.4%), followed by much smaller groups of Black or African (5.9%), Hispanic or Latino (3.1%), Asian (1%), and American Indian/Alaska

TABLE 5.1 Gender, Race, and Information Regarding Era of Service among Living Older Veterans[a] in the US

Characteristic		Living[a]	Served	K-I-A	Wounded
Gender[b]	Male	8,759,028 (97.2%)			
	Female	253,009 (2.8%)			
Race[c]	White (alone; not Hispanic or Latino)	8,234,007 (91.4%)			
	Black or African American (alone)	529,410 (5.87%)			
	American Indian/Alaska Native (alone)	37,122 (0.41%)			
	Asian (alone)	88,512 (1.0%)			
	Native Hawaiian and Other Pacific Islander (alone)	5,736 (0.1%)			
	Some other race (alone)	44,661 (0.5%)			
	Two or more races	72,589 (0.8%)			
	Hispanic or Latino origin[d]	282,998 (3.1%)			
Era(s)					
	World War II	1,246,000 (13.8%)	16,112,566	405,399	670,846
Service	Korean Conflict	2,100,000 (23.3%)	5,720,000	54,246	103,284
	Vietnam War	7,300,000 (81%)	8,744,000	291,557	303,644
Served					
two wars	WWII and Korean	147,000 (1.6%)			
	Korean Conflict and Vietnam	211,000 (2.3%)			
three wars	WWII, Korean Conflict, and Vietnam era	54,000 (0.6%)			
	Vietnam era and both Gulf Wars	49,500 (0.5%)			

Notes: K-I-A = killed in action. WWII = World War II (WWII; December 7, 1941–December 31, 1946); Korean Conflict: (June 27, 1950–January 31, 1955); Vietnam War Era (February 28, 1961–May 7, 1975) (Torreon, 2011).
a Of living Veterans, 9,012,037 (41.2%) were aged 65 and older.
b Figures are from the American Community Survey (VA, 2009a).
c Reflects percentage of total Veteran population (21,854,374 Veterans).
d Of note from this research, Hispanic or Latino origin may refer to any race.

Native (0.4%; US Census Bureau, 2012b). Their military service occurred during one or more periods or eras: 1,000,000 served during World War II; 1,900,000 during the Korean Conflict; 7,200,000 during the Vietnam War era; and others served during peacetime years (US Census Bureau, 2012b).

Overall, the US Veteran population continues to get older. Today, there are 9.4 million Veterans aged 65 and over (US Census Bureau, 2012a), approximately 45% of the 22 million total Veteran population (VA, 2014b). In fact, over the next 30 years, the older Veteran population is projected to double and will exceed half of the total living Veteran population (VA, 2011).

Considerations Relevant to Older Veterans over Time

It is important to consider the extent to which military service factors in the lives of older Veterans as they reach advanced/old age (Settersten, 2006). Over the long term, some effects of military service (e.g. combat exposure) may confound or even accelerate older Veterans' aging process (Spiro & Settersten, 2012). This section presents four specific influences in relation to older Veterans: (a) era, cohort membership, and historic events; (b) military service and its effects over the life span; (c) aging as a process; and (d) health.

Era, Cohort Membership, and Historic Events

The era in which Veterans were born influences their life experiences – before, during, and after military service – and has implications for them as they age (see Table 5.1). Prior to joining the service, Veterans who are now age 65 and older – who, in 2015, were born in 1950 or earlier – may have been raised in an array of varying circumstances. Growing up, Veterans may have lived through and been influenced by one or more historic events in American history: World War I (April 6, 1917–November 11, 1918); the Great Depression (1929–mid 1930s); World War II (December 7, 1941–December 31, 1946); the Korean Conflict (June 27, 1950–January 31, 1955); the Cold War era (1947–1991); and the Vietnam War era (February 28, 1961–May 7, 1975; Torreon, 2011). Similarly, military-related policy may have affected their decision to join the service: conscription (also known as the draft, 1940–1973); movement to an all-volunteer force (AVF; 1973–present; Rostker, 2006); benefits such as guaranteed housing loans and educational benefits through the Servicemen's Readjustment Act of 1944 (the GI Bill); and the passage of Executive Order 9981 (issued in 1948; which led to desegregation in the military; McFarland, 2012).

Military Service and Its Subsequent Effects

Invariably, military service permanently affects the lives of older Veterans and their loved ones. Hypothetically, military service and its effects over the life course may be viewed in one of two ways: as a turning point, or as a life-course disruption.

Military as a Turning Point

On one hand, military service may be viewed as a turning point, whereby early entry into the military at a young age both can positively influence life-course redirection chances and reduce the potential for disruption to established life trajectories (Wilmoth & London, 2011). This perspective posits that although entry into the service required sacrifice by taking a moratorium (e.g. social, psychological) from what others were doing when they entered the service and thereby delaying their subsequent transition into adulthood, doing so allowed them to take full advantage of their benefits upon discharge from the military (Wilmoth & London, 2011). For those who grew up poor, serving in the military afforded the opportunity to leave difficult life circumstances as well as the opportunity to make use of housing, healthcare, and education benefits throughout life upon return (Wilmoth & London, 2011).

Military as a Life-course Disruption

On the other hand, a second corollary hypothesis considers life-course disruption, whereby military service may disrupt life-course trajectories (e.g. established marital, parenting, occupational trajectories) for those who serve and its consequences for the subsequent life course and with regard to later-life outcomes (Wilmoth & London, 2011). Veterans may have come from more advantaged backgrounds or have already completed their education prior to pre-military service and therefore had less time to take advantage of and/or less opportunity to use educational benefits. Serving in the military was of less benefit to them (Wilmoth & London, 2011).

Aging as a Process

Aging is characterized by ongoing deterioration that transpires over time (Kane, Ouslander, Abrass, & Resnick, 2013). According to Goldsmith (2014), aging occurs differently among people, but often involves increased weakness and vulnerability to disease and environmental conditions, decreasing dexterity, changes in mobility, and physiological changes (Kane et al., 2013, p. 3). Additional dimensions further refine aging: life expectancy (the statistical formulation of how long an individual is likely to live); life span (e.g. the maximum number of years that one can expect to live); chronological aging (e.g. one's actual age in years); gerontological aging (e.g. one's risk of dying); normal aging (e.g. typical or natural processes that take place over time); and pathologic aging/changes (e.g. occurring with the presence of disease; Kane et al., 2013).

For Veterans and non-Veterans alike, "everyone does not age in the same way or at the same rate" (Kane et al., 2013, p. 4). Compared with a generation ago, health disparities between healthy and unhealthy adults have become increasingly visible among older adults (Kane et al., 2013). For those who embody successful or optimal aging, their longevity may be characterized in terms of their physical, cognitive, and social functioning as well as factors such as genetics and lifestyle choices (e.g. physical activity, nutrition, and social support; McReynolds & Rossen, 2004). For others, factors such as health may contribute negatively to the aging process. A health summary of older Veterans is discussed in the next section.

Health

For older Veterans, health effects of military service may appear later in life (VA, 2009b) Older Veterans are susceptible to disease and disability. They have higher rates of physical and mental morbidities and functional impairment (Sherwood, Shimel, Stolz, & Sherwood, 2004) than the general population. Research suggests that health status among older Veterans may correspond to that of non-Veterans 10 to 20 years older (Shay, Hyduke, & Burris, 2013). Although hard to measure, the effects of military service are complex, and the following section shines a light on how military service may negatively affect the physical and psychological health of older Veterans.

Among older Veterans, the effects of military service – both positive and negative – remain influential across one or more domains: physical health, mental health, cognitive functioning, social well-being, economic well-being, and relationships (family and other social relationships; Spiro & Settersten, 2012). Health comparisons between older Veterans and their non-Veteran counterparts and the general population demonstrate these differences both with regard to the management of chronic disease and with regard to causes of death. Compared with the general population, Veterans have poorer health outcomes. For example, within the general population, the most frequent chronic diseases and the rates of each disease in the over-65 population are as follows: arthritis (50%), heart disease (30%), any cancer (24%), diagnosed diabetes (20%), and hypertension (72%; Centers for Disease Control [CDC], 2012).

Overall, the main causes of death among older Veterans remain largely unknown (Maynard & Boyko, 2006) and nongeneralizable (Sohn, Arnold, Maynard, & Hynes, 2006). A lack of integrated records results in fragmentation between the Department of Veterans Affairs (e.g. of VA healthcare users; of VA benefit recipients) and other sources (e.g. Medical Vital Status files Social Security Administration Master Files; Sohn et al., 2006). Furthermore, known factors are nongeneralizable; for example, of Veterans who received mental healthcare when they were younger, more die from maladies such as infectious diseases, accidents, or suicide (Maynard & Boyko, 2006). The record of known causes of death among the older adults in the general US population – which comparatively is documented in a more accessible way – offers some basis for comparison. Among older adults in the general population, the main causes of death are heart disease (25.6%), malignant neoplasms (tumors; 22.06%), chronic respiratory diseases (6.56%), cerebrovascular diseases (6.11%), and Alzheimer's disease (4.59%; CDC, 2012).

Possible Implications for Exposure during Service

Today, older Veterans may still be managing injuries they incurred while in the service. Many saw combat or served during eras (e.g. Korean Conflict, Vietnam War) when emerging healthcare (e.g. mobile Army surgical hospitals) and improved transportation (e.g. helicopters) technologies helped them survive injuries incurred while in serving (Boettcher & Cobb, 2006).

Military service remains an important albeit largely unseen variable that influences older Veterans throughout their lives (Settersten, 2006). In the following section, physical and psychological health implications of military service are described. Special consideration is paid to Agent Orange and post-traumatic stress disorder (PTSD) – two "signature" injuries among older Veterans.

Physical

Exposure to hazardous conditions during service may affect the physical health of older Veterans over time (VA, 2015g). Risk of exposure in the line of duty may be general in nature, related to living or working in a particular geographic area or connected with serving during one or more eras. Generally, older Veterans may live with a degree of hearing loss and/or tinnitus (ringing in the ears; American Tinnitus Association, n.d.) resulting from exposure to excessive noise during their service, or a degree of chronic pain resulting from years of physical work and/or wearing heavy equipment (VA, 2015c). Location-wise, older Veterans may be at risk for contaminant-related exposure: herbicide tests and storage outside Vietnam (1944–1969); Edgewood/Aberdeen (1955–1975); Camp Lejeune Water supply (1950s–1980s); Project 112/Project SHAD (1960s–early 1970s); and Atsugi, Japan Waste incinerator (1985–2001) (VA, 2015g). By era of service, World War II Veterans may have been exposed to mustard gas, World War II and Korean War Veterans may have been exposed to cold injuries, and Vietnam Veterans may have been exposed to hepatitis C – which if untreated irreparably damages the liver – or to Agent Orange (VA, 2015g), which will be discussed briefly in the next section.

Agent Orange

From a physical health perspective, Agent Orange is a "signature injury" among older Veterans. Veterans who served during Vietnam and in some other locations may have chronic diseases connected to Agent Orange exposure. Public Law 102-4 – the Agent Orange Act of 1991 – has acknowledged that Veterans who served in Vietnam were exposed to herbicides sprayed over jungle canopies in Vietnam by the US military from 1962 to 1971 (Institute of Medicine [IOM], 2014, 2015). Additionally, Veterans may have been exposed in other ways: serving in Korean demilitarized zones (1968–1971); working on provider aircrafts that had once been used to spread the herbicide; serving on open sea ships during the Vietnam war (off the shore of Vietnam); working on military bases in Thailand; or working at storage facilities and testing sites at various locations throughout the United States (IOM, 2015; VA, 2015g).

As a result of their exposure to Agent Orange, the health-related quality of life among older Veterans over time may suffer. Anecdotally, Agent Orange has been linked to numerous cancers, nervous disorders, skin diseases, and congenital effects (e.g. birth defects in children). Research, however, makes distinctions between exposure to "chemicals of interest" and to health outcomes:

- *sufficient evidence* links "soft-tissue sarcoma (including heart); Non-Hodgkin's lymphoma; Chronic lymphocytic leukemia (including hairy cell leukemia and other chronic B-cell leukemias); Hodgkin lymphoma; and Chloracne";
- *limited to suggestive evidence of an association* links "laryngeal cancer; Cancer of the lung, bronchus, or trachea; Prostate cancer; Multiple myeloma; AL amyloidosis; Early-onset peripheral neuropathy; Parkinson disease; Porphyria cutanea tarda; Hypertension; Ischemic heart disease; Stroke; Type 2 diabetes (mellitus); Spina bifida in offspring of exposed people"; and
- *limited or suggestive evidence of no association:* Spontaneous abortion after paternal exposure to TCDD. (IOM, 2014, p. 937)

Psychological

Psychologically, the effects of military service – and of combat especially – have affected older Veterans to varying degrees over time (Jennings, Aldwin, Levenson, Spiro, & Mroczek, 2006). Although research findings from the National Health and Resilience in Veterans Study suggests most older Veterans rate their aging experience as successful (81%; Pietrzak et al. 2010), a small percentage indicated that they have suicidal ideations (6%; Fanning & Pietrzak, 2013). At the same time, mental health and substance use concerns remain higher among older Veterans than non-Veterans (e.g. Tanielian & Jaycox, 2008). Among Veterans 65 and older seen at the VA, 11% are depressed, a rate more than twice that of non-Veterans (VA, 2015i).

PTSD

The lasting and detrimental effects of war have long been observed (Freud & Dann, 1951) yet perhaps not always well understood. Prior to World Wars I and II, two distinct phenomena occurred: In the 1860s, John Erichsen observed neurological symptoms in individuals involved in railway accidents and later dubbed this "syndrome" as "railway spine"; in the late 1880s, Jean-Martin Charcot, Pierre Janet, William James, and Sigmund Freud observed unexplainable symptoms (e.g. blindness, paralysis of the hand) that did not always dissipate with time among women, and called this "hysteria" (Ellenberger, 1970, cited in Herman, 1992, p. 10). After WWI until the Vietnam War, "war neurosis" or "shell shock" was seen in soldiers who broke down in large numbers after being subjected to annihilation and began to act like the hysterical women observed in years past. British psychologist Charles Myers thought "shell shock" might be due in part to the concussive effects of exploding shells on the battlefield (Myers, 1940, cited in Herman, 1992, p. 20). During the years leading up to the Vietnam War, trauma shifted from something thought to afflict those with weak moral character, to something that could happen to high moral character, to something that could happen to anyone under fire or severe combat exposure (Herman, 1992).

An understanding of trauma and its treatment has really only begun to develop over the past 40 years. In the United States during the Vietnam War, anti-war Veterans organized rap groups to meet with their peers and talk about war (Herman, 1992). The VA began to provide services, and the Vet Centers were established in 1979 to help Veterans address readjustment concerns (VA, 2015h). Theory, research, and treatment dedicated to understanding trauma and stress of Vietnam Veterans were established (e.g. Figley, 1978). PTSD became a diagnosis in the third edition of the *Diagnostic and Statistical Manual of Mental Disorders* (American Psychiatric Association, 1980). Since then, much has happened in relation to better understanding and treating trauma and its sequelae (covered in more depth elsewhere in this book).

From a psychological health perspective, PTSD is a "signature injury" among older Veterans. Those who served in combat during World War II, Korea, or Vietnam and later returned home were said to have developed chronic PTSD, whereas even greater numbers developed post-traumatic stress symptoms (PTSS; Hobbs, 2008, p. 338). Data has most widely been collected and observed among Vietnam-era Veterans. According to the National Vietnam Veterans Readjustment Study, roughly 15% of Vietnam Veterans were diagnosed with PTSD, whereas another 30% had a past PTSD diagnosis (Card, 1987; VA, 2014c).

Over time, an array of life events may have helped or hindered now older Veterans in their attempts to manage their symptoms. For many who experienced trauma upon or soon after their return from service, their PTSD or PTSS may have lessened over time. For others, symptoms persisted or worsened and were dealt with through attempts to cope such as continued substance use or avoidance. In recent years, the emergence of late-onset stress symptoms has also become known as another form of trauma among Veterans. For these Veterans – whose experience after they came home and in the years to follow were absent of trauma – the onset of trauma symptoms arise after being seemingly latent for years. According to Davidson and colleagues (2006, cited in Spiro & Settersten, 2012), these symptoms may surface in the wake of losses (e.g. deterioration of health; loss of a partner) or even seemingly positive changes (e.g. retirement) that occur later in life.

Healthcare for Older Veterans

Several considerations factor into assessing the current state of healthcare for older Veterans. This section highlights: (a) a brief history of healthcare; (b) considerations relevant to accessing healthcare today; and (c) geriatric care. Within each section, care specific to Veterans and more broadly for older adults is considered.

A Brief History of Healthcare

For Older Adults

In early America, the care of older adults was considered the responsibility of family members, sometimes in exchange for land or a home (Williamson, 1984). Prior to the 20th century, older adults without family to support them were sometimes forced to live in poorhouses (Ogden & Adams, 2009). In the 1800s, care for the elderly was partially paid for through local taxes, but the majority of the cost was provided by family (Ogden & Adams, 2009). Since the 19th century, the concept of entitlements for older adults has continued to evolve. The financial burden of care for the elderly began to gradually shift from local taxes, to the state level, and finally moved to the federal level (Ogden & Adams, 2009). Initially established as part of the Social Security Act of 1965, the Federal Medicare Program was created to give older adults access to medical benefits (Karger & Stoesz, 2014). Healthcare provisions for older adults have continued to expand, with the addition of prescription drug benefits and other healthcare benefits added to Medicare in the early part of the 21st century (Karger & Stoesz, 2014). Particularly since the late 19th century, the combination of medical advances resulting in improved longevity and a growing number of older adults has helped shape today's system of healthcare for older adults.

Healthcare for Veterans

Healthcare for Veterans was established as a means to provide lifelong support to military service members. This concept has been evolving since the origins of the United States. Initially established as a means to provide lifelong support to service members, Veteran healthcare has continued to evolve over the past 200 years. During each century, key legislation helped shape today's system of healthcare. In the 1700s, the colonies were mandated to support disabled soldiers (VA, n.d., 2015a). Also, pension systems were devised as an incentive for enlistment in the Revolutionary War (1775–1783; Brogan, 2010). In the 1800s, the federal government began funding healthcare (in 1812; VA, n.d., 2015a). In the 1900s, healthcare within the Veterans Administration (now Veterans Affairs) was established (in 1930; VA, n.d., 2015a) and Vet Centers were opened (in 1979; VA, 2015h); and Geriatric Research, Education, and Clinical Centers (GRECCs) began to further support geriatric medicine-related research (in 1980; Supiano et al., 2012). In the 2000s, healthcare policy such as the Veterans Benefits, Healthcare, and Information Technology Act of 2006 (Public Law 109-461) and Veterans Millennium Healthcare and Benefits Improvement Act (Public Law 106-117) brought increased parity for long-term and acute care for Veterans (e.g. Russell & Figley, 2014).

Considerations Relevant to Accessing Healthcare Today

In recent years, Veteran-related healthcare has become a complicated enterprise. Veterans' benefits within the VA are largely influenced by current events, political changes, and evolving legislation, and are therefore an ever-changing framework to work within. Likewise, the profit-driven private healthcare industry that has changed over time has similarly influenced supports that aging Veterans may access outside of the VA system. For healthcare providers today, understanding the current landscape of the system is crucial.

Consequently, it is not surprising that providers who work with older Veterans (particularly those who work in the community) may feel unsure or underprepared regarding how best to support them. Navigation of healthcare, Veteran-/military-specific resources, geriatric care, and community-based resources can get tricky. Because healthcare for older Veterans is complicated, it is important to briefly summarize relevant considerations of healthcare for older Veterans. This section provides an overview – albeit cursory – of factors that are relevant to care for older Veterans: (a) healthcare coverage and benefits; (b) systems of care; and

(c) geriatric care. Because older Veterans, family members, and others involved in their care may not be aware of resources and where to find them, the considerations discussed in the following section are important for providers to have on their radar.

Healthcare Coverage and Benefits

Healthcare Coverage

Veterans 65 and older receive their healthcare coverage from one of six primary sources (US Census, 2012d). In fact, four out of five (80%) have multiple types of healthcare coverage. The greatest number of older Veterans are enrolled in Medicare (9.2 million); followed by employer-sponsored insurance (4.1 million); VA healthcare (3.1 million); direct purchase (3.1 million); TRICARE (1.3 million); and Medicaid (878,000; US Census, 2012d). Compared with non-Veterans, relatively few older Veterans are uninsured (US Census Bureau, 2012e).

Because older Veterans use various types of healthcare coverage, it is beneficial to have a working sense of how to apply these benefits to care rendered. Medicare (or Title XVIII), an insurance program for older adults, can be used often as a first line of coverage to help older Veterans defray their healthcare costs (e.g. acute-care hospital services; Kane et al., 2013). Generally, Veterans 65 and over are automatically enrolled in Medicare (Parts A and B) if they have social security retirement benefits (Passages, 2011). Employer-sponsored insurance, plans chosen through the older Veteran or partner's employer, may be another option (Department of Health and Human Services, 2004). Direct purchase healthcare, or insurance purchased on an individual basis, is an option for older Veterans who do not have or are ineligible for VA benefits or other VA health coverage (US Centers for Medicare & Medicaid Services, 2015). Older Veterans may also use TRICARE, a healthcare program serving those who served active duty or in the reserve component (Reserves or National Guard), are retired military (e.g. career military) or family members (Russell & Figley, 2014; US Census, 2012d). At age 65, TRI-CARE itself ends and Veterans are from that point on eligible for TRICARE for life (Military.com, n.d.). Medicaid (Title XIX), a welfare program, may help low-income older adults offset the costs of their long-term care (e.g. nursing home costs; Kane et al., 2013).

VA healthcare benefits – not a healthcare plan per se – are healthcare services that may be free of cost or with a co-pay for qualifying Veterans based on factors such as their eligibility status and presence of service-connected injuries (which will be further discussed in the following sections; VA, 2015b, 2015e). Among Vietnam-era Veterans (the only cohort of Veterans over 65 in the sample) surveyed during the 2010 National Survey of Veterans, the majority of respondents did use or considered using the VA as a safety net when needed (36.5%) as their primary source of healthcare (18.8%), for some services (11.8%), for prescriptions (2.7%), for specialized care (0.8%), or in some other way (1.4%), whereas more than one-quarter of respondents said they did not plan to use the VA (27.9%; VA, 2011).

Benefits

Older Veterans are eligible to receive compensation and pension benefits related to their time served in the military. Although a detailed topic, given the high costs of care for older adults, it is helpful for providers to understand what the types of benefits are and how to access further information accordingly.

In the VA system, compensation is a term that refers to a payment that Veterans receive for their service-connected disabilities (Bingham County Clerks' Office, n.d.). These service-connected

(SC) disabilities are deemed by the VA based upon medical examination and evaluation to have been caused or been exacerbated by military service or in relation to an existing SC disability (VA, 2015e). Veterans may have one or more SC disabilities (e.g. cardiovascular, digestive, neurological, mental health, dental, and oral conditions; VA, 2014d). Those disabilities receive a rating (0–100%) whereby the amount of monthly tax-free compensation and the ability to receive care provided in relation to the rating are determined (VA, 2015b, 2015e).

In the VA system, *pensions* are payments to low-income war-time Veterans who are totally and permanently disabled from their non-service-connected injuries (Bingham County Clerks' Office, n.d.). Older Veterans who have non-service-connected (NSC) disabilities are considered disabled due to injury or illness not related to military service (Bingham County Clerks' Office, n.d.). As with SC disabilities, NSC disabilities have been vetted during a compensation and pension exam process.

In 2010, more than 4 million beneficiaries received Veteran's compensation and benefits (US Census, 2012c). Of the roughly 3.5 million beneficiaries who received benefits or compensation, 3.2 million were for SC, and 314,000 were for NSC (US Census, 2012c). Of the just over half-million dependents of deceased Veterans who continued to draw benefits or compensation, just under 350,000 were for SC, whereas just under 200,000 were for NSC (US Census, 2012c). Among Veterans aged 65 and their beneficiaries from the WWII era there were an estimated 529,000 beneficiaries of deceased Veterans and 298,000 living Veterans; from the Korean Conflict era there were 275,000 beneficiaries of deceased Veterans and 209,000 living Veterans; and from the Vietnam era 1,447,000 beneficiaries of deceased Veterans and 1,261,000 living Veterans received compensation and benefits (US Census, 2012c).

With regard to other benefits, older Veterans and often their dependents and survivors are eligible for additional federal benefits (e.g. caregiver support; memorial benefits). For more information, access the VA website (www.va.gov/opa/publications/benefits_book.asp; VA, 2014e) or contact the closest Veteran service officer (www.va.gov/vso) to help explain potential resources in greater detail (VA, 2013a).

Eligibility

For older Veterans, the eligibility to receive care intersects with aforementioned factors of healthcare coverage and benefits and is further determined by additional considerations. Discharge status – honorable, general, other than honorable, bad conduct, or dishonorable – may have implications for whether older Veterans may access certain benefits regarding their healthcare (Lawyers.com, 2015).

Older Veterans may be eligible to receive benefits through the VA, Military Hospital System (MHS)/TRICARE, as well as at the state level and community level. With regard to VA healthcare, eligibility hinges upon variables such as meeting minimum duty requirements, basic eligibility (important particularly for those who served in the Reserves or the National Guard), and enrollment process (which, once processed, places Veterans in one or more enrollment priority groups; VA, 2015e), outlined at www.va.gov/healthbenefits/apply/Veterans.asp. With regard to MHS/TRICARE, eligible older Veterans can use their TRICARE benefits to access healthcare in the community (e.g. civilian healthcare facilities; Air Force Retiree Services, 2011). With regard to state-specific support, state Veterans homes (National Association of State Veterans Homes, 2015) can be an important source of housing. At the community level, resources for older Veterans can be found either through Veteran-/military-specific local websites (e.g. Beyond the Yellow Ribbon, 2015) or ones more specific to older adults (e.g. Seniorresource.com). Additional resources can also be found in Table 5.2.

TABLE 5.2 Selected Resources for Older Veterans, Providers, and Caregivers

Source	Internet address
Crisis	
Veterans Crisis Line 1–800–273–TALK (8255)	www.Veterancrisisline.net
Mental health suicide prevention	www.mentalhealth.va.gov/suicide_prevention
Crisis Center Senior Talk Line	www.crisiscenterbham.com/senior-help-line.php
Professional/workforce	
American Geriatrics Society	www.oundation.americangeriatrics.org
Healthcare and Aging	www.asaging.org/han
Mental Health and Aging Network	www.asaging.org/mhan
Eldercare Workforce Alliance	www.eldercareworkforce.org
Training/education	
National Center for Health and the Aging	www.healthandtheaging.org
Network on Multicultural Aging	www.asaging.org/noma
Healthy People Report Card for Seniors	www.cdc.gov/features/agingandhealth/state_of_aging_and_health_in_america_2013.pdf
Care	
Program of All-Inclusive Care of the Elderly	www.npaonline.org/website/article.asp?id=12
Care locator	
VA geriatrics and extended care	www.va.gov/GERIATRICS
Aging and Disability Resource Center	www.adrc-tae.acl.gov/tiki-index.php? page=ADRCLocator
Eldercare Locator	www.eldercare.gov/Eldercare.NET/Public/Index.asp
Seniorresource.com	www.seniorresource.com
HealthinAging.org	www.healthinaging.org
VA	www.va.gov
Centers for Medicare & Medicaid Services	www.cms.gov
TRICARE	www.mytricare.com/internet/tric/tri/tricare.nsf
Caregiver/Geriatrics and extended care	
VA caregiver support	www.caregiver.va.gov
respite Care.com	www.care.com
Research	
Geriatric Research and Clinical Center	www.va.gov/grecc
RAND Center for Study in Aging	www.rand.org/labor/aging.html
VA Office of Research and Development	www.research.va.gov
Mental illness Research Education Clinical Center	www.mirecc.va.gov
National Institute on Aging	www.nia.nih.gov

Source	Internet address
Assessment related	
Activities of Daily Living	www.healthcare.uiowa.edu/igec/tools/function/lawtonbrody.pdf
Montreal Cognitive Assessment	www.mocatest.org
RAND's Assessing Care in Vulnerable Elders	www.rand.org/health/projects/acove.html
VA Clinical Practice Guidelines	www.healthquality.va.gov/guidelines/MH/ptsd
US Preventive Services Task Force	www.uspreventiveservicestaskforce.org
National Health Interview Survey	www.cdc.gov/nchs/nhis.htm

Notes: VA = US Department of Veterans Affairs; TRICARE = Military healthcare system; RAND = research and development. All links accessed: December 17, 2015.

Geriatric Healthcare

Older adults are known to be the largest – and most expensive – consumers of healthcare, particularly during their last 18 months of life (Beard, 2014).

In recent years, increasing interest in support provided outside of the VA-/military-supported settings has emerged. The following section highlights briefly the increasing importance of one support in particular, that of caregiving support.

Caregiver Support

The subject of caregiving is an important concern for many older Veterans, who may either be recipients of caregiving or function within the role of caregiver. This section briefly addresses each.

Older Veteran as Recipient of Caregiver Support

Care recipients are the people for whom military caregivers and military care providers are providing care (Ramchand et al., 2014). Care is needed for a variety of behavioral, health, and mental health outcomes, ranging from depression to hearing loss to chronic pain (Ramchand et al., 2014). VA care provision encompasses a variety of services, including adult day healthcare centers, home-based primary care, skilled home care, the homemaker and home health aide program, home telehealth, respite care, and home hospice care. Further information on these services can be found online (www.caregiver.va.gov/support/support_services.asp).

Military caregivers are most often family members, including partners, spouses, children, or siblings who help care for service members and Veterans. These caregivers serve an essential role in facilitating the recovery, rehabilitation, and reintegration of the wounded, ill, and injured. Military care providers are most often healthcare professionals or allied health professionals that render treatment, therapy, rehabilitation, or care management services. These individuals often have specific professional licenses or certifications and are reimbursed for their contributions.

Older Veteran as Caregiver

Increasingly, Veterans find that they are caregivers for someone's day-to-day health needs. Some research suggests that approximately 20% of all older Veterans are caregivers (Monin, Levy, & Pietrzak, 2014). In that position, they may find that they are unprepared for and overwhelmed by the daily care needs of their ill family member or friend. Such care needs may include long- and short-term physical conditions, memory problems, emotional, and mental health problems, and behavioral issues.

These caregiving experiences may be perceived as both challenging and satisfying, and can result in caregiver stress, strain, and various health consequences, including increases in anxiety, depression, challenges in social relationships, and physical symptoms (Pinquart & Sorensen, 2003). Interestingly, some research suggests that combat exposure is associated with less emotional strain in older Veteran caregivers (Monin et al., 2014).

Given the majority of Veterans do not use VA services (Nelson, Starkebaum, & Reiber, 2007), if older Veteran caregivers are seeking support, including respite care, various forms of psychosocial support, and information and communication technology, then it is likely from community-based service sectors instead of the VA. This suggests the need for increased awareness by civilian providers of the potential ongoing effects of military service on Veteran caregivers; their associated health behaviors and related decision-making; and specific needs of Veteran caregivers in the creation and delivery of integrated support services by providers.

Implications for Clinical Practice

Currently, support for older Veterans is undergoing a paradigm shift away from expecting military-supported settings (VA, 2015e) to be the sole source of support for older Veterans toward care that also takes place outside of military-supported settings within community- and home-based settings (VA, 2013c). As the substantial knowledge base needed to work with aging Veterans continues to change, providers in all settings benefit from specialized training, education, and supervision opportunities relevant to working with this population. It is important for providers to understand the ever-changing nature of healthcare challenges older Veterans may be adjusting to (e.g. Agent Orange), culturally relevant treatment barriers that exist (e.g. stigma against seeking care), and what resources are currently available (e.g. in the community, in the home, in hospitals; preventative/secondary/tertiary). Providers may benefit from incorporating awareness regarding how best to support older Veterans and the management of their care in a manner that reflects gerontological competence.

Kane and colleagues (2013) provide several recommendations of good care for older adults that generalize also to work with older Veterans. These recommendations speak to the importance of remembering that the aims of geriatric care are not to feel better, be fixed, or to feel good as new. For older adults, no change in health status following an intervention may actually be a good thing compared with potential outcomes within care (Kane et al., 2013). Slowing or delaying disease progression may be helpful goals from a quality-of-life perspective (Kane et al., 2013). In addition, even if decline is imminent, investing in care and the support of older adults is worth doing (Kane et al., 2013).

For all older adults, chronic disease management and preventative care are two of the most important elements of good healthcare (Kane et al., 2013). Assessment is central to both of these elements, and tools for assessment are increasingly available to a range of healthcare professionals and caregivers (Kane et al., 2013). Cognitive screening tools such as the Mini Mental Status Exam or the Montreal Cognitive Assessment can be used to measure cognitive ability and detect any changes. Screening tools such as the Lawton Instrumental Activities of Daily Living measure a person's functional ability in their activities of daily living. This screening tool can identify areas where support is needed, and help to determine what the individual may need in order to live independently in the community (Graf, 2013).

CASE EXAMPLE: "GEORGE"

George is a 70-year-old, African American, widowed, 80% service-connected disabled (70% for PTSD; 10% for tinnitus) male Marine Vietnam combat Veteran who presents for his first counseling appointment. He is here today both because he is feeling "slightly more depressed about his declining health and loss of his wife than usual" and wants to discuss his sadness and frustrations with someone other than his "well-intended daughter" and providers whom he feels are trying to push him out of his home prematurely.

George's military service began when he was drafted. He served one tour in South Vietnam, which lasted approximately a year. Although he describes the majority of time he spent in the country as being "rather uneventful," twice he had what he calls close encounters. More bothersome than either of the close calls he experienced were the events that occurred back home while George was away. First, his fiancée ended their relationship, which was both devastating and difficult to understand, given how well things were going when he left. Then, he also unexpectedly lost his grandmother, who had helped raise him and was dear to him.

When George returned home, he tried to go back to the way things were but life had moved on. His former ambitions no longer seemed to matter. He smoked to distract himself, and drank both to go to sleep at night as well as to numb his pain. Psychologically, he knew on some level he had been traumatized yet did not want to open Pandora's box, so to speak, and delve into things he wished to forget. Physically, soon after his return he began to notice he was having pain that he should get checked out but simply did not want to go to the doctor.

He settled into his life for the years to come. He found a stable job that "paid the bills." He met and married Marie. They went on to have three children, one daughter, Sam (now 40); and two sons, Carlos (now 41), and James (now 42). The years went by and the frenzy of everyday life seemed to help George push any disturbing thoughts he had to the back of his mind. With a moderate amount of alcohol, he found that he could sleep.

Life first took a difficult turn for George during the first several years after his children left home. Too much time on his hands led to more drinking, and more drinking led to fighting with his wife, which George found very upsetting yet was helpless to repair. His long-unmanaged health concerns became hard to ignore, which prompted him to finally seek help.

About ten years ago, Marie's insistence finally convinced George to take care of himself. She physically drove him to the emergency room after he was experiencing chest pain, shortness of breath, and dizziness. This served as a wake-up call for George, who knew he was long overdue to come in and wished he'd started to take care of himself earlier. He felt he had aged far beyond his years. He knew he had made lifestyle choices that hadn't helped. He was disappointed – but not surprised – to be diagnosed with multiple medical concerns including chronic obstructive pulmonary disease, adult onset diabetes, tinnitus, hypertension, peripheral neuropathy, and chronic pain. He finally felt ready and sought therapy to address trauma from Vietnam.

For the next several years, things were going pretty well for George. With Marie's support, George was able to really start managing his care. He sought and was awarded service-connected disability benefit for PTSD (70%) and tinnitus (10%). He engaged with primary care support and specialty care through his closest VA, which was about an hour away from his home. More locally, he was both able to see providers for more holistic care (e.g. massage, chiropractic care) and to attend Alcoholics Anonymous to help him maintain sobriety. From the comfort of home, he was able to talk to his care manager on a regular basis by phone.

Four years ago, George retired, then lost Marie to a heart attack quite unexpectedly. Things spiraled out of control quickly. His adult children intervened, and his daughter began to keep a close eye on him. At her suggestion, he started to see someone to talk to about his grief over losing Marie. Other things rose to the surface, including depressive symptoms about the past and some degree of anxiety about the future.

In the present, George's health is "okay" in general even though his body continues to fall apart. His daughter is threatening to either move in with him or make him move somewhere in the community with assisted living if he does not more actively address his medical needs. With the help of his team, he hopes to address his ongoing physical and mental health needs while maintaining as much independence as possible, preferably while still living in his own home.

Conclusion

The shifting landscape of healthcare will continue to have implications for providers who work with aging Veterans in the coming years. As the Veteran population continues to grow older, the provision of support inside and outside of military-supported settings as well as within the home will become increasingly important. Care that honors older Veterans will require providers to understand who older Veterans are, what their health concerns are, and how these healthcare needs may be addressed. Integration of knowledge specific to gerontology, military, health, and healthcare needs will help providers in their efforts to support and work with older Veterans.

References

Air Force Retiree Services (2011). Turning 65: Understanding TRICARE, Medicare. Retrieved from www.retirees.af.mil/news/story.asp?id=123264617

American Psychiatric Association (1980). *Diagnostic and statistical manual of mental disorders* (3rd ed.). Washington, DC: Author.

American Tinnitus Association (n.d.). Demographics. Retrieved from www.ata.org/understanding-facts/demographics

Beard, J. (2014). We were older then, we are younger now. World Health Organization. Retrieved from www.who.int/mediacentre/commentaries/ageing/en

Beyond the Yellow Ribbon (2015). Beyond the Yellow Ribbon is united in bringing service members all the way home. Retrieved from www.beyondtheyellowribbon.org

Bingham County Clerk's Office (n.d.). Frequently asked questions. Retrieved from www.co.bingham.id.us/clerk/Veteran_faq.html

Boettcher, W. A. & Cobb, M. D. (2006). Echoes of Vietnam? Casualty framing and public perceptions of successes and failures in Iraq. *Journal of Conflict Resolution*, 206(50), 831–854. doi: 10.1177/0022002706293665

Brogan, R. F. (2010). Elder law's new frontier. *New Jersey Lawyer Magazine*, 265, 49–52.

Card, J. J. (1987). Epidemiology of PTSD in a national cohort of Vietnam Veterans. *Journal of Clinical Psychology*, 43(1), 6–17.

Centers for Disease Control (2012). Deaths: Final data for 2010. *CDC/NCHS, National Vital Statistics Report*, 61(4). Retrieved from www.cdc.gov/nchs/data/nvsr/nvsr61/nvsr61_04.pdf

Damron-Rodriguez, J. (2011). Aging Veterans and their caregivers. National Center for Gerontological Social Work Education. Retrieved from www.cswe.org/CentersInitiatives/GeroEdCenter/GECPublications/agingtimes/47004/47009/47011.aspx

Fanning, J. R. & Pietrzak, R. H. (2013). Suicidality among older male Veterans in the United States: Results from the National Health and Resilience in Veterans Study. *Journal Psychiatric Research*, 47, 1766–1775.

Figley, C. R. (1978). Introduction. In C. R. Figley (Ed.), *Stress disorders among Vietnam Veterans: Theory, research, and treatment* (pp. xiii–xxvi). New York: Brunner/Mazel.

Freud, A. & Dann, S. (1951). An experiment in group upbringing. *Psychoanalytic study of the child*, 6, 127–168.

Goldsmith, T. C. (2014). *The evolution of aging: How new theories will change the future of medicine* (3rd ed.) Crownsville, MD: Azinet Press.

Graf, C. (2013). The Lawton Instrumental Activities of Daily Living (IADL) scale. *Try this: Best practices in nursing care. From the Hartford Institute for Geriatric Nursing, New York University, College of Nursing*, 23, 1–2. Retrieved from http://consultgerirn.org/uploads/File/trythis/try_this_23.pdf

Herman, J. (1992). *Trauma and recovery: The aftermath of violence – from domestic abuse to political terror.* New York: Basic Books.

Hobbs, K. (2008). Reflections on the culture of Veterans. *American Association of Health Nurses*, 56(8), 337–341.

Institute of Medicine (2014). *Veterans and Agent Orange: Update 2012.* Washington, DC: National Academies Press.

Institute of Medicine (2015). *Post-Vietnam dioxin exposure in Agent Orange–Contaminated C-123 aircraft.* Washington, DC: National Academies Press.

Jennings, P. A., Aldwin. C. A., Levenson, M. R., Spiro, A., & Mroczek, D. K. (2006). Combat exposure, perceived benefits of military service, and wisdom in later life: Findings from the Normative Aging Study. *Research on Aging*, 28(1), 115–134.

Kane, R. L., Ouslander, J. G., Abrass, I. B., & Resnick, B. (2013). *Essentials of clinical geriatrics* (7th ed.). New York: McGraw Hill.

Karger, H. J. & Stoesz, D. (2014). *American social welfare policy: A pluralist approach.* Boston, MA: Pearson.

Lawyers.com (2015). *Discharges and their effect on Veteran benefits.* Retrieved from http://military-law.lawyers.com/Veterans-benefits/discharges-and-their-effect-on-Veteran-benefits.html

McFarland, S. L. (2012). *A concise history of the Air Force.* Maxwell Air Force Base, AL: Air University, United States Air Force Jeanne M. Holm Center for Officer Accessions and Citizen Development.

McReynolds, J. L. & Rossen, E. K. (2004). Importance of physical activity, nutrition, and social support for optimal aging. *Clinical Nurse Specialist*, 18(4). Retrieved from www.medscape.com/viewarticle/484344_2

Maynard, C. M. & Boyko, E. J. (2006). Differences in cause of death of Washington State Veterans who did and did not use Department of Veterans Affairs healthcare services. *Journal of Rehabilitation, Research, and Development*, 43(7), 825–830.

Military.com (n.d.). *TRICARE benefits overview.* Retrieved from www.military.com/benefits/tricare/your-tricare-benefits-explained.html

Monin, J. K., Levy, B. R., & Pietrzak, R. H. (2014). From serving in the military to serving loved ones: Unique experiences of older Veteran caregivers. *American Journal of Geriatric Psychiatry*, 22(6), 570–579.

National Association of State Veterans Homes (2015). *State homes. Directory of state homes.* Retrieved from www.nasvh.org/StateHomes/statedir.cfm

Nelson, K. M., Starkebaum, G. A., & Reiber, G. E. (2007). Veterans using and uninsured Veterans not using Veterans Affairs (VA) health care. *Public Health Reports*, 122(1), 93–100.

Ogden, L. L. & Adams, K. (2009). Poorhouse to warehouse: Institutional long-term care in the United States. *Publius*, 39(1), 138–163.

Passages (2011). *Veterans and Medicare.* Retrieved from www.passagescenter.org/medicare-counseling/Veterans

Pietrzak, R. H. & Cook, J. M. (2013). Psychological resilience in older U.S. Veterans: Results from the National Health and Resilience in Veterans Study. *Depression and Anxiety*, 30(5), 432–443.

Pietrzak, R. H., Johnson, D. C., Goldstein, M. B., Malley, J. C., Rivers, A. J., Morgan, C. A., & Southwick, S. M. (2010). Psychosocial buffers of traumatic stress, depressive symptoms, and psychosocial difficulties in veterans of Operations Enduring Freedom and Iraqi Freedom: The role of resilience, unit support, and post-deployment social support. *Journal of Affective Disorders*, 120(1), 188–192.

Pinquart, M., & Sorensen, S. (2003). Differences between caregivers and noncaregivers in psychological health and physical health: A meta-analysis. *Psychology and Aging*, 18(2), 250–267.

Ramchand, R., Tanielian, T., Fisher, M. P., Vaughan, C. A., Trail, T. E., & Epley, C. et al. (2014). *America's military caregivers*. Retrieved from www.rand.org/content/dam/rand/pubs/research_reports/RR400/RR499/RAND_RR499.pdf

Rostker, B. (2006). *The evolution of the all-volunteer force*. Thousand Oaks, CA: RAND. Retrieved from www.rand.org/content/dam/rand/pubs/monographs/2007/RAND_MG265.pdf

Russell, M. C. & Figley, C. R. (2014). Overview of the Affordable Care Act's impact on military and Veteran's mental health services: Nine implications for significant improvements in care. *Journal of Social Work in Disability & Rehabilitation*, 13, 162–196. doi: 10.1080/1546710X.2013.870514

Senior Resource (2015). *Resources by state, Canada, and US territory*. Retrieved from www.seniorresource.com/mn.htm

Settersten, R. A. (2006). When nations call: How wartime military service matters for the life course and aging. *Research on Aging*, 28(1), 12–36.

Shay, K., Hyduke, B., & Burris, J. F. (2013). Strategic plan for geriatrics and extended care in the Veterans Health Administration: Background, plan, and progress to date. *Journal of American Geriatric Society*, 61(4), 632–638.

Sherwood, R. J., Shimel, H., Stolz, P. &, Sherwood, D. (2004). Aging Veterans: Re-emergence of trauma issues. *Journal of Geronotological Social Work*, 40(4), 73–86. doi: 10.1300/J083v40n04_06

Sohn, M. W., Arnold, N., Maynard, C., & Hynes, D. (2006). Accuracy and completeness of mortality data in the department of Veterans affairs. *Population Health Metrics*, 4(2). Retrieved from www.pophealthmetrics.com/content/4/1/2

Spiro, A. & Settersten, R. A. (2012). Long-term implications of military service for later-life health and well-being . *Research in Human Development*, 9(3), 183–190. doi: 10.1080/15427609.2012.705551

Supiano, M. A., Alessi, C., Chernoff, R., Goldberg, A., Morley, J. E., Schmader, K. E. et al., and GRECC Directors Association (2012). Department of Veterans affairs geriatric research, education and clinical centers: Translating aging research into clinical geriatrics. *Journal of the American Geriatrics Society*, 60(7), 1347–1356. doi: 10.1111/j.1532-5415.2012.04004.x

Tanielian, T. & Jaycox, L. H. (Eds.) (2008). *Invisible wounds of war: Summary and recommendations for addressing psychological and cognitive injuries*. Thousand Oaks, CA: RAND.

Torreon, B. S. (2011, December 29). *U.S. periods of war and dates of current conflicts*. Congressional Research Service Report for Congress: Prepared for Members and Committees of Congress. Retrieved from www.fas.org/sgp/crs/natsec/RS21405.pdf

US Census Bureau (2012a). *Table 521. Veterans living by period of service, age, and sex: 2010*. Retrieved from www.census.gov/compendia/statab/2012/tables/12s0520.pdf

US Census Bureau (2012b). *Table 522. Veterans living by period of sex, race, and Hispanic origin: 2010*. Retrieved from www.census.gov/compendia/statab/2012/tables/12s0522.pdf

US Census Bureau (2012c). *Table 524. Veterans compensation and pension benefits – Number on rolls by period of service and status: 1990 to 2010*. Retrieved from www.census.gov/compendia/statab/2012/tables/12s0522.pdf

US Census Bureau (2012d). *Today, there are 9.4 million Veterans ages 65 and over*. Retrieved from www.agingstats.gov/main_site/data/2012_documents/population.aspx

US Census Bureau (2012e). *Where do Veterans get health insurance coverage?* Retrieved from www.census.gov/newsroom/releases/pdf/cb13ff27_graphic.pdf

US Centers for Medicare & Medicaid Services (2015). *Military Veterans. Health care coverage options for military Veterans*. Retrieved from www.healthcare.gov/Veterans

US Department of Health and Human Services (2004). Employer-sponsored health insurance: Trends in cost and access. *Research in Action*, 17, 1–12. Retrieved from http://archive.ahrq.gov/research/findings/factsheets/costs/empspria/empspria.pdf

US Department of Veterans Affairs (n.d.). *VA history in brief*. Retrieved from www.va.gov/opa/publications/archives/docs/history_in_brief.pdf

US Department of Veterans Affairs (2009a). *Profile of Veterans 2011: Data from the American Community Survey.* Retrieved from www.va.gov/vetdata/docs/SpecialReports/Profile_of_Veterans_2011.pdf

US Department of Veterans Affairs (2009b). *PTSD Research Quarterly.* Retrieved from www.ptsd.va.gov/professional/newsletters/research-quarterly/v20n3.pdf

US Department of Veterans Affairs (2011). *2010 National Survey of Veterans: Reported plan to use VA Healthcare in the future, for selected group of Veterans.* Retrieved from www.va.gov/vetdata/docs/QuickFacts/2010NSV_Quick_Fact_Final.pdf

US Department of Veterans Affairs (2013a). *Directory of Veteran service organizations.* Retrieved from www.va.gov/vso/

US Department of Veterans Affairs (2013b). *Profile of Veterans: 2011. Data from the American Community Survey.* Retrieved from www.va.gov/vetdata/docs/SpecialReports/Profile_of_Veterans_2011.pdf

US Department of Veterans Affairs (2013c). *Veterans: Elderly Veterans.* Retrieved from www.benefits.va.gov/PERSONA/Veteran-elderly.asp

US Department of Veterans Affairs (2014a). *National Center for Veterans Analysis and Statistics.* Retrieved from www.va.gov/vetdata/Veteran_Population.asp

US Department of Veterans Affairs (2014b). *National Center for Veterans Analysis and Statistics. Department of Veterans Affairs statistics at a glance.* Retrieved from www.va.gov/vetdata/docs/Quickfacts/Stats_at_a_glance_12_31_14.pdf

US Department of Veterans Affairs (2014c). *National Center for PTSD. PTSD history and overview: PTSD assessment and treatment in older adults.* Retrieved from www.ptsd.va.gov/professional/treatment/older/assessment_tx_older_adults.asp

US Department of Veterans Affairs (2014d). *Web automated reference material system. 38 CFR book C, schedule for rating disabilities.* Retrieved from www.benefits.va.gov/warms/bookc.asp#a

US Department of Veterans Affairs (2015a). *About VA – VA History.* Retrieved from www.va.gov/about_va/vahistory.asp

US Department of Veterans Affairs (2015b). *Health benefits.* Retrieved from www.va.gov/HEALTHBENEFITS/cost

US Department of Veterans Affairs (2015c). *Helping Veterans cope with chronic pain.* Huntington, VA Medical Center. Retrieved from www.huntington.va.gov/HUNTINGTON/features/Chronic_Pain.asp

US Department of Veterans Affairs (2015d). *National Center for Veterans Analysis and Statistics.* Retrieved from www1.va.gov/vetdata

US Department of Veterans Affairs (2015e). *Office of Public Affairs. Federal benefits for dependents and survivors. 2014 online edition.* Retrieved from www.va.gov/opa/publications/benefits_book/benefits_chap13.asp

US Department of Veterans Affairs (2015f). *Patient care services.* Retrieved from www.patientcare.va.gov/Geriatrics.asp

US Department of Veterans Affairs (2015g). *Public health. Military exposures.* Retrieved from www.publichealth.va.gov/exposures/

US Department of Veterans Affairs (2015h). *Vet Center Program. Who we are.* Retrieved from www.vetcenter.va.gov/About_US.asp

US Department of Veterans Affairs (2015i). *Veterans Health Administration. One in ten older Veterans is depressed.* Retrieved from www.va.gov/health/NewsFeatures/20110624a.asp

University of Georgia Institute of Gerontology (n.d.). *What is gerontology?* College of Public Health. Retrieved from www.publichealth.uga.edu/geron/what-is

Williamson, J. B. (1984). Old age relief policy prior to 1900: The trend toward restrictiveness. *American Journal of Economics and Sociology*, 43(3), 369–384.

Wilmoth, J. M. & London, A. S. (2011). Aging Veterans: Needs and provisions. In R. A. Setterson & J. L. Angel (Eds.), *Handbook of sociology and aging* (pp. 661–672). New York: Springer. doi: 10.1007/978-1-4419-7374-0_28

6

MILITARY FAMILIES: STRENGTHS AND CONCERNS

Reintegration and Beyond

Eugenia L. Weiss, Deborah Hino, Julie Canfield and David L. Albright

More than 2.2 million US military service members have been deployed in support of Operation Iraqi Freedom (OIF), Operation Enduring Freedom (OEF), and Operation New Dawn (OND) since 2001 (US Department of Defense [DoD], 2013). Many of these service members have children and spouses or significant others that are greatly impacted by this service. The deployment cycle consists of phases including the mobilization, deployment, and reintegration of the service member and his or her family. There are multiple factors that influence military family life and contribute to the overall resiliency of that family as an operating system.

Reintegration is the period of time commonly referred to when military service members return home after a deployment to previously established roles in their civilian environments (Currie, Day, & Kelloway, 2011). As in all adjustments, the process of reintegration can be accompanied by stress and upheaval as service members and their families shift back into civilian roles and routines of daily living. In the case of a military family and for service members with children, there are additional stressors that impact their physical, emotional, cognitive, and social health.

This chapter will discuss some of the challenges and strengths associated with being a military family or a family impacted by military service during the Global War on Terrorism (GWOT). In the wake of the drawdown of US military involvement in Iraq and Afghanistan, we are experiencing a significant shift in terms of the repercussions of a protracted war that has relied on the use of an all-volunteer force. A case vignette at the end of the chapter is provided to illustrate some of the significant issues discussed, and is followed by suggestions for human service providers intervening with military-connected families across all areas of helping including clinical work, programmatic/policy development, and applied research.

Deployment and the Military-Connected Family

Active duty service members have represented approximately 1.3 million of the 2.2 million deployed with 55.2% married; 42.8% with two or more children; and 5% single parents (DoD, 2013). The Reserves and National Guard have deployed more than 800,000 service members in the GWOT and when compared with the rates of active-duty service members, have slightly lower rates of marriage and a higher likelihood of being a single parent (DoD,

2013). Service members have been deployed multiple times and 46% of active-duty service members who have two or more children have served on more than one deployment (Bello-Utu & DeSocio, 2015; McGuinness & McGuinness, 2014).

Families are sometimes given short notice before service members are deployed and return dates can change frequently depending on multiple factors involved which can create additional stressors to a family system (Paley, Lester, & Mogil, 2013). When a spouse or significant other is deployed, the non-deployed partner usually takes over the sole responsibility of the household and the children. This shift in role responsibility can leave these partners feeling overwhelmed and lonely, especially for those without good support systems (Esposito-Smythers et al., 2011). Situations of infidelity are sometimes added stressors and conflicts for military couples during this period (Sayers, 2011). Military service members and their partners may also have unresolved issues prior to the deployment that can resurface during the separation and lead to additional conflicts in the family (Sayers, 2011). As many of the majority of service members are under 25 years of age, their marriages are not necessarily "long term," having stood the test of time.

At-home partners who experience elevated stressors have increased risks for related emotional challenges such as depression, anxiety, and sleep disorders (Mansfield et al., 2010). As a result, such challenges can negatively impact the attachment between the caregiver and the children in the home (Paley et al., 2013). In the absence of a strong external support system to buffer children from the negative effects of such stress, children can experience their own difficulties with emotions and behaviors (Flake, Davis, Johnson, & Middleton, 2009). In cases where the caregiver's mental health continues to be compromised throughout the deployment cycle, this can in turn exacerbate problems that the children in the home experience (Chandra et al., 2010).

Due to advanced technology today, increased communication via audio and video can occur between a deployed service member and his or her family, which can also increase family stress levels as they may become more aware of the challenges that their loved ones are facing both on deployment and at home (Paley et al., 2013). As well, many of the technological interactions are "edited" keeping the most troubling family or service member experiences out of the communication.

Children from military-connected families may also experience anxiety and fear for their parent's safety while they are deployed (Leskin et al., 2013). It has been reported that when a parent is deployed, military-connected youth have higher rates of hospital visits, mental health issues, behavioral problems, and academic problems (Chandra et al., 2010; Creech, Hadley, & Borsari, 2014). Where the duration of the service member's deployment is longer, this relates proportionally to the severity of the problems that the children experience (Chandra et al., 2010).

When a parent is deployed, the children's roles in the family may significantly change, similar to the changing roles of the non-deployed spouse (Chandra et al., 2010). The developmental, emotional, and cognitive capabilities to understand a parent's deployment normatively increases with age in childhood and older youth are often placed in caregiver roles to younger children in the home (Leskin et al., 2013). In one study, adolescents were at higher risk for substance use during or shortly after a parent's deployment (Acion, Ramirez, Jorge, & Arndt, 2013). Adolescents from military-connected families have also reported high rates of hopelessness, sadness, depression, and suicidal ideations (Cederbaum et al., 2014). In addition to this, another study reported that an increased rate of psychiatric hospitalization in children between the ages of 9 to 17 years was related to a longer cumulative duration of parental deployment (Millegan, Engel, Liu, & Dinneen, 2013).

Reintegration

Military-connected families who believe that reintegration will be quick or easy soon discover that it can be a difficult and lengthy process that is often a major stressor for both the service member and his or her family. It can take up to a year or more in some situations for military family members to be able to adjust to the service member's return (Marek & D'Aniello, 2014). Some returning service members might feel like a stranger or guest in their own family due to the changed family dynamics since they were deployed and can feel emotionally separated from their family and avoid discussing details about their deployment as a result (Sayers, 2011). When a military partner returns home, such a response can be stressful for the spouse or at-home partner, and one study found that approximately 50% of military couples experienced an initial honeymoon period, followed by a decline in martial satisfaction, and later improvement in the marriage (Sayers, 2011). Another study found that reunited military couples tend to avoid issues that cause them anxiety including but not limited to: household stressors, financial difficulties, discussing feelings of the service member, politics, and future redeployment possibilities (Knobloch, Ebata, McGlaughlin, & Theiss, 2013). Families that avoid topics such as finances or other household stressors or conflicts can leave these issues unresolved over time and make them more difficult to approach when it is necessary to do so. These families become more at risk for significant problems related to these issues due to the parental collusion of avoidance of these topics and lack of healthy and adaptive communication patterns concerning them.

During a deployment, the at-home spouse or partner assumes decision-making for the family and when the deployed member returns, the family has to renegotiate individual roles and responsibilities; if the at-home partner has difficulty relinquishing this authority and responsibility, the service member may feel that they are no longer valued or needed in their family (Bowling & Sherman, 2008). Although military-connected children are often highly resilient and adaptable to change, some may have difficulties during the reintegration phase with their military parent (Leskin et al., 2013). Children may exhibit difficulties in the attachment with the parent during the reintegration phase, especially if the parent is struggling with psychosocial issues that impact that attachment. Children of military parents with post-traumatic stress symptoms from combat deployments may be particularly impacted by such symptoms and can exhibit signs of fearfulness or anxiety in these relationships (Chandra et al., 2010; Sayers, 2011). Military-connected youth may also be anxious and concerned about the relationship between their parents as the family negotiates the reintegration process (Marek & D'Aniello, 2014).

One study found that adolescents had the most difficult time with reintegration when compared with younger children due to having had more responsibility in the household while the parent was gone and needing to readjust their roles to the new situation when the family member returned (Chandra et al., 2010). This study found that adolescents with a parent who had been deployed and had difficulties with academics and/or behavior problems reported a worsening of these issues as they grew older (Chandra et al., 2010).

Another study found that deployment and reintegration negatively impacted the mental health of 33.7% of the military-connected adolescents studied who reported feelings of hopelessness and/or sadness; 24.8% of these adolescents reported that they had contemplated suicide with girls reporting a higher rate of ideation than the boys in the study (Cederbaum et al., 2014). A different study found that children who had high levels of anxiety during a parent's deployment also had high levels of anxiety when the parent reintegrated into the family with their academics and sleep negatively impacted (Lester et al., 2010).

When service members separate from the military after deployment, they face additional reintegration issues because civilian life may feel like culture shock (Coll, Weiss, & Yarvis, 2011). The reintegration is more difficult for recently separated Veterans because they have to learn how to transition from the structured environment of the military to the more unstructured life of being a civilian (Demers, 2011). Some Veterans believe that "civilians do not understand us," and that the general population cannot understand what happened during their deployment (Demers, 2011, p. 170). In this study, the author noted that Veterans reported that they felt disrespected and had difficulty connecting with civilians during reintegration. Other reintegration challenges for Veterans can include housing insecurity, substance abuse, financial difficulties, and legal involvement/incarceration (Savitsky, Illingworth, & DuLaney, 2009).

Mental Health Issues in the Service Member/Veteran and Impact on the Family

In addition to the difficulty of reintegration, active-duty members and Veterans may also be dealing with mental health problems and/or physical ailments. Research studies indicate that physical ailments and trauma are the two main hindrances for a smooth adjustment from military to civilian life (Leskin et al., 2013). Hoge, Milliken, and Auchterlonie (2007) found that rates for behavioral health problems rose after the Veteran had been home for three to six months. Military service members who had multiple deployments had a greater risk of being diagnosed with a mental health disorder such as depression or post-traumatic stress disorder (PTSD) (Sher, 2009). Research suggests that female Veterans are more likely than male Veterans to report mental health problems like PTSD and depression. Using data from the 2012 Behavioral Risk Factor Surveillance Survey, a survey conducted by the Centers for Disease Control and Prevention, a recent study analyzed data from a national sample of over 50,000 Veterans and found that over 25% of all female Veterans reported being medically diagnosed with depression, with an additional 12% with symptoms of undiagnosed depression (Hendricks Thomas et al., in press). Extrapolating from these results suggests that depression in female Veterans is a serious problem and likely plays some role in their family functioning.

In one study, Veterans who suffered from depression or PTSD had five times higher rates of difficulty with the reintegration period with their families than Veterans without these conditions (Sayers, Farrow, Ross & Oslin, 2009). In a survey of service members with depressive symptoms, 40% of respondents reported feeling like strangers in their own homes (Sayers, 2011). PTSD is known as one of the invisible wounds from combat and can be a lifelong struggle with rates that are difficult, if not impossible, to quantify. Many Veterans experience a range of post-traumatic stress symptoms on a continuum of severity from mild and transient to chronic and severe during reintegration and many never report these symptoms to the military or a healthcare provider. In one study with Army spouses seeking primary care, almost 70% of the respondents who screened positive for a mental health problem with functional limitations sought mental health treatment for these compared with 23% to 40% of soldiers who sought treatment for a mental health condition (Eaton et al., 2008).

Although the rate of PTSD is disputed, one study estimated it to be approximately 20% of returning service members (Fisher, 2014). The comorbidity of mental health problems and substance abuse is well documented with regard to the Veteran community (Meis, Erbes, Polusny, & Compton, 2010). Consequently, many service members with PTSD will often attempt to manage these painful feelings and alleviate disrupted sleep patterns or nightmares through alcohol misuse and/or other substances such as illicit drugs (Tinney & Gerlock, 2014).

Along with PTSD impairing a service member's daily life, it also affects the family as a functioning system filled with relationship dynamics and competing demands. PTSD symptoms such as anxiety, avoidance, and withdrawal can negatively impact the functioning of the family (Sayers, 2011). In addition to this, PTSD symptoms can produce difficulties with the reintegration process for service members and spouses (Marek & D'Aniello, 2014). Service members with PTSD tend to have higher rates of poor relationships, irritability, frustration in expressing their feelings, problems with intimacy, and difficulties in concentration (Dekel & Monson, 2010; Meis et al., 2010). Spouses of service members who have PTSD have reported higher rates of marital dissatisfaction and poor communication patterns (Paley et al., 2013; Renshaw, Campbell, Meis, & Erbes, 2014). Combat-related PTSD in a military parent during reintegration can be damaging to the attachment bonds in a family and children may become fearful of that parent's symptoms of traumatic stress and develop associated behavioral problems themselves (Riggs & Riggs, 2011).

Traumatic brain injury (TBI) is another major health concern among the current cohort of Veterans from GWOT. Recently, one study reported the prevalence of TBI in the military to be estimated at more than a quarter million injuries (Tinney & Gerlock, 2014). Another study reported that approximately 320,000 or 20% of the service members who have served in OEF, OIF, and OND have experienced a mild-TBI (Hyatt, Davis, & Barroso, 2014). This study with service members with mild-TBI reported a decrease and resolution of symptoms within three months (Hyatt et al., 2014). Many TBI symptoms, however, occur in combination with PTSD symptoms due to the traumatic nature of sustaining a brain injury and behaviors such as withdrawing, isolating, being irritable, depressed and angry or agitated can become difficult to tease apart, and can contribute to overall family stress levels (Bowling & Sherman, 2008; Savitsky et al., 2009; Tinney & Gerlock, 2014). Veterans with TBI and PTSD may also tend to shut out their families through a lack of communication about these and other reactions, which can in turn lead to more marital distress (Straits-Troster et al., 2013). In addition to the emotional/behavioral reactions, TBI symptoms can also include physical and cognitive problems such as poor balance, speech impairment, and significant impairments in short-term memory functioning (Boyd & Asmussen, 2013).

Generally, family members become the main caregivers for service members who have medium to severe TBI (Phelan et al., 2011). Depending on the severity of the TBI and associated post-traumatic stress, caregivers face many new responsibilities such as planning and driving to physical and mental healthcare appointments, organizing and assisting in the patient's daily requirements, as well as providing social and emotional support (Kreutzer et al., 2009). Additionally, according to Kreutzer et al., caregivers who positively cope with patients with TBI may see higher recovery rates in the service member. On the other hand, dealing with TBI and associated post-traumatic stress can negatively affect caregivers if they become socially isolated and experience discrimination and stigma from others, all of which can lead to decreases in self-esteem as well as increases in stress, depression, and further isolation (Phelan et al., 2011).

Secondary Traumatic Stress and the Family

The stressors from deployment and reintegration may result in military couples being more vulnerable to anxiety, depression, post-traumatic stress, and relationship problems (Knobloch et al., 2013). The family is a system and when a member in that system has chronic or unresolved PTSD it impacts the entire family's functioning (Paley et al., 2013). Nelson and Wright (1996) noted that secondary traumatic stress occurs when a person who closely interacts with individuals with PTSD demonstrates similar symptoms. In addition to these risk factors, another study reported that parents with PTSD symptoms had difficulties with adjustment to family life and parenting (Gewirtz et al., 2010).

Franciskovic et al.'s (2007) study with Croatian Veterans from the Croatian War of Independence (1991–1995) reported that 63% of non-deployed women spouses had emotional difficulties in dealing with their partners' avoidance in discussing traumatic war experiences and that 50% of the non-deployed spouses suffered from secondary traumatic stress resulting in shorter marriages and higher rates of unemployment. Depression and anxiety may also be a result of secondary trauma reactions for military spouses or partners (Herzog, Everson, & Whitworth, 2011). When a service member has PTSD, depression can be experienced by the spouse and family members if the traumatized person acts in ways that cause pain and loss to the family, such as restricting social activities and not being able to work (Carlson & Ruzek, 2014). Non-deployed spouses or partners who struggle with depression may also have a difficult time assisting the service member in his or her reintegration back into civilian life which further exacerbates an already tenuous familial situation (Verdeli et al., 2011). Research has shown that the mental health of the non-deployed parent can also influence the child's mental health (Chandra et al., 2010). Another study determined that having a parent with PTSD may cause some children in a family to exhibit separation anxieties, nighttime fears, academic difficulties in school, and higher rates of depressive issues (Klaric et al., 2008).

Children suffering from secondary trauma have been reported to have an increased risk for maladaptive coping skills such as substance abuse, greater health problems, and even shorter life expectancies (Bello-Utu & DeSocio, 2015; Brown et al., 2009). Children with secondary stress disorders may over-identify with a parent with PTSD and may either exhibit the same symptoms, take on the responsibilities of a parent and become a rescuer, or become emotionally detached and uninvolved with the parent (Price, 2014). Given the lack of school-based interventions for military-connected children (Brendel, Maynard, Albright, & Bellomo, 2014), these children are likely going to seek some forms of support from their families and/or from other community organizations or activities that they engage in.

Intimate Partner Violence

Although the rates of intimate partner violence (IPV) have been decreasing in the military, incidence of IPV in military families is higher than in civilian families (LaMotte et al., 2015; Schmaling, Blume, & Russell, 2011). When TBI or PTSD is present, then IPV is more prevalent in military-connected families (Tinney & Gerlock, 2014). Strong correlation exists between intimate partner relationships that have high dissatisfaction and the rates of aggression and IPV (LaMotte et al., 2015). IPV may also be related to PTSD and some of the cluster symptoms are "dysfunctional affect, alternating numbness, alternative numbness and hyperarousal, and occasional outburst of rage" (Basham, 2013, p. 450). TBI correlates with higher rates of depression, aggression, anxiety, and emotional dysfunction, which can all play a role in IPV (Bowling & Sherman, 2008; Tinney & Gerlock, 2014).

IPV in general is often directed at women; one in three women is physically or sexually assaulted in their lifetime, and 22% to 35% of female emergency room visits are a result of IPV (Chavis & Hill, 2009; Kubany, Hill, & Owens, 2003). Another report estimated this number to be as high as two-thirds of all women in the US (Flaherty, 2010) and these statistics have implications for the female spouses or partners of military service members. Historically, the incidence of IPV has been higher in military than in civilian families (Cronin, 1995; Griffin & Morgan, 1988; McCarrol et al., 2000; Miller & Veltkamp, 1993). The prevalence of IPV among female service members ranges from 17% to 39% and 22% to 74% for Veterans (Brown & Joshi, 2014). In addition to this, women Veterans are more likely than non-Veterans to experience IPV (Dichter, Cerulli, & Bossarte, 2011). Women Veterans that reported unwanted sexual experiences during military service were over two times more likely to report IPV than those not reporting those experiences (Iverson et al., 2013).

IPV is defined as the misuse of power to exert emotional, financial, physical, psychological, and/or sexual control (Peled, Davidson–Arad, & Perel, 2010). Abusive tactics include coercion and threats, emotional abuse, intimidation, or physical and sexual violence (Chavis & Hill, 2009), verbal aggression, and the use of physical force to resolve conflict (Straus & Gelles, 1990). IPV is associated with a variety of mental and physical sequelae (Campbell, 2002). The most frequent mental health sequelae include depression and PTSD (Golding, 1999), along with alcohol and drug abuse (Goodwin , Spitz, Petersen, & Saltzman, 2000).

Within military-connected populations, IPV is seen as an even more significant problem because of unique factors and stresses of military life (Gerlock, 2004). Those factors include frequent moves, prolonged separation, financial stress, military mission priority (Gerlock, 2004); and combat exposure and subsequent PTSD (Gerlock, 2004; Kulka et al., 1988; Melvin, 2011; Taft et al., 2009).

PTSD can have a significant impact on family life and relationships. For example, active-duty service members and Veterans with PTSD show higher rates of marital instability and partner violence than those without PTSD (Sherman et al., 2006). A study conducted with Veterans and their spouses to determine the impact of PTSD on IPV and other issues found that 33% of Veterans with PTSD reported occurrences of IPV, while only 13.5% of those without PTSD reported such occurrences within the last year (Marshall, Panuzio, & Taft, 2005).

In 1990, a National Vietnam Veterans Readjustment Study was conducted through the US Department of Veterans Affairs (VA) with Vietnam Veterans and their partners. Veterans with direct combat exposure accounted for 42% of IPV cases that year (Marshall, Panuzio, & Taft, 2005). In another study with male combat Veterans, 33% of Veterans reported acts of physical aggression, such as pushing, shoving, slapping, and 91% reported psychological aggression, such as insulting and yelling toward intimate partners (Taft et al., 2009).

Due to multiple deployments and the increased risk for PTSD, the ability to readjust to a non–combat setting is often increasingly difficult. The basic tenets of military training, the use of aggression and violence to achieve mission goals, may cross over into other areas of life where they can lead to damage (Bradley, 2007). Unfortunately, this often occurs in relationships, as violence becomes a tool for resolving interpersonal conflict. An additional consideration is the long-term consequences on military children who witness IPV. Military-connected children have a tendency to join the military as adults (Hall, 2011), and this could potentially lead to a vicious cycle.

Long-term consequences for military families affected by IPV may include the loss of financial security provided by the military. This includes a steady paycheck, insurance, and housing allowance (DoD, 2015). If the service member was dishonorably discharged due to IPV, his or her dependents are eligible for transitional compensation (Sullivan, 2006). It is important to note that the amount of transitional pay is dependent on many variables outlined in the statutes of 38 USC (Sullivan, 2006). In addition, if medical attention was needed as a result of the IPV, the family may be left with high medical bills and serious long-term health issues. Along with these material losses, a family may also lose the "head of household" or parental figure, be required to separate, and deal with the guilt of speaking out against a loved one (DoD, 2015).

Accused batterers also deal with long-term consequences in these situations. In most cases, the commander decides what punishment will ensue for the service member. These punishments include court-martial, discharge from military service, denial of retirement benefits, and the requirement to make compensation payments to the IPV victim(s). If a civilian jurisdiction handles the situation, the batterer could face a conviction appearing on his/her permanent record, possible prison time, and increased difficulty in finding a civilian job.

Child Maltreatment

Military-connected children are also at risk for maltreatment, physical, and emotional abuse as when a service member is deployed, the rate of physical abuse and neglect by the remaining parent increases (Gibbs, Martin, Kupper, & Johnson, 2007). Yearly, about 6,500 incidents of children maltreatment in the military are reported (Gibbs et al., 2011). In 2011, the Army had 4.5 cases of child abuse per 1,000 children, and in 2012, 3,698 cases were reported which representing a 40% increase from 2009; the Marine Corps had 1,591 cases of child abuse and the Navy had 3,336 cases of abuse and 42 children died from abuse (Sandza, 2013).

During the time of the Iraq and Afghanistan wars, the maltreatment of military children also rose (Sandza, 2013). Also, the additional stress upon the non-deployed spouses may be a contributing factor to the maltreatment (Gibbs et al., 2007). In some cases, the returned service members during the reintegration stage may lack the skills to deal with a child's outburst or behavior, resulting in frustration and aggression toward the child (Bowling & Sherman, 2008). Gibbs and colleagues (2013) concluded when an IPV incident occurs with the parents, 24% of the children will also experience maltreatment in the same day. The same study showed that alcohol use increases the rates of IPV and child maltreatment incidents. Children who have experienced maltreatment in their childhood will be more predisposed to depression and health problems in adulthood (Gibbs et al., 2007).

Service Member/Veteran Suicide and the Family

In recent years, suicide has become one of the highest forms of death in the military. Since 2001, military suicides rates have been steadily increasing and the rates have surpassed civilian rates (Bryan, Jennings, Jobes, & Bradley, 2012). In 2014, 268 active-duty members died by suicide which included 122 Army members and 59 Air Force members (DoD, 2014). Suicide is not only prominent in active-duty members, but also in the National Guard and Reserves as in one year, 166 of these members died by suicide (DoD, 2014). Among military service members, in 2012, the suicide rate was estimated to be 22.7 out of 100,000 (Kemp & Bossarte, 2012; Smolenski et al., 2013). At least 40% of all service members and Veterans know someone who has died by suicide (Frances, 2012). In 2009, the Army lost more soldiers to suicides and accidental deaths than combat fatalities (Mastroianni & Scott, 2011). Some of the factors that have been linked with suicides in the military are mental health problems, loss associated with physical injuries, substance abuse, and relationship problems (Black, Gallaway, Bell, & Ritchie, 2011).

Increased suicide rates in the military means increased stress and trauma for the survivors. Formulas on how to grieve or how long to grieve may actually hinder the grieving process for grieving is an individual and subjective process (Harrington-LaMorie, 2012). When faced with a death by suicide, military families may feel a mixture of emotions such as sadness, anger, confusion, and physical symptoms (Harrington-LaMorie, 2012). Survivors may be at risk for physical and mental health problems such as depression, PTSD, and anxiety disorders

(Mitchell et al., 2009). Family survivors have a greater risk of also committing suicide (Jordan, 2008). The sudden death of their loved one may cause the family members to be confused and overwhelmed with questions and a common theme reported by survivors is self-blame, believing they could have prevented the death (Harrington-LaMorie, 2012). Stigma and shame with regard to suicide can also affect the family, leading members to feel embarrassed and become socially isolated (Harrington-LaMorie, 2012). Due to these factors, survivors might keep the suicide secret from others, which can cause tension within the family and hinder the family's ability to heal (Harrington-LaMorie, 2012; Jordan & McIntosh, 2010).

Mental Health Stigma and Help Seeking

In military culture, mental illness is highly stigmatized, therefore active-duty members and Veterans tend to not seek treatment (Kim et al., 2010). Mental illness is often seen as a weakness and service members believe that mental illness to be detrimental to their careers (Hoge et al., 2008). Tanielian and Jaycox (2008) found that in 2008, there were 850,000 OIF and OEF service members that were qualified to receive Veteran Affairs (VA) services but only 40% of those eligible actually sought care. Approximately 58% of Veterans in one study that reported symptoms related to PTSD from the wars in Afghanistan or Iraq were only seen for treatment once at a VA facility (Shiner et al., 2012). Previously, studies have demonstrated that the majority of Veterans are receiving community-based mental health services but not government programs (Koblinsky, Leslie, & Cook, 2014). Multiple research shows the importance of civilian providers understanding military culture, as this will improve the treatment and therapeutic alliance (Koblinsky et al., 2014).

Because most service members are not receiving adequate treatment, their symptoms often become worse over time, making the family dynamics more difficult. When family members perceive mental illness as a weakness and feel the shame and stigma of this perception, this increases stress and frustration for the family (DeCarvalho & Whealin, 2012). Oftentimes the negative stigma that reduces the service member's desire to get treatment is also experienced by their families who may also not receive mental health services (Mansfield et al., 2010). Despite this risk factor, on the positive side, active-duty military spouses have reported greater rates of seeking out mental health services than Veterans (Eaton et al., 2008).

Family-based Assessment and Interventions

Solution-focused brief therapy (SFBT) has been increasingly recognized as a promising approach when working with families and across cultures (Franklin & Montgomery, 2014; Kim et al., 2010). Genograms that are specific to military families from a solution-based perspective can be used as an assessment that can help interpret the family strengths, patterns, and relationships (Weiss et al., 2010). While the ecomap is similar to the genogram, an ecomap provides a graphic depiction of information about the connections between family, community, and external resources (Weiss, DeBraber, Santoyo, & Creager, 2013). Weiss et al. (2013) argue that the use of an ecomap with military connected families is a helpful assessment tool from a macro perspective since these families are part of a larger system such as the military.

The origins and details with regard to SFBT as originally developed is beyond the scope of this chapter, however, it is recognized to include techniques that assist clients in creating solutions from a strengths-based perspective (De Jong & Berg, 2013). The common therapeutic techniques associated with SFBT include the behavioral health counselor's utilization of exception-finding questions, coping questions, relationship questions, scaling questions, the use of indirect compliments, and the use of the miracle question (de Shazer, 1985; Greene & Lee, 2011). These will be further discussed in the vignette in the next section of this chapter.

Other approaches that are worthy of mention here include trauma-focused CBT (TF-CBT) for children who have had traumatic experiences, such as physical abuse, sexual abuse, and grief (Cohen & Mannarino, 2011). Families Overcoming under Stress (FOCUS) was developed by a team from the University of California, Los Angeles and Harvard University that supports military families when a parent returns from deployment (Lester et al., 2010). FOCUS is provided at various military bases in the US and in Japan. FOCUS uses a family-centered intervention that integrates a strengths-based perspective, provides education, and improves coping skills for parents and children regarding the deployment experience (Lester et al., 2010).

Another important tool for use with families is psychoeducation. Psychoeducation provides the families with knowledge about the Veteran's illness and injury, and they also learn coping skills to deal with the illness or injury (Fisher, 2008). The VA provides a psychoeducation curriculum called Support and Family Education (SAFE). These educational family sessions address how mental illness impacts the family and introduces problem-solving techniques (Sherman, 2008). An offspring of SAFE is Operation Enduring Families, which is also offered at the VA, and its goal is to support family members by equipping them with resources and coping skills when the Veteran returns from deployment (Bowling, Doerman, & Sherman, 2011). Operation Enduring Families' goal is to create an atmosphere that is supportive and encouraging to the service member and family.

MILITARY FAMILY CASE SUMMARY

(All names and circumstances have been altered to protect client confidentiality.)

Sergeant First Class (SFC) John Coyne joined the Army right out of high school. A recruiter for the New York National Guard had visited his high school and given a talk to the students about the benefits of enlistment. In his junior year, with permission from his parents, he enlisted in the military and completed eight weeks of basic training requirements during the summer between his junior and senior years of high school. He graduated and was assigned to a unit as a mechanic since he had some basic skills in that area that he had learned in his shop class at his high school. John spent the next six years of his contract working as a mechanic at a local garage in his civilian life and as a support staff engineer with his unit on the drill weekends. He met Catherine when she brought her car into his garage, married soon thereafter, and they bought a house and had two children one after another, 18 months apart. When their children were out of preschool, Catherine became pregnant again and they decided that they needed to find a good school for the children, make more money, and gain some financial stability to support their growing family. John filled out the forms and was accepted to join the active-duty Army at the rank of sergeant which allowed him to earn a good salary with benefits. John was assigned to a unit at Fort Hood Texas and the whole family moved into a small house on base and enrolled the children Maggie (6 years old) and Bryan (5 years old) in the elementary school on base and when the baby, Tyler, was born that year put him into daycare when he reached 6 months.

John was deployed to Iraq in 2007 almost immediately after starting with his new unit of combat engineers assigned the job of fixing and maintaining vehicles that were used for route clearance. John spent the year of his first deployment on these routes, repairing vehicles that hit improvised explosive devices on a daily basis. He was tasked with leaving the forward operating base to go out to where the vehicles had been hit to repair the damage done to them following these explosions. John was often unarmed when he was underneath the vehicles doing repairs. There were several incidents of firefights when he was in this situation and one day early into the deployment he witnessed his staff sergeant take fire while John was under a vehicle fixing it and had no time to get out to help. As SSG Tollard gasped for breath looking at John directly, he died within minutes. In the weeks and months that followed, John began to have anxiety and difficulty sleeping at night, with repetitive dreams of being under a vehicle without protection for himself or the ability to rescue his battle buddy in the midst of a firefight. He felt helpless in these dreams and guilty when he was awake for not having done more to help SSG T.

John returned home 12 months later with nightmares every night on the same theme, often thrashing about in his sleep to the point of hitting his wife, dreaming that she was his battle buddy and he was pushing him out of the line of fire. He would waken in the middle of the dream to find his wife yelling and crying because she had just been pushed out of bed and onto the floor from a sound sleep. These incidents often woke up the oldest child, Maggie, who would come running into the room to see if everything was okay and then Catherine would need to comfort her and to get her back to sleep would lay down with her in her bed. Many nights, Catherine woke up in Maggie's bed, and eventually they bought Maggie a queen-sized bed for this reason. Catherine grew increasingly worried because John's reactions weren't like "the old John" as she told her friends on base who understood what she meant, because as she told them, the old John would have been upset by his behaviors. John began to drink heavily to fall asleep at night to stop the nightmares and prevent the incidents of pushing Catherine out of bed and he would pass out into a sleep that was neither restorative nor healthy. John went to see a therapist at the Veterans Administration Medical Center, was diagnosed with PTSD, and prescribed a combination of several medications including sertraline, prazosin, and lorazepam. The couple grew distant from one another, intimacy was rare, and John's bad moods easily escalated into outbursts of uncontrollable rage that ended in him punching doors or walls.

John had become angry and irritable on a daily basis from the combination of lack of sleep in his life mixed with the increased alcohol consumption and he withdrew from his friends and family. Catherine and the children stopped inviting their friends over to the house because of the unpredictability of John's anger and sudden mood swings. Catherine delivered a fourth baby, a girl named Emily, and within a few months, John never wanted to hold her, and never felt bonded to her like he did to his other children. John received orders that he was being mobilized again, this time to Afghanistan in 2012 and the couple was relieved to have the separation to get some distance and try to make sense of what was going on in their family.

John was considered deployable even though he held a diagnosis of PTSD, was cleared as Fit for Duty by the Behavioral Health Officer and mobilized a second time. John continued to have nightmares of SSG Tollard but they were less debilitating because he wasn't sleeping well or much since he was on deployment and his adrenaline was always flowing. His deployment was extended to 15 months and he didn't communicate as much with Catherine or the children during this deployment because he never knew what to say and was unsure of himself about how to act when he saw them on video. He was feeling depressed and anxious, and didn't want to pretend that everything was fine like he did during the first deployment, so he made excuses for not talking or getting off the phone with them.

When John returned home the second time, his children had grown up significantly: Maggie was 14 years old and starting high school as an over-achiever; Bryan was 13 and having academic trouble in middle school; Tyler was 8 years old and in third grade; and the baby was 2 years old. His reintegration was even more difficult than the first time: he couldn't talk to civilians and was angry at them all the time, even when he was just walking down the street, because he thought they were superficial and spoiled and he didn't know how to relate to or communicate with them. He had sustained an injury to his back fixing a vehicle on duty and had degenerative arthritis and problems ever since that time. He was regularly prescribed medications to relieve the pain such as OxyContin and Percocet and eventually became addicted to them since they helped him to sleep at night. He received service-connected disability benefits from the Veterans Administration that came in a monthly check on the first of the month and these funds ran out by the end of the month. He would become irritable at that time of the month when he no longer had medications for his pain or the ability to buy these from a buddy of his in his unit who also had prescriptions. At his Post-Deployment Health Reassessment, John admitted that he was in treatment for chronic and severe PTSD in addition to his physical injury and was placed on a duty-limiting profile that he referred to as a "Dead Man Walking" ticket in terms of his future military career. He would need to find another career and make the transition to civilian employment quickly but with limited skills that he deemed transferrable to the civilian world.

The anxiety John felt about this transition would cause him to fluctuate between angry outbursts at his wife and children when he was sober and a euphoric, albeit superficial, closeness to them when he was high or intoxicated. He eventually stopped going to his children's school events and sports like his son's basketball games and daughter's soccer matches because the crowds were too stressful and he constantly worried that bombs would go off while they were playing. John also stopped driving and rarely left the house because he had flashbacks of his buddy whenever he attempted to go anywhere by himself indicating that his PTSD wasn't going away and was actually getting worse with time. Catherine insisted on driving if John needed to get to appointments or when he joined the family to social events because she was fearful for everyone's safety. She was concerned that he was unstable and also worried that he would become physically aggressive if pushed too much or at the wrong time if he was in a bad mood. She and the children began to feel like they were "walking on eggshells" when he was around and could not relax in their own home or when out in public places with him or even on their own time. The oldest daughter's grades began to slip at school because she was having trouble sleeping at night and had gotten caught smoking marijuana in the school locker room one day which prompted the parents to be called to school to come up with an immediate response, a plan, and a solution to her downward spiral. They family entered family therapy with a licensed mental health counselor on base that was referred by her pediatrician to try to ameliorate the situation and return to the loving family that they once had been and wanted to get back to being in this post-deployment phase of their lives.

Clinical Assessment/Formulation

An assessment of this family's functioning suggests that John, Catherine, and the children are all going through a difficult readjustment following the last deployment with post-traumatic and secondary traumatic stress symptoms activated. John is experiencing a chronic (so far unsuccessfully treated) PTSD with substance abuse and a growing opiate dependency and agoraphobia. He is coping with his PTSD by attempting to avoid reminders and triggers of his traumatic memories of situations that occurred while he was deployed to Iraq. The result of these attempts to cope with the very difficult and painful images of his friend being killed in action have led him to become isolated and without social support that could be helpful to him as he goes through this process. John is attempting to manage these memories and current difficulties in his family and career on his own in a manner that is consistent with the military culture. John is also perceiving himself to be a burden to his family since he is not managing his reactions and daily behaviors in a healthy, adaptive way, and he has no plan for a future career once his is medically separated from the military. John is aware of the fact that he hasn't been able to resolve his post-traumatic stress and feels that he "should" be able to do so, which has led to profound feelings of weakness in his self-perception. Given this combination of factors, John is at a high risk for suicide, which will need to be assessed in the early phases of treatment and then monitored regularly throughout the intervention. As such, John will need to be treated for his current depression as well as his post-traumatic stress and substance abuse.

John and Catherine are having a disrupted attachment bond in their marriage that will need to be repaired as will the bonds between John and his children that have become weakened by John's emotional unavailability to them since his return from the last deployment. John withdraws from the family to keep his distance because he doesn't trust himself and wants to make sure he keeps them safe this way. However, Catherine does not know this because he has never communicated it to her and she in turn experiences this withdrawal as a rejection and believes that he fell out of love with her on the deployment. In addition to this loss she feels, she believes that her needs are unimportant compared to John's PTSD and substance abuse to control these that have become the primary focus in the family's day-to-day living and in their routines developed to accommodate these behaviors. John had become extremely irritable and could express anger as his only emotion and often spoke to her and the children in threatening tones of voice if they challenged his authority in the home. There was one instance where John had been drinking heavily and although Catherine would usually avoid such topics, she needed to figure out a financial issue with him that night regarding a bill that had to be paid immediately with limited funds in their checking account. He perceived this as an attack against him as a provider because he wasn't working at the time and pushed her against the wall in an impulsive rage that she had never seen before that moment. Catherine realized at that point that she had been cast into a new role in the family as caregiver for John and mediator between him and the children and him and their outside world of family and friends. She also came to the conclusion that she and the children were at risk of domestic violence if they proceeded further down this path and that she would no longer have help from her life partner in major decision-making. These realizations were significant losses for her and she became overwhelmed by the sadness of the situation and, not knowing where to turn for help or what to do next, she began to cry.

Suggested Treatment Plan

The best treatment approach for this family is an SFBT, since it is a very useful intervention for counselors working with military families with children, especially those who may need collateral work done with their schools (Hall, 2008). It will involve a great deal of psychoeducation about their father's symptoms, how they've developed since his last deployment, and what effects they have on individual members as well as the family's functioning as a system. The family will be encouraged to create an "ecomap" of their family's resources, community resources, and social networks that can provide enhanced resiliency for the family (Weiss et al., 2013).

The language used in this educational piece will need to be adjusted to the developmental stages of the children when explained to them in a family meeting and normalized so that they do not feel to blame or in any way responsible for the situation. John will need to be supported in an empathic manner that does not scapegoat him as the cause of the family's problems nor alienate him from the treatment. SFBT focuses on solutions rather than problems so the counseling is specific, measurable, brief, and changes comes quickly in incremental steps (Sklare, 2005). The intervention will focus on looking for successes in the family's readjustment since John returned from both deployments also known as "exception finding" for the family going through their current challenging time. The family would identify situations when they engaged with one another in appropriate, healthy ways that were adaptive in terms of the family's coping strategies. They will be encouraged to think of "the miracle question" of SFBT which asks what would be different if a miracle happened in their sleep and the family's problems were all gone the next day (Sklare, 2005, p. 7). They would also be asked to rate their satisfaction with their lives on a scale from 0 to 10, with 10 being completely satisfied and what measurable changes needed to occur to move them up the scale toward their goals as a family. Small positive changes and shifts in their functioning would be highlighted and as they begin to seek out these changes, a ripple effect will occur that will create a chain reaction and add up to a major shift for them.

SFBT holds the perspective that all clients have the strengths for adaptive change within them and the family's goals would be treated as positive steps for present and future actions rather than insights gained through problem analysis (Sklare, 2005). Since the intervention was targeted for the oldest daughter's current problematic behaviors, substance abuse, and defiance of authority by smoking marijuana in school, these behaviors would be addressed for her and she would be asked what she needs to move up the satisfaction scale, to reduce her anxiety and improve her feelings regarding authority figures in her life.

The entire family would be asked to commit to the treatment and to establish goals by and for each individual member moving forward: if any of the children had become parentified, for example, then a goal for them would be to let go of these roles in a slow, methodical, manner that does not feel threatening or scary for them as they will be giving up the sense of control that is associated with this role. They will need to identify ways in which they can act as children again and these would be communicated openly and assessed regularly as a concrete and measurable goal for them in the treatment. Parents and children are often very open to focusing on solutions and short-term interventions and these can be as simple as finding more time to spend together or learning new parenting or communication skills (Hall, 2008).

Catherine and John will need to commit to working on these issues as a team and in this goal, problem-solve ways in which they can open up their currently closed lines of communication. The couple will need to assess whether Catherine's role of caregiver is inadvertently reinforcing and strengthening John's symptoms and how they might best achieve a healthy level of interdependency. Likewise, they will also need to identify how John's coping skills may not be adaptive and consider implementing skills that have worked for him individually and together as a couple in the past. The couple would be encouraged to have an honest dialog about suicide, with increased education about the risks for military, and identify how they will manage this if it becomes a real choice in either partner's decision-making process.

The focus of the treatment should not be on "changing John" and highlighting all of the struggles in their lives that he is the "cause of" which would only make the situation worse and place him more at risk. Instead, it should be treated as a collaborative endeavor that the family takes on together with the confidence that the situation can be managed – with the right amount of commitment on the part of the family and the right amount of empathy on the part of the treating provider.

Conclusion

It is important to remember that the effects of deployment and reintegration are not limited to the service member/Veteran, but include the entire family. Every day, roughly 1,300 recent Veterans and families start the process of reintegration back to civilian life (Joint Chiefs of Staff, 2014). These families likely face varying levels of relational uncertainty that might manifest in poor communication practices (Cox & Albright, 2014), and other opportunities for clinical intervention.

Family members should be included in their service member's treatment and receive individual therapy as well. In order to treat the whole family, more resources from civilian and/or military providers are needed for families of both combat and non-combat Veterans. Research shows that having a supportive family can reduce mental health problems (Clark, Jordan, & Clark, 2013).

As you've read in this chapter, there are many areas of potential strength and concern when working with military families and/or a member of a military family. It is important to remember that there is no "standard" or "uniform" military family unit. Each familial unit is individual in its composition, internal dynamics, and ways in which it has reacted both to military culture and the stresses of military service. Given the majority of Veterans (and their families) do not use VA care (Nelson, Starkebaum, & Reiber, 2007), it imperative for civilian mental health practitioners both to ask clients whether or not they or a family member served in the US Armed Forces, and seek ongoing training opportunities on military cultural competencies, current challenges facing the population, and appropriate evidence-supported treatments.

References

Acion, L., Ramirez, M. R., Jorge, R. E., & Arndt, S. (2013). Increased risk of alcohol and drug use among children from deployed military families. *Addiction*, 108(8), 1418–1425. doi: 10.1111/add.12161

Basham, K. (2013). Couple therapy for redeployed military and Veteran couples. In A. Rubin, E. L. Weiss, & J. E. Coll (Eds.), *Handbook of military social work* (pp. 443–465). Hoboken, NJ: Wiley.

Bello-Utu, C. F. & DeSocio, J. E. (2015). Military deployment and reintegration: A systematic review of child coping. *Journal of Child and Adolescent Psychiatric Nursing*, 28(1), 23–34. doi: 10.1111/jcap.12099

Black, S. A., Gallaway, M. S., Bell, M. R., & Ritchie, E. C. (2011). Prevalence and risk factors associated with suicides of army soldiers 2001–2009. *Military Psychology*, 23(4), 433–451. doi: 10.1037/h0094766

Bowling, U., Doerman, A., & Sherman, M. (2011). Operation enduring families: Information and support for Iraq and Afghanistan Veterans and their families. Oklahoma City, OK: Oklahoma City VA Medical Center. Retrieved from: www.ouhsc.edu/oef/pdf/OEFMANUAL_3rd_ed_FINAL_110902.pdf

Bowling, U. B. & Sherman, M. D. (2008). Welcoming them home: Supporting service members and their families in navigating the tasks of reintegration. *Professional Psychology: Research and Practice*, 39(4), 451–458. doi: 10.1037/0735-7028.39.4.451

1, C. & Asmussen, S. (2013). Traumatic brain injury (TBI) and the military. In A. Rubin, E. L. Weiss, & Coll (Eds.), *Handbook of military social work* (pp. 163–178). Hoboken, NJ: Wiley.

Bradley, C. (2007). Veteran status and marital aggression: Does military service make a difference? *Journal of Family Violence*, 22, 197–209.

Brendel, K. E., Maynard, B. R., Albright, D. L., & Bellomo, M. (2014). Effects of school-based interventions with US military-connected children: A systematic review. *Research on Social Work Practice*, 24, 649–658.

Brown, D. W., Anda, R. F., Tiemeier, H., Felitti, V. J., Edwards, V. J., & Croft, J. B. (2009). Adverse childhood experiences and the risk of premature mortality. *American Journal of Preventive Medicine*, 37(5), 389–396. doi: 10.1016/j.amepre.2009.06.021

Brown, A. & Joshi, M. (2014). Intimate partner violence among female service members and Veterans: Information and resources available through military and non-military websites. *Social Work in Mental Health Care*, 53, 714–738.

Bryan, C. J., Jennings, K. W., Jobes, D. A., & Bradley, J. C. (2012). Understanding and preventing military suicide. *Archives of Suicide Research*, 16(2), 95–110. doi: 10.1080/13811118.2012.667321

Campbell, J. C. (2002). Health consequences of intimate partner violence. *The Lancet*, 359, 1331–1336.

Carlson, E. & Ruzek, J. (2014). PTSD and the family. US Department of Veterans Affairs. Retrieved from: www.ptsd.va.gov/professional/treatment/family/ptsd-and-the-family.asp

Cederbaum, J. A., Gilreath, T. D., Benbenishty, R., Astor, R. A., Pineda, D., DePedro, K. T., & Atuel, H. (2014). Well-being and suicidal ideation of secondary school students from military families. *Journal of Adolescent Health*, 54(6), 672–677. doi: 10.1016/j.jadohealth.2013.09.006

Chandra, A., Lara-Cinisomo, S., Jaycox, L. H., Tanielian, T., Burns, R. M., Ruder, T., & Han, B. (2010). Children on the homefront: The experience of children from military families. *Pediatrics*, 125(1), 16–25. doi: 10.1542/peds.2009-1180

Chavis, A. Z. & Hill, M. S. (2009). Integrating multiple intersecting identities: A multicultural conceptualization of the power and control wheel. *Women & Therapy*, 32, 121–149.

Clark, M. G., Jordan, J. D., & Clark, K. L. (2013). Motivating military families to thrive. *Family and Consumer Sciences Research Journal*, 42(2), 110–123. doi: 10.1111/fcsr.12046.

Cohen, J. A. & Mannarino, A. P. (2011). Trauma-focused CBT for traumatic grief in military children. *Journal of Contemporary Psychotherapy*, 41(4), 219–227. doi: 10.1007/s10879-10011-9178-0

Coll, J., Weiss, E., & Yarvis, J. (2011). No one leaves unchanged: Insights for civilian mental health care professionals into the military experience and culture. *Social Work in Health Care*, 50(7), 487–500. doi: 10.1080/00981389.2010.528727

Cox, J. & Albright, D. L. (2014). The road to recovery: Addressing the challenges and resilience of military couples in the scope of Veterans' mental health. *Social Work in Mental Health*, 12, 560–574.

Creech, S. K., Hadley, W., & Borsari, B. (2014). The impact of military deployment and reintegration on children and parenting: A systematic review. *Professional Psychology: Research and Practice*, 45(6), 452–464. doi: 10.1037/a0035055

Cronin, C. (1995). Adolescent reports of parental spousal violence in military and civilian families. *Journal of Interpersonal Violence*, 10, 117–122.

Currie, S. L., Day, A., & Kelloway, E. K. (2011). Bringing the troops back home: Modeling the post-deployment reintegration experience. *Journal of Occupational Health Psychology*, 16(1), 38–47. doi: 10.1037/a0021724

DeCarvalho, T. L. & Whealin, M. J. (2012). *Healing stress in military families: Eight steps to wellness.* Hoboken, NJ: Wiley.

De Jong, P. & Berg, I. K. (2013). *Interviewing for solutions.* Belmont, CA: Brooks/Cole.

de Shazer, S. (1985). *Keys to solution in brief therapy.* New York: Norton.

Dekel, R. & Monson, C. M. (2010). Military-related post-traumatic stress disorder and family relations: Current knowledge and future directions. *Aggression and Violent Behavior*, 15(4), 303–309. doi: 10.1016/j.avb.2010.03.001

Demers, A. (2011). When Veterans return: The role of community in reintegration. *Journal of Loss and Trauma*, 16(2), 160–179. doi: 10.1080/15325024.2010.519281

Dichter, M. E., Cerulli, C., & Bossarte, R. M. (2011). Intimate partner violence victimization Among women Veterans and associated heart health risks. *Women's Health Issues*, 21, S190–S194.

Dinshtein, Y., Dekel, R., & Polliack, M. (2011). Secondary traumatization among adult children of PTSD Veterans: The role of mother–child relationships. *Journal of Family Social Work*, 14(2), 109–124. doi: 10.1080/10522158.2011.544021

Eaton, K. M., Hoge, C. W., Messer, S. C., Whitt, A. A., Cabrera, O. A., McGurk, D., & Castro, C. A. (2008). Prevalence of mental health problems, treatment need, and barriers to care among primary care-seeking spouses of military service members involved in Iraq and Afghanistan deployments. *Military Medicine*, 173(11), 1051–1056. doi: 10.7205/MILMED.173.11.1051

Esposito-Smythers, C., Wolff, J., Lemmon, K. M., Bodzy, M., Swenson, R. R., & Spirito, A. (2011). Military youth and the deployment cycle: Emotional health consequences and recommendations for intervention. *Journal of Family Psychology*, 25(4), 497–507. doi: 10.1037/a0024534

Fisher, M. E. (2008). The use of psychoeducation in the treatment of PTSD with military personnel and their family members: An exploratory study from a clinician's perspective. Unpublished master's thesis, Smith College, Northampton, MA.

Fisher, M. P. (2014). PTSD in the US military, and the politics of prevalence. *Social Science & Medicine (1982)*, 115, 1–9. doi: 10.1016/j.socscimed.2014.05.051

Flaherty, M. P. (2010). Constructing a world beyond intimate partner abuse. *Affilia*, 25(3), 224–235.

Flake, E. M., Davis, B. E., Johnson, P. L., & Middleton, L. S. (2009). The psychosocial effects of deployment on military children. *Journal of Developmental and Behavioral Pediatrics*, 30(4), 271.

Frances, A. (2012). The epidemic of military suicide. *Psychiatric Times*, 29(11), 1.

Franciskovic, T., Stevanović, A., Jelusić, I., Roganović, B., Klarić, M., & Grković, J. (2007). Secondary traumatization of wives of war Veterans with posttraumatic stress disorder. *Croatian Medical Journal*, 48(2), 177–184.

Franklin, C. & Montgomery, K. L. (2014). Does solution-focused brief therapy work? In J. S. Kim (Ed.), *Solution-focused brief therapy: A multicultural approach* (pp. 32–54). Thousand Oaks, CA: Sage.

Gerlock, A. A. (2004). Domestic violence and post-traumatic stress disorder severity for participants of a domestic violence rehabilitation program. *Military Medicine*, 169, 470–474.

Gewirtz, A. H., Polusny, M. A., DeGarmo, D. S., Khaylis, A., & Erbes, C. R. (2010). Posttraumatic stress symptoms among National Guard soldiers deployed to Iraq: Associations with parenting behaviors and couple adjustment. *Journal of Consulting and Clinical Psychology*, 78(5), 599–610. doi: 10.1037/a0020571

Gibbs, D. A., Clinton-Sherrod, A. M., Wheeless, S. C., Johnson, R. E., & Gable, C. (2013). Child exposure to intimate partner violence after soldiers' deployment. *Military Behavioral Health*, 1(2), 121–128.

Gibbs, D., Martin, S., Clinton-Sherron, M., Walter, J., & Johnson, R. (2011). Child Maltreatment with military families. *RTI International*. Retrieved from: www.rti.org/pubs/rb-0002-1105-gibbs.pdf

Gibbs, D., Martin, S., Kupper, L., & Johnson, R. (2007). Child maltreatment in enlisted soldiers' families during combat-related deployments. *Journal of the American Medical Association*, 298(5), 528.

Golding, J. M. (1999). Intimate partner violence as a risk factor for mental disorders: a meta-analysis. *Journal of Family Violence*, 14, 99–132.

Goodwin, M., Spitz, A., Petersen, R., & Saltzman, L. (2000). Screening for intimate partner violence by health care providers: Barriers and interventions. *American Journal of Preventative Medicine*, 19, 230–237.

Greene, G. J. & Lee, M. Y. (2011). *Solution-oriented social work practice: An integrative approach to working with client strengths*. New York: Oxford University Press.

Griffin, W. A. & Morgan, A. R. (1988). Conflict in maritally distressed military couples. *American Journal of Family Therapy*, 16, 14–22.

Hall, L. K. (2008). *Counseling military families: What mental health professionals need to know* (215–250). New York: Routledge.

Hall, L. K. (2011). The military culture, language, and lifestyle. In R. B. Everson & C. R. Figley (Eds.), *Families under fire: Systemic therapy with military families* (pp. 31–52). New York: Routledge.

Harrington-LaMorie, J. (2012). Grief, loss, and bereavement in military families. In A. Rubin, E. L. Weiss, & J. E. Coll (Eds.), *Handbook of military social work* (pp. 383–407). Hoboken, NJ: Wiley.

Hendricks Thomas, K., Albright, D. L., Shields, M., Kaufman, E., & Michaud, C. (in press). Predictors of depression diagnoses and symptoms in female Veterans: Results from a national survey and implications for programming. *Journal of Military and Veterans' Health*.

Herzog, J. R., Everson, R. B., & Whitworth, J. D. (2011). Do secondary trauma symptoms in spouses of combat-exposed National Guard soldiers mediate impacts of soldiers' trauma exposure on their children? *Child and Adolescent Social Work Journal*, 28(6), 459–473. doi: 10.1007/s10560-10011-0243-z

Hoge, C. W., McGurk, D., Thomas, J. L., Cox, A. L., Engel, C. C., & Castro, C. A. (2008). Mild traumatic brain injury in US soldiers returning from Iraq. *New England Journal of Medicine*, 358(5), 453–463. doi: 10.1056/NEJMoa072972

Hoge, C. W., Milliken, C. S., & Auchterlonie, J. L. (2007). Longitudinal assessment of mental health problems among active and reserve component soldiers returning from the Iraq war. *JAMA*, 298(18), 2141–2148. doi: 10.1001/jama.298.18.2141

Huebner, A. & Mancini, J. (2008). Supporting youth during parental deployment: Strategies for Professionals and Families. *Prevention Researcher*, 15(suppl.), 10–13.

Hyatt, K., Davis, L. L., & Barroso, J. (2014). Chasing the care: Soldiers experience following combat-related mild traumatic brain injury. *Military Medicine*, 179(8), 849–855. doi: 10.7205/MILMED-D-13-00526

Iverson, K. M., Mercado, R., Carpenter, S. L., & Street, A. E. (2013). Intimate partner violence among women Veterans: Previous interpersonal violence as a risk factor. *Journal of Traumatic Stress*, 26, 767–771.

Joint Chiefs of Staff (2014). *Enabling collaborative support to reintegrate the military family*. Retrieved from: www.jcs.mil/Portals/36/Documents/CORe/141119_Enabling_Collaborative_Support.pdf

Jordan, J. R. (2008). Bereavement after suicide. *PscyhiatricAnnalsOnline.com*, 38(10), 679–685.

Jordan, J. R. & McIntosh, J. L. (2010). Suicide bereavement: Why study survivors of suicide loss. In J. R. Jordan & J. L. McIntosh (Eds.), *Grief after suicide: Understanding the consequences and caring for the survivors* (pp. 403–411). New York: Routledge.

Jordan, J. R. & McIntosh, J. L. (2010). Is suicide bereavement different? A framework for rethinking the question. In J. R. Jordan & J. L. McIntosh (Eds.), *Grief after suicide: Understanding the consequences and caring for the survivors* (pp. 19–42). New York: Routledge.

Kaplow, J. B., Layne, C. M., Saltzman, W. R., Cozza, S. J., & Pynoos, R. S. (2013). Using multidimensional grief theory to explore the effects of deployment, reintegration, and death on military youth and families. *Clinical Child and Family Psychology Review*, 16(3), 322–340. doi: 10.1007/s10567-10013-0143-0141

Kemp, J. & Bossarte, R. (2012). Suicide data report, 2012. Department of Veteran Affairs. Retrieved from: www.va.gov/opa/docs/suicide-data-report-2012-final.pdf

Kim, J. S., Smock, S., McCullom, E., Trepper, E., & Franklin, C. (2010). Is solution focused brief therapy evidence based? *Families in Society*, 91, 300–306.

Kim, P. Y., Thomas, J. L., Wilk, J. E., Castro, C. A., & Hoge, C. W. (2010). Stigma, barriers to care, and use of mental health services among active duty and National Guard soldiers after combat. *Psychiatric Services*, 61(6), 582–588. doi: 10.1176/ps.2010.61.6.582

Klarić, M., Frančišković, T., Klarić, B., Kvesić, A., Kaštelan, A., Graovac, M., & Diminić Lisica, I. (2008). Psychological problems in children of war Veterans with posttraumatic stress disorder in Bosnia and Herzegovina: Cross-sectional study. *Croatian Medical Journal*, 49(4), 491–498.

Knobloch, L. K., Ebata, A. T., McGlaughlin, P. C., & Theiss, J. A. (2013). Generalized anxiety and relational uncertainty as predictors of topic avoidance during reintegration following military deployment. *Communication Monographs*, 80(4), 452. doi: 10.1080/03637751.2013.828159

Koblinsky, S. A., Leslie, L. A., & Cook, E. T. (2014). Treating behavioral health conditions of OEF/OIF veterans and their families: A state needs assessment of civilian providers. *Military Behavior Health*, 2, 162–172.

Kreutzer, J. S., Rapport, L. J., Marwitz, J. H., Harrison-Felix, C., Hart, T., Glenn, M., & Hammond, F. (2009). Caregivers' well-being after traumatic brain injury: A multicenter prospective investigation. *Archives of Physical Medicine and Rehabilitation*, 90(6), 939–946. doi: 10.1016/j.apmr.2009.01.010

Kubany, E. S., Hill, E. E., & Owens, J. A. (2003). Cognitive trauma therapy for battered women with PTSD. *Journal of Traumatic Stress*, 16, 81–91.

Kulka, R. A., Schlenger, W. E., Fairbank, J. A., Hough, R. L., Jordan, B. K., Mannar, C. R., & Weiss, D. S. (1988). *National Vietnam Veterans Readjustment Study: Contractual report of findings from the National Vietnam Veterans Readjustment Study, volumes I and II*. Research Triangle Park, NC: Research Triangle Institute.

LaMotte, A. D., Taft, C. T., Weatherill, R. P., Scott, J. P., & Eckhardt, C. I. (2015). Correlates of intimate partner violence perpetrated by female partners of operation Iraqi freedom and operation enduring freedom Veterans. *Partner Abuse*, 6(2), 143–156. doi: 10.1891/1946-6560.6.2.143

Leskin, G. A., Garcia, E., D'Amico, J., Mogil, C. E., and Lester, P. E. (2013). Family-centered programs and interventions for military children and youth. In A. Rubin, E. L. Weiss, & J. E. Coll (Eds.) *Handbook of military social work* (pp. 427–441). Hoboken, NJ: Wiley.

Lester, P. E. (2012). War and military children and families: Translating prevention science into practice. *Journal of the American Academy of Child and Adolescent Psychiatry*, 51(1), 3–5. doi: 10.1016/j.jaac.2011.10.008

Lester, P., Peterson, K., Reeves, J., Knauss, L., Glover, D., & Mogil, C. et al. (2010). The long war and parental combat deployment: Effects on military children and at-home spouses. *Journal of the American Academy of Child and Adolescent Psychiatry*, 49, 310–320. doi: 10.1016/j.jaac.2010.01.003

McCarroll, J. E., Ursano, R. J., Liu, X., Thayer, L. E., Newby, J. H., Norwood, A. E., & Fullerton, C. S. (2000). Deployment and the probability of spousal aggression by US Army soldiers. *Military Medicine*, 165, 41–46.

McGuinness, T. M. & McGuinness, J. P. (2014). The well-being of children from military families. *Journal of Psychosocial Nursing and Mental Health Services*, 52(4), 27. doi: 10.3928/02793695-20140304-01

Mansfield, A. J., Kaufman, J. S., Marshall, S. W., Gaynes, B. N., Morrissey, J. P., & Engel, C. C. (2010). Deployment and the use of mental health services among US army wives. *New England Journal of Medicine*, 362(2), 101–109. doi: 10.1056/NEJMoa0900177

Marek, L. I. & D'Aniello, C. (2014). Reintegration stress and family mental health: Implications for therapists working with reintegrating military families. *Contemporary Family Therapy*, 36(4), 443–451. doi: 10.1007/s10591-10014-9316-9314

Marshall, A. D., Panuzio, J., & Taft, C. T. (2005). Intimate partner violence among military Veterans and active duty service men. *Clinical Psychology Review*, 25, 862–87.

Mastroianni, G. R. & Scott, W. J. (2011). Reframing suicide in the military. *Parameters*, 41(2), 6–12.

Meis, L. A., Erbes, C. R., Polusny, M. A., & Compton, J. S. (2010). Intimate relationships among returning soldiers: The mediating and moderating roles of negative emotionality, PTSD symptoms, and alcohol problems. *Journal of Traumatic Stress*, 23(5), 564–572. doi: 10.1002/jts.2056

Melvin, K. (2011). Couple functioning and posttraumatic stress in operation Iraqi Freedom and Operation Enduring Freedom Veterans and spouses. Doctoral dissertation, Johns Hopkins University.

Millegan, J., Engel, C., Liu, X., & Dinneen, M. (2013). Parental Iraq/Afghanistan deployment and child psychiatric hospitalization in the US military. *General Hospital Psychiatry*, 35(5), 556–560. doi: 10.1016/j.genhosppsych.2013.04.015

Miller, T. W. & Veltkamp, L. J. (1993) Family violence: clinical indicators among military and post-military personnel. *Military Medicine*, 158, 766–771.

Mitchell, A. M., Sakraida, T. J., Kim, Y., Bullian, L., & Chiappetta, L. (2009). Depression, anxiety and quality of life in suicide survivors: A comparison of close and distant relationships. *Archives of Psychiatric Nursing*, 23(1), 2–10. doi: 10.1016/j.apnu.2008.02.007

National Advisory Council on Violence Against Women (2001). The role of the US Military in preventing and responding to violence against women. In *US Department of Justice, Toolkit to end violence against women* (pp. 1–9). Rockville: National Institute of Justice.

Nelson, B. S. & Wright, D. W. (1996). Understanding and treating post-traumatic stress disorder symptoms in female partners of Veterans with PTSD. *Journal of Marital and Family Therapy*, 22, 455–467.

Nelson, K. M., Starkebaum, G. A., & Reiber, G. E. (2007). Veterans using and uninsured Veterans not using Veterans Affairs (VA) health care. *Public Health Reports*, 122(1), 93–100.

Paley, B., Lester, P., & Mogil, C. (2013). Family systems and ecological perspectives on the impact of deployment on military families. *Clinical Child and Family Psychology Review*, 16(3), 245–265. doi: 10.1007/s10567-10013-0138-y

Peled, E., Davidson-Arad, B., & Perel, G. (2010). The mothering of women abused by their partner: An outcome evaluation of a group intervention. *Research on Social Work Practice*, 20, 391–402.

Phelan, M. S., Griffin, M. J., Hellerstedt, L. W., Sayer, A. N., Jense, C. A., & Burgess, J. D. (2011). Perceived stigma, strain, and mental health among caregivers of Veterans with traumatic brain injury. *Disability and Health Journal*, 4(3), 177–184. doi: 10.1016/j.dhjo.2011.03.003

Price, J. (2014). When a child's parent has PTSD. US Department of Veterans Affairs. Retrieved from: www.ptsd.va.gov/professional/treatment/children/pro_child_parent_ptsd.asp

Renshaw, K. D., Campbell, S. B., Meis, L., & Erbes, C. (2014). Gender differences in the associations of PTSD symptom clusters with relationship distress in US Vietnam Veterans and their partners. *Journal of Traumatic Stress*, 27(3), 283–290. doi: 10.1002/jts.21916

Riggs, A. S. & Riggs, S. D. (2011). Risk and resilience in military families experiencing deployment: The role of the family attachment network. *Journal of Family Psychology*, 25(5), 675–687. doi: 10.1037/a0025286

Sandza, R. (2013). The Army's hidden child abuse epidemic. *Army Times*. Retrieved from: http://archive. armytimes.com/article/20130729/NEWS06/306170030/The-Army-s-hidden-child-abuse-epidemic

Sandza, R. (2013). Pentagon launches major child abuse study. *Marine Corps Times*. Retrieved from: http://archive.marinecorpstimes.com/article/20131116/NEWS/311160007/Pentagon-launches-major-child-abuse-study

Savitsky, L., Illingworth, M., & DuLaney, M. (2009). Civilian social work: Serving the military and Veteran populations. *Social Work*, 54(4), 327–339. doi: 10.1093/sw/54.4.327

Sayers, S. L. (2011). Family reintegration difficulties and couples' therapy for military Veterans and their spouses. *Cognitive and Behavioral Practice*, 18(1), 108–119. doi: 10.1016/j.cbpra.2010.03.002

Sayers, S. L., Farrow, V. A., Ross, J., & Oslin, D. W. (2009). Family problems among recently returned military Veterans referred for a mental health evaluation. *Journal of Clinical Psychiatry*, 70(2), 163–170. doi: 10.4088/JCP.07m03863

Schmaling, K. B., Blume, A. W., & Russell, M. L. (2011). Intimate partner violence and relationship dissolution among reserve soldiers. *Military Psychology*, 23(6), 685.

Sher, L. (2009). A model of suicidal behavior in war Veterans with posttraumatic mood disorder. *Medical Hypotheses*, 73(2), 215–219. doi: 10.1016/j.mehy.2008.12.052

Sherman, M. D. (2008). *SAFE program: Mental health facts for families* (3rd ed.). Retrieved from: www.mirecc.va.gov/VISN16/docs/SAFE_Manual.pdf

Sherman, M. D., Sautter, F., Jackson, M. H., Lyons, J. A., & Han, X. (2006). Domestic violence in veterans with posttraumatic stress disorder who seek couples' therapy. *Journal of Marital and Family Therapy*, 32(4), 479–490. doi: 10.1111/j.1752-0606.2006.tb01622.x

Shiner, B., Drake, R. E., Watts, B. V., Desai, R. A., & Schnurr, P. P. (2012). Access to VA services for returning Veterans with PTSD. *Military Medicine*, 177(7), 814–822. doi: 10.7205/MILMED-D-12-00009

Sklare, G. B. (2005). *Brief counseling that works: A solution-focused approach for school counselors and administrators.* Thousand Oaks, CA: Corwin Press.

Smolenski, D. J., Reger, M. A., Alexander, C. L., Skopp, N. A., Bush, N. E., Luxton, D. D. et al. (2013). *DoDSER: Department of Defense suicide event report/calendar year 2012 annual report*. Retrieved from: http://t2health.dcoe.mil/sites/default/files/dodser_ar2012_20140306_0.pdf

Straits-Troster, K., Gierisch, J. M., Strauss, J. L., Dyck, D. G., Dixon, L. B., Norell, D., & Perlick, D. A. (2013). Multifamily group treatment for Veterans with traumatic brain injury: What is the value to participants? *Psychiatric Services*, 64(6), 541–546. doi: 10.1176/appi.ps.001632012

Straus, M. A. & Gelles, R. J. (1990). *Physical violence in American families: Risk factors and adaptations to violence in 8,145 families.* New Brunswick, NJ: Transaction Publishers.

Sullivan, M. (2006). *The military divorce handbook: A practical guide to representing military personnel and their families.* Chicago, IL: American Bar Association.

Taft, C. T., Weatherill, R. P., Woodward, H. E., Pinto, L. A., Watkins, L. E., Miller, M. W., & Dekel, R. (2009). Intimate partner and general aggression perpetration among combat Veterans presenting to a posttraumatic stress disorder clinic. *American Journal of Orthopsychiatry*, 79(4), 461–468.

Tanielian, T. & Jaycox, L. H. (Eds.) (2008). *The invisible wounds of war: Psychological and cognitive injuries, their consequences, and services to assist recovery*Santa Monica, CA: RAND. Retrieved from: www.rand.org/content/dam/rand/pubs/monographs/2008/RAND_MG720.pdf

Tinney, G. & Gerlock, A. A. (2014). Intimate partner violence, military personnel, Veterans, and their families. *Family Court Review*, 52(3), 400–416. doi: 10.1111/fcre.12100

US Department of Defense (2013). Demographics 2013: Profile of the military community. Retrieved from: www.militaryonesource.mil/12038/MOS/Reports/2013-Demographics-Report.pdf

US Department of Defense (2014). *Department of Defense quarterly suicide report*. Defense Suicide Prevention Office. Retrieved from: www.suicideoutreach.org/Docs/Reports/DoD-Quarterly-Suicide-Report-CY2014-Q4.pdf

US Department of Defense (2015). Domestic abuse involving DOD military and certain affiliated personnel (6400.06). Retrieved from: www.dtic.mil/whs/directives/corres/pdf/640006p.pdf

Verdeli, H., Baily, C., Vousoura, E., Belser, A., Singla, D., & Manos, G. (2011). The case for treating depression in military spouses. *Journal of Family Psychology*, 25(4), 488–496. doi: 10.1037/a0024525

Weiss, E. L., Coll, J. E., Gerbauer, J., Smiley, K., & Carillo, E. (2010). The military genogram: A solution-focused approach for resiliency building in service members and their families. *Family Journal*, *18*(4), 395–406. doi: 10.1177/1066480710378479

Weiss, E., DeBraber, T., Santoyo, A., & Creager, T. (2013). Theory and practice with military couples and families. In A. Rubin, E. L. Weiss, & J. E. Coll (Eds.), *Handbook of military social work* (pp. 467–492). Hoboken, NJ: Wiley.

7

THE IMPACT OF WAR AND DEPLOYMENTS ON YOUNG MILITARY-CONNECTED CHILDREN

Eugenia L. Weiss, Don Moncrief, Tara DeBraber and David L. Albright

Introduction

Military-connected families and children have faced tremendous challenges since the beginning of the US involvement in the Global War on Terrorism (GWOT), which began over ten years ago. These families have been exposed to the stressors of continuous separations as a result of service member deployments, as well as coping with the readjustment process when a deployed parent returns home. The entire readjustment process, which can be stressful enough, is often exacerbated when the returning service member displays symptoms associated with combat stress, as well as any physical limitations due to wounds suffered in battle. There has been research conducted on active duty, military-connected school-aged children and adolescents, but there is a scarcity of empirical studies on the effects of military wartime deployment separation and accompanying stressors on early childhood (0–5 years old). The purpose of this chapter will be to provide a review of the current research that has been conducted on this segment of the military-connected population, a population that continues to be an afterthought among civilian and government policymakers. Three case vignettes of a young military-connected children are provided, along with potential applications of evidence-informed interventions. Implications for human service providers will conclude this chapter.

Background

The GWOT in the last ten plus years has resulted in increased attention to the mental health consequences for service members and returning Veterans from Iraq and Afghanistan. The literature has also included the effects of military service and deployments on the overall functioning of military-connected families. However, this literature has largely focused on adolescents and empirical studies on the mental health and stressors of young military-connected children (ages 0–5) has been scarce. The topic of stress and mental health in developing infants and young children is necessary since "deployment is a family issue and the military employs over two million active duty personnel" demographically comprising young families (Kelley & Jouriles, 2011, p. 459); with 40% of children being younger than 5 years of age (Chartrand, Frank, White, & Shope, 2008). This population will undoubtedly continue to rise as a result of the social and legal changes toward same-sex marriage and the acceptance of gay and lesbian service members into the military. This will allow for a richer diversity within the culture of the military family, as well as increase the number of families as a whole. Additionally, early childhood for military-connected youth has been "defined by the context of a parent deploying to war" (Lester, 2012, p. 3) with young children experiencing, "a deployed parent that was gone, on average, half of their lifetime" (Barker & Berry, 2009, p. 1037).

In order to understand the effects of the common stressors associated with military life on this youngest population of military-connected children, it is essential to briefly examine the various developmental stages and theories of the development of infancy and young childhood, in order to recognize how these stressors can affect normal psychosocial development. In terms of a general understanding of physical development, it is common to refer to the 0–2-age range as infants/babies and the 3–5-age range as toddlers, which each group will be referred to for the purposes of this chapter. A major reason for the utilization of school-aged students for past studies of military-connected children is largely due to their ability to adequately verbalize their emotions, and researchers can more easily access them through schools. However, it is well established that infant and toddler development, or the first years of life, are crucial periods of human development.

Human Development and Attachment

The most influential theories which help to provide a window in the growth and development of a child, from infancy through early adulthood, are Erikson's theory of psychosocial development, as well as the findings of the attachment theorists and researchers such as Bowlby (1969/1982), Ainsworth et al. (1978) and others. These theories provide a foundation to understanding the impact of stress and separation on these young children. Lieberman and Van Horn (2013) remind us that there are "developmentally expectable early anxieties that all children experience in the first years of life across cultures and circumstances" and that "normative anxieties are exacerbated by the events of deployment, reunification and associated circumstances that are specifically relevant to young children in military families" (p. 282).

Erikson identified eight psychosocial development stages that, when successfully resolved, allow for the psychological and social development of an individual from infancy through late adulthood. The three earliest stages, identified as "trust versus mistrust," "autonomy versus shame," and "initiative versus guilt," all occur through the first five years of a child's life. Erikson believed that an underlying psychosocial crisis occurs in each stage of development, in which the needs of the individual are conflicted with the needs of the society (Erikson & Erikson, 1998). According to Erikson's theory, the successful completion of the individual stages will result in the establishment of a healthy personality as well as the creation of basic human virtues. The failure of an individual to successfully complete any of the developmental stages can diminish a person's ability to successfully navigate the further stages, thereby leaving an individual vulnerable to various personality flaws and an unhealthy sense of one's self (Erikson & Erikson, 1998).

Within the first year of life a child exhibits a sense of uncertainty about the environment in which they reside. An infant will inevitably have to look toward the primary caregiver in order to find stability, affection, and an overall sense of consistency in their otherwise chaotic world. If the caregiver can provide the infant with consistent and reliable care, then the child will eventually develop an ability to trust which will aid them in the establishment of other relationships throughout life (Erikson, 1993).

However, what happens to an infant's development when a mother or primary caregiver is either too emotionally distraught over the deployment of her spouse serving in the military to provide consistent care, or if a mother is forced to deploy herself, in service to her country, and therefore cannot provide any care to her child? Recent studies have found that mothers who experienced military deployments, both first hand and as the wives of deployed service members, are at a greater risk for and may experience effects such as separation anxiety, inadequate maternal role functioning, poor emotional functioning, depression, and anxiety (Goodman et al., 2013). In the case of a deployed mother serving her country away from her child, it becomes essential that there is a substitute primary caregiver present to provide the child with proper care and affection to allow for an infant to develop trust. However, when a mother has difficulty providing adequate care for a young child due to the absence of her husband, it becomes essential that sources of support within the environment be readily available to women and their children through family readiness groups and behavioral health resources. It is therefore essential that the military recognize the struggles that primary caregivers must endure during the absence of a deployed family member and provide such services for the families to utilize.

The essence of attachment theory as described by Bowlby (1969/1982) is that an infant must develop a relationship with a primary caregiver in order to foster a child's successful social and emotional development. This process is crucial for a child to learn how to effectively regulate their emotions. Ainsworth and her colleagues (1978) identified different patterns of attachment that develop in response to the different levels of social interaction a child experiences within the first year of life. A total of four different attachment styles have been identified: secure attachment, anxious–ambivalent attachment, anxious–avoidant attachment, and disorganized attachment. Secure attachment is considered to be the most well-adjusted attachment style. Children who exhibit a secure attachment style feel secure in the presence of their primary caregiver. If the caregiver leaves the infant alone, the infant will inevitably experience a sense of separation anxiety. Anxious–ambivalent attachment occurs when an infant feels this same sense of separation anxiety if separated from the primary caregiver. However, the infant will not feel reassured once the caregiver returns to the infant, in contrast to the reassurance experienced by toddlers who have a secure attachment style. Anxious–avoidant attachment occurs when an infant avoids their primary caregiver. Disorganized attachment can be summarized by a general lack of any attachment behavior. If a child's primary caregiver is either ambivalent or distracted, it becomes inconceivable that a toddler will learn to effectively manage the stressors present within their caretaking environment, thereby potentially preventing the development of a secure attachment pattern.

A recent study conducted by Vincenzes, Haddock, and Hickman (2014) examined the emotions experienced by military wives when their husbands were deployed for extended periods of time (at least six months), using attachment theory. The study determined that, within the group of 58 women who took part in the study (49.3% of whom were mothers of at least two or more children of various ages), as the length of deployments increased so did the level of stress experienced by the wives left at home (Vincenzes et al., 2014). In addition, the research supported the belief that those wives who were able to develop secure attachment styles when they were young appeared to be better equipped at coping with separations resulting from military deployments.

The Effects of Parental Deployment

Limited research has been published on the effects of parental combat deployments (i.e. unaccompanied tours overseas to war zones) on the mental health of young military-connected children particularly from the current conflicts that are markedly different from previous conflicts in terms of duration of parental deployments (i.e. longer in length) and frequency of deployments (i.e. multiple deployments) as well as service members' greater exposure to danger due to the lack of "clear or green zones" in combat theaters (Tanielian & Jaycox, 2008). For instance, past research on children whose parents deployed to Operation Desert Storm showed that there was a higher risk of mental health disorders for those children who had preexisting emotional or behavioral problems and for those children ages 3–5 with a deployed parent than those without a deployed parent (Lemmon & Chartrand, 2009). Barker and Berry (2009) asserted that "home discipline problems, sadness, and increased demands for attention may be present in 25–50% of children younger than 5 with a deployed parent" (p. 1033); additionally, "behavioral problems may be more pronounced in younger than older children, especially for boys" (p. 1033). Younger children also experienced sleep disruptions or changes in appetite. Research has shown that the stay-at-home parent (i.e. the non-deployed remaining parent) may experience difficulties in maintaining a regular household routine, which can result in behavioral- and mood-related problems in young children (Park, 2011).

Davis (2010) found that "65% of the services provided to children for mental health problems and behavioral issues occur 'outside the gate' – by civilian pediatricians" (p. 1216). In this study, outpatient visits included reports of increased anxiety, behavioral, and stress disorders in children ages 3–8 as evidenced by "sleep problems, separation issues, and regressive behaviors" (Davis, 2010, p. 1216). A separate study by Gorman, Eide, and Hisle-Gorman (2010) found that in 11% of outpatient visits of military-connected children aged 3–8 years old the children had "clinically significant" pediatric behavioral issues and stress disorders and that this figure increased to 19% when a parent was deployed (p. 1062). Additionally, the length of parental deployments has been associated with greater levels of anxiety and somatic symptoms in children, where the longer deployments result in an increase in reported symptomatology (Chandra et al., 2010).

Children often respond to separation from a parent during deployment as a type of loss or grief experience and it is hypothesized that their reactions will vary based on several factors: age and levels of cognitive, emotional and social skill development; temperament; the non-deployed parent's psychological health and level of distress; as well as whether or not the deployment was combat related and length of deployment (Park, 2011; US Department of Defense [DoD], 2010). The literature showed that the duration of parental deployments produced higher levels of stress rather than the total number of deployments (DoD, 2010). An Army family study discovered that children aged 0–5 were least able to adaptively cope when a parent was deployed (DoD, 2010). Children aged 3–5 tended to use externalizing behaviors in reaction to a parent's deployment, and probably due to lack of sufficient verbal skills to be able to adequately express and articulate thoughts, feelings, and emotions (DoD, 2010). Barker and Berry (2009) point out that infants tend to exhibit clingy behaviors toward caregivers and excessive crying; whereas toddlers exhibit an increase in temper tantrums and/ or regressive behaviors, while children aged 3–5 respond to separation with confusion and/or disruptive behaviors. Furthermore, the mental health of young military-connected children tends to be directly correlated with the stay-at-home parent's level of distress (Murray, 2002), and in particular the mother's mental health (Jensen, Martin & Watanabe, 1996). A study by Flake et al. (2009) found that "the most significant predictor of child psychosocial functioning during wartime deployment was parental stress" (p. 276). Jensen et al. (1996) claimed that the "functioning of the remaining parent and the children are closely intertwined" (p. 439). Chandra et al. (2010) have echoed these findings in that "caregivers with poorer mental health reported more child difficulties … and deteriorating caregiver mental health may exacerbate child difficulties during the deployment and reintegration period" (pp. 20, 23).

Attachment

Multiple developmental models and neurobiological studies state that early secure attachments are vital in the cognitive, emotional, and social development of children (National Infant & Toddler Child Care Initiative, 2010; National Research Council & Institute of Medicine, 2000). Chartrand et al. (2008) noted that the critical time for developing attachment relationships is between 18 to 35 months of age and because of the high deployment tempo in the recent conflicts, infants will often be separated from the service member parent during these critical times of brain development and formation of secure attachments. Parental service member deployments result in an infant spending more time with the primary attachment figure, that is, the remaining parent (in the majority of the cases, the mother), who can provide "a continuous secure base for them during the parental separation" (p. 1013). However, Barker and Berry (2009) documented that some young children can experience confusion and distress when the deployed parent returns home. The majority of children are able to quickly adjust to the deployed parent's return; however, some experience problems including "trouble sleeping in their own bed, not seeking comfort from returning parent, not wanting returning parent to leave the house, returning parent losing authority as disciplinarian, and preferring nondeployed caregiver over returning parent" (Barker & Berry, 2009, p. 1038).

Parental Distress and Risk for Child Maltreatment

Wartime service member deployments have been associated with an increase in the rates of child abuse and neglect. A study comprising enlisted Army soldiers and their families found child maltreatment rates to be 42% higher during deployments (during actual deployment or separation and post-deployment or reintegration) as compared with pre-deployment (before the service member departs) (Gibbs et al., 2007). Mental health issues in the returning service member can also increase the risk for physical abuse of military-connected young children as well as lower education levels of enlisted service members (Campbell, Brown, & Okwara, 2010).

Injury or Death of the Service Member Parent

In addition to the experience of deployment separations and reintegration, young military-connected children can also face other significant stressors, namely, the death or serious injury of the service member parent. A service member's death may occur during a deployment or after returning from combat (i.e. during post-deployment) as a result of injuries or death by suicide. The rates of suicide in both active-duty and Veteran populations have shown a substantial increase over the last decade (Cato, 2013; Mills et al., 2011). Military-connected children who experience the death of a service member can develop what is often referred to as "childhood traumatic grief," whereby young children can experience feelings of horror, fear, or helplessness and children sometimes "fill in the details" to tragic parental deaths through fantasy and "avoid any reminders of the deceased parent" (Cohen & Mannarino, 2011, p. 220). The death of a parent as a result of a deployment is traumatic for the entire family and young children's expression of grief may be misinterpreted due to their inability to properly communicate emotions. Children aged 0–5 experience grief of a parent as intense feelings and display specific behaviors that may be inconsistent and emerge later during times of stress (DoD, 2010). The very young children between 0 and 2 years old may stop speaking, while slightly older children aged 3–5 may present with problems sleeping, eating, and using the bathroom (DoD, 2010).

A child's mental health can be further compromised as a result of a parent returning home with combat-related polytraumatic injuries (e.g. physical injuries to multiple body systems) and/or mental health challenges such as post-traumatic stress disorder (PTSD) and/or mild traumatic brain injury (mTBI), the signature injury of the GWOT (Tanielian & Jaycox, 2008). Infants and young children are thought to be "particularly vulnerable to the stressors associated with deployment and reintegration experiences" and rely on adults to "assist in their management of strong emotions" (Zero to Three, 2012, p. 2). Furthermore, as a result of exposure to parental PTSD, the child may develop secondary stress reactions and be at risk of more serious psychiatric disorders and other behavioral problems in adolescence and into adulthood (Campbell et al., 2010, p. 133). However, there are several protective factors to keep in mind, for example, maintaining previously established family routines (pre-injuries) and the availability of supportive networks (Cozza & Guimond, 2011).

PTSD and associated co-morbidities have been estimated to affect 15 to 30% of those service members returning from combat; alcohol abuse and aggression have been reported in almost half of those with PTSD and related symptoms (Tanielian & Jaycox, 2008). Intimate partner violence (IPV) in military and Veteran couples has also been correlated with combat PTSD and the prevalence rates of IPV in the literature vary widely, from 13.5% to 58% (Marshall, Panuzio, & Taft, 2005). Obviously, all of these significant stressors in military and Veteran families increase the risk of negative child outcomes.

The next section of the chapter outlines three case scenarios with common elements, that is, the challenges associated with military deployment and reintegration and the responses of very young children and their parents along with potential interventions for human service providers.

CASE VIGNETTE 1

(All names and identifying information for each case vignette have been altered.)

A young Caucasian mother, Melissa Chapman, aged 20, brings her 19-month-old daughter, Marie, to the pediatrician for a routine medical check-up. Melissa appears somewhat disheveled and when speaking to the physician she reports that Marie is "irritable and cries all of the time" since her husband left for deployment, and that she is exhausted as the primary caregiver and has no family support close by. Melissa had recently moved with her husband to his new duty station at Fort Hood, Texas and away from her family in Florida. Her husband, an Army Corporal (E-4), Marcus Chapman, Caucasian, age 23, also from Florida, has been deployed to Afghanistan with the 2nd Ranger Battalion and involved in the training of Afghan forces. This is Marcus's first deployment and he has been away for three months. Melissa feels isolated and unsure of what do to about their irritable baby and questions her parenting abilities as well as the stability of their marital relationship. Melissa and Marcus were recent newlyweds, and had decided to marry when he received his orders to deploy. Additionally, Marcus had recently joined the military after spending a few years in college without obtaining a degree, working at odd jobs. According to Melissa, a new marriage, unfamiliarity with the military lifestyle, a baby, and being away from family were significant adjustments for both Marcus and Melissa.

Upon further medical examination, the physician determines that Marie has infant acid reflux, a fairly common digestive condition in babies and prescribes medications to treat it. Marie had suffered from this condition starting at 6 months of age and had been successfully treated, however, it appeared as though the symptoms had resurfaced about three months ago, coinciding with Marcus's deployment. The physician recommends that

Melissa receive counseling and/or attend a parent support group on a military installation to help her cope emotionally with the demands associated with being a young new mother who is also isolated and acting as an only parent while worrying about Marcus being deployed overseas, whom she has had some communication with over the Internet via Skype. Melissa agrees to participate in counseling, and, once in therapy, she reveals to the psychotherapist that she feels abandoned by Marcus (given her own history of abandonment by her own biological father) and that their baby, Marie, seems to long for Marcus as she insists on holding on to a toy that she associates with her father, and, even with the medication for her digestive problem, Marie still seems to be "unhappy." It is important to note that Melissa reported that Marie has met all of her developmental milestones, seemed securely attached to her mother and did not start to exhibit symptoms until Marcus left for his deployment. There were no signs of child maltreatment while Marie was in Melissa's care. Upon Marcus's return from deployment, Marie seems to act detached from her father, where Marcus feels rejected. At times Marie is seemingly angry toward him, as she pinches him and pulls his hair while simultaneously throwing herself on the floor in a fit of rage (i.e. temper tantrum) every time he leaves the house and whenever she does not get her way. Both Melissa and Marcus are baffled by Marie's behaviors upon reunification and the couple is also working on getting re-acclimated to each other and to their relatively new marriage and their seemingly different attachment needs.

Potential Intervention for Vignette 1

The mental health practitioner in this case can utilize an evidence-informed intervention, such as, parent–child interaction therapy (PCIT). PCIT is a behavioral family therapy and parenting approach used in diverse populations and originally designed for use with preschool-aged children to decrease externalizing behaviors, enable parents to feel more effective in their parenting, and increase positive interactions between the child and her parents (Eyberg, 1988). Although it has not been evaluated specifically with military-connected children and their parents, there are various empirical studies that support treatment efficacy (for a review, see Cooley et al., 2014). PCIT involves not only a thorough observational coding of parent–child interactions and externalizing behaviors as part of the assessment, but also includes two intervention phases, the first is the child-directed interaction (CDI) comprising play therapy followed by the parent-directed interaction (PDI), in which parents practice their parenting skills while being observed by the therapist (see Eyberg, 1988). This approach seems feasible given the case vignette scenario where Marie is seemingly suffering from anxiety related to separations (ambivalent attachment-related reactions) and is exhibiting externalizing behaviors such as pinching and pulling of her father's hair as well as temper tantrums when he leaves the house. PCIT can also assist the parents with their sense of competency in their parenting skills and also help them to work together in the parenting of their young child. It could also be argued that Marie's physical symptoms (digestive problem) returned as a result of the separation stress and her mother's stressful response to her husband's deployment. The therapist could also refer Marie and Marcus for couples' therapy. Basham (2013) recommends a phase-oriented trauma-informed and integrative couples' therapy for military couples that is grounded in attachment theory (see Ainsworth, 1989, on affectional bonds throughout the life cycle). Another attachment-based approach that has been empirically supported would be emotionally focused couples' therapy originally developed by Johnson (2004) and applied to military couples by Sneath and Rheem (2011).

CASE VIGNETTE 2

Anabel Garcia is a 4-year-old Latina female who is the daughter of Rosa Garcia (20 years old) and Carlos Garcia (22 years old). Anabel's father, Carlos, is a US Marine rifleman assigned to a battalion in North Carolina. Carlos is currently on his second deployment to Afghanistan and recently informed his wife Rosa that he has volunteered to extend his combat tour and will be conducting security for convoys. Carlos told Rosa that he felt he had to extend his deployment in order to "get payback" for the death of his best friend James, who was killed a month ago as a result of the detonation of an improvised explosive device (IED) while his squad was on a patrol.

Rosa and Carlos report that they come from very traditional Mexican-American families. The couple began dating in high school, when Carlos was a senior and Rosa was a sophomore. Toward the end of that school year, Rosa became pregnant with Anabel, prompting Carlos to enlist in the Marine Corps after his graduation, in order to make a "better life" for his family. Rosa completed her junior year of high school, however, after Carlos had graduated boot camp and completed infantry school, Rosa quit school and took Anabel to North Carolina to be with Carlos. The couple married as soon as Rosa turned 18 and the family currently reside in base housing at Camp Lejeune.

When Carlos enlisted in the Marine Corps, Rosa had thought that he would be stationed in southern California, which was only a little more than an hour from her parents' home, but when Carlos told her that they would be moving to North Carolina, she was emotionally devastated. Rosa's family was her entire support system and she had never traveled outside of the state of California. Rosa was incredibly unhappy from the time she initially arrived in North Carolina. Rosa felt like an outsider both on the military installation and around Jacksonville, the closest city to Camp Lejeune.

For the first two years of Anabel's life, Carlos was the ever-present care provider to his daughter. This is not to say that Rosa was not a "good enough" mother, but Carlos not only handled the majority of Anabel's feedings, he interacted with her on a regular basis, often singing and speaking to her in both Spanish and English. "Dada" was Anabel's first word and her face would light up as soon as she saw her father. After Anabel turned 2, Carlos was deployed to Afghanistan where he served an eight-month combat deployment in which his platoon came under frequent small arms fire and received mortar fire on an almost daily basis. That first deployment was difficult on Rosa but Carlos managed to keep the majority of the details of his activities in Afghanistan from Rosa which helped her overall emotional state. However, Rosa discovered that being the sole primary care provider for Anabel was frustrating. Rosa's parents and other family members were in California and with Carlos deployed, Rosa felt as if she had no additional support. Anabel was often "fussy" and cried frequently. Oftentimes the only thing that would calm Anabel was when Rosa would give her a stuffed bear that held a plastic picture frame of Carlos (Carlos had inserted a photo of his face so that Anabel would not forget about him while he was gone).

Once Carlos returned from his first deployment he was visibly different toward both his wife and his daughter. Carlos preferred spending time with his fellow Marines, most of whom did not have a wife or a child. Carlos spent a large amount of the money he had saved while on deployment, on a sport motorcycle, without discussing the purchase with Rosa. When Rosa confronted Carlos about the motorcycle, Carlos became angry and yelled at Rosa, telling her that he risked his life and deserved to buy whatever he wanted with the money he was paid. Carlos was much more unresponsive toward Anabel's needs as well. Carlos rarely interacted with his daughter and left the parenting responsibilities entirely up to Rosa. Carlos and Rosa argued a great deal and on a few occasions the couple would push each other when the arguments intensified. Anabel would cry throughout the altercations between her parents and neither her father nor her mother would respond to her needs until hours after an argument.

Rosa was worried about Carlos as he would often go about his day with very little sleep because when he tried to sleep he would often complain of having violent nightmares. It was common for Carlos's body to make sudden and violent movements in his sleep and she was often awakened at night by Carlos yelling and crying in his sleep. Anabel would sometimes sleep in their bed at night but Rosa no longer allowed her to sleep in the bed out of fear that she might be hurt or accidentally injured by Carlos.

A month prior to Anabel's fourth birthday, Carlos was deployed for a second time to Afghanistan. Rosa had told Carlos that she was going to return to California while he was deployed so that her family could help her with Anabel. However, Carlos refused to agree to this arrangement, mainly out of fear that Rosa would have an affair with one of her old boyfriends in California. Once Anabel turned 4, Rosa enrolled her for preschool/day care. When Rosa would drop Anabel off at the program, she would cling onto Rosa's leg and the day-care providers would have to physically restrain Anabel from chasing after her mother as she left. Once Rosa would return to retrieve her daughter, Anabel would begin crying again, refusing to leave with her mother. Anabel would throw herself on the ground and often repeatedly hit her head on it, multiple times, on purpose.

In addition to Anabel's seemingly insecure attachment style, her language was minimal when compared with the other 4-year-old children. Anabel would usually point at an object and grunt. When the day-care providers would prompt Anabel to use her words, Anabel would throw herself on the ground or throw objects around the room. Anabel was also physically aggressive with her peers. It was not uncommon for Anabel to push the other children off of the tricycles that all the children would share and take turns riding, just so she could ride them without waiting her turn. Anabel also began struggling with encopresis, even though she has not needed to wear a diaper since she was 2 years old.

Recently, Anabel cut her head on the corner of a desk, when she was in the middle of a tantrum: the cut required six staples. While in the emergency room, Nancy Rodriguez, a social worker assigned to the ER, interviewed Rosa regarding the accident. Rosa confided that Anabel had been difficult to control since her husband has been deployed to Afghanistan. Rosa admitted that she becomes easily frustrated over her own inability to control her daughter and she sometimes resents Anabel and her husband Carlos because she is unable to be closer to her own family in California. Rosa stated, "If I had not become pregnant and married so early I feel like I would have a lot more options in my life today."

It is important to note that Rosa confirmed that Anabel had met most of her important developmental milestones, up to the age of 3. However, Rosa feels that within the last year, Anabel's vocabulary has become much more limited and she had recently begun having "accidents in her pants" (encopresis) and often cried easily. Rosa states that she believes Anabel is only acting this way because she is trying to make her life more difficult and Anabel probably just misses her father. Ms. Rodriguez tells Rosa that she recommends that she seek assistance through the Fleet and Family Support Services, available on base at Camp Lejeune, to obtain assistance in parenting skills. In addition, Ms. Rodriguez explains that she will be referring both Rosa and Anabel to the base mental health clinic for further evaluation.

Potential Intervention for Vignette 2

The focus of therapy would be to improve communication skills of all members of the family, reduce the conflict between the family members, as well as identify and address the effects of combat stress on both the service member and the family as a whole. In addition, special attention should be made to foster a more secure attachment style within Anabel, which could be aided by increasing parental sensitivity.

An evidence-based intervention that might prove to be extremely useful in this case would be BSFT (brief strategic family therapy). BSFT establishes that problems are created as a result of dysfunctional interaction patters, namely communication (or lack of) and the resulting behaviors (Rambo et al., 2012). Therefore, the dysfunctional interaction patterns actually work to maintain the family problems, which, if left unaddressed, will often worsen with time. A counselor utilizing BSFT would typically see the preservation of the family as the most desirable outcome of therapy (Szapocznik et al., 2012). In order to achieve this, a therapist would challenge and eventually change the overall family dynamics, specifically, the interaction process that is associated with maladaptive and problematic behaviors. Ultimately, the result would be a substantial alteration in the way that the individual family members behave toward each other.

Although there has not been a great deal of research examining the use of BSFT on the 0–5-age range of children, the technique has been determined to be efficient in treating child and adolescent behavior problems and can be easily applied and utilized with clients and families from multiple ethnic and cultural backgrounds (Szapocznik et al., 2012). However, one important factor to be considered is that the therapist needs to understand the military culture and cultural nuances of military life (Coll, Weiss, & Metal, 2013). Understanding military culture and lifestyle is especially important for civilian human service providers who will more than likely be treating military families within their practices due to the overwhelming number of clients inundating the military mental health system (Everson & Figley, 2011).

In addition to BSFT, child–parent psychotherapy (CPP) would be another alternative evidence-informed treatment method that has been utilized to treat maladaptive attachment styles observed within preschool-aged children exposed to family violence. The goal of CPP is to foster an infant's, a toddler's, or preschooler's ability to regulate affect as well as promote interpersonal skills. This is achieved through teaching the primary-care providers to establish a secure foundation in which the child's developmental and social needs can be better met through improved interaction (Lieberman & Van Horn, 2009).

When examining Anabel's recent difficulties with encopresis, one must recognize that this is a symptom that is commonly treated under both biological and psychological perspectives. Studies have identified numerous psychological and emotional factors which may play a role in encopresis, such as separation from close family members or primary-care providers, inconsistent attention especially related to toilet training, as well as the mental health of the mother. It was noted in one study that psychiatrically distressed mothers were more likely to have children suffering from encopresis due to their inability to manage the stress associated with a child's soiling problems (Akdemir et al., 2015). Thus, an evaluation of the family situation and the mother's overall mental health as well as the incorporation of a family-based therapy technique, similar to CPP or BSFT, has the potential to be an effective intervention for encopresis and the improvement of family functioning.

Once in therapy, upon discovering Carlos's behavior prior to his second deployment, a therapist would undoubtedly be concerned, not only with the fact that it would appear that Carlos is suffering from combat stress or possibly PTSD, but any therapist would also be concerned with IPV that may have occurred and could continue to occur upon Carlos's return from Afghanistan. Rosa might be helped through a program called FOCUS, a family-centered, resiliency-training intervention program that serves active-duty personnel and their children conducted on military bases, schools, clinics, and through telehealth services (Leskin et al., 2013). The goal of the FOCUS program is to increase positive family relationships and foster coping skills for healthy child and family development. The family could also be referred to the Fleet and Family Support Services, where Carlos would be required to be assessed for PTSD and participate in individual, as well as family therapy with Rosa and Anabel. Past studies examining Veterans and active-duty service members diagnosed with PTSD and their family situations have revealed that the romantic partners of service members suffering from PTSD report high levels of family dysfunction and severe relationship problems when compared with their counterparts of those not suffering from PTSD symptoms (Monson, Taft, & Fredman, 2009). Additionally, the PTSD symptom cluster of avoidance/numbing symptomology has been identified as having the strongest association with both relationship dissatisfaction and the likelihood of impaired intimacy (Solomon, Dekel, & Mikulincer, 2008). This can play a vital role in the need for an evidence-informed therapy that can aid in the instances of avoidance in order to establish improved communication. Lastly, findings have also identified a substantial link between Veterans suffering from PTSD and the likelihood for perpetrating acts of psychological and physical aggression and abuse toward both intimate partners and children, alike (Glenn et al., 2002).

In terms of an evidence-informed approach to jointly treating both the symptoms of PTSD, as well as enhancing the functioning of intimate partner relationships, cognitive-behavioral conjoint therapy (CBCT) has proven to be highly effective. CBCT emphasizes conflict management strategies in order to foster safe communication between intimate partners, interventions aimed at decreasing instances of avoidance thereby increasing effective communication, as well as utilization of cognitive restructuring practices to initially challenge and then alter the maladaptive thought processes which are common with PTSD (Fredman, Monson, & Adair, 2011).

VIGNETTE 3

Robbie is a 3-year-old, Caucasian boy and the only child of his parents. His 30-year-old father is a staff sgt. in the Marine Corps, an infantry unit leader, and his 27-year-old mother is a stay-at-home mom. Robbie's father has been in active duty for 12 years and has been deployed overseas five times. Robbie's parents met while his father was on leave with a buddy visiting his family on pre-deployment leave and they were married within two weeks. Shortly after his parents were married and his mother moved to the base, his father deployed for his fourth tour. Robbie was an infant when his father deployed on his fifth tour and his mother moved back home to be near family and friends. When his father is not deployed, he is often away from the home for field operations, schooling, and other training. Robbie lives with his mother in base housing in North Carolina which is far away from his grandparents and other extended family members who live in Oregon. His mother, who is typically outgoing when his father is home, spends most days sitting on the couch in her pajamas leaving Robbie to entertain himself. She has a difficult time when her husband is away stating she feels unmotivated and has no purpose. Robbie's mother does not have many friends at the base but she will occasionally talk to the neighbors if they are outside at the same time. Robbie's father calls home when he is able to, but he is rarely able to Skype or Face Time due to lack of reliable internet. His parents frequently argue on the phone when his father calls and his mother will cry silently after the call ends. The family has no significant financial stressors but report there is never any extra money left over after paying bills. Robbie's father feels stressed when he is away from the family for extended periods since he knows his wife has difficulties in his absence. Robbie's father has asked her to see a counselor since his fourth deployment but she has always told him everything will be fine when he returns home. Since having Robbie, his father is increasingly telling his spouse to see a counselor as he plans to stay on active duty and will continue to deploy. His father wants to have more children and worries that his wife will not be able to manage herself, the children, and the household in his absence.

Robbie has been attending a preschool program part-time and his teachers are reporting behavior problems. When Robbie is dropped off in the morning, he cries inconsolably for 15 minutes. He is able to follow some of the routines of the classroom but often clings to the teachers instead of playing with his peers. The teachers have reported to his mother that Robbie is wetting (enuresis) the cot at nap time most days he attends preschool and has been hitting other children instead of asking to play with a toy or book. The teachers have noticed Robbie struggling to hold a pencil as the students are learning to write their letters and has difficulty with outside play preferring to engage in solitary activities indoors. Robbie's mother reported the concerns to Robbie's pediatrician at his well visit check-up. Robbie's mother states he was potty-trained by two and a half years old, but he started to have daytime accidents and bedwetting during naps and bedtime ever since his father has been away. Upon further questioning, Robbie's mother reported to the physician that she does not feel she is able to handle Robbie's misbehavior when her husband is gone and stated she will sometimes ignore him, yell at him, or spank him on the buttocks. The physician diagnosed Robbie with a developmental coordination disorder and a referral was placed for occupational therapy to address his coordination issues. The physician referred both Robbie and his mother to a case manager at the clinic and notified the Family Advocacy Program (FAP) on base for further assessment for potential child abuse based on the mother's self-reported disciplinary style.

Robbie was evaluated at occupational therapy and requires assistance with his fine motor skills and hand–eye coordination and was scheduled for therapy every two weeks. Robbie's mother vented to the occupational therapist about his reported behaviors at school and the occupational therapist stated she will also work on assisting Robbie with positive ways to deal with his anger and anxiety as it comes up during each session. Robbie and his mother also met with the case manager at the clinic who will assist the mother in developing a local support system. The case manager contacted the Family Readiness Officer of the unit to inquire about any groups or other activities for Robbie's age group.

Potential Intervention for Vignette 3

Military families continue to face challenges at home even during times of non–deployment. This is often due to separations for training and schooling and the long and unpredictable work hours a service member may have (Park, 2011). Since military families face frequent separations it is essential for them to have social supports to cope with associated stressors (Drummet, Coleman, & Cable, 2003). Robbie's family faces several challenges, with the primary issue identified as the poor coping of Robbie and his mother in the absence of Robbie's father. Helpful interventions were set in place with the referrals to the FAP, case management, and occupational therapy.

The Department of Defense developed the FAP to address the psychosocial needs of military members and families (Franklin, 2013). FAP provides information and education to identify and prevent family violence and child maltreatment (Weiss & DeBraber, 2013). Robbie and his mother met with an FAP clinician who assessed Robbie's mother was reacting to stress in a negative way and providing confusing signals to Robbie with her inconsistent discipline. The clinician did not determine Robbie's discipline to be maltreatment at the time of the assessment and made several recommendations to continue to monitor the family's functioning. Robbie and his mother were scheduled for a monthly home visit and Robbie's mother was referred to psychoeducation classes on stress management and parent education. In addition to psychoeducation groups, Robbie's mother was scheduled to meet with an individual counselor biweekly for treatment. Childcare was provided for all scheduled groups and individual appointments. Robbie's mother reported an increase in her confidence to appropriately respond to Robbie as a result of the parenting classes. The group assisted her with a plan on how to react to Robbie's acting out behaviors in a calm and controlled manner. She also learned that younger children often exhibit regressive behaviors such as bedwetting as a response to stress (Riggs & Riggs, 2011). To further address her inconsistent discipline, Robbie's mother was encouraged to create a list of desired, ignorable, and punishable behaviors to help her manage her expectations of him on a developmentally appropriate level (Campbell et al., 2010). During her individual sessions, Robbie's mother was able to identify sources of support and increase her identification of positive coping skills. She was educated on the importance of building her support network and reaching out for assistance since, oftentimes, children's responses to stressful situations are reflections of the mother's reactions (Drummet et al., 2003).

A second helpful intervention for this family was the establishment of case management services. The case manager met with Robbie and his mother and explained the role as being a source of support, assistance with navigating the military system, and providing oversight and follow-up for all recommendations and services received. The case manager coordinated the referral to the occupational therapist to a provider that accepted the military health insurance and was in a convenient location for Robbie's mother. The case manager recommended Robbie's mother meet with a financial counselor, a free service, to discuss developing a budget and ways to track spending in order to address the stress surrounding the family's finances. The case manager also assessed a lack of support and increased stress as a primary cause for the difficulties Robbie and his mother were experiencing with each other and those in their environment. Similar to Vignette 1 in this chapter, the case manager placed a referral to a counselor certified in PCIT which has been found to reduce physically abusive discipline (Campbell et al., 2010). According to the Child Welfare Information Gateway, PCIT has proven effective with children aged 2–8 as parents learn effective parenting to improve the relationship with the child and the behavior problems decrease (2013). PCIT is an evidence-based practice, which treats the parent and child together. PCIT addresses the negative interaction patterns that have resulted in poor behavior to help parents bond with the child and effectively respond to the child's needs (Child Welfare Information Gateway, 2013). PCIT sessions are 1–1.5 hours in length and are typically provided between ten and 20 sessions. Robbie and his mother were scheduled for ten sessions, with approval to increase if needed. During the sessions, the counselor placed an audio device in the ear of Robbie's mother to be able to provide her with cues to guide her with strategies to reinforce Robbie's positive behavior. Over the course of the sessions, the counselor noted a secure bond between Robbie and his mother along with a consistent approach to discipline that resulted in an improved relationship. Robbie's mother reported feeling more confident in managing challenging behaviors and stated she and his teachers noticed a decrease in Robbie's acting out and bedwetting behaviors.

Implications for Human Service Providers

Human service providers can help parents understand normal development trajectories and the stressors associated with military deployments on the family system and particularly in the varying child reactions and that children's reactions can be manifestations of fear of abandonment, separation-related anxieties, or anger at the parent for leaving or the military parent not being emotionally available upon reunification (due to his or her injuries). Thus addressing the emotional needs of young children is important and having ways of maintaining the connection or bond through the deployment with the use of technology if possible, such as Skype. Also being familiar with resources such as Zero to Three (zerotothree.org) and the National Child Traumatic Network (www.nctsn.org) and Sesame Street program for military families with young children (www.sesameworkshop.org/what-we-do/our-initiatives/military-families) are important sources of information and provide materials for parents and family members to utilize in order to assist their young children with the challenges associated with military deployments and separations. Daddy Dolls (http://daddydolls.com) are also a resource used for young military children to maintain their connection with their deployed parent through a doll that depicts the parent or loved one. United through Reading is yet another resource of personalized books and videos of parents reading to their children as a way of maintaining the emotional connections once a parent deploys, the child can see the personalized book and view the video of the parent reading to the child (www.unitedthroughreading.org/military-program/military-book). Lastly, for civilian human service providers, participating in workshops or trainings on military culture will be a benefit in providing military culturally responsive services to this population (Coll, Weiss, Draves & Dyer, 2012).

Conclusion

The chapter highlights what is currently known about the effects of military wartime deployment separation and accompanying stressors on military-connected children between 0 and 5 years old. However, early childhood mental health and the impact of military lifestyle and the stressors associated with combat deployment have not been adequately addressed in the empirical literature. In addition, current studies have been scrutinized by leading investigators as being based on "self-reported data, small or highly selective samples, narrow age ranges, and cross-sectional designs or were conducted during peacetime" (Mansfield, Kaufman, Engel, & Gaynes, 2011, p. 1000). Research conducted with military-connected children during peacetime or from other conflicts can impact the generalizability to military-connected children during these particularly stressful and enduring conflicts (GWOT) with multiple and lengthy combat deployments. Furthermore, studies conducted on older children and adolescents do not necessarily apply to an early childhood population that is so developmentally different from the older-aged children and youth. Thus, this chapter serves to highlight current knowledge in terms of the challenges and potential intervention programs with the youngest and most vulnerable aged youth who also happen to be military connected and are faced with unique and extreme family stressors during times of war and separation. Despite the current drawdown of US military involvement in the Middle East, as mentioned in the family chapter, human service providers will be encountering military-connected families and their young children in community settings for years to come.

Note

Thank you to Therese Reynolds for her contributions to the original draft.

Bibliography

Ainsworth, M. D. S. (1989). Attachments beyond infancy. *American Psychologist*, 44(4), 709–716.

Ainsworth, M. D. S., Blehar, M. C., Waters, E., & Wall, S. (1978). *Patterns of attachment: A psychological study of the strange situation*. Hillsdale, NJ: Erlbaum.

Akdemir, D., Çengel Kültür, S. E., Saltık Temizel, İ. N., Zeki, A., & Şenses Dinç, G. (2015). Familial psychological factors are associated with encopresis. *Pediatrics International*, 57(1), 143–148.

Allen, M. & Staley, L. (2007). Helping children cope when a loved one is on military deployment. *National Association of the Education of Young Children*, 62(1), 82–86.

American Psychological Association (2007). *The psychological needs of US military service members and their families: A preliminary report*. Washington, DC: American Psychological Association. Retrieved from: www.apa.org/about/policy/military-deployment-services.pdf

Barker, L. H. & Berry, K. D. (2009). Developmental issues impacting military families with young children during single and multiple deployments. *Military Medicine*, 174, 1033–1040.

Basham, K. (2013). Couple therapy for redeployed military and Veteran couples. In A. Rubin, E. L. Weiss, & J. E. Coll (Eds.), *Handbook of military social work* (pp. 443–465). Hoboken, NJ: Wiley.

Bowlby, J. (1969/1982). *Attachment and loss: Volume 1: Attachment* (rev. ed.). New York: Basic Books.

Campbell, C. L., Brown, E. J., & Okwara, L. (2010). Addressing sequelae of trauma and interpersonal violence in military children: A review of the literature and case illustration. *Cognitive and Behavioral Practice*, 18, 131–143.

Cato, C. (2013). Suicide in the military. In A. Rubin, E. L. Weiss, & J. E. Coll (Eds.), *Handbook of military social work* (pp. 225–244). Hoboken, NJ: Wiley.

Chandra, A., Lara-Cinisomo, S., Jaycox, L. H., Tanielian, T., Burns, R. M., Ruder, T., & Han, B. (2010). Children on the homefront: The experience of children from military families. *Pediatrics*, 125, 16–25. doi: 10.1542/peds.2009-1180

Chartrand, M. M., Frank, D. A., White, L. F., & Shope, T. R. (2008). Effect of parents' wartime deployment on the behavior of young children in military families. *Arch. Pediatr. Adolesc. Med.*, 162(11), 1009–1014.

Child Welfare Information Gateway (2013). *Parent–child interaction therapy with at-risk families*. Washington, DC.

Clark, J. C. & Messer, S. C. (2006). Intimate partner violence in the US Military: Rates, risks, and responses. In C. A. Castro, A. B. Adler, & C. A. Britt (Eds.), *Military life: The psychology of serving in peace and combat* (4 vols.). Bridgeport, CT: Praeger.

Cohen, J. A. & Mannarino, A. P. (2011). Trauma-Focused CBT for traumatic grief in military children. *Journal of Contemporary Psychotherapy*, 41, 219–227. doi: 10.1007/s10879-10011-9178-0

Coll, J. E., Weiss, E. L., Draves, P., & Dyer, D. (2012). The impact of military cultural awareness, experience, attitudes, and education on clinician self-efficacy in the treatment of Veterans. *Journal of International Continuing Social Work Education*, 15(1), 39–48.

Coll, J. E., Weiss, E. L., & Metal, M. (2013). Military culture and diversity. In A. Rubin, E. L. Weiss, & J. E. Coll (Eds.), *Handbook of military social work* (pp. 21–36). Hoboken, NJ: Wiley.

Cooley, M. E., Veldorale-Griffin, A., Petren, R. E., & Mullis, A. K. (2014). Parent–child interaction therapy: A meta-analysis of child behavior outcomes and parent stress. *Journal of Family Social Work*, 17, 191–208. doi: 10.1080/10522158.2014.888696

Cozolino, L. (2012). *The neuroscience of psychotherapy: Healing the social brain* (2nd ed.). New York: Norton.

Cozza, S. J. & Guimond, J. M. (2011). Working with combat-injured families through the recovery trajectory. In S. MacDermid Wadsworth & D. Riggs (Eds.), *Risk and resilience in US military families* (pp. 259–277). New York: Springer.

Davis, B. E. (2010). Parental wartime deployment and the use of mental health services among young military children. *Pediatrics*, 126, 1215–1216. doi: 10.1542/peds.2010-2543

Davis, B. E., Blaschke, G. S., & Stafford, E. M. (2012). Military children, families, and communities: Supporting those who serve. *Pediatrics*, 129, S3–S9. doi: 10.1542/peds.2010-3797c

Drummet, A. R., Coleman, M., & Cable, S. (2003). Military families under stress: Implications for family life education. *Family Relations*, 52, 279–287.

Erikson, E. H. (1993). *Childhood and society*. New York: Norton.

Erikson, E. H. & Erikson, J. M. (1998). *The life cycle completed (extended version)*. New York: Norton.

Everson, R. B. & Figley, C. R. (Eds.) (2011). *Families under fire: Systemic therapy with military families*. New York: Routledge.

Eyberg, S. M. (1988). Parent–child interaction therapy: An integration of traditional and behavioral concerns. *Child & Family Behavior Therapy*, 10, 33–46.

Flake, E. M., Davis, B. E., Johnson, P. L., & Middleton, L. S. (2009). The psychosocial effects of deployment on military children. *Journal of Development and Behavioral Pediatrics*, 30(4), 271–278.

Franklin, K. (2013). Cycle of deployment and family well-being. In A. Rubin, E. L. Weiss, & J. E. Coll (Eds.), *Handbook of military social work* (pp. 313–333). Hoboken, NJ: Wiley.

Fredman, S. J., Monson, C. M., & Adair, K. C. (2011). Implementing cognitive–behavioral conjoint therapy for PTSD with the newest generation of Veterans and their partners. *Cognitive and Behavioral Practice*, 18(1), 120–130.

Gewirtz, A. H. & Zamirt, O. (2014). The impact of parental deployment to war on children: The crucial role of parenting. *Advances in Child Development and Behavior*, 46, 89–112.

Gibbs, D. A., Martin, S.Kupper, L., & Johnson, R. (2007). Child maltreatment in enlisted soldiers' families during combat-related deployments. *Journal of the American Medical Association*, 298, 528–535.

Glenn, D. M., Beckham, J. C., Feldman, M. E., Kirby, A. C., Hertzberg, M. A., & Moore, S. D. (2002). Violence and hostility among families of Vietnam Veterans with combat-related posttraumatic stress disorder. *Violence & Victims*, 17(4), 473–489.

Goodman, P., Turner, A., Agazio, J., Throop, M., Padden, D., Greiner, S., & Hillier, S. L. (2013). Deployment of military mothers: supportive and nonsupportive military programs, processes, and policies. *Military Medicine*, 178(7), 729–734.

Gorman, G. H., Eide, M., & Hisle-Gorman, E. (2010). Wartime military deployment and increased pediatric mental and behavioral health complaints. *Pediatrics*, 126, 1058–1066. doi: 10.1542/peds.2009-2856

Haas, D. M. & Pazdernik, L. A. (2007). Partner deployment and stress in pregnant women. *Journal of Reproductive Medicine*, 52, 901–906.

Harnett, C. (2013). Supporting National Guard and Reserve members and their families. In A. Rubin, E. L. Weiss, & J. E. Coll (Eds.), *Handbook of military social work* (pp. 335–357). Hoboken, NJ: Wiley.

Hughes, D. A. (2000). *Facilitating developmental attachment: The road to emotional recovery and behavioral change in foster and adopted children*. Northvale, NJ: Jason Aronson.

Jensen, P. S., Martin, D., & Watanable, H. (1996). Children's response to parental separation during operation desert storm. *Journal of American Academy of Child and Adolescent Psychiatry*, 35(4), 433–441.

Johnson, S. M. (2004). *The practice of emotionally focused couple therapy: Creating connection* (2nd ed.). New York: Brunner-Routledge.

Kelley, M. L. & Jouriles, E. N. (2011). An introduction to the special section on U.S. military operations: Effects on military members' partners and children. *Journal of Family Psychology*, 25(4), 459–460. doi: 10.1037/a0024569

Lemmon, K. M. & Chartrand, M. M. (2009). Caring for America's children: Military youth in time of war. *Pediatrics in Review*, 30, e42–e48. doi: 10.1542/pir.30-36-e42

Leskin, G. A., Garcia, E., D'Amico, J., Mogil, C. E., & Lester, P. (2013). Family centered programs and interventions for military children and youth. In A. Rubin, E. L. Weiss, & J. E. Coll (Eds.), *Handbook of military social work* (pp. 427–441). Hoboken, NJ: Wiley.

Lester, P. E. (2012). War and military children and families: Translating prevention science into practice. *Journal of the American Academy of Child and Adolescent Psychiatry*, 51(1), 3–5.

Lieberman, A. F. & Van Horn, P. (2009). Child–parent psychotherapy: A developmental approach to mental health treatment in infancy and early childhood. In C. H. Zeanha Jr. (Ed.), *Handbook of infant mental health* (3rd ed.) (pp. 439–449). New York: Guilford Press.

Lieberman, A. F. & Van Horn, P. (2013). Infants and young children in military families: A conceptual model for intervention. *Clinical Child Family Psychology Review*, 16, 282–293. doi: 10.1007/s10567-10013-0140-0144

MacDermid, S. M., Samper, R., Schwarz, R., Nishida, J., & Nyaronga, D. (2008). Understanding and promoting resilience in military families. *Military Family Research Institute at Purdue University*, 1–28.

Mansfield, A. J., Kaufman, J. S., Engel, C. C., & Gaynes, B. N. (2011). Deployment and mental health diagnoses among children of US Army personnel. *Arch. Pediatr. Adolesc. Med.* 165, 999–1005. doi: 10.1001/archpediatrics.2011.123

Marshall, A. D., Panuzio, J., & Taft, C. T. (2005). Intimate partner violence among military Veterans and active duty service men. *Clinical Psychology Review*, 25, 862–876.

Mikulincer, M., Shaver, P., & Pereg, D. (2003). Attachment theory and affect regulation: The dynamics, development, and cognitive consequences of attachment-related strategies. *Motivation and Emotion*, 27(2), 77–102.

Miller, G. E., Chen, E., & Zhou, E. S. (2007). If it goes up, must it come down? Chronic stress and hyptothalamic–pituitary–adrenalcortical axis in humans. *Psychological Bulletin*, 133, 25–45.

Mills, P., Huber, S., Watts, B., & Bagian, J. (2011). Systemic vulnerabilities to suicide among Veterans from the Iraq and Afghanistan conflicts: Review of case reports from a national Veterans Affairs database. *Suicide and Life-Threatening Behavior*, 41(1), 21–32.

Monson, C. M., Taft, C. T., & Fredman, S. J. (2009). Military-related PTSD and intimate relationships: From description to theory-driven research and intervention development. *Clinical Psychology Review*, 29(8), 707–714.

Murray, J. S. (2002). Helping children cope with separation during war. *Journal for Specialists in Pediatric Nursing*, 7, 127–130.

National Infant & Toddler Child Care Initiative (2010). *Relationships: The heart of development and learning*. Chapel Hill, NC: National Training Institute for Child Care Health Consultants, Department of Maternal and Child Health at the University of North Carolina at Chapel Hill, pp. 12–24.

National Research Council and Institute of Medicine (2000). *From neurons to neighborhoods: The science of early childhood development*. Washington, DC: National Academy Press.

Orlans, M. & Levy, T. M. (2014). *Attachment, trauma, and healing: Understanding and treating attachment disorder in children, families and adults*. Philadelphia, PA: Jessica Kingsley.

Park, N. (2011). Military children and families. *American Psychologist*, 66(1), 65–72. doi: 10.1037/a0021249

Pulley, L. & James, L. C. (2011). The need for child mental health services within a department of Defense setting. *Journal of Clinical Psychological Med Settings*, 18, 196–197. doi: 10.1007/s10880-10011-9232-9239

Rambo, A., West, C., Schooley, A., & Boyd, T. V. (2012). *Family therapy review*. New York: Taylor & Francis.

Riggs, S. A. & Riggs, D. S. (2011). Risk and resilience in military families experiencing deployment: The role of the family attachment network. *Journal of Family Psychology*, 25(5), 675–687. doi: 10.1037/a0025286

Saltzman, W. R., Lester, P., Beardslee, W. R., Layne, C. M., Woodward, K., & Nash, W. P. (2011). Mechanisms of risk and resilience in military families: Theoretical and empirical basis of a family-focused resilience enhancement program. *Clinical Child and Family Psychology Review*, 14(3), 213–230.

Sneath, L. & Rheem, K. D. (2011). The use of emotionally focused couples' therapy with military couples and families. In R. Blaine Everson & C. R. Figley (Eds.), *Families under fire: Systemic therapy with military families* (pp. 127–151). New York: Routledge.

Sogomonyan, F. & Cooper, J. L. (2010). Trauma faced by children of military families: What every policymaker should know. *National Center for Children in Poverty*, 1–12.

Solomon, Z., Dekel, R., & Mikulincer, M. (2008). Complex trauma of war captivity: A prospective study of attachment and post-traumatic stress disorder. *Psychological Medicine*, 38(10), 1427–1434.

Szapocznik, J., Schwartz, S. J., Muir, J. A., & Brown, C. H. (2012). Brief strategic family therapy: An intervention to reduce adolescent risk behavior. *Couple and Family Psychology: Research and Practice*, 1(2), 134.

Tanielian, T. & Jaycox, L. H. (2008). *Invisible wounds of war: Psychological and cognitive injuries, their consequences, and services to assist recovery*. Santa Monica, CA: RAND Corporation.

US Department of Defense (2010). *Report on the impact of deployment of members of the armed forces on their dependent children* (Section 571). Retrieved from www.militaryonesource.mil/12038/MOS/Reports/ Report_to_Congress_on_Impact_of_Deployment_on_Military_Children.pdf

US Department of Defense Demographics (2009). *A profile of the military community.* Retrieved from www.militaryhomefront.dod.mil

Van Horn, P. (2012). Child–parent psychotherapy. In C. H. Zeanah Jr. (Ed.), *Handbook of infant mental health* (pp. 439–443). New York: Guilford Press.

Vincenzes, K. A., Haddock, L., & Hickman, G. (2014). The implications of attachment theory for military wives: Effects during a post-deployment period. *Professional Counselor, 122.*

Weiss, E. L. & Coll, J. E. (2013). Children and youth impacted by military service: A school-based resilience building and behavioral health perspective. In C. Franklin, M. B. Harris, & P. Allen-Meares (Eds.), *The school services sourcebook: A guide for school-based professionals* (2nd ed.) (pp. 695–706). New York: Oxford University Press.

Weiss, E. L. & DeBraber, T. (Fall 2012). *Child maltreatment in military families: Risk & resilience factors.* Washington, DC: NASW.

Weiss, E. L. & DeBraber, T. (2013). Women in the military. In A. Rubin, E. L. Weiss, & J. E. Coll (Eds.), *Handbook of military social work* (pp. 37–49). Hoboken, NJ: Wiley.

Zero to Three (2009). *Honoring our babies and toddlers: Supporting young children affected by a military parent's deployment, injury, or death.* Retrieved from: www.ok.gov/odva/documents/militaryparents.pdf

Zero to Three (2012). *Research and resilience: Recognizing the need to know more.* Retrieved from:www. zerotothree.org/about-us/funded-projects/militaryfamilies/march30researchandresilience.pdf

8

CARING FOR CAREGIVERS

Understanding and Helping Those Who Support the Veterans of Iraq and Afghanistan

Ilysa R. Michelson and Cory Chen

Understanding the Context of Caregiving for Iraq/Afghanistan Veterans

Most of us will take on the role of "caregiver" at some point in our lifetime. In 2014, 43.5 million Americans provided unpaid but essential care for partners, parents, and/or children. These caregivers spent an average of 18 hours a week providing care, including help or protection to assist someone with a medical or behavioral condition, personal needs, household chores, finances or other assistance (AARP Public Policy Institute; National Alliance for Caregiving, 2015). Caregiving can involve assisting loved ones in "Activities of Daily Living," the basic and essential tasks of everyday life, which include bathing, feeding, transferring, and others. Caregiving also extends to "Instrumental Activities of Daily Living" which involve tasks that support an individual's capacity to live independently such as meal preparation or management of finances (Lawton & Brody, 1969). Additionally, caregivers provide emotional and social support in both times of crisis and in managing chronic stressors. Today's caregivers often manage a range of complex illnesses in the home. In fact, three in five care recipients have a long-term physical condition (59%), more than one-third have an acute physical and condition (35%), and one-quarter have a memory problem (26%). Over one-third of care recipients have more than one chronic illness or problem (AARP Public Policy Institute; National Alliance for Caregiving, 2015).

The population of individuals caring for Veterans of the wars in Iraq and Afghanistan has grown immensely, now nearing approximately 1.1 million. Often referred to as "Post 9/11 caregivers" or "OEF/OIF/OND caregivers" (Operation Enduring Freedom/Operation Iraqi Freedom/Operation New Dawn), this group of Iraq and Afghanistan "Veteran caregivers" is unique in several ways. They tend to be younger than the average American caregiver, with more than 40% between the ages of 18–30. They are likely to be caring for children as well as the Veteran. And they are more likely to be Veterans themselves. Additionally, these caregivers may maintain their caregiving role for longer periods of time due to the relative youth of these Veterans. Most notably, in addition to caring for Veterans with more obvious physical disabilities, these caregivers are also often caring for injuries that have not been as well studied in the caregiving literature and may be less visible, such as post-traumatic stress disorder (PTSD), depression, or substance abuse. One-third of Iraq/Afghanistan Veteran caregivers are spouses, one-quarter are parents, and approximately one-quarter are unrelated neighbors or friends. Siblings, partners, or other relatives also serve as post 9/11 caregivers in smaller numbers. These caregivers most often report needing the following: knowledge about their Veterans' condition, strategies to provide better care and effectively advocate for their Veterans' healthcare needs, help with housing and financial difficulties, assistance with future planning, and ways to take care of themselves as caregivers (Ramchand et al., 2014).

Many healthcare or behavioral health providers outside of military, Department of Defense (DoD), or Veterans Affairs (VA) settings have little specialized training in how to support caregivers of recently returning Veterans. In this chapter, we address the unique challenges of many Veteran caregivers, who not only struggle to meet the physical needs of recently returning service members, but also often manage the less visible challenges related to adjustment to civilian life. These may include the ruptures of relationships and family structure, identity and spiritual challenges after returning from a war zone, serious mental health conditions, and the difficulty of navigating healthcare that may not be specific to a Veteran population. Our goal is to guide healthcare workers in providing support to this unique but growing group of caregivers. Numerous anecdotes and case examples will be provided to illustrate common struggles that Veteran caregivers express. All names have been changed to preserve anonymity, and the situations described represent the aggregate experiences of numerous caregivers of Iraq or Afghanistan Veterans. Throughout this chapter, we use the terms "Post-9/11 Veteran caregivers," "OEF/OIF/OND caregivers," and "Caregivers of Iraq or Afghanistan Veterans" interchangeably, to reflect current terms used in the literature. We have also included several assessment tools and resources healthcare workers may use to ask pertinent questions, elicit more information, and suggest referral sources to help our Veteran caregivers in healthcare or home settings. While these resources are most relevant for treating caregivers of Veterans, we think they may also be valuable for those working with caregivers in the general population.

The main questions we hope to address in this chapter are: (1) What are the common problems Iraq/Afghanistan caregivers face? and (2) What are the best ways of addressing their needs? The next section will present an overview of the caregiver experience, followed by a discussion of the types of physical daily caregiving tasks that caregivers may be faced with when assisting an OEF/OIF/OND Veteran. Next we will discuss the potential mental health issues Veterans may experience, and how to assess and assist them and their caregivers in a brief healthcare or counseling interaction. We will provide tips throughout the chapter to help counselors ask questions to elicit the information you need to address and steer a caregiver toward relevant resources. Finally, we discuss some lessons learned from our experiences and research, and guide you to additional information about VA programs for Iraq/Afghanistan Veterans and their caregivers.

The Caregiver Experience: Who Are They and What Challenges Do They Face?

The role of Veteran caregivers is, in some ways, a specialized one, which many family members and friends may feel unprepared to handle. Caregivers of civilians are most likely to be managing chronic illnesses and those related to older age, such as dementia (including Alzheimer's), or long-term medical problems and disabilities. Many injuries for which Iraq/Afghanistan Veterans require care are quite different, as are the early age at which many of these Veteran caregivers start their roles. In a sample of Veteran caregivers enrolled in the Department of Veterans Affairs (VA) Caregiver Support Program, all of whom provide care for seriously injured Iraq/Afghanistan Veterans, 63% of caregivers were under 40 years old, significantly younger than the average age of civilian caregivers (approximately 50 years old) (US Department of Veterans Affairs, 2015). A large number of post-9/11 caregivers are spouses or partners and are typically women, 39% of post-9/11 Veteran caregivers have children living in the home, adding to financial burdens, creating potential power struggles, and leading to additional caregiving responsibilities. Due to the younger age of Iraq/Afghanistan Veterans, many have not been married or in partnerships with the Veteran for long periods of time, and thus in some cases, may not have had the long relationship history with the Veteran care recipient that civilian caregivers often do with their care recipients. Frequent or numerous deployments resulting in separations during military tours of duty, as well as pressured courtships further contribute to the more limited time post-9/11 caregivers and their Veterans have had together before transitioning to this new relationship dynamic.

The significant shifts for caregivers and Veterans as they inhabit new social and household roles can be trying. For example, the identity shift from breadwinner to care recipient, or from friend to caregiver may be a profound and stressful one, inevitably changing the relationship dynamic. These factors, in addition to the higher rates of preexisting family instability and mental health problems in the Iraq/Afghanistan Veteran population, appear to increase the likelihood of marital distress when these inevitable stressors occur. When compared with pre-9/11 caregivers and civilians, post-9/11 caregivers also reported lower relationship quality with their spouses or partners (Ramchand et al., 2014).

Many caregivers work full or part-time jobs out of financial necessity, as they are rarely compensated for their caregiving responsibilities. While there is a federal program administered through the VA which provides post-9/11 caregivers support and payment for the daily aid they provide, many are not aware of, or connected to, these resources. Additionally, communities vary in the range of supportive programs available to caregivers, and the lack of consistency can create confusion for those trying to navigate the system (see Assessment Tool at the end of this chapter for national and community caregiver resources). For all of these reasons, many caregivers must be employed outside of the home. Some caregivers report that it is a relief to have a professional identity and time away from their role as caregiver. Although the literature on the relationships between multiple life roles – for example, professional accountant, wife, mother – on stress is complex, it does appear to have the potential for both detrimental and beneficial effects (Martire, Stephens, & Townsend, 2000). Thus, Veteran caregivers are often juggling these multiple roles and can struggle with unmanageable logistical and relationship stressors, and may be in desperate need of support. It is especially important for healthcare providers to find out about the additional responsibilities a Veteran caregiver may have that could be heightening their experience of "caregiver burden," which increases the likelihood of burnout and emotional detachment (US Department of Veterans Affairs, 2015).

Leanne, the wife and caregiver for her 36-year-old Veteran husband, notes the numerous roles she has in her family in addition to caregiving, and the stresses and fears that result:

> Every morning, after washing up the kids, I bathe him and then get ready for work as a secretary. Then I have to stop feeling sorry for myself and put on my work hat. It's different now – sometimes those moments when I'm bathing him feel like the only intimacy we have left. I don't get to be the wife anymore like I imagined I would be. I worry about the future, thinking about raising my kids and trying to manage it all. But I try to let go of all that and just be practical. We need to make ends meet. At night the fears set in. I can't stop thinking about what would happen if I died. How would my family manage?

Veteran Readjustment to Civilian Life

Regardless of the condition in which a caregiver is helping a returning Veteran, all Veterans face the formidable challenge of readjustment and integrating back into civilian and family life. After living in unfamiliar settings, often for many years, Iraq and Afghanistan Veterans return to a home life that has adjusted to the absence of the military member. Frequently, both the Veteran and their family must work together to figure out how to integrate the Veteran back into a family system that has learned to function without them. Additionally, there are times when the behaviors that kept a solider alive in the battlefield, such as maintaining a high state of alertness and intense reactivity, may not translate well to the more mundane daily tasks of civilian life. Even in the case of unproblematic adjustment, a returning Veteran will struggle to adapt to a new daily pace, rhythm, and structure in their family, professional, and interpersonal life.

As they transition from their life as a soldier, Veterans may struggle with feeling misunderstood and disconnected from the concerns and problems of civilian life. They may be reluctant and unsure of how to share their military experiences with civilians whom they suspect cannot understand and so many Veterans begin to isolate themselves. The existential elements of war should not be ignored – the scope of combat, injury and death many Iraq/Afghanistan Veterans have been exposed to can be profound and life-altering and in fact are experiences that few civilians can relate to. For caregivers, a more nebulous challenge may be helping them communicate their support to their loved one without pressuring the Veteran to share details or implying they may ever fully understand their experience. Caregivers themselves may feel enormous stress as they adjust to the feeling (or reality) that their loved one's identity has shifted as they incorporate their war experience into their personal narrative. Referring a caregiver to psychotherapy can be essential in helping them to navigate the deep shift in identity for themselves and for their Veteran.

Caregiving and Veteran Physical Disabilities

For recently returning service members, devastating physical injuries and pain conditions are all too common. Of all injuries experienced by Iraq/Afghanistan Veterans, the vast majority are musculoskeletal. More than 80% of OIF/OEF/OND Veterans who are care recipients have a disability that impairs physical movement (Ramchand et al., 2014). Caregivers may be tasked with assisting their Veterans with problems related to back pain (more than 73% of post-9/11 Veteran care recipients), or joint pain (42% have knee impairment, 18% traumatic arthritis), frequently from carrying body armor and heavy supplies during their tours of duty. Some of the most visible injuries are, ironically, due to improved technologies. More Veterans than in any previous conflict are surviving serious, life-threatening combat injuries due to body armor and helmets made with bullet- and heat-resistant materials such as Kevlar. Additionally, fast-acting trauma teams are treating soldiers on the battlefield, getting the average soldier to a hospital within four days, compared with an average of 45 days during the Vietnam War era. For these reasons, over 90% of Veterans survive their combat wounds, the highest percentage in US history (Gawande, 2004).

The darker side to this survival rate is the high incidence of devastating head and limb injuries. More than 1,500 service members to this date (approximately 4%) have had amputations (Ramchand, et al., 2014) due to bomb and/or rocket attacks, including IEDs (improvised explosive devices), a signature weapon of the Iraq and Afghanistan wars (Gawande, 2004) and 15% of our post-9/11 Veterans have a spinal cord injury or paralysis (Ramchand et al., 2014);

37% of Veterans from these conflicts return with tinnitus, chronic ringing in the ears which is often associated with hearing loss, a condition which can trigger depression and difficulty functioning in social settings. Others return with concussions from the force of bomb blasts, as well as chronic headaches. There are also numerous physical conditions that are less understood but may result in significant disabilities, such as respiratory problems related to exposures at "burn pits," which are areas in Iraq and Afghanistan devoted to open-air combustion of trash. Additionally, it is important to recognize that physical disabilities often occur in conjunction with mental health issues, making the task of caregiving particularly challenging.

Rhonda, a caregiver for her 33-year-old OIF Veteran husband, describes the sometimes overwhelming nature of mental health and physical injuries when there are many other responsibilities:

> I am the wife of a disabled Veteran who has PTSD and terrible back and joint pain since coming back from Iraq in 2006. I just learned my husband will no longer be able to work because of his disabilities. That's a tough thing to take no matter your age, but when he's only 33, that's pretty impossible. We have 2 children, I have a part time job, and he isn't able to get around well by himself. He is angry a lot because he used to be the breadwinner and the head of the family. He is becoming more and more detached and frustrated, and why wouldn't he be? I am the one holding our family together now and I don't know how long I can do it anymore. My body is hurting from all the heavy lifting. He needs help going from his bed to his walker. Now I'm also the one doing all the home repairs, housework and physical labor to keep our home together. I don't have any time to myself. This was so NOT the plan I had for my life. All I want is to be alone.

Caregivers of Veterans with physical disabilities vary in their roles and responsibilities based on the nature of the injury or disability, the way that the Veteran is coping with that injury, and the resources available to support the caregiver. Asking caregivers about these areas in addition to asking what the caregiver is doing for the Veteran will allow healthcare providers to gain a better picture of the caregiver's tasks and what could be done to further support him or her. The nature of the specific injury and disability will often define the needs of the Veteran, such as assistance with specific tasks, management of pain, or modifications to living environments. Veterans vary in their ability and motivation to cope with these changes in functioning, particularly if they are also experiencing depression, anxiety, or PTSD. These conditions may interfere with their ability to function as independently as they might otherwise. Both Veteran and caregiver *strengths* as well as factors that may interfere with physical functioning and caregiving should be identified. Finally, caregivers vary in the range of resources available to them. Factors that influence this may include the services available in their community, differences in availability of social support networks, and differences in financial situations. Providers need to be mindful of these individual differences as they assess how best to assist the caregiver around managing the challenges faced as a result of Veteran physical disabilities.

Caregiving and Veteran Mental Health Challenges

In addition to these physical challenges, the "signature" injuries of the Iraq and Afghanistan wars are often invisible. The high incidence of PTSD, depression, substance abuse, and traumatic brain injuries (TBI) – sometimes occurring together – is a defining feature of these recent conflicts (Patel, 2015). Thus, in addition to the inevitable adjustment challenges of returning stateside, caregivers must sometimes adapt to a Veteran returning with a diagnosed mental health condition. Although estimates of the prevalence of mental health disorders vary depending on the sample studied, recent data found that 35% of OEF/OIF Veterans had received a mental health diagnosis: 21.5% had received a diagnosis of PTSD; 18.3% had been diagnosed with depression; and 8.4% had received substance use disorder diagnoses (Cohen et al., 2010). Additionally, the co-occurrence of multiple mental health issues is extremely common. For caregivers this means coping with Veterans' mental health symptoms that may seriously interfere with the ability to function in a work or school setting, and/or maintain satisfying social or family relationships. Caregivers are often tasked with assisting their Veteran in managing emotions and daily experiences that the Veteran once took for granted, especially those that require tolerating frustration and stress, such as the emotions evoked during child care, waiting on lines, or making complex decisions. As PTSD, depression, or other mental health conditions cloud the emotional life of a Veteran, daily activities may begin to feel unmanageable. A retreat into solitude, while not effective in the long run, may feel like a more appealing choice for many Veterans.

While many returning Veterans are diagnosed with these mental health issues, many go undiagnosed and may avoid treatment, due to the stigma of mental health treatment or thoughts that acknowledging one's mental health problem equates to a mental "weakness." It is also common for Veterans to avoid treatment due to concerns about future job prospects, such as fears that the documentation of treatment may be used to imply a Veteran is "unfit" for a future career in law enforcement or the military. Below we describe some of the most common mental disorders that Veterans struggle with and their implications for caregiving.

Traumatic Brain Injury (TBI)

The reports of mild TBI in military personnel varies widely from 4.2% to 23% (Galarneau, Woodruff, Dye, Mohrle, & Wade, 2008). Common causes of TBI include blast injury caused by IEDs, vehicular accidents or crashes, fragment or bullet wounds, and falls (Nelson, Lamberty, Sim, Doane, & Vanderploeg, 2012). The cognitive impairment associated with TBI can manifest in a variety of ways and can include memory problems or lapses, balance problems or dizziness, sensitivity to bright lights, irritability, headaches, sleep problems, as well as changes in personality. Additionally, TBI appears to be significantly associated with other mental health issues including depression and PTSD.

The example of Dan, and his caregiver wife, Liz, illustrates some of the common challenges associated with TBI. Dan is a Veteran who lost consciousness during an IED explosion in Afghanistan. He struggles to remember his appointments and stay focused on tasks, often starting and then stopping tasks before completing them. Liz, his wife, notices that Dan often becomes frustrated and impatient with himself and has been growing increasingly depressed and withdrawn. Liz has had to take over many of the tasks that they once shared such as managing their finances, coordinating their kids' activities and schedules as well as Dan's own medical appointments. Dan often appears to want to help but has become unreliable in the tasks he takes on which frustrates both Dan and Liz. Dan is often depressed and angry as he wants to hold onto an image of himself as "capable and competent" but also recognizes that his efforts to manage the tasks that he once experienced as simple often result in more stress and frustration. Liz is unsure of how to think about Dan's continued desire to be involved and whether she should encourage or prohibit it and how to support Dan emotionally as he struggles to come to terms with this new level of functioning.

Caregivers of Veterans with cognitive impairment are often forced to take on an expanded range of responsibilities, as Veterans may no longer be able to function at work or assist with the everyday tasks involved in managing a household. Caregivers may also need to take on tasks that were once shared as well as new tasks to help Veterans better navigate their environment. These may include the range of responsibilities associated with managing a household, including finances, childcare, and coordinating and managing medical care. Caregivers can respond to the expanded responsibilities in a variety of ways and often have mixed feelings about the demands they face. Often caregivers feel stressed and overtaxed with their new responsibilities, particularly if the Veteran had previously handled certain responsibilities and the caregiver struggles to learn new skills to manage tasks previously handled by the Veteran. On the positive side, sometimes caregivers may also experience a sense of mastery and competence, particularly if they are able to competently take on these responsibilities. Caregivers must also face the range of emotions that come with facing and mourning the loss of the Veterans as they once were and the future with the Veteran that caregivers had imagined they might have.

Asking caregivers about the specific changes in Veteran cognitive functioning can help healthcare providers understand the nature of the challenges the caregiver is facing. Additionally, healthcare providers should encourage caregivers to have the Veteran's cognitive functioning evaluated – by a neurologist, psychologist specializing in neuropsychological testing, or by asking their primary care physician for a referral – so that they can better understand the pattern of strengths and weaknesses present, anticipate what to expect as the Veteran attempts to adjust to the demands of civilian life, and better understand the cause of the changes they might observe.

Post-traumatic Stress Disorder (PTSD)

PTSD is among the most common mental health issues faced by Veterans returning from Iraq and Afghanistan. Veterans with PTSD have experienced a traumatic event and display four types of symptoms: (1) re-experiencing; (2) avoidance; (3) negative changes in cognition and mood; and (4) changes in arousal and reactivity. Re-experiencing may include spontaneous memories of the trauma, nightmares about the trauma, or "flashbacks" which refer to moments of disorientation when the Veteran may feel or act as if they are experiencing the trauma again. Avoidance refers to the efforts many Veterans make to limit contact with things that would remind them of their trauma (e.g. people, places, or activities) as well as attempts to avoid remembering, thinking about, or feeling things that are associated with the trauma. Avoidance is among the most pernicious of PTSD symptoms as it temporarily relieves distress, but often maintains PTSD symptoms and robs Veterans of the rewarding aspects of their lives.

Many meaningful aspects of life may also remind the Veteran of their trauma, but avoiding these reminders often results in a shrinking of the Veteran's world as they withdraw from the people and activities that were once meaningful to them. Changes in cognition and mood associated with PTSD may include difficulty remembering aspects of the trauma; negative beliefs about themselves, others, or the world; distressing feelings like fear, anger, guilt or shame; detachment from others; and difficulty experiencing positive emotions or pleasure. Finally, changes in arousal and reactivity may include symptoms like being easily startled and hyper vigilant, irritability, reckless or self-destructive behavior, difficulties with concentration, or sleep difficulties (e.g. problems falling asleep or staying asleep).

Beyond the diagnostic criteria, a Veteran's sense of existential distress brought on by psychological trauma can be equally profound. David J. Morris, a war correspondent and Iraq Veteran with PTSD described his combat traumas as destroying "the fabric of time," corroding "everything that came before, eating at moments and people from your previous life, until you can't remember why any of them mattered" (Morris, 2015).

Providing care to a Veteran with PTSD can be extremely challenging. Many Veterans, in part due to the avoidance symptoms associated with the disorder, will not talk about the trauma they experienced directly and so caregivers may be at a loss as to how to explain the changes they observe in their loved one. Education about the signs and symptoms of PTSD can help caregivers make sense of what the Veteran is experiencing, allow for early detection and treatment, as well as allow the caregiver to better understand how to be most helpful to the Veteran. It is understandable that many caregivers might misinterpret a Veteran's disengagement and withdrawal from their relationship as a reflection of a shift in the Veteran's feelings about the caregiver. Many caregivers may fear that the Veteran no longer loves them or worry that the Veteran no longer feels invested in their family. Sometimes caregivers blame themselves and worry that they have done something wrong. Assisting caregivers to recognize the ways that PTSD may impact the Veteran's interpersonal experience may help caregivers shift these attributions and remain engaged in the Veteran's care.

Also, many well-meaning caregivers may exacerbate the Veteran's avoidance symptoms as they attempt to accommodate to the Veteran's desire to limit contact with situations that the Veteran finds upsetting (Fredman, Vorstenbosch, Wagner, & McDonald, 2014). Effective treatment of PTSD often depends on a Veteran gradually facing the situations that are anxiety provoking. These situations, which vary based on the nature of the trauma, may include being in crowds or tight spaces, driving, or loud noises. The situations often trigger anxiety and lead Veterans to avoid these situations, negatively impacting the Veteran's ability to function in society. A well-intentioned caregiver may attempt to help the Veteran avoid these upsetting situations, which may decrease the Veteran's distress in the short term, but, in the long run, this avoidance may result in the Veteran's world shrinking as they spend their days increasingly isolated. Avoiding these situations makes integrating back into civilian life, which necessarily requires interaction with individuals and groups of people outside the home, more difficult. It is tricky for caregivers to know how to balance being respectful and responsive to the Veteran's feelings while also not enabling behaviors that may ultimately maintain the disorder.

For example, Shania reported to her counselor that she has brought her Veteran husband, Ben, dinner in his room for the past four months because he has become increasingly anxious and irritable being outside of the home, and then was "less comfortable" eating at the family table. As a healthcare provider it is important to ask a caregiver not only which symptoms their Veteran experiences, but also *how* they are providing this support so they can be gently educated about effective interventions. In this case, slowly expanding Ben's social interactions rather than narrowing them, would be a way to slowly increase his exposure to stimuli that are uncomfortable, but essential, in improving his social functioning. Shania could be encouraged to ask the Veteran's mental health providers how best to support Ben's treatment and navigate these issues. Some mental health clinics even offer couples' therapy for PTSD or caregiver support groups that can directly address some of these challenges.

Finally, PTSD may sometimes be associated with violence and aggression. In the midst of a flashback, disoriented during a nightmare, or in a moment of heightened irritability and anger, some Veterans may become violent toward their caregivers or other family members. Healthcare providers should be attuned to this possibility and assess the caregiver's safety and the safety of other family members, particularly children. Helping caregivers create safety plans that identify high-risk situations, recognize signs of increased risk of violence, and map out what the caregiver can do to keep themselves and others safe is critical. Healthcare providers should also be familiar with laws regarding mandated reporting of abuse if children, elderly, or other vulnerable populations are involved.

Substance Abuse

Veterans have tended to use substances to "self-medicate" after exposure to combat or other war stressors. Among these Veterans, 11% have been diagnosed with a substance abuse disorder, most of which is accounted for by alcohol. For some Veterans, "binge drinking" – defined here as a pattern of drinking that brings blood alcohol concentration levels to 0.08 g/dL, typically after four drinks for women and five drinks for men in about two hours (National Institutes of Health, n.d.) – was part of military culture, sometimes a tool for relief from the daily stresses of combat or part of how soldiers bonded and socialized. After deployments and returning home, some Veterans describe alcohol abuse as a way to numb themselves from the persistent fear and agitation of PTSD, and a temporarily effective way to avoid the uncomfortable feelings associated with traumatic memories. It has been suggested that increased combat exposure and human trauma is associated with drinking greater quantities of alcohol and higher rates of abuse. Additionally, cannabis abuse has been increasing among the Veteran population (Bonn-Miller, Harris, & Trafton, 2012). Some Veterans have been found to use marijuana to cope with other psychiatric disorders like PTSD and studies are beginning to find significant negative effects of cannabis abuse including increased risk of depression and less improvement in Veterans undergoing PTSD treatment (Bovasso, 2001; Bonn-Miller, Boden, Vujanovic, & Drescher, 2013).

It is worth noting that Veterans may also be at risk after receiving prescription drugs from their healthcare providers. In particular, Iraq/Afghanistan Veterans receiving VA healthcare are prescribed opioid painkillers at high rates, often to appropriately address severely debilitating pain conditions. The darker side of opioid prescription is the high potential for abuse or addiction, a challenge that has led to much debate in the healthcare community. Clinicians, particularly those working with younger Veterans, struggle with the ethics of adequately managing a Veteran's pain condition while simultaneously limiting health risks. Risks of addiction or overdose are especially notable for Veterans with mental health diagnoses, as they tend to be prescribed opioids at significantly higher rates. In one study of more than 15,000 Iraq/Afghanistan Veterans, 17.6% with a mental health condition were prescribed opioid pain medication within one year of receiving a pain-related diagnosis, versus 6.5% of this cohort who did not have a diagnosed mental health condition. This is significant because Veterans receiving prescription opioids have more adverse outcomes, including accidents and overdoses, than those who are not prescribed opioid medications (Seal et al., 2012).

Caregiving for Veterans with substance abuse or addiction can be extremely stressful. Veterans with substance abuse or addiction can have varying levels of insight into the problems they are facing. Caregivers must vary the kind of communication, involvement, and support they provide to Veterans depending on what "stage of change" they are in (Miller & Rollnick, 2012). For example, Veterans who are not yet ready to acknowledge the negative impact their substance use has on their lives can be extremely frustrating to caregivers. At this stage, caregivers are often in danger of engaging in power struggles with Veterans around whether their substance use is a problem. Caregivers need guidance to support their Veterans' recognition of the impact of their substance use and help to keep themselves from shielding Veterans from the negative consequences of their substance use. Frequently, well-intentioned caregivers may "clean up" or "cover for" a Veteran's substance use, which may ultimately delay the Veteran's recognition of the problems and build increasing resentment in the caregiver.

Darren is the husband of Wendy, an Army Veteran, who has recently returned from Afghanistan. Darren has noticed that Wendy's drinking has increased significantly since returning from her deployment and he will often come home from work to find her passed out with empty whiskey bottles next to her. Despite multiple fights about her drinking,

Wendy is adamant that this is not a problem and she claims that she drinks just "a few" to relax. Darren has given up trying to talk with Wendy about her drinking and has instead started to get home from work early so that he can hide the bottles and take Wendy up to bed before their two teenage children get home from school. He often makes excuses to his kids or their friends telling them that Wendy has a headache and should not be disturbed. Increasingly, Darren is becoming resentful and frustrated and Wendy remains unaware of the negative consequences of her actions. Collaborating with the Veterans' mental health team may allow Darren to find ways to more effectively communicate with Wendy and to not protect her from the negative consequences of her actions so that she may begin to realize the negative effect that her drinking is having on her life.

Later on, as Veterans become more aware that their substance use is problematic and begin actively working on changing, caregivers may help to further problem-solve and facilitate the Veteran's efforts to avoid triggers or use alternative strategies to manage the situations when substance abuse most often occurs. Collaboration with the Veteran's treatment team throughout this process can be very useful as what would be most helpful will vary over time and depend on the unique relationship between the caregiver and the Veteran. Additionally, various community agencies such as Al-anon or Nar-anon provide support and guidance to family members caring for individuals with substance abuse disorders.

Major Depressive Disorder (MDD)

Another extremely common mental health condition experienced by returning Veterans is MDD, often commonly referred to as "depression," which is characterized by depressed mood and/or loss of interest in things that were once enjoyable. It is also associated with sleep difficulties, changes in weight, lack of energy, restlessness or feeling slowed down, feelings of worthlessness, difficulty concentrating, or recurrent thoughts of death or suicide. MDD is more than a temporary feeling of sadness, as Veterans suffering from MDD experience these symptoms most of the day, nearly every day for at least a two-week period. MDD is the most common psychiatric disorder in the world and the leading cause of disability (Blanco et al., 2010; WHO, 2011). Also, given its association with suicide, it is critical that caregivers are made aware of the signs and symptoms of the disorder as there are a number of highly effective psychotherapy treatments and antidepressant medications that have been developed for MDD. Additionally, there are some medical conditions, like hypothyroidism, that can cause symptoms that mirror MDD and if correctly identified are highly treatable.

Caregivers of Veterans with MDD may be unsure of how to help their loved one. Some may be surprised that upon finally returning home, some Veterans may appear sad and withdrawn. Caregivers can be made aware of the difficulties that Veterans face around the many transitions in role, environment, and culture that are associated with returning to civilian life (Blanco et al., 2010). Additionally, some Veterans may have experienced significant losses that are both concrete (e.g. fellow soldiers that may have been killed or friendships that are harder to maintain after returning from deployment) or symbolic (e.g. a loss of purpose, connection, identity). Once again, helping caregivers to recognize and understand these aspects of their Veterans' experience may help them to remain empathic and supportive. Additionally, caregivers of depressed Veterans need to take care of themselves and preserve their own lives, which may include maintaining friendships and routines, continuing with interests and hobbies, and setting appropriate limits on what the caregiver is and is not willing to do.

Also, many caregivers struggle with what to say in order to support Veterans with depression. They may find that their well-meaning attempts to be reassuring with statements like, "You'll be fine" or "God never gives you more than you can bear," do not seem to help and may lead the Veteran to feel unheard, patronized, or judged. Healthcare providers can help caregivers to identify and listen to the underlying feelings behind the Veteran's statements, validate the Veteran's experience, reassure the Veteran in the caregiver's willingness to be present and consistent, and know that sometimes empathic silence is the best response (Golant & Golant, 2007). Finally, encouraging caregivers to help Veterans obtain the necessary evaluation for medical issues as well as psychological treatment, if necessary, is important for successfully addressing MDD. Given the high frequency of suicide among Veterans, the next section will specifically attempt to provide further elaboration on the phenomenon, risk assessment, and treatment options to address suicidality for our Veteran population.

Suicidal Thoughts and Behaviors

Darien, brother of a 27-year-old female Veteran, assists her with caretaking for her 6-year-old child since she has been unable to work after returning from the Marines in 2009. He relates his experience of worrying about how to help her:

> My sister has been through a lot. She saw a lot of children being hurt and killed in Afghanistan during her tours there. But she also told me that what really destroyed her trust in people is that one of her officers raped her. She was never the same after that, since they were supposed to be the ones protecting her. She seems more withdrawn than ever before. She once said she feels so ashamed that she wishes she were dead. I don't know what to do. I try to tell her that she's okay now and she's safe, but she's stopped taking her medicine and she's been a lot quieter lately.

Darian's story is one that should trigger referrals for professional treatment. Suicide is a tragically common phenomenon among Iraq/Afghanistan Veterans, with an overall rate of 21.9 per 100,000 (not including active-duty service members). This is striking when compared with the overall rate of suicide in the US, which was reported as 12.6 per 100,000 in 2013 (American Foundation for Suicide Prevention, 2015). Suicidal thoughts and attempts are even more common, often fueled by high rates of depression, PTSD, substance abuse, and perception of identity loss – the diminishment of identity as a "strong" or "healthy" person, soldier, provider, breadwinner, and so on. Many healthcare workers are afraid to ask caregivers and Veterans about the presence of suicidal thoughts, intent, or plans. They worry that by bringing up questions about suicide that they might "plant" ideas which otherwise would not be there. The opposite, in fact, is true. Clinical practice and research suggests that honestly addressing suicidal thoughts and eliciting a person's reasons to live, along with discussing coping skills and social supports to get through crises, can be life-saving in some cases and decrease the likelihood of future attempts. Asking these questions is an essential part of an intake interview or brief encounter with a caregiver of a Veteran. It is particularly important for healthcare providers to recognize warning signs that Veterans (or caregivers) may be suffering from mental health issues that could result in dangerous or even life-threatening behaviors. Healthcare providers also serve an important function as they help caregivers to notice these signs in their Veterans so that they can get the care they need as quickly as possible.

Healthcare providers should describe warning signs of suicide to help caregivers remain aware of risk factors, which include talking about wanting to die or killing oneself, planning for ways to kill oneself (e.g. searching online, seeking access to pills, weapons, or other means), talking about feeling trapped, being in unbearable pain or hopeless, increased alcohol or drug use, or withdrawal from friends or family. These warning signs represent an "acute risk" of suicide, meaning that their presence signals a heightened risk based on the Veteran's current mental state. A comprehensive list of warning signs is available at www.suicidep reventionlifeline.org/GetHelp and may be a palatable take-home resource for a caregiver so they can remain aware of potential signs.

Additionally, caregivers should be made aware of "chronic risk" factors for suicide. These are characteristics of the Veteran that are relatively stable and although are not the "cause" of a suicide attempt, they do represent factors that are statistically associated with risk. For example, caregivers may keep in mind the helpful adage "past behavior is the best predictor of future behavior." In fact, a prior suicide attempt is among the strongest predictors of future suicide attempts. Additionally, prior history of psychiatric diagnoses, history of impulsivity, recent losses (e.g. physical, financial, or personal), family history of suicide, history of abuse, and health problems are all factors associated with increased risk of suicide. Finally, elderly or young adults, unmarried, white, male, living alone are also demographic factors associated with increased risk (Rudd et al., 2006). Protective factors that decrease the risk of suicide also exist and include social support, spirituality, sense of responsibility to family, positive coping skills, problem-solving skills, and a positive relationship with a mental health professional.

When meeting with a caregiver and Veteran, the healthcare provider should be sure to gently but openly ask about current suicidal thoughts. Even if a caregiver–Veteran dyad is not open to discussing specifics about suicide, it can be helpful to give the aforementioned resources if there should ever be a future need. For example, it can be helpful to offer information by saying "Please keep this on hand in case you ever meet someone who needs this information."

More importantly, giving information to a Veteran or any civilian caregiver allows them access to resources that can be used during an emotional crisis. The Veterans Crisis Line at 1-800-273-TALK (8255) – callers should press "1" to be connected directly to a VA professional – was developed to support Veterans experiencing any type of mental health or emotional crisis, not just a suicidal crisis. All calls are kept confidential. The VA also created a website to communicate with a professional online if that is preferred: www.Veteranscrisis line.net.

If you learn that a Veteran is experiencing acute risk of suicide, helping the caregiver get the Veteran to an emergency room for evaluation is critical. For Veterans with chronic suicidal thoughts or exhibiting suicidal signs or behaviors, it is an opportunity to connect that caregiver and Veteran with a qualified professional who can provide psychotherapy. A variety of psychotherapy approaches exist and are available in both group and individual formats. Encourage the caregiver to discuss the options available with the Veteran's medical team. Given the challenges faced by a recently returning Veteran, many Veterans feel most comfortable pursuing treatment through the VA or a clinic specifically for military and their families, where clinicians are familiar with the challenges faced by this population.

Caregiving for Veterans with Multiple Challenges

It is important to note that many Veterans present with multiple physical and mental health issues. A large number of Veterans who have PTSD, up to 22% (SAMHSA, 2012), also abuse alcohol or other substances to cope with their symptoms and find temporary relief. They may also be diagnosed with a combination of physical and mental health conditions that exacerbate difficulty functioning and leave them feeling unmoored or hopeless. Frequently, there is a complex relationship between various conditions that tend to occur at the same time. For example, a relatively high percentage of Iraq/Afghanistan Veterans have both MDD and PTSD. When both disorders are present, these Veterans are more likely to experience pain, including head, back and muscle aches. This presents additional challenges from a caregiving perspective, as Veterans with comorbid PTSD/MDD also report higher levels of depression, trauma symptoms, service-connected disability, and unemployment than Veterans with either with PTSD or MDD alone (Runnals et al., 2013). For healthcare providers, this highlights the importance of an integrated approach to treatment, intervening in practical ways that may increase a sense of purpose and competence in the Veteran, as well as with pharmacological and psychological treatments.

Monica notes her efforts to understand her husband, David, who returned from combat with severe PTSD and substance abuse:

> Every time he sees a piece of trash or a ditch in the road he freezes. He has nightmares that are so bad he hides under a mat while he sleeps. I hear him crying out at night. He told me that before he met me, he drank 10 shots of whisky every night to so he didn't have to feel anything. But since he stopped drinking (I made him stop, or else I wouldn't marry him) he hides in the basement most of the day. I think it's because it's too upsetting for him to see all the media coverage of the Middle East and things outside that remind him of being in combat. Every time I ask him about it he zones out, stops talking to me. I'm afraid I'm losing him.

When Veterans present with multiple issues, helping caregivers identify and prioritize the various issues can be important. Collaborating with the caregiver on identifying what issues are most important to the Veteran, as well as to them as the caregiver, and providing information regarding areas that caregivers may not have recognized as potential targets of intervention can be important clinical interventions.

Lessons Learned and Additional Resources Available to Veterans and Their Caregivers

In conclusion, it is important to remember that a variety of services are available to US Veterans and their caregivers, and being aware of these resources can be extremely helpful to caregivers and other healthcare providers. The VA provides individual and group psychotherapies – with clinics specializing in PTSD, traumatic brain injury, and readjustment for returning Iraq/Afghanistan Veterans – and this is care that combat Veterans are entitled to receive through legislation (the Caregivers and Veterans Omnibus Health Services Act of 2010). If a Veteran feels stigma related to pursuing mental health treatment, the VA provides Primary Care Mental Health (PCMH) Integration at all medical centers. When a Veteran attends a primary care appointment, the Veteran or caregiver can mention to the physician that the Veteran is experiencing mental health symptoms, and the Veteran can be seen right away (usually the same day) by a mental health provider on-site. Through the VA Caregiver Support Program (see the Assessment Tool at the end of this chapter for additional resources), all *caregivers* are also entitled to free individual or group psychotherapy to address caregiving stressors and their own mental health conditions. As of the writing of this chapter, free respite care is also available to caregivers, so that they may take a break and receive support while a trained professional cares for their Veteran. Information about enrolling a caregiver in this program is provided in Table 8.1 at the end of this chapter, accessible with the link next to "Department of Veterans Affairs, Caregiver Support website."

TABLE 8.1 Resources for Caregivers of Post 9-11 Veterans

Resource / program	Description	Website
Caregiver Resource Directory	This directory includes the most commonly referenced resources for caregivers of recovering Service members, most at the national level	http://warriorcare.dodlive.mil/files/2015/04/April-2015-Caregiver-Resource-Directory.pdf
Department of Veterans Affairs, Caregiver Support website	Provides information and links to resources for post-9/11 caregivers, including the VA's Caregiver Support Program	www.caregiver.va.gov
National Alliance on Caregiving	Research, advocacy and policy related to caregiving. Resources for professionals and caregivers	www.caregiving.org
Veterans Crisis Line	Confidential support 24 hours a day, 7 days a week, 365 days a year. Support for deaf and hard-of-hearing individuals is also available	www.Veteranscrisisline.net
Veterans Affairs' Caregiver Benefits & National Support Line	Financial and emotional support and information for Veterans, active-duty service members and their caregivers	www.realwarriors.net/family/support/caregiversupport.php
Vet Center Programs	Information about "Vet Centers," where combat Veterans and/or survivors of military sexual trauma can receive free counseling	www.vetcenter.va.gov
Operation Homefront	Financial, food, housing and other practical assistance for military families and returning Veterans	www.operationhomefront.net
Easter Seals Dixon Program for Military & Veterans Services	Advocacy and training programs for caregivers of Veterans	www.easterseals.com/our-programs/military-Veterans
Family of a Vet	Resources and online support for families of returning Veterans	http://familyofavet.com
PTSD Coach (mobile app)	Free mobile application that teaches about managing symptoms occurring after trauma	www.ptsd.va.gov/public/materials/apps/PTSDCoach.asp

Resource/ program	Description	Website
Wounded Warrior Project	Advocacy and a range of programs for professional development, readjustment, rehabilitation, and mental health issues of Veterans	www.woundedwarriorproject.org
National Alliance on Mental Illness	Education, advocacy, and support including a Helpline for families of individuals with mental illness	www.nami.org
Al-Anon	Organization that provides support for friends and families of individuals with alcohol use problems	http://al-anon.org
Nar-Anon	Organization that provides support for friends and families of individuals with substance use problems	www.nar-anon.org

Our hope for this chapter is that it provides an accessible and pragmatic overview of the various things to consider in caring for those who care, the families of those who support US Veterans. One of the challenges we face as clinicians and program administrators is that the experience of post-9/11 caregivers is highly varied. Given our effort to make this chapter relatively brief, we focus on the challenges faced rather than the joys and meaning that caregivers often derive from their relationships with Veterans. We realize this as a limitation of what we present but hope that readers will recognize that caregiving can also be a powerful and rewarding experience. That said, given the range of complex issues that Veterans may experience while on active duty (or may have had prior to their military service) and the unique characteristics of the couple, family, and community that Veterans return to after military service, a comprehensive assessment of these variables is critical to understanding how healthcare providers can be most helpful to the caregiver and the Veteran. In general, caregivers will benefit from additional information about the problems that the Veteran may be experiencing, the resources available to address the Veteran's specific problems, and the importance of caregiver self-care. The solution to any given issue often involves collaboration between medical and mental health services, community services, and family coordination and support. Caregivers often require assistance in navigating these complicated systems. This is where healthcare and behavioral health providers can help.

Many caregivers can also benefit from help in navigating their daily interactions with the Veteran. Often, caregivers' well-meaning efforts to support the Veteran and minimize their stress can paradoxically exacerbate or maintain Veterans' difficulties. Thus, the caregiver's love and willingness to support Veterans is critical, but not enough, and may sometimes even backfire. Collaboration with the Veteran's healthcare or behavioral health providers can help caregivers ensure that their dedication fuels efforts that move the Veteran's life *forward* rather than inadvertently holding them back. The Assessment Tool offers a brief guide to assess a caregiver's and Veteran's functioning, challenges, and coping skills. This may be particularly helpful if healthcare or behavioral health providers only have a single or infrequent interaction with a caregiver–Veteran pair. In this brief assessment tool, we offer concrete suggestions for how to ask caregivers difficult questions and also recommend resources to assist them.

As healthcare providers increasingly begin to work more with caregivers and their Veterans, it is essential to remember that ambivalence is a normal part of the caregiving experience. We should expect that caregivers will experience a full range of feelings their role, including love, dedication, pride, obligation, sadness, resentment, frustration, loss, and sometimes hopelessness. Even if caregivers are not voicing these feelings directly, it can be helpful for healthcare providers to normalize and provide supportive services for caregivers in anticipation of these experiences. Acknowledging these feelings can help caregivers to recognize their limits, take better care of themselves, and get the help that they need in order to continue to provide the invaluable care they do to these US heroes.

Getting to Know You and Your OEF/OIF/OND Veteran: Brief Caregiver Assessment Tool

Many people feel stress in their role as a caregiver. We would like to help identify the areas that are the most distressing to you, in order to guide your treatment. Note to clinician: *Circle items that caregiver endorses or is concerned about, for follow-up. Italics indicate examples, or topics to pay attention to.*

Understanding the Context of Caregiving

- To begin, please tell me how things have been going as you try to take care of (Veteran name). What stresses you out most these days? Please also share which aspects of your life are going well.

Factors to Pay Attention to

1. *Feelings of uncertainty about how to best help*
2. *Changes in roles*
3. *Struggles around Veteran-specific issues*
4. *Getting the Veteran the mental or physical healthcare that he/she needs*
5. *Both the most stressful aspects of the caregiver's life as well as potential areas of strength*
6. *Environmental issues (unstable, unsafe housing, or not adapted for disability)*

- What is your social network like? Do they provide you with the support you need?

Factors to Pay Attention to

1. *Sources of support*
2. *Sources of additional conflict*

Follow up with questions about family, friends, colleagues, military organizations, spiritual communities, etc. if relevant.

- In addition to (the Veteran) are there others who you are involved in helping to care for (e.g. kids, parents, friends, other family) him/her?
- Tell me a little about the other responsibilities in your life and the things you are involved in (e.g. work, spiritual institutions, community involvement)?
- Do you have any medical or mental health issues that I should be aware of?
- What medical or psychological services or community agencies are currently helping you to care for him/her?

Follow-up Questions, If Needed

- Are you connected with VA healthcare (at a hospital, clinic or Vet Center)?
- Are you connected with any treatments or support groups that help with your coping skills or mood?

Understanding the Veteran's Readjustment to Civilian Life

- Since (the Veteran) has returned home, have there been any challenges the two of you have faced adjusting to life with him home?

Factors to Pay Attention to

1. *Shifting responsibilities and roles*
2. *Incongruent expectations of what the Veteran's return would be like*
3. *Veteran difficulties adjusting to pace, rhythm, structure of civilian life*

- How do you and (Veteran name) communicate about issues that come up? Please tell me about any trouble you may have talking about your worries or getting those issues addressed.

Factors to Pay Attention to

1.   *Veteran barriers (e.g. not expressing his/her feelings, angry reactions)*
2.   *Caregiver barriers (e.g. fears of upsetting the Veteran, difficulty knowing what to say)*
3.   *Situational barriers (e.g. finding the time to talk, interference of other family members)*
4.   *Cultural factors (e.g. Military culture, gender roles, religious beliefs)*
5.   *Violence in the home (physical, sexual, emotional)*
6.   *Financial stress*

- How do you feel you've been coping with the stress of caregiving?

Follow-up Questions, If Needed

- *How do you relieve your stress? (positive examples may be exercise, talking with others, spiritual activities, hobbies, etc.)*
- *How are you managing your own healthcare needs?*
- *How have you been feeling lately given (insert significant stressors mentioned above)?*

Follow-up Questions, If Needed

- Have you been feeling sad or depressed lately?
- Have you had any difficulties sleeping?
- Do you ever feel anxious or worried?
- Do you ever find yourself feeling angry or resentful?
- Do you feel like you don't have enough time to yourself?
- Do you ever feel burnt out?
- Do you ever feel hopeless?
- Any feelings of shame or guilt?
- Do you ever find yourself crying more than usual?
- Do you ever have thoughts of hurting yourself or killing yourself? (if yes, discuss safety planning and/or refer to mental health provider)
- Are you concerned about any sexual difficulties?

If yes to any of the above, say: Our emotional and physical health is connected, so it is important to get the support you need to keep your mind and body strong. May I share some resources that might help? (*See Table 8.1, for resources.*) *If caregiver declines, offer your contact information for future follow-up.*

Understanding the Caregiving Tasks/Roles for Physical Disabilities

- Many caregivers help with Veterans' physical, mental health, or organizational challenges. Please tell me about the ways you're involved in helping (Veteran name). Of the things you've just described, what is most stressful?

Examples, If Needed

- Does he/she have a physical injury?
- Does he/she use a prosthetic device, or other medical equipment?
- Does he/she have an amputation?
- Does he/she have chronic pain, or pain that interferes with his/her life?
- Does he/she need assistance with feeding?
- Does he/she need assistance taking medication?
- Does he/she need help getting to medical appointments?
- Does he/she need help bathing and/or toileting?
- Does he/she need help with grooming?
- Does he/she need significant help with childcare?
- Do you manage many household tasks (laundry, shopping, cleaning)?

Understanding Veteran Mental Health Challenges

- Many Veterans struggle to manage their emotions, including anger, sadness, or others. Have you noticed this with your Veteran? Please tell me what this looks like for him/her.

Examples, If Needed

- Does he/she have difficulty managing his/her anger, frustration, or mood swings?
- Does he/she have any memory problems, difficulty concentrating, or problems managing things he/she used to be able to manage?
- Does he/she seem emotionally numb or disconnected?
- Does he/she have frequent nightmares?
- Does he/she avoid things that remind him/her of his military experiences?
- Does it feel like he/she has frequent emotional crises?
- Does he/she drink more alcohol than you think he/she should?
- Are you concerned about his/her drug use (including prescription drugs)?
- Does he/she seem sad or down?
- Does he/she not seem to enjoy the things that he/she used to?
- Does he/she have trouble sleeping many nights?
- Has he/she ever done anything to hurt him/herself?
- Has he/she ever talked about wanting to hurt him/herself?

Offer resources in Table 8.1, emphasizing that both Veterans and caregivers often need support.

Other: Are there any other concerns you have about caregiving that I haven't asked about?

For more information on coping with caregiving stress, see the VA caregiver support program www.caregiver.va.gov or call 1-855-260-3274. If you are in emotional crisis, call: 1-800-273-8255.

References

AARP Public Policy Institute; National Alliance for Caregiving (2015, June). *Executive summary: Caregiving in the US*. Retrieved July 30, 2015, from: www.caregiving.org/wp-ontent/uploads/2015/05/2015_CaregivingintheUS_Executive-Summary-June-4_WEB.pdf

American Foundation for Suicide Prevention (2015). *Understanding suicide: Facts and Figures*. Retrieved from: https://s3-us-west-2.amazonaws.com/afsp120/AFSP_PDF_ForWebsite/AFSP_PDF_ForWebsite/book.swf

Blanco, C., Okuda, M., Markowita, J. C., Liu, S., Grant, B., & Hasin, D. (2010). The epidemiology of chronic major depressive disorder and dysthymic disorder: Results from the national Epidemiologic Survey on Alcohol and Related Conditions. *Journal of Clinical Psychology*, 71(12), 1–47.

Bonn-Miller, M., Boden, M., Vujanovic, A. A., & Drescher, K. D. (2013). Prospective investigation of the impact of cannabis use disorders on posttraumatic stress disorder symptoms among veterans in residential treatment. *Psychological Trauma: Theory, Research, Practice, and Policy*, 5(2), 193.

Bonn-Miller, M. O., Harris, A. H., & Trafton, J. A. (2012). Prevalence of cannabis use disorder diagnoses among veterans in 2002, 2008, and 2009. *Psychological Services*, 9(4), 404–416.

Bovasso, G. (2001). Cannabis abuse as a risk factor for depressive symptoms. *American Journal of Psychiatry*, 158(12), 2033–2037.

Cohen, B., Gima, K., Kim, S., Marmar, C. R., & Seal, K. H. (Jan 2010). Mental health diagnoses and utilization of VA non-mental health medical services among returning Iraq and Afghanistan veterans. *Journal of General Internal Medicine*, 25(1), 18–24.

Family Caregiver Alliance (2012, December 31). *Selected Caregiver Statistics*. Retrieved July 31, 2015, from: https://caregiver.org/selected-caregiver-statistics

Fredman, S. J., Vorstenbosch, V., Wagner, A., & Macdonald, A. (2014). Partner accommodation in posttraumatic stress disorder: Initial testing of the significant others' responses to trauma scale (SORTS). *Journal of Anxiety Disorders*, 28(4), 372–381.

Galarneau, M., Woodruff, S. I., Dye, J. L., Mohrle, C. R., & Wade, A. L. (2008). Traumatic brain injury during Operation Iraqi Freedom: Findings from the United States Navy-Marine Corps Combat Trauma Registry. *Journal of Neurosurgery*, 108, 950–957.

Gawande, A. (2004). Casualties of war – Military Care for the wounded from Iraq and Afghanistan. *New England Journal of Medicine*, 351, 2471–2475.

Golant, M. & Golant, S. K. (2007). *What to do when someone you love is depressed* (2nd ed.). New York: Holt.

Lawton, M. & Brody, E. M. (1969). Assessment of older people: Self-maintaining and instrumental activities of daily living. *Gerontologist*, 9(3), 179–186.

Martire, L., Stephens, M. P., & Townsend, A. L. (2000). Centrality of women's multiple roles: beneficial and detrimental consequences for psychological well-being. *Psychology and Aging*, 15(1), 148.

Miller, W. & Rollnick, S. (2012). *Motivational interviewing: Helping people change* (3rd ed.). New York: Guilford Press.

Morris, D. J. (2015). *The evil hours*. Boston: Houghton Mifflin Harcourt.

National Institutes of Health (n.d.). *National Institute on Alcohol Abuse and Alcoholism: Drinking levels defined*. Retrieved from: www.niaaa.nih.gov/alcohol-health/overview-alcohol-consumption/moderate-binge-drinking

Nelson, N. W., Lamberty, G. J., Sim, A. H., Doane, B. M., & Vanderploeg, R. D. (2012). Traumatic brain injury in Veterans. In *Neuropsychological practice with Veterans* (ch. 5). New York: Springer.

Patel, B. (2015). Caregivers of Veterans with invisible injuries: What we know and implications for social work. *Social Work*, 60(1), 1–9.

Ramchand, R., Tanielian, T., Fisher, M. P., Vaughan, C. A., Trail, T. E., Epley, C., et al. (2014). *RAND health*. Retrieved July 28, 2015, from Summary: 2014 RAND corporation study, "hidden heroes: America's military caregivers": www.rand.org/content/dam/rand/pubs/research_reports/RR400/RR499/RAND_RR499.pdf

Rudd, M. D., Berman, A. L., Joiner, T. E., Nock, M. K., Silverman, M. M., Mandrusiak, M., Witte, T. et al. (2006). Warning signs for suicide: Theory, research, and clinical applications. *Suicide and Life-Threatening Behavior*, 36(3), 255–262.

Runnals, J., Voorhees, E. V., Robbins, A. T., Brancu, M., Straits-Troster, K., Beckham, J. C., et al. (2013, August 7). Self-reported pain complaints among Afghanistan/Iraq era men and women Veterans with comorbid posttraumatic stress disorder and major depressive disorder. *Pain Medicine: Psychology, Psychiatry & Brain Section*, 1529–1533.

SAMHSA (n.d.). Retrieved August 6, 2015, from National Suicide Prevention Lifeline: www.suicidepreventionlifeline.org

SAMHSA, Knowledge Application Program (2012, Summer). *Behavioral health issues among Afghanistan and Iraq US War Veterans*. Retrieved July 30, 2015, from: http://store.samhsa.gov/shin/content/SMA12-4670/SMA12-4670.pdf

Seal, K., Shi, Y., Cohen, G., Cohen, B. E., Maguen, S., Krebs, E. E., et al. (2012). Association of mental health disorders with prescription opioids and high-risk opioid use in US Veterans of Iraq and Afghanistan. *JAMA*, 307(9), 940–947.

US Department of Veterans Affairs (2015, June 3). Services for family caregivers of post-9/11 Veterans. Retrieved August 6, 2015, from: www.caregiver.va.gov/support/support_benefits.asp

World Health Organization (2011). Depression. What is depression?, WHO, Geneva: Switzerland. Retrieved from: www.who.int/mental_health/management/depression/definition/en

9

UNDERSTANDING OUR MILITARY SURVIVORS OF SEXUAL ASSAULT

Kristi L. Mueller

Current data has revealed that more service members are making reports of sexual assault (US Department of Defense, 2015). As more service members come forward seeking help, the need is increasing for providers to be well informed of the assessment and treatment of these experiences and the effects on mental health, physical health, and overall well-being. This chapter aims to inform and update clinicians about the experience of sexual trauma in military members, both male and female.

Background

Definitions

Sexual harassment and sexual assault have specific legal definitions that may differ across settings, but for the purposes of clinical intervention, definitions arising from a behavioral health perspective will be used in this discussion. From a clinical perspective, *sexual harassment* refers to an unwanted sexual experience that occurred in the workplace. Within the military context, *the workplace* is broadly defined since the military is a 24/7 occupation and oftentimes military members work and live in the same geographical location. This is especially the case during military deployments and at times it may be difficult to escape sexually harassing behavior. From a legal perspective, unwanted sexual experiences become sexual harassment when the behaviors create an intimidating, hostile, or offensive working environment (US Equal Employment Opportunity Commission, 1990). This broad range of behaviors may include sexually offensive comments (e.g., "catcall" whistles as you walk by, or repeated comments about wanting to "hook up" or "hit that") or the display of sexually demeaning objects (e.g., pornographic materials).

Sexual assault is defined as "intentional sexual contact characterized by use of force, threats, intimidation, or abuse of authority or when the victim does not or cannot consent. Sexual assault includes rape, forcible sodomy (oral or anal sex), and other unwanted sexual contact that is aggravated, abusive, or wrongful (including unwanted and inappropriate sexual contact), or attempts to commit these acts" (Department of Defense Directive, 2012). One form of sexually harassing behavior that may not involve physical force involves *quid pro quo* (or "this for that") harassment; this can occur when there is a power differential between the individuals. This behavior consists of coerced sexual involvement through the promise of reward (e.g., a preferred job assignment), threats of punishment (e.g., a negative evaluation which may impact future promotions), or the abuse of authority (e.g., when a higher-ranking member makes sexual demands of a lower-ranking member). Sexual assault also includes forced sexual contact in situations where the victim does not or cannot consent (e.g., due to intoxication effects).

Another term that is important to be aware of is *military sexual trauma* (MST), defined by the Department of Veterans Affairs (VA) to refer to experiences of sexual assault or repeated, threatening sexual harassment that a Veteran experienced during his or her military service.

Prevalence

It is challenging to compare the prevalence rates of sexual assault in the military with those found in civilian populations due to the high variance of demographic and environmental factors (age, gender balance, education levels, duty hours, alcohol availability, and many other risk factors that differ between active-duty populations and comparison groups). However, comparisons have been made between different military components. The 2014 RAND Military Workplace Study (RMWS) found that active-duty Air Force service members experienced lower rates of sexual harassment and assault when compared with other branches of the military (Morral, Gore, & Schell, 2015). In contrast, a significantly higher proportion of women in the Marine Corps and Navy are estimated to have experienced a sexual assault in the past year than women in other services.

Common demographic trends are shared among all services. For both men and women, junior enlisted members (E1–E4) have the highest rates of sexual assault (1.4% of junior enlisted men and 7.3% of junior enlisted women). The majority (85%) of the assaults were committed by another member of the military, and over one-half of both men and women indicated that the offender was higher in rank than the victim.

According to the RMWS, rates of reported sexual harassment declined in active-duty women since 2012. No statistically significant change was noted in active-duty men. Recent estimates suggest that approximately 1.5% of the active-duty component population (approximately 20,300 service men and women) including Army, Air Force, and Marine Corps were sexually assaulted during 2014. This represents approximately 1% of men and 4.9% of women. Since there are more men than there are women serving in the US military, the number of men assaulted in the past year was higher than women (10,600 men reported sexual assault compared with 9,600 women). Notably, this data represents the number of active-duty service members who have experienced at least one sexual assault during 2014, rather than the number of sexual assault episodes. The actual number of sexual assault episodes during the time frame is estimated to be higher, approximately 2.5 incidents per 100 men and 9.6 incidents per 100 women (Morral et al., 2015).

Although military sexual trauma had been previously documented in Veterans of previous war eras (Skinner et al., 2000; Wolfe, Sharkansky, Read, Dawson, Martin, & Ouimette, 1998), Operation Enduring Freedom (OEF) and Operation Iraqi Freedom (OIF) Veterans are the first generation of Veterans Health Administration users to return from a large-scale deployment to such comprehensive screening and treatment services. Data from a large-scale study of 125,729 deployed OEF and OIF Veterans indicated that 15.1% of the women and 0.7% of the men endorsed sexual trauma during their military service (Kimerling et al., 2010). This study emphasizes the prevalence of sexual trauma during military service, both during peacetime as well as in deployed contexts.

Of the reported sexual assaults in 2014 across all military services, 43% of assaults against women and 35% of assaults against men were classified as *penetrative sexual assaults*. These figures are higher than previously estimated, especially among men. Higher numbers of reported assaults do not necessarily indicate a higher occurrence; rather, it indicates that the number of service members making reports is rising.

In addition to enhancing the formal reporting process, the Army's Sexual Harassment/ Assault Response and Prevention (SHARP) program has enhanced focus on increasing education and prevention efforts. In part, the increased awareness of inappropriate sexual behavior may be contributing to the rise of formal reports, especially with male victims.

The Experience of Sexual Assault

PFC SANDRA MILLER

PFC Miller was 19 years old and just arrived to her first duty station in the Army. She was happy to finally be on her own and living the dream, traveling the world. She was getting to know others in her unit and was excited to be invited to a barracks party in one of the other soldier's room. She felt special to be invited and to have free beer and alcohol, since she was underage. Later that night she was raped by another soldier in her unit. She was embarrassed and didn't remember much of the evening. Since she didn't want to get in trouble for underage drinking, she didn't report the assault and she didn't seek medical attention related to the assault. She became quiet, withdrawn, and over the course of the next year, she missed numerous days of work due to various medical ailments.

It is essential that clinicians realize the possible relationship between physical and psychological illness stemming from sexual trauma. Sexual assault victims tend to have more physical symptoms during the first year post-assault and symptoms may persist (Frayne et al., 1999; Golding, 1994; Skinner et al., 2000). Physical health symptoms and medical comorbidities include pelvic pain, menstrual problems, headaches, chronic fatigue, and having poorer overall health functioning and health satisfaction as compared with those who have not experienced sexual trauma (Kimerling, Gima, Smith, Street, & Frayne, 2007; Surís & Lind, 2008).

Mechanisms of physical illness vary from direct to indirect. Direct health effects of the assault include the contraction of a sexually transmitted infection/disease during the assault, sustainment of a physical injury, or pregnancy. Indirect health effects through behaviors can lead to future health problems such as tobacco use, substance use disorders, or high-risk sexual behaviors (e.g., multiple partners, unprotected sex, prostitution).

There is also literature suggesting physiologic mechanisms of physical illness, which may explain in part why sexual assault survivors have more physical illness. Traumatic exposure can produce lasting alterations in the endocrine, autonomic, and central nervous systems (Friedman, Charney, & Deutch, 1995; van der Kolk, 1996). Other research has documented the occurrence of complex changes in the regulation of stress hormones in trauma victims (Charney, Deutsch, Krystal, Southwick, & Davis, 1993; DeBellis & Putnam, 1994; Southwick et al., 1993). Additionally, abnormalities have been found in areas of the brain, especially the amygdala and the hippocampus (Bremner, Krystal, Southwick, & Charney, 1995; Bremner, Randall, Scott, et al., 1995), brain structures that create a link between fear and memory. Some of these physiological changes, such as the dysregulation of the hypothalamic–pituitary–adrenal axis (HPA) and adrenalin production dysfunction, can persist for years after the trauma (Resnick, Yehuda, Pitman, & Foy, 1995; Yehuda, 2002).

Survivors of sexual trauma also tend to have higher prevalence rates of depression, post-traumatic stress disorder (PTSD), difficulty readjusting after deployment, eating disorders, alcohol abuse, and other mental health comorbidities compared with those who have not experienced sexual trauma (Kimerling et al., 2007; Surís & Lind, 2008). Some of the general experiences may include strong emotions (sudden and intense emotional responses to benign stimuli); feelings of numbness (difficulty experiencing pleasant emotions); difficulty sleeping; difficulty with attention, concentration, and memory; substance abuse; hypervigilance; and difficulty with interpersonal relationships. Although many trauma survivors recover spontaneously without professional help and are remarkably resilient, others may experience some level of difficulty and functional impairment that develop into clinical disorders. Like many other behavioral health conditions, early intervention leads to improved outcomes.

In the case described above, PFC Miller was seen for various medical ailments over the course of a year. Although she was treated for legitimate medical conditions (pelvic pain, heavy menstrual bleeding, and persistent fatigue), she always suspected that her physician didn't believe her symptoms. Her experience following the sexual assault was focused around shame and avoidance. A year after the assault, she eventually presented to a behavioral health counselor after the recommendation of a friend. Although initially guarded and tearful, PFC Miller opened up to her counselor and eventually worked toward becoming more authentic with herself. She stated that the most beneficial thing was having a counselor who "didn't judge me." She noted the validation and unconditional support from the counselor to be the most healing part to her progress in therapy. This case is important to highlight because forming a trusting therapeutic relationship is essential when treating survivors of sexual assault. More will be discussed in the next section, below. Over time, her medical conditions were stabilized and she began to feel more like herself. Although she had some symptoms of both anxiety and depression, her core issues were based around self-worth and trust; through collaborative treatment planning, therapy focused on those key components. Her therapist utilized a combination of supportive therapy and cognitive behavioral therapy, and she responded well to treatment.

Military sexual trauma appears to be a unique predictor of psychiatric symptoms after controlling for combat exposure and other life stressors (Murdoch, Polusny, Hodges, & Cowper, 2006). In a study examining OEF/OIF Veterans, Kimerling et al. (2010) found that women who experienced MST were over three times more likely to be diagnosed with PTSD compared with women in the military who did not experience MST. Similarly, the researchers found that men who experienced MST were more than two times likely to be diagnosed with PTSD compared with men in the military who did not experience MST. These psychological illnesses may present in social settings as difficulty with trust, psychological defense mechanisms (repression, denial, or normalization of the trauma), poor self-esteem and body image, sexual problems, impulsivity, anger, work difficulties, and relationship problems (Katz, Cojucar, Beheshti, Nakamura, & Murray, 2012). As in the case of PFC Miller above, she withdrew from her peer group partly because she was unsure of who she could trust, and partly due to her lowered self-esteem following the assault. Eventually, treatment progress was evident when she subjectively "felt better" as well as when she resumed social interactions and relationships.

Treatment Recommendations

SGT. KENDRA JAMES

I didn't know what to do. I made an appointment with my primary care doctor and asked to get tested for any sexually transmitted diseases. I made an excuse and said that I just got a new boyfriend and just wanted to be safe. But I guess she figured me out. She was really nice. She asked me if someone hurt me. She reassured me that she was there to help me, and things were confidential. She even gave me a choice. She gave me options. I don't know why, but I felt safe talking to her. Then she recommended that I talk to a counselor. I can't explain why, but I trusted her. I felt like she took time with me, and it made it easier to open up about what really happened to me.

Considering the aforementioned physical and psychological effects associated with sexual trauma, early intervention is critical at preventing long-term illness. Both medical practitioners as well as behavioral health clinicians are encouraged to develop skills that allow them to inquire about sexual trauma in the least threatening way possible.

A pioneer in the field, Judith Herman (2015) discusses that the core experiences of psychological trauma are disempowerment and disconnection from others. Therefore, recovery from psychological trauma is based upon the empowerment of the survivor and the creation of new connections. She stresses the importance of the need for recovery to occur in the context of relationships rather than in isolation.

In her well-known book *Trauma and Recovery*, Herman (2015) proposed a three-stage model of recovery which has been widely recognized as the foundation of trauma treatment, and formed the basis of the *Expert Consensus Guidelines for Treatment of Complex PTSD in Adults* (Cloitre et al., 2012). The three stages of her model include: (1) establishing safety; (2) remembrance and mourning; and (3) reconnection with ordinary life.

Helping the Survivor Regain Control

It may help to provide survivors of sexual trauma with a choice. For example, the clinician might say, "You mentioned that since the incident, you've struggled with depression and difficulty with sleeping through the night. I recommend further treatment to discuss the incident, but it is *your* choice, and I fully support which ever decision you make."

Validating the survivor's experiences, both past and present, is a simple way to develop lasting rapport with the survivor. When Kendra James presented to her first behavioral health counseling session, she was open to receive support and care, thanks in large part to the primary care physician who referred her. Through discussion with the counselor, Kendra identified that she was placing erroneous blame on herself for the non-consensual sex with a male acquaintance whom she continued to work with. This guilt was leading to sleep impairment and she noticed slow withdrawal from her social network. Since she was unwilling to report the assault (despite the strong recommendation by the counselor), she continued to see the male offender daily in the workplace. Initially, Kendra felt like she was constantly being reminded of the incident, which led to further self-blame. To aid in Kendra's feeling of control and power, her counselor suggested a room make-over, which changed the environment of her surroundings. Kendra moved furniture, put artwork on the walls, and got new curtains.

She took control of something, and she felt empowered. Her counselor validated her motivation level and reminded Kendra that she was on the path of recovery; she was not letting the assault define her.

Helpful suggestions to avoid during clinical interviews or therapy sessions include: negative questioning (e.g., "you were never sexually assaulted, were you?"), labeling (e.g., "people like you"), implicit assumptions about the client (e.g., "she brought it on by drinking"), and controlling the session (e.g., the provider controlling the session with a loud voice, or allowing little time for the client to talk).

It is important that providers ensure that appropriate boundaries are set (and maintained) throughout the therapeutic process. As previously mentioned, recovery occurs best in the context of interpersonal connections. However, it is important for providers to carefully navigate the power differential within the therapeutic relationship, while gently setting limits when needed. Oftentimes, setting limits can be highly therapeutic and patient feelings can be validated. To prevent additional feelings of shame and punishment, the provider may consider gently (yet assertively) explaining the rationale for setting boundaries (e.g., limiting phone calls outside of true emergencies, minimizing unscheduled walk-in visits).

Navigating Through the Recovery Process

Generally, psychotherapy for sexual trauma often involves some or all of the following elements: addressing immediate health and safety concerns, normalizing post-trauma reactions by providing education about trauma and psychological reactions to traumatic events, providing the patient with validation, supporting existing adaptive coping strategies and facilitating the development of new coping skills, and exploring affective and cognitive reactions including fear, self-blame, anger, and disillusionment.

Although clinicians may prefer to follow empirical treatment models when treating certain behavioral health issues, there is no "one size fits all" treatment approach to treating sexual assault victims. Rather, the clinician should tailor the treatment approach to the individual's unique symptoms and needs. Although clinicians should be trained to recognize the unique experiences of various client backgrounds and cultural settings (e.g., male victims, military service members), the more important aspect of providing quality behavioral healthcare is the ability to appreciate the wide variability in responses to sexual assault.

Some victims prefer same-gender process groups whereas other victims may prefer a mixed-gender approach. Some victims explicitly do not want (or perhaps they are not ready for) group-based therapy; they prefer individual therapy only, to work through their sexual assault experience. Yet, there are others who prefer to solely address the *symptoms* of their sexual assault (versus the experience of the assault) and may want to focus only on the depression, insomnia, etc. Therefore, clinicians should be well versed in the general principles of trauma therapy, while maintaining the sensitivity and awareness of working with victims of sexual assault.

Revictimization

It is important for clinicians to be aware of the risk associated with revictimization. Rates of childhood abuse and other pre-military sexual trauma are higher in victims who experienced sexual trauma in the military (Coyle, Wolan, & Van Horn, 1996; Merrill et al., 1999). This is also true in civilian samples; childhood sexual abuse is associated with increased odds of being sexually victimized as an adult (Messman–Moore & Brown, 2004). However, a recent study suggests that high levels of maternal care may act as a protective factor against future revictimization among military service members (Wilson, Kimbrel, Meyer, Young, & Morissette, 2015). Therefore, it doesn't mean that all individuals with a history of childhood sexual abuse will become adult victims of sexual trauma. Once an individual has experienced sexual trauma in the military, they are statistically at higher risk for additional sexual trauma (Sadler, Booth, Cook, & Doebbeling, 2003) and women are more likely to experience more severe forms of *intimate partner violence* (Murdoch & Nichol, 1995).

Gender Differences

1LT. DAVID GREEN

1Lt. Green is a 25-year-old Caucasian unmarried Army Infantry Officer, recently returned from Afghanistan, who presented to the Behavioral Health Clinic at the recommendation of his primary care provider related to insomnia. During clinical interview, 1Lt. Green vaguely admitted to "having a lot on his mind" which sometimes interfered with sleep, but he emphasized his passion for leading soldiers. Being an Army Officer was his life dream and he was proud to serve. Although 1Lt. Green's platoon was exposed to several enemy engagements during the deployment, he proudly reported none of his men were wounded. During the interview, he repeatedly emphasized that he was a good leader and his motto was to "lead from the front" by setting a good example for his troops. He minimized his stress-related problems, but admitted to using alcohol and over-the-counter sleep medicine to fall asleep on a routine basis since he's been back. After rapport and trust were developed, 1Lt. Green disclosed that he had an unwanted sexual experience with another male during the deployment. The incident occurred late one evening on his way to the showers. He recalled the assault as "an out of body experience." Although 1Lt. Green was not under the influence of drugs or alcohol at the time, he recalled being unable to move and felt "frozen." Despite knowing that another man was on top of him, he "did nothing to get away"; this was the image that he thought about most. Although the rape occurred just that one time, he went through the remainder of the nine-month deployment afraid that it was going to happen again. He even questioned himself often about his sexuality. He asked himself, "Does this mean I'm gay? Did I send the wrong signal somehow? Did I bring this on myself?" 1Lt. Green was a physically strong, young, infantry officer. He "should've done something" was a thought that crossed his mind often, and continues to keep him up at night.

Although men and women experience many of the same psychological difficulties following sexual assault or trauma, they also face distinct challenges (Peterson, Voller, Polusny, & Murdoch, 2011). Male victims of sexual assault may have difficulty reconciling their masculine identity (Davies, 2002). In our society, men typically associate their identity with strength and control; this is even more pronounced with the military subculture. Following a sexual assault, if a male survivor identifies himself as a "victim" it may be in contrast to the normative "masculine identity" and may further exacerbate the inner experience of confusion and turmoil related to the sexual assault. This may lead the client to question his own sexuality.

Statistical Differences

The Rand Military Workplace Study (Morral et al., 2015) was the first survey of the military that included a large enough sample of men to provide details on their sexual assault experiences. Several distinct characteristics of assaults against men and women were identified through the study. Men who experienced a sexual assault were more likely to have been assaulted repeatedly, and more likely to have been assaulted by two or more offenders. Penetrative assaults against men were more likely to involve injuries and threats of violence, as compared with assaults against women. Male victims were four times more likely than female victims to indicate that their worse incident of sexual assault involved hazing. Men were also more likely than women to describe the incident as serving to humiliate or abuse them, as opposed to having a sexual intent. Assaults against men were more likely to occur at work, during work hours, and were less likely to involve alcohol than assaults against women.

Treatment Differences

When men seek medical attention after a sexual assault, they may seek assistance for secondary injuries without revealing the sexual assault that led to the injuries (Isley & Gehrenbeck-Shim, 1997). For example, men may request STD testing because they had unprotected sex with a partner, but they may not disclose the entire truth to the medical provider.

The same may be true for behavioral health issues; male victims may seek behavioral health treatment for secondary symptoms such as depression or insomnia. As introduced previously, the RMWS demonstrated that although many men experienced oral and anal penetration, they did not necessarily perceive these acts as "sexual." Instead, many of these acts were perceived as *hazing* (Morral et al., 2015). Men in these circumstances may see little need for help from a "sexual assault" program or therapist, because they perceive the behavior as non-sexual misconduct. Therefore, if a male client in this circumstance presented to a behavioral health provider, he may seek assistance with self-esteem issues, depression, or other symptoms not directly identified as related to sexual trauma.

In the case study of David Green, above, his presenting issues focused on insomnia and anxiety. The underlying issues were predominantly guilt and shame. The initial phase of treatment with this individual focused on rapport building and validation. Psychoeducation about the trauma response was essential with this client to address the overwhelming shame he felt for "not doing anything" during the assault. According to TeBockhorst, O'Halloran, and Nyline (2015), survivors who experience *tonic immobility* may also experience greater shame and guilt about the sexual assault. TeBockhorst and colleagues (2015) define tonic immobility as "diminished or absent volitional movement in response to a traumatic event, accompanied by diminished vocal capacity" (p. 171). Providing survivors with some evidence that they did not choose the path their bodies ultimately went down is a critical first step in helping them navigate toward recovery. Additionally, providing evidence that others have also experienced a similar response can be especially validating and normalizing.

Dispelling Myths

Enhancing the education and training of behavioral health providers about sexual assault with both male and female victims is of the utmost importance. Research on the civilian population suggests that myths about rape persist even among service providers, including behavioral health counselors, crisis workers, and medical personnel (Anderson & Quinn, 2009; Dye & Roth, 1990). Expanded training and education for professionals who work with sexual assault victims can enhance awareness and dispel socially endorsed myths about male rape. For example, given that male victims may seek medical care without referencing the sexual assault, providers can utilize more subtle ways to inquire about possible sexual victimization. Additionally, treatment approaches for male victims may address gender and sexual identity issues as well as externalizing behaviors (e.g., alcohol and drug abuse) since statistics suggest male victims exhibit these issues more frequently than female victims (Cucciare, Ghaus, Weingardt, & Frayne, 2011).

Impact on Clinician

Providing therapeutic care to survivors of trauma can be highly rewarding, yet challenging at the same time. It takes a great deal of sensitivity and therapeutic skill to provide clinical support to survivors of sexual trauma, and recovery can be a long-term process. In addition, many of the presenting issues with those in the military are colored by aspects of the military culture: being strong, cohesion of the unit and "watching each other's back" which makes reporting instances of sexual assault that much more complicated. This suggests that an awareness of military culture as well as experience with trauma in general is a necessity for providing good care.

Providers have the complex task of guiding survivors through the difficult process of trauma recovery, while remaining grounded and external to the emotional chaos that often surrounds the survivor.

Clinicians need to remain vigilant at caring for themselves, and to avoid potential burnout from the emotionally demanding work we do. Some providers who work closely with survivors of trauma can develop symptoms that often mimic the survivor's psychological distress (Figley, 1995). Compassion stress may include feelings of helplessness, confusion, isolation, and some degree of secondary traumatic stress symptoms (hyper-arousal, anxiety, depression, avoidance, intrusive symptoms).

Helpful strategies to prevent such burnout include remaining aware of your internal and external processes, both in and out of session. It can help to have friends and family act as your "eyes" when they notice a change in demeanor. It is always a good idea to maintain collegial relationships to consult with and/or debrief following emotionally draining sessions. Oftentimes, we are guilty of not taking our own advice, and self-care is not done routinely. However, the importance of self-care cannot be stressed enough. It is highly beneficial to consistently maintain replenishing self-care activities; it will ensure your continued emotional strength during and outside of therapy.

Above all, it can sometimes be helpful to remind ourselves about *why* we chose the mental health field, and particularly why we chose to work with Veterans. Undoubtedly, working with survivors of sexual trauma can be complex; however, it is one small way that we can do our part in bettering the future of the US.

Note

The view expressed in this chapter solely belongs to the author and does not necessarily reflect the position or policy of the US government, the Department of Veterans Affairs, or the Department of Defense. Case examples are used to illustrate the experience of sexual assault. The experiences described in each case example are composites.

References

Anderson, I. & Quinn, A. (2009). Gender differences in medical students' attitudes towards male and female rape victims. *Psychology, Health & Medicine*, 14, 105–110.

Bremner, J. D., Krystal, J. H., Southwick, S. M., & Charney, D. S. (1995). Functional neuroanatomical correlates of the effects of stress on memory. *Journal of Traumatic Stress*, 8, 527–554.

Bremner, J. D., Randall, P., Scott, T. M., Bronen, R. A., Seibyl, J. P., Southwick, S. M., & Innis, R. B. (1995). MRI-based measures of hippocampal volume in patients with posttraumatic stress disorder. *American Journal of Psychiatry, 152*, 973–981.

Charney, D. S., Deutsch, A. Y., Krystal, J. H., Southwick, S. M., & Davis, M. (1993). Psychobiologic mechanisms of post-traumatic stress disorder, *Archives of General Psychiatry*, 50, 294–305.

Cloitre, M., Courtois, C. A., Ford, J. D., Green, B. L., Alexander, P., Briere, J., & van der Hart, O. (2012). *The ISTSS Expert Consensus Treatment Guidelines for Complex PTSD in Adults*. Retrieved from: www.istss.org/ISTSS_Main/media/Documents/ComplexPTSD.pdf

Coyle, B. S., Wolan, D. L., & Van Horn, A. S. (1996). The prevalence of physical and sexual abuse in women Veterans seeking care at a Veterans Affairs medical center. *Military Medicine*, 161(10), 588–593.

Cucciare, M. A., Ghaus, S., Weingardt, K. R., & Frayne, S. M. (2011). Sexual assault and substance use in male Veterans receiving a brief alcohol intervention. *Journal of Studies on Alcohol and Drugs*, 72, 693–700.

Davies, M. (2002). Male sexual assault victims: A selective review of the literature and implications for support services. *Aggression and Violent Behavior*, 7, 203–214.

DeBellis, M. D. & Putnam, F. W. (1994). The psychobiology of childhood maltreatment. *Child and Adolescent Psychiatric Clinics of North America*, 3, 663–677.

Department of Defense Directive (2012) *Glossary, 6495.01*, "Sexual Assault Prevention and Response Program" 23 January.

Dye, E. & Roth, S. (1990). Psychotherapists' knowledge about and attitudes toward sexual assault victim clients. *Psychology of Women Quarterly*, 14, 191–212.

Figley, C. R. (1995). *Compassion fatigue: Coping with secondary traumatic stress disorder in those who treat the traumatized*. New York: Brunner/Mazel.

FrayneS. M., Skinner, K. M., Sullivan, L. M., Tripp, T. J., Hankin, C. S., Kressin, N. R., & Miller, D. R. (1999). Medical profile of women Veterans Administration outpatients who report a history of sexual assault occurring while in the military. *Journal of Women's Health & Gender Based Medicine*, 8(6), 835–845.

Friedman, M. J., Charney, D. S., & Deutch, A. Y. (1995). *Neurobiological and clinical consequences of stress: From normal adaptation to post-traumatic stress disorder*. Hagerstown, MD: Lippincott-Raven.

Golding, J. M. (1994). Sexual assault history and physical health in randomly selected Los Angeles women. *Health Psychology: The Official Journal of the Division of Health Psychology*, 13(2), 130.

Herman, Judith. (2015). *Trauma and recovery: The aftermath of violence – from domestic abuse to political terror*. New York: Basic Books.

Isley, P. J. & Gehrenbeck-Shim, D. (1997). Sexual assault of men in the community. *Journal of Community Psychology*, 25, 159–166.

Katz, L. S., Cojucar, G., Beheshti, S., Namakura, E., & Murray, M. (2012). Military sexual trauma during deployment to Iraq and Afghanistan: Prevalence, readjustment, and gender differences. *Violence and Victims*, 27(4), 487–499.

Kimerling, R., Gima, K., Smith, M. W., Street, A., & Frayne, S. (2007). The Veterans Health Administration and military sexual trauma. *American Journal of Public Health*, 97(12), 2160–2166. doi: 10.2105/AJPH.2006.092999

Kimerling, R., Street, A. E., Pavao, J., Smith, M. W., Cronkite, R. C., Holmes, T. H., & Frayne, S. M. (2010). Military-related sexual trauma among Veterans Health Administration Patients returning from Afghanistan and Iraq. *American Journal of Public Health*, 100(8), 1409–1412. doi: 10.2105/AJPH.2009.171793

Merrill, L. L., Newell, C. E., Thomsen, C. J., Gold, S. R., Milner, J. S., Koss, M. P., & Rosswork, S. G. (1999). Childhood abuse and sexual revictimization in a female Navy recruit sample. *Journal of Traumatic Stress*, 12(2), 211–225. doi:10.1023/A:1024789723779

Messman-Moore, T. L. & Brown, A. L. (2004). Child maltreatment and perceived family environment as risk factors for adult rape: Is child sexual abuse the most salient experience? *Child Abuse & Neglect*, 28, 1019. doi: 10.1016/j.chiabu.2004.05.003

Morral, A. R., Gore, K. L., & Schell, T. L. (2015). *Sexual assault and sexual harassment in the US Military. Volume 1. Design of the 2014 RAND military workplace study.* Santa Monica, CA: RAND National Defense Research Institute. Retrieved from RAND website: www.rand.org/content/dam/rand/pubs/research_reports/RR800/RR870z2/RAND_RR870z2.pdf

Murdoch, M. & Nichol, K. (1995). Women Veterans' experiences with domestic violence and with sexual harassment while in the military. *Archives of Family Medicine*, 4(5), 411–418.

Murdoch, M., Polusny, M. A., Hodges, J., & Cowper, D. (2006). The association between in-service sexual harassment and post-traumatic stress disorder among Department of Veterans Affairs disability applicants. *Military Medicine*, 171, 166–173.

Peterson, Z. D., Voller, E. K., Polusny, M. A., & Murdoch, M. (2011). Prevalence and consequences of adult sexual assault of men: Review of empirical findings and state of the literature. *Clinical Psychology Review*, 31, 1–24.

RAND Military Working Group study (2014). www.sapr.mil/public/socs/reports/FY14_RAND.pdf

Resnick, H. S., Yehuda, R., Pitman, R. K., & Foy, D. W. (1995). Effect of previous trauma on acute plasma cortisol level following rape. *American Journal of Psychiatry*, 152(11), 1675–1677.

Sadler, A. G., Booth, B. M., Cook, B. L., & Doebbeling, B. N. (2003). Factors associated with women's risk of rape in the military environment. *American Journal of Industrial Medicine*, 43(3), 262–273. doi: 10.1002/ajim.10202

SHARP programwww.sexualassault.army.mil/index.cfm

Skinner, K. M., Kressin, N., Frayne, S., Tripp, T. J., Hankin, C. S., Miller, D. R., & Sullivan, L. M. (2000). The prevalence of military sexual assault among female Veterans' Administration outpatients. *Journal of Interpersonal Violence*, 15, 291–310. doi: 10.1177/088626000015003005

Southwick, S. M., Krystal, J. H., Morgan, C. A., Johnson, D., Nagy, L., Nicolaou, A., & Charney, D. S. (1993). Abnormal noradrenergic function in post-traumatic stress disorder. *Archives of General Psychiatry*, 50, 266–274.

Surís, A. & Lind, L. (2008). Military sexual trauma: A review of prevalence and associated health consequences in Veterans. *Trauma, Violence, & Abuse*, 9(4), 250–269. doi: 10.1177/1524838008324419

TeBockhorst, S., O'Halloran, M., & Nyline, B. (2015). Tonic immobility among survivors of sexual assault. *Psychological Trauma*, 7(2), 171–178.

US Department of Defense (2015). *Annual report on sexual assault in the military, fiscal Year 2014.* Washington, DC: Department of Defense.

US Equal Employment Opportunity Commission (1990). *Policy guidance on current issues of sexual harassment.* Retrieved from: www.eeoc.gov/policy/docs/currentissues.html

van der Kolk, B. A. (1996). The body keeps the score: Approaches to the psychobiology of posttraumatic stress disorder. In B. A. van der Kolk, A. D. MacFarlane, & L. Wasaeth (Eds.), *Traumatic stress: The effects of overwhelming experience on mind, body, and society* (pp. 214–241). New York: Guilford.

Wilson, L. C., Kimbrel, N. A., Meyer, E. C., Young, K. A., & Morissette, S. B. (2015). Do child abuse and maternal care interact to predict military sexual trauma? *Journal of Clinical Psychology*, 71(4), 378–386. doi: 10.1002/jclp.22143

Wolfe, J., Sharkansky, E. J., Read, J. P., Dawson, R., Martin, J. A., & Ouimette, P. C. (1998). Sexual harassment and assault as predictors of PTSD symptomatology among US female Persian Gulf War military personnel. *Journal of Interpersonal Violence*, 13, 40–57.

Yehuda, R. (2002). Post-traumatic stress disorder. *New England Journal of Medicine*, 374(2), 108–114.

10

SEXUAL AND GENDER MINORITY VETERANS

Sandra Laski and David L. Albright

Sexual and gender minorities (SGM), including lesbian, gay, bisexual, and transgender individuals, are an increasingly open, acknowledged, and visible part of society. Despite this newfound "openness and acceptance," issues related to sexual identity still abound in the military population.

SGM refers to a broad coalition of groups, including lesbian, gay, bisexual, and transgender individuals. While this chapter focuses on the Veteran and service member community, the authors wish to highlight the importance of recognizing that the various populations represented by the LGBT acronym are distinct groups. These groups are routinely treated as a single population under umbrella terms such as LGBT (lesbian, gay, bisexual, and transgender), though it is critical to understand that each group faces challenges and struggles especially in the service of their country.

Tumultuous changes have taken place in the past decade in regard to the SGM populations in the civilian population as well as the military and Veteran population. As recently as a few years ago, SGM Americans in the Armed Forces were forced to keep their sexuality a secret or risk being discharged, dishonorably.

The following are examples of critical events or changes that affect the medical and mental health of SGM, military and non-military including their overall quality of life:

- In 2010 the Affordable Care Act prohibited sex discrimination in federally funded healthcare facilities, which included discrimination based on transgender status.
- In 2011, the discriminatory US policy known as "Don't Ask, Don't Tell" (DADT) was repealed, eliminating the 17-year ban on openly gay military personnel.
- In 2011 the Veterans Health Administration established Directive 2011-024/2013-003: Providing Health Care for Transgender and Intersex Veterans establishing for the first time in history that transgender and intersex Veterans will receive respectful delivery of health care.
- In 2011, the Guidelines for Psychological Practice with Lesbian, Gay and Bisexual Clients were adopted by the APA Council of Representatives. The function of the guidelines was to inform the practice of psychologists and to provide information for the education and training of psychologists regarding LGB issues.
- In 2011, the Joint Commission (a US-accrediting and certification board recognized nationwide for its efforts to improve healthcare for the public) published the field guide

titled, *Advancing Effective Communication, Cultural Competence, and Patient- and Family-Centered Care for the Lesbian, Gay, Bisexual, and Transgender (LGBT) Community*. The Joint Commission urged US hospitals to contribute to improved healthcare quality for LGBT patients and their families by creating more welcoming, safe and inclusive environments.

- In June 2013, 17 years after Defense of Marriage Act (DOMA) was signed into law, the Supreme Court overturned Section 3 of DOMA, which was a significant advancement for gay and lesbian troops since the repeal of DADT in 2011. While the end of DADT enabled gays to serve openly, healthcare, housing and other benefits remained closed to their spouses and partners because of DOMA.
- While military medical policies still exclude transgender people from serving openly in the US Armed Forces, there are reports that the Pentagon has a plan to end the ban in May 2016.

Prevalence

The Veterans Health Administration (VHA) is the largest integrated healthcare system in the world, with over 8.3 million enrollees receiving care within a network of 1,400 hospitals, clinics, and nursing homes across the country. VHA offers quality healthcare to many individuals who might not otherwise have access to healthcare in repayment for service to their country. Given the size of the population served by the VHA, it is likely the largest single provider of healthcare for SGM individuals in the US. Although the Department of Veterans Affairs (VA) operates the single largest healthcare system in the US, it currently has no way to identify gender or sexual minority status of patients.

SGM individuals have long been an essential part of the US Armed Forces, including the Army, Navy, Coast Guard, Marine Corps, and Air Force (National Defense Research Institute, 2010; Shilts, 1994), and recently SGM Veterans are gaining visibility within VHA, partly as a consequence of the repeal of the DADT policy and the passage of a national VHA Directive on transgender care in 2011. Despite these critical events, the VHA and Department of Defense (DoD) have no exact data on prevalence rates of SGM individuals because sexual or gender minority status is not part of the VHA or DoD data collection strategies. As a result, it is not exactly clear how many SGM Veterans or service members there are, nor how many are using VHA services.

Gates (2010) estimated that approximately one million gay and lesbian Americans are Veterans. Population estimates suggest that gay and lesbian service members represent 2.5% of active duty personnel and 2.8% of all military personnel when Guard and Reserves are included (Gates, 2010). Recent analysis of the 2004 National Behavioral Risk Factor Surveillance System (BRFSS) dataset suggests that same-sex-partnered Veterans may use VA services at the same prevalence as opposite-sex-partnered Veterans (Blosnich, Bossarte, Silver, & Silenzio, 2013).

The prevalence of transgender Veterans and those who use VHA services is even less certain. By extrapolating from existing studies, it can be estimated that there are at least 2,000–6,000 transgender Veterans (Shipherd, Mizock, Maguen, & Green, 2012). Prior to issuance of the 2011 VA directive on transgender care, a study by Shipherd and colleagues (2012) reported that transgender Veterans utilize VA care at higher rates (about three times) than Veterans in the general population. Another study of transgender Veterans using VA services has documented that the rate of gender identity disorder diagnoses in the VA has grown over the past decade; results indicated use of VHA services by transgender Veterans was more than five times higher than what is found with Veterans generally (Blosnich, Brown et al., 2013).

Research on the experience of SGM military personnel is quite limited and narrowly focused on issues involving acceptance of SGM individuals in the military environment, the compatibility of SGM individuals with the organizational culture and values of the military, and the perceived impact of unit cohesion, readiness and effectiveness of the military (Estrada, Dirosa, & Decostanca, 2013). Studies on health disparities between SGM military individuals and non-gay individuals are few. A recent study of Veteran sexual minority women (Blosnich, Foynes, & Shipherd, 2013) compared with non-Veteran heterosexual women noted that sexual minority women Veterans had three times the odds of poor physical health than their non-Veterans peers.

Few empirical studies have inquired about the experiences of the SGM military population as they relate to mental health concerns. Of particular interest is a recent study by Cochran et al. (2013) who examined the mental health characteristics of SGM (transgender not included) Veterans compared with a sample of Veterans who were not of a sexual minority. The study sought to explore the impact of sexual concealment on mental health and anxiety. The study compared 409 GM Veterans with data from 15,000 Veterans, looking at current mental health. Findings showed that SGM Veterans were more likely to screen positive for post-traumatic stress disorder (PTSD), depression, and alcohol problems than the comparison sample. The researchers concluded that there was support for the notion that negative experiences while in the military, especially those related to concealment of one's SGM identity, were predictive of certain mental health problems post-service. This was supported in a study (Mattocks et al., 2013) of 365 women Veterans who served in Afghanistan/Iraq who rated their current mental health as worse than before deployment.

Lesbian and Bisexual Service Members

Katrina is a 25-year-old African American female who served in one deployment to Iraq where she was engaged in combat. Her stepfather sexually abused her in childhood. While stationed overseas, her military superior raped her on several occasion and threatened to destroy her military career if she told anyone. She believed her superior had the power to take away her military career and make her job miserable until the inevitable discharge. As a result, she never told anyone, not even her civilian girlfriend Sara. She felt alone, afraid and angry toward her rapists, herself, and the military. She retired from service a year ago and is now seeking VA medical and mental health services. Katrina started drinking heavily in the military to fit in and make connections with other soldiers, though now she is drinking to deal with painful memories from childhood, the rapes by her superior, and war memories. She has difficulty being touched, being in crowds, feels disconnected from life in general and has difficulty falling and getting back to sleep once awakened from nightmares. Her girlfriend Sara is supportive and loving, though becoming frustrated with the lack of intimacy in their relationship.

Katrina and Sara's case illustrates the profound and enduring impact of past and continued sexual trauma layered onto military experience. Military sexual trauma for the lesbian and bisexual woman impacts all quarters of her life including readjustment after service, mental health comorbidities, emotional numbing, trust and substance abuse issues.

Biopsychosocial Implications for Women

Per data from the US Department of Defense (2011), there have been more than 150,000 US female service members who have been deployed overseas since the start of the Iraq (Operation Iraqi Freedom) and Afghanistan (Operation Enduring Freedom) initiatives.

According to Lehavot et al. (2013), women Veterans in general have reported high rates of trauma across the life span and adverse health outcomes. Up to 93% of female Veterans report a traumatic event in their lifetime, including childhood sexual and physical abuse, adult sexual and physical abuse and intimate partner violence (Zinzow, Grubagh, Suffoletta-Maierle, & Frueh, 2007). Once they enter the military, women Veterans may experience additional violence, including military sexual trauma and combat exposure. Female Veterans also face less overt experiences than assault or combat, such as gender discrimination and sexism.

High rates of exposure to trauma and gender-based violence for female Veterans increase the risk for poor medical and mental health, as well as overall quality of life. Two recent studies indicate that women Veterans report poorer health-related quality of life and elevated rates of depressive and anxiety disorder as compared with civilians (Lehavot et al., 2013). Rates of PTSD are high among women Veterans.

It is reported that LB women Veterans are likely to experience heightened levels of prejudice and discrimination, victimization, including greater incidence of rape, as compared with heterosexual women Veterans, resulting in adverse health and substance use disorders (Booth, Mengeling, Torner, & Sadler, 2011; Lehavot et al., 2013).

Booth and colleagues (2011) indicated that women Veterans who enter the service with a history of childhood sexual abuse are at higher risk for continued abuse. As such, it is imperative to have provisions for substance abuse and mental health services to address and treat ongoing trauma, substance abuse, and comorbid depression, and PTSD for women Veterans.

Gay and Bisexual Service Members

James is a Caucasian male who served in Operation Enduring Freedom. Before enlisting in the service he had been in a two-year relationship with Joshua. During the first 30 months of service, James experienced two nine-month deployments. The length of deployments and concealment of their relationship placed a great amount of stress on the couple. While other straight service men and women had the freedom to speak openly about their loved ones and carried their pictures, James and Joshua were forced to conceal their relationship because of the DADT policy that was enforced at that time. DADT was the official US policy that prohibited any gay or bisexual person from disclosing (or speaking about) his or her sexual orientation while serving in the US Armed Forces. The policy specified that service members who disclose gay or bisexual orientation or engage in same-sex conduct would be dishonorably discharged. When James and Joshua correspond to one another, they were not able to express their love and how much they missed each other out of fear that James may be harassed and discharged from service. Over time, James began to feel that the distance, stress, and strain was negatively impacting their relationship; he wanted to seek counseling, but knew he could not reveal his secret. Consequently, he suffered in isolation. James began drinking excessive amounts of alcohol to escape from the pain of not being able to connect emotionally with Joshua. Further, some of his military comrades were beginning to ask questions like "Why is he not dating?" Alcohol consumption seemed to alleviate the fears James had regarding discharge, which would include losing his career, healthcare, educational benefits, and eligibility for service connected disability payments if needed.

The situation suggested in this case example highlights the continued sense of stigma and fear that pervades the gay/bisexual service member. The military cultural imperatives of strength and cohesion, needs of the unit over the individual, subtle institutional homophobia, etc., are all at play in James's concerns and ultimate behavior. Despite legislation to the contrary, James has felt discrimination and distance from his fellow service members and fears greater reprisals if he declares and is open about his relationship with Joshua.

Biopsychosocial Implications

During the 18 years of the DADT policy, sexual minority military personnel faced increasing risk of manipulation (including blackmail), daily distress and anxiety, along with compromised personal and unit relationships (National Defense Research Institute, 2010). During the time period of DADT, sexual minorities experienced high rates of discrimination and victimization because of their sexual orientation. Over 14,000 LGBT individuals were discharged from the military under DADT, with a disproportionate number of expulsions/dishonorable discharges of women and minorities (Cianni, 2012; Estrada et al., 2013).

With the repeal of DADT, other VHA policy changes and the VHA's efforts to make their healthcare facilities more welcoming of SGM populations, it is hoped that SGM Veterans will feel more comfortable disclosing their sexual and gender identity status to their VA and civilian healthcare providers without fear of reprisal.

Challenges for Gay/Bisexual Men

SGM service members likely will have experienced discrimination on individual and institutional levels from early childhood. They often experience rejection from family members, peers and religious organizations; they commonly are bullied, harassed, and are victims of assault. Such experiences have been tied to increased rates of psychological distress, including depression and anxiety, substance abuse, and internalized heterosexism in LGB individuals. For several generations, SGM military personnel have faced workplace stigma, institutionalized heterosexism, and sexual-orientation-linked barriers to vocational advancement (Cochran et al., 2013).

The term "homosexual" was first created in the 1800s to categorize those who engaged in same-gender sexual behavior as sick or deviant. Over the years the term "homosexuality" has been associated with sin, criminal behavior, uncleanliness, and mental illness, all of which serve to place SGM people in the subordinate role of being categorized as "deviant" individuals who are marginalized by mainstream society. This is still the case in the military where institutionalized homophobia exists despite recent legislation.

Transgender Service Members

Transgender people are among the most socially stigmatized of sexual minorities, facing discrimination in most aspects of their lives. Social and legal institutions in the US predominately condone discrimination, ridicule, and abuse of transgender people within foundational institutions such as the family, the workplace, public settings, and healthcare settings. In addition to discrimination, major data findings show disproportionate rates of violence toward transgender people than the general population with transgender people of color experiencing the highest rates of violence (National Coalition of Anti-Violence, 2013).

Transgender Americans can and do serve in the nation's military; they serve at a rate of double that of the general population. However, the repeal of DADT did not lift the ban on transgender Americans who must still keep their identity a secret while in the Armed Forces. In fact, transgender status and related medical diagnoses immediately disqualify an applicant from joining the service and for actively serving personnel, it is cause for dismissal (Cray, Miller, & Durso, 2013).

After a recent suicide attempt, Jack was being discharged from a VA inpatient psychiatric unit. Staff insists that before he can be discharged he must have a future outpatient appointment scheduled for follow-up with a mental health provider; he is given a business card of a clinical social worker with date/time of return visit to meet with this mental health provider. He is reluctant to keep this appointment because he does not believe mental health providers at the VA are trained in gender therapy and therefore not be able to help him. "They will make it worse by asking about my genitals – and the sex reassignment surgery I have had or plan to have. They are so ignorant about trans needs and will only reject me anyway," Jack thinks to himself. Jack is a soft-spoken 25-year-old Marine who served three deployments to Afghanistan. Being a Marine made him proud and he had hoped to make a career in the military, though his gender dysphoria symptoms were becoming more than he could bear and he decided to not reenlist so he could transition to his true gender identity – male. Jack was born with female genitalia and named Jennifer. Jack struggled with the difficult early stages of transitioning from female to male. He loathed his female anatomy, felt ugly and trapped. Suicide seemed like the only way to stop the chronic internal pain.

Transgender people have a unique set of mental and physical health needs, yet these needs are often not met due to prejudices against transgender people within medical systems (including the VA Health Care Systems) and dominant society (Bockting, Miner, Swinburne Romine, Hamilton, & Coleman, 2013; Yerke & Mitchelle, 2013).

In 2011, the VHA enacted the Veterans Health Administration Directive 2011-024 providing Health Care for Transgender and Intersex Veterans, mandating a national policy covering clinical services for transgender and intersex Veterans (Department of Veterans Health Administration, 2011). As the largest integrated healthcare system in the US (VHA), the Directive represents one of the largest formal expansions of transgender and intersex healthcare ever developed. The Directive, for the first time in VHA history, established the eligibility of Veterans who identify as transgender or intersex for transgender medical and mental health services within the VA system and no aspect of the Veteran's gender disqualifies them from any necessary care included in the VHA benefits package (Department of Veterans Health Administration, 2011). The VHA benefit package does not include any surgeries or procedures deemed "cosmetic." Consequently, important procedures and surgeries are not available to transgender Veterans unless they pay for these out of pocket, which are often cost prohibitive. For example, removal of unwanted facial and body hair via laser and electrolysis is not available and many transvets cannot afford these procedures.

Since the Directive was implemented, large gaps have been identified regarding the lack of staff and provider knowledge in working with this specialized population (Blosnich et al.,

2013). While the Directive incorporates important policies around transgender Veteran healthcare, it also presents a challenge to the VA providers since most staff and healthcare providers have not been trained in this area of care. As a consequence, when Veterans such as Jack seek needed medical and mental health services, their fears are realized with denial of services and/or providers who are not trained to provide sensitive patient-centered care (Sherman et al., 2014; Shipherd et al., 2012).

Challenges for Transgender Service Members in Healthcare Settings

Since the implementation of the VHA Directive, large gaps were identified regarding lack of provider knowledge in working with the transgender population (Blosnich et al., 2013). Yet, transgender Veterans rely on healthcare providers for gender dysphoria diagnosis, which is the gateway for cross-sex hormone treatments, sex reassignment surgeries, and medical clearance when seeking gender-confirming surgical alterations (Coleman et al., 2012).

Historically, the US government and its healthcare systems prohibited treatments for gender identity issues including body alterations for feminizing or masculinizing purposes. As a result, transgender Veterans have many fears about obtaining services at the VA, such as not getting the services they need, fears of being treated poorly by their providers, and fears of harassment by other Veterans (Sherman et al., 2014; Shipherd et al., 2012).

Research has found that transgender people experience elevated rates of health disparities (Budge, Adelson, & Howard, 2013) yet often do not seek out healthcare due to fears of rejection from their healthcare providers (Shipherd et al., 2012). Further, the lack of sensitivity on the part of healthcare providers who do not respect the expressed identity of transgender people can adversely influence whether transgender people will access care and remain connected to their providers.

Very few providers (and even fewer of their staff) are knowledgeable about transgender health (Shipherd et al., 2012). Most providers are not trained to respect transgender patients' gender identity (e.g., use of appropriate pronouns and chosen names) and their special needs for confidentiality (e.g., knowing whether to use a patient's female or male name during phone calls to third parties and/or in the clinic setting).

These distressing observations suggest that civilian and military healthcare providers need to become especially knowledgeable about the issues related to the transgender population. In response to the specific needs of the SGMT service member, the Department of Defense and the Veterans Health Administration (VA) have initiated numerous programs to improve care. Training programs in diversity have been initiated along with non-discrimination policy directives; education on transgender healthcare is being addressed through the VA transgender health policy. The Office of Diversity and Inclusion (ODI) has established the VA Diversity Council to raise awareness of the SGMT community and classes in cultural competency training are held for employees, supervisors, and managers, VA wide.

Challenges for Aging SGM Veterans

Ray is a 75-year-old Vietnam Veteran, Caucasian who has been with his 80-year-old African American partner Vic for 37 years. They have had a wonderful life together. They both lost contact with their biological families many years ago because their families could not accept their gay sexual orientation. Due to states not acknowledging same-sex marriages, the couple did not marry. As a result, Ray's healthcare insurance would not cover Vic. Vic had been diagnosed with Alzheimer's roughly eight years ago and now his healthcare needs are such that Vic needs a long-term care facility. Ray has many fears about transferring the care of Vic to a long-term facility: Will they respect and honor the long-term relationship between Ray and Vic?

Ray and Vic are faced with common issues related to aging as part of the aging SGM populations. While there is an important small body of research on aging SGM, there is very little research that has focused on SGM Veterans and health/mental health disparities. The Institute of Medicine identifies LGB older adults as an at-risk and under-served population. Health disparities related to sexual orientation and gender identity have been identified as one of the most pronounced gaps in health research with health research of LGBT older adults largely absent from the literature (Fredrickson-Goldsen & Muraco, 2010).

Many SGM experience health disparities throughout their lives. While they are a resilient population, they also face distinct challenges. Today, we live in a time of tremendous social change and increasing visibility along with inclusion of SGM. At the same time, it is important to remember that LGBT older adults grew up in an era that was far less accepting of their identities and coming out placed them at risk of being labeled criminals, sinners, and mentally ill. For many, their sexual orientation and gender identity remained hidden out of necessity to obtain and keep employment, housing and family connections. It was commonplace for families to disown LGBT family members. Consequently, LGBT elders have been historically taught that hiding (i.e. presenting as straight and gender conforming) was critical to survival.

Discrimination and fear of discrimination are common and prominent themes in studies of the aging SGM population. The added stress of dealing with lifelong discrimination and stigma has placed LGBT older adults at greater risk of physical and mental illnesses, such as depression, chronic illness, poverty, social isolation, poor nutrition, and premature death (Fredrickson-Goldsen & Muraco, 2010).

Aging, combined with a history of marginalization, discrimination, and victimization increases the potential vulnerability of LGBT older adults. Further, given the heightened risks of discrimination and victimization, the fear of and potential difficulty in accessing culturally responsive services can impact the quality of life and overall health and well-being of SGM. For the Veteran population, these dynamics are present as well, with Veterans equally concerned about their aging status and potential for discrimination and marginalization. Of major concern for Ray and Vic, is whether their relationship as both Veterans and those in a long-term relationship will be honored as they traverse the VA healthcare system. There are numerous long-term care facilities available to Veterans throughout the US where Vic can access care. An issue could be whether Ray will be accorded the status of "spouse" to Vic.

How Best to Care for Our SGM Military

The development of LGBT cultural sensitivity is a process whereby one gains knowledge of SGM people. The process includes critically examining personal and professional attitudes toward sexual orientation and gender identity while considering how factors such as age, culture, religion, media, and larger systems influence attitudes and ethical decision-making. There is also the need to recognize how attitudes and knowledge of SGM issues may be relevant to assessment and treatment and issues related to when to seek consultation or make appropriate referrals. Cultural awareness and military cultural awareness includes understanding the ways in which social stigmatization (i.e. prejudice, discrimination, and violence) poses risks to the mental health and well-being of SGM clients. It is also critical to understand that homosexuality and bisexuality are not indicative of mental illness. Further, recognition of the families of SGM people may include people who are not legally or biologically related. Practitioners need to understand how a person's gender identity and sexual orientation might impact his or her family and the relationships within that family.

Practitioners should strive to be knowledgeable about and respect the importance of SGM relationships and understand the particular circumstances and challenges SGM face. This is especially true in the military population where, historically, these relationships have been grounds for dismissal from military service. SGM people cross all socioeconomic, ethnoracial, age, gender, religious, geographical location, educational, and relationship status lines. It is essential to recognize the particular life issues or challenges that are related to multiple and often conflicting cultural norms, values, and beliefs that SGM members of racial and ethnic minorities face especially while serving in the military and as Veterans. Clinicians are charged with engaging in culturally competent SGM practice by applying theories of social and mental health perspectives with the most up-to-date knowledge available.

VHA and VA New Offices, Policies and Programs Developed

The VHA is committed to patient-centered care by acknowledging and implementing the Joint Commission standards on non-discrimination. In so doing, the VHA has endorsed a patient and family members' rights and responsibilities policy stating that Veterans and their family members will not be subject to discrimination for any reason, including for reasons of age, race, ethnicity, religion, culture, language, physical or mental disability, socioeconomic status, sex, sexual orientation, or gender identity or expression (www.va.gov/health/rights/familyrights.asp).

To implement nondiscrimination policies, the VHA created the Veterans Health Administration Office of Health Equity (OHE), which is committed to addressing the special health needs of LGBT Veterans and reducing health disparities for them and members of other vulnerable communities. VHA's commitment to SGM Veterans includes:

- Promoting a welcoming health and work environment that is inclusive of LGBT Veterans and employees.
- Providing information, guidance, and education to VHA providers about LGBT health issues (VHA Fact Sheet, 2011).

In terms of healthcare delivery, VHA is committed to a patient-centered approach that focuses on the needs and values of the SGM Veterans. As such, in 2010, VHA issued a policy statement providing for patient visitation rights in support of the needs of SGM family members. Also in 2010, VHA issued, VHA Directive 2013-003: Providing Health Care for Transgender and Intersex Veterans, a policy directive on respectful delivery of healthcare to transgender and intersex individuals, and is currently providing training for healthcare providers on services for transgender Veterans (Department of Veterans Health Administration, 2011) (excluding sex reassignment surgery, and cosmetic procedures)

In addition, the VHA created the US Department of Veterans Affairs (VA) Office of Diversity and Inclusion (ODI), whose mission is to foster a diverse workforce and an inclusive work environment that ensures equal opportunity through national policy development, workforce analysis, outreach, retention, and education to best serve US Veterans (www.diversity.va.gov). ODI has established a formal SGM special emphasis program in its effort to increase education and awareness of the SGM community. To enhance that program, an LGBT employee resource group under the auspices of the VA Diversity Council was also established. To bolster their efforts, the ODI is developing cultural competency training in this area for employees, supervisors, and managers, nationally throughout the VA system. In addition to ongoing cultural competency training within VA facilities, in 2013, VA's commitment to LGBT healthcare resulted in an impressive 91 VA facilities being awarded the Human Rights Campaign Health Equity Index 2013 Equality Leader status.

For the civilian clinician, it is imperative that SGM cultural competence be achieved and kept current. Civilian practitioners further need to be aware of the broad band of services offered at the VHA level. In civilian settings, care must be taken to be respectful and aware of the multiplicity of stressors in the lives of the SGM service member, with the multiple layering of the military and civilian environments.

References

American Psychiatric Association. (2013). *Diagnostic and statistical manual of mental disorders* (5th ed.). Arlington, VA: American Psychiatric Publishing.

Blosnich, J., Bossarte, R., Silver, E., & Silenzio, V. (2013). Health care utilization and health indicators among a national sample of US Veterans in same-sex partnerships. *Military Medicine*, 178(2), 207–212. doi: 10.7205/MILMED-D-12-00325

Blosnich, J. R., Brown, G. R., Shipherd, J. C., Kauth, M., Piegari, R. I., & Bossarte, R. M. (2013). Prevalence of gender identity disorder and suicide risk among transgender Veterans utilizing Veterans Health Administration (VHA) care. *American Journal of Public Health*, 1023(10), e27–32. doi: 10.2105/AJPH.2013.301507

Blosnich, J., Foynes, M. M., & Shipherd, J. C. (2013). Health disparities among sexual minority women Veterans. *Journal of Women's Health*, 22(7), 631–636. doi: 10.1089/jwh.2012.4214

Bockting, W. O., Miner, M. H., Swinburne Romine, R. E., Hamilton, A., & Coleman, E. (2013). Stigma, mental health, and resilience in an online sample of the US transgender population. *American Journal of Public Health*, 103(5), 943–951.

Booth, B. M., Mengeling, M., Torner, J., & Sadler, A. G. (2011). Rape, sex partnership, and substance use consequences in women Veterans. *Journal of Traumatic Stress*, 24, 287–294.

Budge, S. L., Adelson, J. L., & Howard, K. (2013). Anxiety and depression in transgender individuals: The roles of transition status, loss, social support, and coping. *Journal of Consulting and Clinical Psychology*, 81(3), 545–557. doi: 10.1037/a0031774

Center for Disease Control and Prevention (CDC) (2007). Compendium of HIV prevention interventions with evidence of effectiveness [Internet]. Atlanta: CDC. Available from: www.cdc.gov/hiv/resources/reports/hiv_compendium/index.htm

Cianni, V. (2012). Don't ask don't tell and gays in the military. *Journal of Gay and Lesbian Mental Health*, 16, 322–333.

Cochran, B. N., Balsam, K., Flentje, A., Malte, C. A., & Simpson, T. (2013). Mental health characteristics of sexual minority Veterans. *Journal of Homosexuality*, 60(2–3), 419–435. doi: 10.1080/00918369.2013.744932

Coleman, E., Bockting, W., Botzer, M., Cohen-Kettenis, P., DeCuypere, G., Feldman, J., & Zucker, K. (2012). Standards of care for the health of transsexual, transgender, and gender-nonconforming people, version 7. *International Journal of Transgenderism*, 13(4), 165–232.

Cray, A., Miller, K., & Durso, L. E. (2013). Seeking shelter: The experiences and unmet needs of LGBT homeless youth. *Washington: Center for American Progress*, 4.

Department of Veterans Affairs, Office of Policy and Planning (2011). Analysis of unique Veterans' utilization of VA benefits and service. http://britannica,com/EBchecked/topic/1553878/Don't-ask-don't-tell-DADT

Estrada, A., Dirosa, G., & Decostanza, A. (2013). Gays in the US military: Reviewing the research and conceptualizing a way forward. *Journal of Homosexuality*, 60, 327–355.

Fredrickson-Goldsen, K. & Muraco, A. (2010). Aging and sexual orientation: A 25-year review of the literature. *Research on Aging*, 32(3), 372–413.

Gates, G. J. (2010). Lesbian, gay, and bisexual men and women in the US military: Updated estimates. Williams Institute, UCLA School of Law. See: https://escholarship.org/uc/item/0gn4t6t3

Lehavot, K., Hoerster, K. D., Nelson, K. M., Jakupcak, M., & Simpson, T. L. (2013). Incorporating lesbian and bisexual women into women Veterans' health priorities. *Journal of General Internal Medicine*, 28(Suppl. 2), S609–S614. doi: 10.1007/s11606-11012-2291-2292

Mattocks, K. M., Sadler, A., Yano, E. M., Krebs, E. E., Zephyrin, L., Brandt, C., & Haskell, S. (2013). Sexual victimization, health status, and VA healthcare utilization among lesbian and bisexual OEF/OIF Veterans. *Journal of General Internal Medicine*, 28(Suppl. 2), S604-S608. doi: 10.1007/s11606-11013-2357-2359

National Coalition of Anti-Violence (2013). See: glad.org

National Defense Research Institute (2010). *Sexual orientation and US military personnel policy: an update of RAND's 1993 study*. Santa Monica: RAND.

RAND (2010). Annual Report: Focus on making a difference. Corporate Publications.

Sherman, M., Kauth, M., Ridener, L., Shipherd, J. C., Bratkovich, K., & Beaulieu, G. (2014). An empirical investigation of challenges and recommendations for welcoming sexual and gender minority Veterans into VA care. *Professional Psychology: Research and Practice*, 11(2), 235–242.

Sherman, M., Kauth, M., Shipherd, J. C., & Street, R. (2014). Communication between VA providers and sexual and gender minority Veterans: A pilot study. *Professional Psychology: Research and Practice*.

Shilts, R. (1994). *Conduct unbecoming: Gays and lesbians in the US military*. New York: St. Martin's Griffin.

Shipherd, J. C., Mizock, L., Maguen, S., & Green, K. E. (2012). Male-to-female transgender Veterans and VA health care utilization. *International Journal of Sexual Health*, 24(1), 78–87. doi: 10.1080/19317611.2011.639440

US Department of Veteran Affairs (2011). Minority Veterans. Retrieved from: www.va.gov/vetdata/docs/Special Reports/MinorityVeterans_2011.pdf

VHA Fact Sheet (2011). VHA Health Administration, Washington, DC.

Yerke, A. & Mitchell, V. (2013). Transgender people in the military: Don't ask, don't tell, don't enlist. *Journal of Homosexuality*, 60(2–3), 436–457.

Zinzow, H., Grubaugh, J., Suffoletta-Maierle, S., & Frueh, B. (2007). Trauma among female Veterans: a critical review. *Trauma Violence Abuse*, 8, 384–400.

PART III

Clinical Challenges and Perspectives

11

VETERANS AND SUICIDE

Risk Factors, Assessment, and Treatment

Christie Jackson

> My PTSD is a vicious, terminal parasite. It burred its way through my mind for years; its toxic filth spewing poison without abandon throughout my mind, body and ultimately my soul. Its darkness began to advance, ravaging me, especially emotionally, robbing me of any ability to exist. Hopelessness, helplessness and utter defeat of all that was human inside of me followed. A deeply tragic death of my humanity. It made me into an impulsive and repulsive mockery of my true self. My mind no longer my own, my body polluted and wracking with pain. My disease, my PTSD brought a total, suffocating darkness which enveloped my soul in putrid, filthy, decaying layers upon layers of physical and emotional agony. PTSD took away the only life I knew. All that remained was my excruciating, inescapable mental agony and an insatiable search for any means to arrest it.

"Bob," an Army combat Veteran with three tours in Iraq and Afghanistan, wrote this moments before he tried to kill himself by overdosing on alcohol and prescription psychotropic medication. Fortunately, Bob survived his suicide attempt and *did not* become a statistic – one of the 22 Veterans who commit suicide every day. As a combat Veteran, he had to face violence, suffering, and death on a scale that civilians will never know (Sherman, Harris, & Erbes, 2015). The Operation Iraqi Freedom (OIF), Operation Enduring Freedom (OEF), and Operation New Dawn (OND) conflicts have evolved into our nation's longest war, and there are now approximately 2.5 million military troops who have served in Iraq and Afghanistan. The psychological toll of serving in combat is associated with a number of serious mental health concerns (Mental Health Advisory Team Six, 2009), and these mental health concerns persist or even worsen in the months and years following deployment (Thomas et al., 2010). Sadly, since 2001 more service members have died by suicide than in combat.

Mental health providers treating Veterans should be equipped with an understanding of the particular risk factors of suicide associated with military service, know how to perform a thorough suicide risk assessment, and provide evidence-based treatment as well as other resources for individuals at risk of suicide. In this chapter, information regarding all of these key areas will be presented, beginning with a discussion of help-seeking barriers among military Veterans.

Stigma and Help-Seeking

Veterans are especially reluctant to ask for help. While the stigma of seeking mental health treatment is widespread in our society, military culture is entrenched with this unfortunate attitude (e.g. Greene-Shortridge, Britt, & Castro, 2007). Indeed, often the individuals who need help the most are the ones least likely to get it. According to Hoge et al. (2004), OIF/OEF Veterans who met criteria for a mental disorder were twice as likely to report stigma and barriers to care than those who did not meet criteria.

Veterans may also resist seeking treatment because of perceived concerns relating to non-military mental health providers. In fact, data from a recent study of community mental health providers revealed that only 33% of clinicians explicitly asked clients about military status (Miller, Finn, & Newman, 2014). Clearly, it is important for clinicians to routinely inquire about histories of military service during a standardized intake; this can pave the way for eliciting more details about the potential impact of serving. Cornish et al. (2014) also recommend that clinicians increase awareness and normalize the help-seeking process, including stories of other Veterans who had difficulties and then sought help.

Risk Factors for Suicide and Important Characteristics of OIF/OEF Veterans

Veterans are thought to comprise as much as 20% of all suicides (Posey, 2009), and suicide is now the third leading cause of death in the Army population (US Department of Defense, 2010). This is partially due to the difficulties of surviving the challenges of a war zone coupled with the particular strains a soldier must face in his/her transition back to civilian life. To illustrate the common challenges an OIF/OEF Veteran must face, Jennifer Senior quotes an Army suicide report in an article in *New York* magazine:

> At 24 years of age, a Soldier, on average, has moved from home, family, and friends and resided in two other states; has traveled the world (deployed); been promoted four times; bought a car and wrecked it; married and had children; has had relationship and financial problems, seen death; is responsible for dozens of Soldiers; maintains millions of dollars' worth of equipment; and gets paid less than $40,000 a year (2011, p. 30).

Clinicians can begin by educating themselves about the nature of the conflicts in Iraq and Afghanistan, as well as other factors pertinent to this group of Veterans. Importantly, in contrast to previous wars, the current conflicts have been characterized by repeated and extended deployments, thus exacerbating the potential of psychological distress (Tanielian & Jaycox, 2008). This war was distinguished by the constant threat of suicide bombers and roadside explosives. In Iraq and Afghanistan, marketplaces and any other crowded areas, as well as motor vehicles, were frequent targets and some soldiers may find similar situations at home especially difficult to navigate. Therefore, Veterans may be particularly sensitive to driving and being in crowds. Traveling through tunnels or over bridges or overpasses may be especially triggering. Other reminders may even include conditions such as extreme heat, sand, and city noises. It is also not uncommon for returnees to experience distress when dealing with individuals of Muslim or Middle Eastern origin, and some individuals have expressed extreme guilt over these reactions. Other Veterans have noted that prayer calls often preceded war-zone attacks, and so now even walking past a mosque can be frightening for them. It is important for clinicians to normalize these reactions as learned behavioral responses that can be "unlearned" over time as the Veteran safely confronts these stimuli under the supervision of his/her therapist.

Difficulties with relationships, career plans, housing, and financial stressors are common for returning/retiring service members. Veterans sometimes feel that civilians could never understand their wartime experiences and subsequently isolate themselves more and more over time. Providers can normalize these feelings while simultaneously helping the Veteran find appropriate, encouraging sources of social support. Indeed, having strong social support and a sense of connectedness are associated with reduced risk of suicide (Resnick et al., 1997; Stroebe, Stroebe, & Abakoumkin, 2005). It may be helpful to urge a Veteran to attend local Veterans Organizations, a support group, or a Vet Center in the community. Vet Centers, part of the Department of Veterans Affairs and located throughout the US, offer confidential counseling and support where individuals can connect to other Veterans and learn about resources. Often, family members and significant others are encouraged to participate as well.

Disappointments while transitioning home can be compounded by psychiatric symptoms such as insomnia, hyperarousal, and guilt or confusion about their roles while in service or during deployment. It is helpful to normalize the fear and frustration the Veteran may be experiencing relative to his/her symptoms by explaining how combat-ready skills can interfere with readjustment to civilian life (see Castro et al., 2006). Clinicians can gently point out that the very skills and talents that kept a Veteran alive during combat may no longer be skillful in the civilian world (Mallen et al., 2014).

Often these problems are related to the hesitation to allow one's guard down and the difficulties of actually doing so. Surviving in combat requires emotional control, focused aggression, and hyperawareness. Relating to loved ones, controlling anger, and relaxing one's defenses to life as usual is challenging for many (Maguen et al., 2010). Risky and thrill-seeking behaviors, including reckless driving and unprotected sex, as well as impulsivity and overreacting, may be common. Since research reflects that impulsivity increases risk of suicide (Brent et al., 1994), clinicians should be careful to assess for these factors. Normalizing and dealing with these symptoms and stressors directly can ease a Veteran's transition back home and reduce the risk of accidental death or suicide.

Certain demographic factors are also important to keep in mind. Male Veterans are twice as likely to kill themselves as male civilians (Kaplan et al., 2007). Female Veterans are also at a higher risk of suicide than non-Veteran females. One recent study suggested that young female Veterans, aged 18–34, are *three* times more likely to commit suicide than their non-military peers (McFarland, Kaplan, & Huguet, 2010). As in the civilian population, Veterans who are male, over 65 or 18–25 years old, living alone, white or American Indian/Alaska Native may be particularly at risk (Pearson, Conwell, Lindesay, Takahashi, & Caine, 1997).

For Veterans and civilians alike, *the single most important predictor of suicidal behavior is past suicidal behavior* (Harris & Barraclough, 1997; Nordstrom, Asbert, Aberg-Wistedt, & Nordin, 1995; Paykel & Dienelt, 1971). Other factors that increase risk include a family history of suicide (Moscicki, 1995), hopelessness (Beck, Rush, Shaw, & Emery, 1979), and stressful life events. It is a disturbing fact that many of the same issues that returning Veterans face-interpersonal conflict or loss, work difficulties, financial or legal problems, major illness, and chronic pain-are listed as precipitating events linked to suicidal behavior.

Chronic pain is common among those returning from military service, and has been linked to elevated risk of suicide (Ratcliffe, Enns, Belik, & Sareen, 2008; Tang & Crane, 2006). Chronic pain is also a frequent complication of traumatic brain injury (TBI; Nampiaparampil, 2008). Service members are at high risk of TBI resulting from blast injuries, motor vehicle accidents, falls, or gunshot (Warden, 2006). TBIs further exacerbate suicidal risk because of their propensity to increase impulsivity, thought to be due to damage to the frontal lobes (Banasik, 2005), especially among those with a concussion, cranial fracture, or a cerebral contusion and hemorrhage (Teasdale & Engberg, 2001). Taking all of these factors into consideration, it is not surprising that a Veteran's suicide risk increases along with the number of deployments, the length of deployments, and number of injuries sustained.

Although serving in combat is associated with a host of factors known to increase suicidal risk, research also points to the critical importance of assessing for other traumas, including those related to sexual, physical, and emotional abuse. Tiet, Finney, and Moos (2006) reported that among a large nationally representative sample of male treatment-seeking Veterans, recent sexual abuse, recent physical abuse, and lifetime sexual abuse were significantly associated with higher likelihoods of recent suicide attempts. LeBouthillier and colleagues (2015) conducted a similar epidemiological study investigating types of traumas and suicidal risk among a large US sample of individuals with PTSD. They found that childhood mal-treatment was associated with the highest rate of suicidal ideation, followed by assaultive violence and peacekeeping traumas. Not surprisingly, multiple traumas increased suicidality, in that each additional trauma was associated with an increase of 20.1% in rate of suicidal ideation and 38.9% in rate of suicide attempts.

Finally, clinicians should not assume that just because a Veteran did not serve in combat that s/he is not at risk of PTSD and/or suicide, as illustrated in this poignant case example: "Dan" is a young Veteran who served in the Marines, but was involved in a motor vehicle accident during basic training and was never deployed. His dreams of fighting for his country were destroyed, a crushing disappointment only compounded by the fact that his twin brother went on to become a military war hero. Crippled by his chronic pain, sense of defeat, and social alienation, Dan ended his life at a tragically young age, leaving behind his parents, brother, and young wife to pick up the pieces.

Suicide Risk Assessment

It is encouraging to note that clinicians, armed with the right knowledge and tools, *can* help to prevent suicide. A comprehensive suicide risk assessment should be performed on every Veteran that is new to one's practice, and an abbreviated assessment should be conducted at periodic intervals as needed, depending on the Veteran's diagnosis, functionality, and current stressors. Immediate warning signs of suicide include threatening to hurt or kill self, looking for ways to kill self; seeking access to pills, weapons, or other means, and talking or writing about death, dying, or suicide (Knox & Kemp, 2009). The presence of any of these signs requires immediate attention and further evaluation, which may include hospitalization and/or involving local emergency services as needed.

Other warning signs indicate that the Veteran may be at increased risk of suicide, alerting the clinician to put precautions in place to protect his or her safety. These signs include: hope-lessness; rage, anger, or seeking revenge; acting reckless or engaging in risky activities (including driving recklessly); feeling trapped; increasing alcohol or drug abuse; withdrawing from friends, family, or society; anxiety, agitation, unable to sleep or sleeping all the time; dramatic changes in mood; no reason for living, no sense of purpose in life; giving away valued possessions.

It is recommended that clinicians ask the following types of questions to assess suicidal ideation:

- Have you been feeling so sad lately that you were thinking about death or dying?
- Have you been thinking that life is not worth living?
- How often are you thinking about suicide?
- What kind of thoughts have you had about hurting yourself?
- Do you feel you have control over the thoughts and/or responses to them?

These questions are helpful at determining suicidal plan and intent:

a   Have you thought about how you would kill yourself? What would you do?
b   Have you thought about when and where you might do it?
c   Do you have access to (guns, knives, pills, whatever means the Veteran identifies)?
d   How much do you want to die right now?
e   How likely are you to kill yourself today? This week?
f   Have you ever rehearsed how you might commit suicide?

As noted above, previous suicidal behavior is the most important risk factor and should be assessed next. Clinicians can ask:

- Have you ever tried to commit suicide before? Where? When? How? Did you get medical treatment? What happened? Were there any injuries?
- Did you attempt to avoid discovery or rescue?
- What triggered the crisis?
- What was your perception of the lethality of the behavior?
- How did you feel about the fact that you were still alive?
- Have you ever started to kill yourself but stopped? What happened?

A comprehensive suicide risk assessment should include other factors such as history of mental illness, recent losses (financial, emotional, or physical), family history of suicide, and sexual orientation (American Psychiatric Association, 2003). The assessment should also include protective factors that may decrease risk, such as positive social support, spirituality, dependents, and positive coping skills (American Psychiatric Association, 2003). Ascertaining the severity of risk depends on consideration of relevant risk factors, present symptoms, social support (or lack thereof), and the Veteran's current behavior (i.e. is the affect and behavior congruent with what s/he is reporting?). Clinicians should not hesitate to seek consultation or supervision, and risk will need to be reassessed throughout treatment, as risk level will wax and wane. Often, it is not enough to ask just once about suicidal behaviors and risk factors. People sometimes report conflicting information at different time points to the same mental health provider or to different individuals. The value of obtaining consent to get collateral information and consult with all members of the treatment team cannot be overstated. In Appendix 11.A, a comprehensive suicide risk assessment template is detailed. For periodic reassessment of suicidal risk, a brief suicide risk assessment template is provided in Appendix 11.B.

Therapeutic Interventions and Resources

Acute Risk

If a Veteran endorses wanting to kill him or herself, has specific plans with the intent of acting on those plans, has already made or begun to make an attempt, or otherwise leads the clinician to feel s/he is at imminent risk, emergency action should be taken. In this case, clinicians should either hospitalize the Veteran or involve emergency services. Clinicians can call 911 to assist in bringing the Veteran to a local hospital, preferably a VA hospital if feasible, or dispatch local emergency responders to the Veteran's location. Another option is to call the local police precinct, explain the situation, and request a "wellness check." Finally, there may be mobile outreach services available to check on a patient whose safety is in question. These units are available in most metropolitan areas and can usually be found either with a quick Internet search using the patient's residential zip code or through the local hospital. Mobile crisis units have a 24–48-hour window in which they will go to a Veteran's home, evaluate the patient for suicidal risk, and then report back to the provider.

If a Veteran is willing to be hospitalized, it is imperative that s/he never be left alone. Depending on the Veteran's preference and situation, it may be helpful to involve family members or significant others during the hospitalization process. If the Veteran is not willing to go to the hospital and it is determined s/he is at imminent risk, then s/he may need to be hospitalized involuntarily.

It is recommended that an emergency contact person be assigned for every patient during the first session, so that in the event family or others need to be involved, the information is available. Whenever safety is in question, err on the side of caution. In other words, it is better to break confidentiality and risk therapeutic rupture if it means saving a Veteran's life. Veterans and all clients should be warned that in the event their safety or that of someone else is threatened, confidentiality may be broken.

It is important to note the steps for appropriate care for suicidal Veterans before a crisis occurs. It is recommended that community therapists working with Veterans make contact with their local Suicide Prevention Coordinator (SPC). Every VA Medical Center has at least one SPC, and these individuals can share valuable resources as well as offer support and consultation to community clinicians. Contact with the VA has shown to be a protective factor in Veteran suicidality (Maze, 2010) and does not preclude outside care; it is a way to enhance Veteran support. It is also helpful to know that not every VA Medical Center has an emergency department or inpatient unit. Additionally, if there is no VA Medical Center nearby, identify the closest community hospital in case of emergency.

Finally, every clinician working with Veterans should be aware of the VA's 24-hour Suicide Prevention Lifeline. The Crisis Line, designed by the VA in part to address the difficulties some Veterans may have asking for help, was the subject of a recent Oscar award-winning documentary, *Crisis Hotline Veterans Press 1* (2013). Calls are routed to a call center located in Canandaigua, New York, where trained responders will speak to the Veteran and/or family members and assess risk. The hotline personnel can arrange for emergency medical or police dispatch, and can make direct referrals to the Veteran's local SPC. There is also a corresponding website with a chat line that has been established as an effort to appeal to OIF/OEF Veterans, www.suicidepreventionlifeline.org, and even a number that Veterans can text for immediate assistance, 838255.

At the time of the documentary, the Crisis Line had received a total of over 900,000 calls since its inception, or roughly 22,000 calls per month. There are 250 responders, all trained in mental health intervention, and 25% of the responders are Veterans themselves. This poignant film highlights some of the issues that suicidal Veterans might face, such as PTSD, as well as the emotional challenges faced by the mental health practitioners that are doing their best to save them.

Ongoing Management of Safety: Suicide Safety Plans

If a Veteran is not at imminent risk, then s/he and the therapist will need to work together to determine ways the Veteran can remain safe. This collaborative effort should include the development of a Suicide Safety Plan, described below. Other options include increasing the number of therapy contacts and/or telephone check-ins over the next few weeks or as needed. Continuing to work on building the Veteran's coping strategies and distress tolerance skills, assisting him/her in regaining control and a sense of balance, involving social supports, and removing or securing lethal means of self-harm should be the focus of treatment during this time.

It is essential to realize that a patient continues to be at heightened risk once an acute risk subsides. In fact, individuals are most vulnerable to making a suicidal attempt during the first month following an inpatient stay. Clinicians should be attuned to all the risk factors articulated above and continue to check in regarding suicidal ideation and safety throughout treatment.

The "No-Suicide Contract" is not recommended for use with suicidal individuals, Veterans or otherwise (Rudd, Mandrusiak, & Joiner, 2006). Experts contend that suicide contracts on their own are insufficient to prevent suicide, should never be used in lieu of a formal suicide assessment, and provide a false sense of security if a patient is willing to sign one. Rather, clinicians should work with clients to develop a suicide safety plan (Stanley & Brown, 2008). VA clinicians nationwide have been mandated to develop safety plans for any high-risk Veteran. A suicide safety plan is a hierarchical list of coping skills that can be used to manage distress or suicidal crises, and is designed so that any clinician working with a Veteran may implement it as part of an overall treatment package. Safety plans include six basic steps. When the first step fails to decrease the level of suicide risk, the Veteran is instructed to move on to the next step, and so forth. The steps of a safety plan are as follows:

1. recognizing warning signs;
2. using internal coping strategies;
3. socializing with family members or others who may offer support or distraction from the crisis;
4. contacting family members or friends who may offer help to resolve a crisis;
5. contacting professionals or agencies; and
6. reducing access to means.

Clinicians should establish a working rapport with the Veteran and explain that the safety plan is a list of strategies to help him/her tolerate suicidal feelings and other times of extreme distress. It is recommended that plans be written out on paper in a collaborative fashion using the Veteran's own words. A copy should always be given to the Veteran and efforts made to increase the likelihood that s/he will actually use the plan when needed (i.e. recommend the plan be put on the refrigerator or carried in a wallet, problem-solve ways to overcome obstacles to its implementation, encourage sharing the plan with trusted significant others).

Clinicians should generate no more than five responses at most for each step of the plan. Listing too many options can be just as overwhelming as not having any skills to draw from during a psychiatric emergency. In short, the plan should be clear, written in the words of the Veteran, and easily accessible. Although the plan is brief and concrete, much can be learned through the process, such as an individual reporting s/he has no social support, or what mental health professionals a Veteran feels most connected to or would call upon in a time of crisis. The plan should accompany patients as part of overall treatment or life circumstances and evolve, with ongoing refinements as new skills are learned and personal contacts change. Clinicians should inquire about its use and efficacy, problem-solving barriers and reinforcing its implementation. Safety plans should be the focus of any mental health visit when safety is in question.

CASE STUDY – SUICIDE SAFETY PLAN

"Tara" is a young African American female OEF Veteran who returned from Afghanistan four years ago, and she presented to the mental clinic complaining of depressed mood and problems with irritability. She answered yes when asked if she experienced any military sexual trauma (MST), but refused to give any details. She was quiet and withdrawn for most of the initial intake session, but did reluctantly admit to engaging in self-harm behavior. Tara reported that several times a week she would tie a scarf or belt around her neck and pull it until she could not breathe. She also endorsed suicidal ideation ever since she first came home from deployment. She had one previous suicide attempt two years ago when she tried to kill herself by overdosing on all the medications she could find. She denied any current intent or plan to kill herself. Tara stated she was willing to collaborate with her clinician to develop a Suicide Safety Plan as long as she did not have to discuss any details of her trauma.

Tara's Suicide Safety Plan

Step 1 – Warning Signs

Feeling hopeless
Not eating
Having the thought "It doesn't matter anyway"

Step 2 – Internal Coping Strategies

Listen to music
Do Sudoku puzzles
Make some herbal tea

Step 3 – Social Contracts Who May Distract from the Crisis

Take dog to the dog park
Go to Starbucks
Go to farmer's market

Step 4 – Family Members or Friends Who May Offer Help

Call sister XXX-XXXX
Call friend XXX-XXXX

Step 5 – Professionals and Agencies to Contact for Help

Call therapist XXX-XXXX
Call Veteran Suicide Hotline 800-273-TALK (8255)

Step 6 – Making the Environment Safe

Denied access to guns. Agreed to clear medicine cabinet of all extra over-the-counter and prescription drugs and put belts and scarves away.

After this initial meeting, Tara's clinician assessed suicidal ideation, risk, and intent at every session and reinforced the use of her safety plan. Tara learned several effective coping skills for dealing with her suicidal thoughts and self-harm behavior in both individual and group therapy. As Tara progressed and her symptoms improved, her clinician reduced the frequency of suicide risk assessments.

Psychotherapy for Suicidal Veterans

Clinicians should be aware that there are a number of evidence-based mental health treatments available for Veterans who may be struggling with suicidal ideation, urges to suicide, and/or self-harm behaviors. Since Veterans may be especially reluctant to ask for help and remain in treatment, motivational interviewing (Miller & Rollnick, 2013) strategies may be helpful in eliciting commitment to and strengthening engagement in therapy, regardless of the therapeutic modality.

Dialectical behavior therapy (DBT; Linehan, 1993) was specifically developed to treat chronically suicidal individuals and should be recommended as a first-line intervention. DBT typically includes individual and group therapy as well as telephone coaching for the patient, and a consultation team for therapists. DBT explicitly organizes treatment to focus first on suicidal and self-harm behaviors and incorporates four modules: mindfulness, distress tolerance, emotion regulation, and interpersonal effectiveness. There are numerous outcome studies that point to the efficacy of DBT in reducing suicidal behavior (e.g. Linehan et al., 2006) and among female Veterans in particular (Koons et al., 2001). Moreover, evidence suggests learning DBT distress tolerance skills in a drop-in group can significantly reduce suicide-related behaviors in high-risk Veterans (Denckla et al, 2014).

Other options include cognitive therapy for suicidal patients (Wenzel, Brown, & Beck, 2009), a form of cognitive behavioural therapy (CBT) that follows a ten-session protocol focusing on suicidal ideation and strategies to deal with suicidal crises. The authors purposefully developed a relatively brief protocol that could easily be adopted by community mental health centers.

Finally, as noted above, numerous studies point to a strong link between interpersonal traumas (e.g. rape, sexual assault, domestic violence, child abuse) and suicidal risk for both male and female Veterans (Sareen et al., 2010; Tiet, Finney, & Moos, 2006). Therefore, clinicians may wish to consider other forms of therapy that address these issues directly, such as Skills Training in Affective and Interpersonal Regulation (STAIR; Cloitre, Cohen, & Koenen, 2006), a type of CBT specifically developed to treat complex trauma, and one that may be particularly suited to Veterans with MST (Cloitre, Jackson, & Schmidt, in press).

CASE STUDY – SEQUENCED TREATMENT TO PROMOTE SAFETY

Tara continued to meet with her therapist and modify her suicide safety plan as she learned more coping skills and became better at identifying the warning signs that she was experiencing escalating distress. She attended the DBT distress tolerance group at her local VA where she learned critical skills for tolerating extreme distress without engaging in self-harm behaviors. She also kept a diary card where she kept track of her urges to suicide and self-harm and presented that to her therapist each week.

Tara began to see the benefits of therapy, and she was ready to join the weekly DBT skills training group, where she learned the distress tolerance skills in more detail and she learned other vital skills (e.g. interpersonal effectiveness, emotion regulation, and mindfulness) as well. Tara also began to slowly open up to her therapist about the details of her MST. Now that she had learned some valuable coping skills and had significantly reduced her self-harm behaviors, she was ready to address her trauma. Tara's therapist referred her for STAIR so that she could slowly and safely begin to heal and live life in the present.

Conclusion

It is imperative that clinicians working with returning Veterans identify those at risk and provide effective interventions (Martin, Ghahramanlou-Holloway, Lou, & Tucciarone, 2009). Clinicians should be aware of the particular readjustment issues and war-related sequelae that might be impacting an OIF/OEF Veteran. In every case, it is always important to assess for any previous suicidal behavior, as that is the strongest predictor of suicidal behavior.

There are a number of evidence-based therapies and important interventions that can save a Veteran's life. DBT, STAIR, and CBT for suicidal individuals are recommended types of psychotherapy that may be particularly helpful for OIF/OEF Veterans. Suicide safety planning is an invaluable tool and should be the initial focus of any therapy work with suicidal Veterans. All clinicians should be aware of the Veterans Crisis Line, which is an immensely helpful resource for Veterans in distress as well as their family members. For further information and resources that may be helpful for community clinicians, see Appendix 11.C.

Note

The author wishes to dedicate the chapter to suicidal Veterans. The case studies are real, but all identifying information has been changed to protect confidentiality.

References

American Psychiatric Association (2003). *Practice guidelines for the assessment and treatment of patients with suicidal behaviors*. Arlington, VA: Psychiatric Publishing.

Banasik, J. L. (2005). Acute disorders of brain function. In L. C. Copstead & J. L. Banasik (Eds.), *Pathophysiology* (3rd ed.). (pp. 1093–1123). St. Louis: Elsevier.

Beck, A. T., Rush, A. J., Shaw, B. F., & Emery, G. (1979). *Cognitive therapy of depression*. New York: Guilford Press.

Brent, D. A., Johnson, B. A., Perper, J., Connolly, J., Bridge, J., & Bartle, S. et al. (1994). Personality disorder, personality traits, impulsive violence, and completed suicide in adolescents. *Journal of the American Academy of Child and Adolescent Psychiatry*, 33, 1080–1086.

Castro, C. A., Hoge, C. W., Milliken, C. W., McGurk, D., Adler, A. B., Cox, A., Bliese, P. D. (2006, November). *Battlemind training: Transitioning home from combat*. Paper presented at the Army Science Conference, Orlando, FL, November. Abstract retrieved from http://oai.dtic.mil/oai/oai?verb=getRecord&metadataPrefix=html&identifier=ADA481083

Centers for Disease Control and Prevention, National Center for Injury Prevention and Control. (n.d.). Injury prevention & control: Data and statistics. [Web-based injury statistics query and reporting system]. Retrieved from: www.cdc.gov/ncipc/wisqars

Cloitre, M., Cohen, L. R., & Koenen, K. C. (2006). *Treating survivors of childhood abuse: Psychotherapy for the interrupted life.* New York: Guilford Press.

Cloitre, M., Jackson, C., & Schmidt, J.A. (in press). STAIR for strengthening social support and relationships among Veterans with military sexual trauma and PTSD. *Military Medicine.*

Cornish, M. A., Thys, A., Vogel, D. L., & Wade, N. G. (2014). Post-deployment difficulties and help-seeking barriers among military Veterans: Insights and intervention strategies. *Professional Psychology: Research and Practice,* 45(6), 405–409.

Denckla, C. A., Bailey, R., Jackson, C., Tatarakis, J., & Chen, C. K. (2014). A novel adaptation of distress tolerance skills training among military Veterans: Outcomes in suicide-related events. *Cognitive and Behavioral Practice,* doi: 10.1016/j.cbpra.2014.04.001

Greene-Shortridge, T. M., Britt, T. W., & Castro, C. (2007). The stigma of mental health problems in the military. *Military Medicine,* 172, 157–161.

Harris, E. C. & Barraclough, B. (1997). Suicide as an outcome for mental disorders. A meta-analysis. *British Journal of Psychiatry,* 170, 205–228.

Hoge, C. W., Castro, C. A., Messer, S. C., McGurk, D., Cotting, D. I., & Koffman, R. L. (2004). Combat duty in Iraq and Afghanistan: Mental health problems and barriers to care. *New England Journal of Medicine,* 351(1), 13–22.

Kaplan, M. S., Huguet, N., McFarland, B. H., & Newsom, J. T. (2007). Suicide among male Veterans: A prospective population-based study. *Journal of Epidemiology and Community Health,* 61, 619–624.

Knox, K. & Kemp, J. (2009). Operation SAVE: Suicide prevention. Education, Training, and Dissemination. Canandaigua, VISN 2 Center of Excellence.

Koons, R., Tweed, L. J., Lynch, T. R., Gonzalez, A. M., Morse, J., & Butterfield, M. I. (2001). Efficacy of dialectical behavior therapy in women Veterans with borderline personality disorder. *Behavior Therapy,* 32, 371–390.

LeBouthillier, D. M., McMillan, K. A., Thibodeau, M. A., & Asmundson, G. J. G. (2015). Types and number of traumas associated with suicidal ideation and suicide attempts in PTSD: Findings from a US nationally representative sample. *Journal of Traumatic Stress,* 28(3), 83–110.

Linehan, M. M. (1993). *Cognitive behavior therapy for borderline personality disorder.* New York: Guilford Press.

Linehan, M. M., Comtois, K. A., Murray, A. M., Brown, M. Z., Gallop, R. J., Heard, H., & Lindenboim, N. (2006). Two-year randomized controlled trial and follow-up of dialectical behavior therapy vs therapy by experts for suicidal behaviors and borderline personality disorder. *Arch Gen Psychiatry,* 63, 757–766.

McFarland, B. H., Kaplan, M., & Huguet, N. (2010). Self-inflicted deaths among women with US military service: A hidden epidemic. *Psychiatric Services,* 61(12), 1177.

Maguen, S., Cohen, G., Cohen, B. E., Lawhon, G. D., Marmar, C. R., & Seal, K. H. (2010). The role of psychologists in the care of Iraq and Afghanistan Veterans in primary care settings. *Professional Psychology: Research and Practice,* 41(2), 135–142.

Mallen, M. J., Schumacher, M. M., Leskela, J., Thuras, P., & Frenzel, M. (2014). Providing coordinated care to Veterans of Iraq and Afghanistan wars with complex psychological and social issues in a Department of Veterans Affairs Medical Center: Formation of seamless transition committee. *Professional Psychology: Research and Practice,* 45(6), 410–415.

Martin, J., Ghahramanlou-Holloway, M., Lou, K., & Tucciarone, P. (2009). A comparative review of US military and civilian suicide behavior: Implications for OEF/OIF suicide prevention efforts. *Journal of Mental Health Counseling,* 31(2), 101–118.

Maze, R. (2010). Eighteen Veterans commit suicide each day. Retrieved from www.armytimes.com/news/2010/04/military_Veterans_suicide_042210w

Mental Health Advisory Team Six (2009). *Operation Iraqi Freedom 07–09.* Washington, DC: Office of the Surgeon General, United States Army Medical Command.

Miller, K. E., Finn, J.A., & Newman, E. (2014). Are communities ready? Assessing providers' practices, attitudes, and knowledge about military personnel. *Professional Psychology: Research and Practice,* 45(6), 398–404.

Miller, W. R. & Rollnick, S. (2013). *Motivational interviewing: Preparing people for change* (3rd ed.). New York: Guilford Press.

Moscicki, E. K. (1995). Epidemiology of suicidal behavior. *Suicide and Life-Threatening Behavior*, 25, 22–35.

Nampiaparampil, D. E. (2008). Prevalence of chronic pain after traumatic brain injury. *Journal of the American Medical Association*, 300(6), 711–719.

Nordstrom, P., Asberg, M., Aberg-Wistedt, A., & Nordin, C. (1995). Attempted suicide predicts suicide risk in mood disorders. *Acta Psychiatrica Scandinavia*, 92, 345–350.

Paykel, E. S. & Dienelt, M. N. (1971). Suicide attempts following acute depression. *Journal of Nervous and Mental Disease*, 153, 234–243.

Pearson, J. L., Conwell, Y., Lindesay, J., Takahashi, & Caine, E. D. (1997). Elderly suicide: A multi-national view. *Aging and Mental Health*, 1(2), 107–111.

Perry, D. (Producer) & Kent, E. G. (Director). (2013). *Crisis Hotline: Veterans Press 1* [motion picture]. United States: HBO Documentaries.

Posey, S. (2009). Veterans and suicide: A review of potential increased risk. *Smith College Studies in Social Work*, 79(3), 368–374.

Ratcliffe, G. E., Enns, M. W., Belik, S.-L., & Sareen, J. (2008). Chronic pain conditions and suicidal ideation and suicide attempts: An epidemiologic perspective. *Clinical Journal of Pain*, 24(3), 204–210.

Resnick, M. D., Bearman, P. S., Blum, R. W., Bauman, K. E., Harris, K. M., & Jones, J. et al. (1997). Protecting adolescents from harm. *Journal of the American Medical Association*, 278(10) 823–832.

Rudd, M. D., Mandrusiak, M., & Joiner, T. E. (2006). The case against no-suicide contracts: The commitment to treatment statement as a practice alternative. *Journal of Clinical Psychology*, 62(2), 243–251.

Sareen, J. et al. (2010). Correlates of perceived need for mental health care among active military personnel. *Psychiatric Services*, 61(1), 50–57. Online: http://ps.psychiatryonline.org/doi/full/10.1176/ps.2010.61.1.50

Senior, J. (2011). The Prozac, Paxil, Xoloft, Wellbutrin, Celexa, Effexor, Valium, Klonopin, Ativan, Restoril, Xanax, Adderall, Ritalin, Haldol, Risperdal, Seroquel, Ambien, Lunesta, Elavil, Trazodone War. *New York*, February 14, 2011, pp. 26–30, pp. 83–84.

Sherman, M. D., Harris, J. I., & Erbes, C. (2015). Clinical approaches to addressing spiritual struggle in Veterans with PTSD. *Professional Psychology: Research and Practice*, 46(4), 203–212.

Stanley, B. & Brown, G. K. (2008). Safety plan treatment manual to reduce suicide risk: Veteran version. Washington, DC: United States Department of Veterans Affairs.

Stroebe, M., Stroebe, W., & Abakoumkin, G. (2005). The broken heart: Suicidal ideation in bereavement. *American Journal of Psychiatry*, 162, 2178–2180.

Tang, N. & Crane, C. (2006). Suicidality in chronic pain: A review of the prevalence, risk factors and psychological links. *Psychological Medicine*, 36, 575–586.

Tanielian, T. L. & Jaycox (Eds.) (2008). *Invisible wounds of war: Psychological and cognitive injuries, their consequences, and services to assist recovery* (Vol. 720). Pittsburgh, PA: RAND Corporation.

Teasdale, T. & Engberg, A. (2001). Suicide after traumatic brain injury: A population study. *Journal of Neurology, Neurosurgery & Psychiatry*, 71, 436–440.

Thomas, J. L., Wilk, J. E., Riviere, L. A., McGurk, D., Castro, C. A., & Hoge, C. W. (2010). Prevalence of mental health problems and functional impairment among active component and National Guard soldiers 3 and 12 months following combat in Iraq. *Archives of General Psychiatry*, 67, 614–623: doi: 10.001/archgenpsychiatry.2010.54

Tiet, Q. Q., Finney, J. W., & Moos, R. H. (2006). Recent sexual abuse, physical abuse, and suicide attempts among male Veterans seeking psychiatric treatment. *Psychiatric Services*, 57(1), 107–113.

US Department of Defense (2010, July 28). Army health promotion, risk reduction, suicide prevention report 2010. Office of the Chief of Public Affairs, press release.

Warden, D. (2006). Military TBI during the Iraq and Afghanistan wars. *Journal of Head Trauma Rehabilitation*, 21, 398–402.

Wenzel, A., Brown, G. K., & Beck, A. (2009). *Cognitive Therapy for Suicidal Patients: Scientific and Clinical Approaches*. Washington, DC: American Psychological Association.

Appendix 11.A Comprehensive Suicide Risk Assessment

1. Ideation

Plan
Intent

2. Previous Attempts

Describe:

3. Impulsivity

For example, "Are you the kind of person who might get into fights? Risk-taker/thrill seeker?"

Violence
Verbal aggression
Impulsive behaviors
Head injury

4. Psychiatric Illness

None
Depression
PTSD
Bipolar disorder
Substance Abuse
Alcohol Abuse
Psychosis
Personality disorder
Describe:

5. Physical Problems

Pain: (*Note*: Tang & Crane (2006) recommend ascertaining helplessness and hopelessness about the pain, the desire for escape from pain, pain catastrophizing and avoidance, and problem-solving deficits related to the pain.)
Chronic illness (clinicians should be aware that medical conditions, such as hepatic encepha-lopathy, unstable diabetes mellitus, and renal failure, can contribute to altered mental status).
Acute illness
Describe:

6. Acute Symptoms

Psychic pain
Anxiety
Panic
Hopelessness
Insomnia
Obsessionality

Recent intoxication
Hallucinations

7. Adherence to Medication

Reliable, poor, other

8. Firearms

Available
Restricted
Other means – medications, heights, razors, extra extension cords, sharp knives, etc.

9. Protective Factors

Religious/spiritual beliefs
Hopes and plans for the future
Positive/explicit reasons for living
Dependent others
Living with others
Regular contacts with supports
Psychic toughness

Appendix 11.B Brief Suicide Assessment

1. Are you feeling hopeless about the present or future?
2. Have you had thoughts about taking your life? Or, have you had thoughts of killing yourself? Or, have you had thoughts of suicide?
3. Do you have a plan for how you would kill yourself?

Appendix 11.C Resources for the Clinician, Veteran, and Family

Clinician

1. Suicide, Guns and Public Health
   www.meansmatter.org
2. Complete list of VA health care facilities
   www.va.gov
3. Veterans Mental Health Coalition of NYC
   www.mha-nyc.org/advocacy/Veterans-mental-health-coalition.aspx
4. American Association of Suicidology (AAS)
   www.suicidology.org
5. American Foundation for Suicide Prevention (AFSP)
   www.afsp.org
6. Suicide Prevention Resource Center
   www.sprc.org
7. VA Mental Health Suicide Prevention
   www.mentalhealth.va.gov/MENTALHEALTH/suicide_prevention/index.asp

8. VISN 19 MIRECC Clinical Services
    www.mirecc.va.gov/visn19/clinical/clinical_vets.asp
9. Department of Defense
    www.defense.gov/home/features/2010/0810_restoringhope/
    www.realwarriors.net/
10. Clinical Records Initiative: Military Addendum
    www.mtmservices.org/NYSCRI_2010F/Program_Pages/All_Forms.html

Veteran/Family

1. US Airforce Suicide Prevention
    www.af.mil/suicideprevention.asp
2. Department of Navy-Minding Your Mental Health™
    www.nehc.med.navy.mil/Healthy_Living/Psychological_Health/Mental_Health/mm
    h_mentalhealth.aspx
3. US Army Suicide Prevention
    http://chppm-www.apgea.army.mil/dhpw/Readiness/SPTRG/GoodCharlotte2.wmv
4. Army Behavioral Health
    www.behavioralhealth.army.mil/sprevention
5. Marine Corps Veterans and Families
    www.usmc-mccs.org/suicideprevent/index.cfm?sid=fl&smid=1
6. TRICARE Military Healthcare Program: Suicide Prevention
    www.tricare.mil/mybenefit/ProfileFilter.do?&puri=%2Fhome%2FMentalHealthAn
    dBehavior%2FConditions%2FSuicidePrevention
7. US Coast Guard-Suicide Prevention
    www.uscg.mil/worklife/suicide_prevention.asp
8. Military OneSource
    24-hour, 7-days-a-week, toll-free information and referral telephone service.
    www.militaryonesource.com
9. Affordable readjustment services and reintegration support
    www.homeagainVeterans.org
10. Veterans Suicide Prevention Hotline and Chatline
    www.suicidepreventionlifeline.org
    1-800–273-TALK (8255), and press "1"
    text 838255
11. Defense Centers of Excellence for Psychological Health and Traumatic Brain Injury
    (DCoE)
    www.realwarriors.net
12. Iraq and Afghanistan Veterans of America (IAVA)
    www.Iava.org

12

TRAUMATIC BRAIN INJURY FROM BLAST EXPLOSIONS

Applications for Non-DoD/VA Mental Health Clinicians

George M. Cuesta

Introduction

This chapter will introduce practicing non-Department of Defense (DoD)/Veterans Administration (VA) affiliated mental health clinicians to traumatic brain injury (TBI). It will describe the epidemiology of brain injury, describe typical signs and symptoms, and offer suggestion for assessment and intervention.

TBI is a major cause of death and disability in the US. According to the Centers for Disease Control and Prevention, TBI contributes to about 30% of all injury deaths (CDC, 2015). Every day, 138 people in the US die from injuries that include TBI (CDC, 2015). Survivors of TBI face effects that can last a few days to disabilities that last a lifetime. The effects of TBI are far-reaching and can include impaired physical, cognitive, and emotional functioning. These issues adversely affect not only the person with TBI, but also their families and the communities in which they live.

Epidemiology of TBI

The Big Picture – TBI in the US General Population

According to the Centers for Disease Control and Prevention, in the year 2010 there were about 2.5 million emergency department (ED) visits, hospitalizations, or deaths associated with TBI (either alone or in combination with other injuries) in the general population of the US (CDC, 2015). In 2010, TBI contributed to the deaths of more than 50,000 Americans. TBI was a diagnosis in more than 280,000 hospitalizations and 2.2 million ED visits (CDC, 2015). Over the decade from 2001 to 2010, while rates of TBI-related ED visits increased by 70%, hospitalization rates only increased by 11% and death rates decreased by 7%. Each year 1.5 million Americans incur a TBI. About 5.3 million persons have enduring disabilities as a direct result of TBI (CDC, 2015).

In the general population, during the period from 2006 to 2010, the leading causes of TBI in the US were from falls (40%), unintentional blunt trauma (15%), motor vehicle crashes (14%), and assaults (10%) in that order (CDC, 2015). During the period from 2006 to 2010, falls accounted for 40% of all TBIs in the US that resulted in an ED visit, hospitalization, or death. The youngest and oldest age groups are disproportionately affected by falls. For example, more than 55% of TBIs among children 0–14 years were caused by falls and more than 81% of TBIs in adults aged 65 and older were caused by falls (Faul et al., 2010).

Among TBI-related deaths in the general US population from 2006 to 2010, risk factors included gender (men were nearly three times as likely to die as women) and older age (rates were highest for individuals 65 years and older). Among non-fatal TBI-related injuries during the same period, risk factors again included male gender and older age (Faul et al., 2010).

TBI in the Military Population

The Defense and Veterans Brain Injury Center (DVBIC) is the Department of Defense's (DoD) Office of Responsibility for tracking TBI data in the US military. The DVBIC website provides numbers for service members diagnosed with TBI since 2000, listed in total and identified by service and injury severity. The numbers are updated each quarter. Information posted here is collected from electronic medical records in cooperation with the Armed Forces Health Surveillance Center (link is external).

Most causes of TBI among US Armed Forces Service members are the same as for the general population (i.e. falls, unintentional blunt trauma, motor vehicle accidents, and assaults). A report from the Defense Medical Surveillance System (DMSS), Theater Medical Data Store (TMDS) indicated that in 2012 alone nearly 30,000 American service members sustained a TBI (DMSS, TMDS Feb. 13, 2013) (see Figure 12.1).

A more recent report indicated the following data: During the war period, there were 2,020,340 deployments to Iraq/Afghanistan by active component members who had not

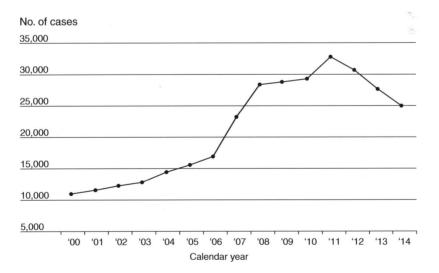

FIGURE 12.1 DoD Numbers for TBI: Number of Service Members Diagnosed
Source: Defense Medical Surveillance System (DMSS), Theater Medical Data Store (TMDS) 2000–2014, as of Dec 8, 2015. Graph taken from the Defense and Veteran Brain Injury Center website. Link: http://dvbic.dcoe.mil/dod–worldwide–numbers–tbi

previously been diagnosed with TBI. Within three years after returning from these deployments, there were 191,052 TBI diagnoses; the cumulative incidence of post-deployment TBI diagnoses was 9.46 per 100 deployments (100 dplys). Among all demographic/military subgroups of Iraq/Afghanistan deployers, the cumulative incidence of TBI diagnoses was highest among those in the Army (11.90 per 100 dplys), older than 24 years (25–35 years and older than 35 years: 10.28 and 10.32 per 100 dplys, respectively), and in combat-specific occupations (10.68 per 100 dplys).

By far the DMSS, TMDS (2013) reported that, among the various branches of the US military (i.e. Army, Air Force, Navy, Marines), the incidence of TBI is greatest in the Army. In 2012, for example, nearly 20,000 Army soldiers sustained a TBI (see Figure 12.2). While TBIs were sustained by members of the other branches of the military, the numbers were far fewer than in the Army.

In terms of incidence of severity, most TBIs sustained by members of the Armed Forces were in the mild range (roughly 25,000). Incidence of moderate to severe TBIs hovered well below approximately 2,000 (see Figure 12.3).

A significant cause for service members who have been deployed to combat zones such as Iraq and Afghanistan are mild-TBI (m-TBI) from blast explosions. An m-TBI, also known as a concussion, is the most prevalent form of TBI. Common symptoms include fatigue, headache, visual disturbances, memory loss, dizziness, and loss of balance. Often the person with a mild TBI does not experience symptoms for days or weeks after the percipient. In the arena of battle, a mild TBI can be caused by an improvised explosive device (IED) that rocks the vehicle in which the service member is riding and the tossing about can cause the brain to swell, creating a mild TBI.

Hoge et al. (2008) surveyed 2,525 US Army infantry soldiers three to four months after return from a year-long deployment to Iraq. Those soldiers with m-TBI, were significantly more likely to report poor general health, missed workdays, medical visits, and a higher

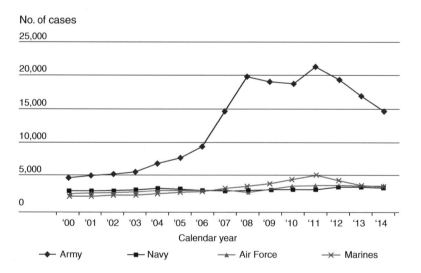

FIGURE 12.2 DoD Numbers for TBI: Number of Service Members Diagnosed by Branch of Service

Source: Defense Medical Surveillance System (DMSS), Theater Medical Data Store (TMDS) 2000–2014, as of Dec 8, 2015. Graph taken from the Defense and Veterans Brain Injury Center website. Link: http://dvbic.dcoe.mil/dod-worldwide-numbers-tbi

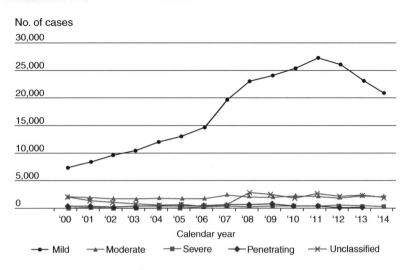

No. of cases

FIGURE 12.3 DoD Numbers for TBI Worldwide: Number of Service Members Diagnosed by Severity

Source: Defense Medical Surveillance System (DMSS), Theater Medical Data Store (TMDS) 2000–2014, as of Dec 8, 2015. Graph taken from the Defense and Veterans Brain Injury Center Website. Link: http://dvbic.dcoe.mil/dod-worldwide-numbers-tbi

number of somatic and post-concussive symptoms than were soldiers with other injuries. Hoge et al. (2008) reported that m-TBI occurring among these soldiers deployed to Iraq was strongly associated with PTSD and physical health problems three to four months after the soldiers returned home.

Mechanisms of TBI from Blast Explosions

While the overwhelming majority (>75%) of TBIs in the current wars in Iraq and Afghanistan (Operation Iraqi Freedom, or OIF and Operation Enduring Freedom, or OEF) are categorized as non-penetrating mild TBI or m-TBI, Warden (2006) reported that the incidence of blast injuries and associated blunt trauma in OIF/OEF was significantly higher than in previous military conflicts.

Brain injury from blast explosions is caused by unique mechanisms. The exact mechanism is unclear, but likely arises from a combination of *primary* and *secondary* effects. The *primary* effect derives from the blast pressure wave as described below.

There are four categories of injuries that can be sustained from a blast explosion. These four categories include the following:

- Primary blast injury – This is injury caused solely by the direct effect of blast overpressure on tissue. Changes in atmospheric pressure cause *primary blast injuries* (PBI). These changes result from conversion of solid or liquid into gases.
- Secondary blast injury – These are injuries caused by flying objects that strike people and cause physical harm.
- Tertiary blast injury – This type of injury occurs when a person is projected through the air and that person strikes another object potentially causing mechanical injury to the brain and other parts of the body.

- Quaternary blast injuries – These encompass all other injuries caused by explosions and may include burns, crush injuries, and toxic inhalations. A person may be injured by more than one of these mechanisms.

Assessment of Functional Impairments Resulting from TBI

Mental health clinicians working with Veterans who have m-TBI should assess for how well individuals are carrying out their activities of daily living (ADLs). ADLs include activities in which all humans engage – i.e. dressing, feeding, bathing, toileting. These can easily be assessed by frank questioning of the client by the clinician. Typically, clients with m-TBI may not have difficulties in this domain. However, instrumental activities of daily living (IADLs) may be a challenge for some of these clients. IADLs should routinely be evaluated by clinicians to determine if there are any functional impairments or weaknesses in these areas. These activities are more complex and require planning, foresight, and problem-solving. Examples of IADLs include preparing a meal, planning a list of items to buy at the grocery store, planning a trip to a destination including how to get there (what subway to take, transfers, and what stop to get off), what is needed to get there (money, documents, Metro Card), money management, medication management and so forth. One example of an instrument that can assist the clinician with measuring IADLs is the Lawton Instrumental Activities of Daily Living Scale (Graf, 2008). The scale takes approximately 10 to 15 minutes to administer. It contains eight items that are rated with a summary score from 0 (low functioning) to 8 (high functioning). This scale can be administered through an interview or by a written questionnaire. The patient or a caregiver who is familiar with the patient can provide the answers (Graf, 2008).

Assessment of Cognitive Impairments Resulting from TBI

Veterans with m-TBI may complain of difficulties with concentration, short-term memory, problem-solving, and other cognitive challenges. Mental health clinicians can administer, score, and interpret brief cognitive screens that will aid in the referral process. Examples of these cognitive screens include the Mini Mental State Examination (MMSE, Folstein et al., 1975), the Modified MMSE (3MS, Teng & Chui, 1987) and the Montreal Cognitive Assessment (MoCA, Nasreddine et al., 2005). These screens briefly tap into cognitive domains including attention, memory, visual spatial abilities, language, and executive functions (e.g. planning, foresight, and problem-solving). They take little time to administer and score. Cut-offs have been established to aid the clinician in reaching a provisional conclusion about the presence or absence of impairments.

Assessment of Psychological Impact of TBI

Veterans with m-TBI may complain of irritability, anxiety, depression, difficulties with managing anger, low frustration tolerance, and so forth. In addition to thorough clinical interviewing and in order to more fully assess these difficulties, mental health clinicians can administer, score, and interpret brief psychological screens that will aid in learning more about how the client is functioning psychologically. Results from these measures can aid the clinician in case formulation and reaching diagnostic conclusions. Examples of psychological screening measures include the Beck Depression Inventory (BDI, Beck et al., 1961), Beck Anxiety Inventory (BAI, Beck & Steer, 1993), Neurobehavioral Screening Inventory (NSI,

Cicerone & Kalmar, 1995), and the Post Traumatic Stress Disorder (PTSD) Checklist for Diagnostic and Statistical Manual of Mental Disorders (DSM), 5th Edition (PCL-5, Weathers et al., 2013).

Impact of m-TBI on Family Dynamics and Caregiver Support

It is well known that TBI affects not only the person with TBI, but all of her or his family and caregivers. Studies show that caregivers of people who have suffered a brain injury may experience feelings of burden, distress, anxiety, anger, and depression. Family members often experience substantial emotional distress and disruption of family functioning. These difficulties can impact the rehabilitation process and the recovery of the Veteran with injury. Family members and caregivers are also an important source of support for individuals with TBI (Sander, 2014). The mental health professional working with Veterans who have m-TBI can make skillful and effective interventions with family members and caregivers. These interventions can include emotional support, encouragement, and, most importantly, education about m-TBI and the course of recovery from the injury.

Treatment of m-TBI Sequelae

McAllister (2008) provided excellent guidelines for clinicians evaluating and treating individuals with moderate to severe TBI. However, these clinical guidelines can reasonably be applied to persons with m-TBI as well. McAllister (2008) makes an excellent point that the evaluator must have a clear picture of what the individual was like prior to the injury in order to more accurately understand the effect of the brain injury on the individual. Therefore, questions in the clinical interview that shed light on the person's premorbid functioning are essential. Following careful neuropsychological assessment, the mental health clinician will have a fairly good idea of what are the cognitive, psychological, and functional impairments in their client.

McAllister (2008) recommended that it is best to have a clear sense of the cause of the challenging behavior before designing a treatment plan. He suggested a hypothesis testing approach based upon the data from the evaluation. For example, a Veteran with increased irritability, increased arousal and activation and significant reduction in sleep might be conceptualized as having an irritable, manic-like syndrome and thus reasonably started on a mood stabilizer (McAllister, 2008). The critical issue is that the interventions developed and implemented spring from testable hypotheses and can be evaluated and reevaluated for their effectiveness over time.

For mental health clinicians, working closely and collaboratively with a neuropsychiatrist, physiatrist, and a neuropsychologist can be invaluable since these professionals typically evaluate and treat individuals with brain injuries. The neuropsychiatrist can assist with antidepressant, anxiolytic, and other medications. The physiatrist, a physical medicine and rehabilitation physician, can assist with all aspects of rehabilitation from acute (inpatient) to post-acute (outpatient) rehabilitation. Physiatrists typically work with other professionals such as occupational therapists, physical therapists and speech/language pathologists. Neuropsychologists typically conduct comprehensive neuropsychological evaluations with the Veteran who has brain injury. Neuropsychologists can assist the mental health clinician in understanding the cognitive strengths and impairments of the individual with m-TBI. They can also shed light on the personality, behavioral, and psychological challenges the Veteran might be experiencing post injury.

Practical Suggestions for Mental Health Professionals Treating Veterans with m-TBI

There is a plethora of resources available for mental health clinicians on the Internet that provide good guidance and advice on how to work with individuals with m-TBI. One excellent resource readily available for the reader is www.brainlinemilitary.org/concussion. For Veterans with cognitive impairments, here are some practical suggestions:

- Encourage your patient to record important information (such as appointments, errands, and medication schedules).
- Promote better sleep hygiene, diet, and exercise to improve mental well-being.
- If cognitive deficits are not improving, refer your Veteran to specialty care for complete neuropsychological testing and assessment, if it has not already been completed. Also consider referrals to rehabilitation medicine professionals who work specifically on cognitive challenges following m-TBI (e.g. neuropsychologists, rehabilitation psychologists, speech-language pathologists, and occupational therapists).
- If the service member or Veteran has documented cognitive difficulties, cognitive rehabilitation can be effective in helping them to either compensate for or treat their cognitive problems. Evidence varies for the specific cognitive problems that present commonly following concussion/mTBI, but clients often find guidance related to how to compensate for their deficits very helpful.

Case Example

The following example is not an actual client, but an amalgam of case history from a variety of clients. The point here is to illustrate some of the assessment, referral, and treatment issues associated with these clients.

> Jane was a 26-year-old, African American, married, mother of two young children; a 1-year-old son and 3-year-old daughter. She recently resigned from the Active Army Reserves. She has a supportive husband, Desmond (age 32), who is a Staff Sergeant in the Active Army. Jane enlisted in the Army Reserves right out of high school at the age of 18. Her military occupational specialty was in supply and logistics. She had two deployment tours in Iraq and the traumatic event occurred on the second tour. She was wounded in a convoy when an IED exploded and hit her vehicle.
>
> Jane sustained shrapnel injuries to her extremities and her left two fingers and left four toes were traumatically amputated. There was a reported loss of consciousness for about two minutes. She was wakened by her fellow soldiers trying to evacuate her with confusion, disorientation, agitation, combativeness, and temporary deafness. She was treated for her injuries in the field (Echelon I) and then at the combat support hospital (Echelon II). Eventually, she was evacuated to the military hospital in Landsthul, Germany and, ultimately, back to the continental US.
>
> Jane had a short stay at the Walter Reed Army Medical Center now in Bethesda, Maryland. She received inpatient acute rehabilitation, outpatient rehabilitation, and then she was discharged to her home and family. She was medically retired from the Army with a Purple Heart. She is now living with her husband and two children. Her parents live nearby and are very involved in helping Jane with child care.

Jane tried to go to community college using her Post 9/11 GI Bill, but had great difficulty with concentration, completing assignments, recalling class meeting times, and had conflicts with professors and fellow students. Jane complained of flashbacks of the traumatic event and nightmares. Her husband complained she was emotionally distant, irritable, had angry outbursts with him and the children.

There was one angry outburst at the commissary when she lost her temper and loudly reprimanded her daughter for misbehavior. Shaken by her behavior, she spoke to her pastor who referred her to the local Vet Center. Her counselor met with her and began the assessment. No brain injury work-up had ever been completed on Jane. At the time of the event, the medical focus was on her orthopedic and other physical injuries. The counselor consulted with one of the clinical psychologists on the team who met with Jane and administered the MoCA and the 3MS. Also administered was the PTSD Checklist and her ADLs and IADLs were also assessed. Here were Jane's assessment scores:

- MOCA total score = 25 out of 30
- MMSE total score = 26 out of 30
- 3MS total score = 79 out of 100
- PCL total score = 67 out of 85
- ADLs = normal
- IADLs = abnormal; e.g. frequent trouble with forgetting items on the grocery shopping list, planning for outings with the children, disorganized approach to school assignments, arranging public transportation, preparing meals.

The psychologist concluded that the provisional diagnosis was PTSD and m-TBI and informed the counselor. The counselor consulted with the Veterans Affairs Medical Center neuropsychologist, with the Veteran's consent, and presented the evidence from the assessment. A referral was made for a comprehensive brain injury work-up with a neurologist and neuropsychologist. Impairments were found in selective and sustained attention, short-term memory, planning, foresight, and problem-solving. From here, the Veteran was referred to an occupational therapist for cognitive remediation of attention, memory, and executive functioning.

The Vet Center counselor consulted with the brain injury team and developed a strategy for tailoring the treatment for PTSD. For the present moment, Jane was not a candidate for cognitive processing therapy (CPT). It was concluded that the extensive verbal instructions in CPT might overwhelm the Veteran. However, the counselor was hopeful she will later be able to participate in this treatment. It was recommended she learn compensatory strategies to overcome her cognitive and behavioral impairments. Parenting skills group was recommended. Couples' counseling was also considered. Education about TBI was provided to Veteran and her spouse. Since Jane's parents were also supportive and involved, this education about TBI was also provided to them.

Conclusions

Brain injury can be a devastating life event. There are potential adverse implications for cognition, psychological, interpersonal, and spiritual functioning. Mental health counselors in the community who work with Veterans have at their disposal ways to help these Veterans make a better readjustment back to civilian life. These counselors can partner with Veterans Health Administration clinicians to maximize readjustment potential of these Veterans.

References

Armed Forces Health Surveillance Center (2010). *Report of the Defense Medical Surveillance System (DMSS) and Theater Medical Data Store (TMDS)*. Silver Spring, MD: Author.

Beck, A. T. & Steer, R. A. (1993). *Beck Anxiety Inventory Manual*. San Antonio: Harcourt Brace and Company.

Beck, A. T., Ward, C. H., Mendelson, M., Mock, J., & Erbaugh, J. (1961). An inventory for measuring depression. *Archives of General Psychiatry*, 4, 561–571.

Centers for Disease Control and Prevention (CDC) (January 2015). Traumatic Brain Injury in the United States: Fact Sheet. National Center for Injury Prevention and Control. Retrieved June 19, 2015 from: www.cdc.gov/traumaticbraininjury/get_the_facts.html

Cicerone, K. D. & Kalmar, K. (1995). Persistent postconcussion syndrome: the structure of subjective complaints after mild traumatic brain injury. *Journal of Head Trauma Rehabilitation*, 10, 1–17.

Faul, M., Xu, L., Wald, M. M., & Coronado, V. G., (2010). Traumatic brain injury in the United States: emergency department visits, hospitalizations, and deaths. Atlanta (GA): Centers for Disease Control and Prevention, National Center for Injury Prevention and Control.

Folstein, M. F., Folstein, S. E., & McHugh, P. R. (1975). "Mini-mental state". A practical method for grading the cognitive state of patients for the clinician. *Journal of Psychiatric Research*, 12(3), 189–198.

Graf, C. (2008). The Lawton Instrumental Activities of Daily Living Scale. *American Journal of Nursing*, 108(4), 53–62.

Hoge, C. W., McGurk, D., Thomas, J. L., Cox, A. L., Engel, C. C., & Castro, C. A. (2008). Mild traumatic brain injury in US soldiers returning from Iraq. *New England Journal of Medicine*, 358(5), 453–463.

McAllister, T. W. (2008). Neurobehavioral sequelae of traumatic brain injury: evaluation and management. *World Psychiatry*, 7, 3–10.

Nasreddine, Z. S., Phillips, N. A., Bedirian, V., Charbonneau, S., Whitehead, V., Collin, I., Cummings, J. L., & Chertkow, H. (2005). The Montreal Cognitive Assessment, MoCA: A Brief Screening Tool for Mild Cognitive Impairment. *Journal of the American Geriatric Society*, 53(4), 695–699.

Sander, A. M. (2014). Treating and collaborating with family caregivers in the rehabilitation of persons with traumatic brain injury. In M. Sherer & Sander, A. M. Sander (Eds.), *Handbook on the neuropsychology of traumatic brain injury* (pp. 271–282). New York: Springer.

Teng, E. L. & Chui, H. C. (1987). The Modified Mini Mental State (3MS) Examination. *Journal of Clinical Psychiatry*, 48, 314–318.

Warden, D. (2006). Military TBI during the Iraq and Afghanistan wars. *Journal of Head Trauma Rehabilitation*, 21, 398–402.

Weathers, F. W., Litz, B. T., Keane, T. M., Palmieri, P. A., Marx, B. P., & Schnurr, P. P. (2013). *The PTSD Checklist for DSM-5 (PCL-5)*. Scale available from the National Center for PTSD at www.ptsd.va.gov

Additional Reading and Resources

Bush, S. S. (Ed.) (2012). *Neuropsychological practice with Veterans*. New York: Springer.

Centers for Disease Control and Prevention (CDC) (2013). *Report to Congress on traumatic brain injury in the United States: Understanding the public health problem among current and former military personnel.* Retrieved July 20, 2015 from www.cdc.gov/traumaticbraininjury/pubs/congress_military.html

Defense & Veterans Brain Injury Center (DVBIC). Retrieved 20 July 2015 from http://dvbic.dcoe.mil/dod-worldwide-numbers-tbi

Hill, J., Lawhorne, C. & Philpott, D. (2011). *Life after the military: A handbook for transitioning Veterans.* Lanham, MD: Government Institutes, Scarecrow Press.

Kennedy, C. H. & Moore, J. L. (Eds.) (2010). *Military neuropsychology.* New York: Springer.

Kennedy, C. H. & Zillmer, E. A. (Eds.) (2006). *Military psychology: Clinical and operational applications.* New York: Guilford Press.

Silver, J. M., McAllister, T. W., & Yudofsky, S. C. (2005). *Textbook of Traumatic Brain Injury*. Washington, DC: American Psychiatric Publishing.

Sloane, L. B. & Friedman, M. J. (2008). *After the war zone: A practical guide for returning troops and their families*. Philadelphia: Da Capo Press.

Southwick, S. M. & Charney, D. S. (2012). *Resilience: The science of mastering life's greatest challenges*. New York: Cambridge University Press.

13

WORKING WITH MILITARY NURSES AND THEIR FAMILY SYSTEMS

Pauline A. Swiger, Eric S. Graybill and Diane L. Vaccarell

A Brief Introduction to the History of Nursing in the Military

The history of nursing and the US military begins in 1775 during the War of Independence when Congress authorized funds for one nurse for every ten patients generated by the war. The purpose of this workforce was to free up the healthy soldiers, who were caring for the sick and wounded, to go back to the front lines. The nurses were paid $2 a month and one meal per day for their work. Nurses cared for service members in conflicts from that point on, although not as part of the service but as an adjunct during wartime. In 1899, the Surgeon General established the criteria for a Reserve Force of nurses that could be activated during times of need; this began the move to make nurses a permanent part of the military's medical department. In 1901, a bill became law which created a female-only corps in which nurses were appointed for a three-year service period but did not give nurses officer status. WWI was the first conflict in which the Armed Forces had an established Nurse Corps. When the conflict began, there were 433 nurses on active duty but by the end of the conflict over 22,000 nurses served either overseas or at home. This equated to one-third of all graduate nurses in the US having served at some time during WWI. In 1920, nurses were finally allowed to wear military rank insignia, second lieutenant through major, in order to identify them as members of the Nurse Corps but were only referred to by name as Miss or Nurse. Females were paid about half what a male officer of the same rank would be paid. During WWII, 56,793 nurses served in all parts of the world. Innovations in nursing care came out of this conflict such as flight nursing, post-operative care, and nurse-administered anesthesia. Nurses were also authorized to wear a military uniform (fatigues) and became more immersed with service members; some were even captured as prisoners of war. In 1947, Public Law 36 officially established the Army Nurse Corps which authorized the military to recruit and retain 2,558 nurses and elevated nurses to commissioned officers. Over the next several years, nurses worked to obtain full pay status for their given rank and several schools were established to increase nursing expertise. Nurses also began teaching enlisted medical personnel. In 1955, the Nurse Corps was opened to male nurses; about 25 years after males could serve as civilian nurses. Beginning in 1962, over 5,000 nurses served in Vietnam where they developed as trauma and intensive-care specialists. Over the next 30 years, nurses grew as experts in their field and as professionals within the military. The Chief of the Army Nurse Corps was commissioned as the first female general and for the first time a nurse was given the position as Commander in a military hospital. These were huge steps toward equality for women in the armed services. In the 1980s and 1990s, nurses served in Dessert Shield, Dessert Storm, Operation Restore Hope (in Somalia, Haiti, and Bosnia), as well as multiple humanitarian missions. Since 2001, military nurses have served in Operation Enduring Freedom in Afghanistan, Operation Iraqi Freedom, and Operation New Dawn, also in Iraq. Military nurses have cared for the sick, injured, forgotten, and persecuted. Along with proud service, nurses have accepted the hazards associated with military service; many have died of disease and suffered the elements; some have served as prisoners of war and even died in combat (Schwab, 2013). As with most military service members, nurses feel a sense of duty and a common loyalty to those they care for; they serve wherever they are needed and therefore are exposed to similar risks, heartbreaks, and tragedies associated with military service.

As this brief history shows, nurses have played a vital role in the care of our military. This chapter will look at the experience of nurses in the military and will inform behavioral health practitioners on issues as they relate to the military experience of nurses and how to best care for these carers as they reenter society after military service.

The Military Nurse Experience

There are numerous factors that define the experience of military nurses: the structure of the military and the military ethos/culture are most prominent.

Rank and the Hierarchal Structure within the Military

The military has many traditions, customs, and courtesies that foster respect for one another. This can cause constraints regarding the freedom with which someone expresses themselves and may limit a service member's autonomy (McManus, Mehta, McClinton, De Lorenzo, & Baskin, 2005). One might expect that this amplifies the divide between nurses and physicians; however, military nurses, especially those in hospital leadership roles, may have equal rank or even outrank a physician. This creates a balance which may explain why military nurses often report very collegial relationships with physicians and generally report good practice environments within military hospitals (Raju, Su, & Patrician, 2014; Zangaro & Kelley, 2010).

Military Ethos

Military or Warrior Ethos is a code of behavior that is based on an idealized image of the warrior. There is often tension within the military ethos between honor and sense of inadequacy. In addition to the beliefs, "protect civilians" and "display moral courage", the role of protector often encompasses other responsibilities and beliefs as well. The Warrior Ethos statement is contained within the new Soldier's Creed: "I will always place the mission first. I will never accept defeat. I will never quit. I will never leave a fallen comrade."

Military Ethos can make high levels of teamwork and mission focus possible, and can serve as an organized way of life and source of lifelong pride. But, it also sets standards that can be difficult to meet, and can sometimes result in conflicting values related to different military roles, and be a reason for some individuals to rebel against its high standards and values. In regards to psychological health, military ethos can serve as both a protective factor and a vulnerability.

Particularly through the worldview of the nursing Soldier as well as the worldview of their family, providers need to ask culturally informed questions about the person(s) unique military experience. This can allow a development of knowledge about the military and medical culture that a particular nursing Soldier has. An example of a question that can help providers to be more informed includes asking "In what ways is taking care of your health consistent with being a good (Soldier, nurse, significant other, parent, etc.)?"

Life as a Military Nurse on Active Duty

The day-to-day patient care activities of military nursing are similar to those of any nurse. They are exposed to shift work; caring for those in high stress situations and the physical demands that are not much different from what a civilian nurse might experience but a military nurse must also balance the additional responsibilities that come along with military service. Nurses in the military maintain a state of readiness in which they must be responsive at a moment's notice to provide care in any number of situations. The possibility of leaving one's family and being called upon to provide care in difficult situations in a distant part of the world, is present even during peacetime as nurses participate in national or global humanitarian crisis relief (Fry, Harvey, Hurley, & Foley, 2002).

Early on in my career as a brand new 2Lt., I was learning my craft as a nurse and also learning my profession as a Soldier. There were many tasks that needed to be completed in addition to my clinical growth: weapons qualification, physical fitness tests, military education, leadership training, and many others. As an Army nurse and officer, you are required to be so much more than a nurse. Inherently, Army officers are leaders, so the assertive transformation from an orienting rookie nurse, to a team leader, to a preceptor, to a charge nurse, a committee chairman, head nurse, and so on ... These character skills bleed over into your clinical performance and you learn to function as an assertive patient advocate and work collaboratively with a medical team to deliver safe patient care. Train-up for deployment includes as much clinical training as it does Soldier training. Learning to put on your gas mask is as important as starting an IV in the back of an ambulance.

Caring for Nurses

Nurses have to be cared for and their experience validated. This is an area of concern in behavioral health. The exigencies of deployment and pre-deployment can take a toll on the military nurse and their family.

In a qualitative study of 367 nurses, researchers found that 80% of the nurses surveyed felt that they were unprepared for deployment. They also felt that although their initial pre-deployment training was inadequate, they were ultimately able to provide adequate or more than adequate care to their patients. These same nurses acknowledged that although they believed clinical and physical preparation was possible, they felt psychological preparation was not possible (Stanton-Bandiero, 1998).

Prior to deploying I sought out as much trauma training as I could get. I was terrified that an injured service member would come in to the hospital and I would not know what to do. Before leaving I had dreams of failing in my job; I'd wake up in a cold sweat wondering how I was going to live with myself if I failed. This was the job I was supposed to do, but was I really prepared? The military provided me with several amazing training opportunities, like TCMC (Tactical Combat Medical Care), but I still didn't feel ready. I was worried that I'd freeze or become overwhelmed with emotion instead of letting my training kick in.

Once nurses realize they are headed for deployment, commonly four to 12 months in length, they may begin to count the "soon to be" missed events and milestones. Missing birthdays, holidays, a child's first step, or a best friend's wedding evoke feelings of guilt and loss. In addition, deployment can create an ethical dilemma for the service member. They may ask themselves, "what is more important, being a parent or a service member?" Choosing one evokes feelings of failure in the other. Military parents are also aware of the impact of deployment on their children. Families experience increased school, family, and peer relationship difficulties during and after deployment (Scannell-Desch & Doherty, 2013). As preparation for deployment begins, so too does anxiety for many service members.

Handing off roles: Me and my wife spent weeks going over things that I usually take care of. From mowing the lawn, changing lightbulbs, how to work the fuse box, where the Christmas lights are and how to put them up and take them down ... So many little things I do without thinking must be handed off to her to take care of for the next year. The guilt I feel for "dumping" these things in her lap is heavy. Heidi must also function in the "manly" father role as well as the loving and nurturing mother role. There are times she had to remember that I wasn't there with my two older boys that needed a pep talk and a fatherly encouraging "man up" when my boys needed some tough love. I had to make sure that she knew how to change a tire, set the house alarm, change batteries in smoke detectors, work the electronics with the TV, etc. ... I also had to build a trust with neighbors. My immediate neighbors needed to know that I would be gone and I had to trust them to watch over my family while I am away. They proved to be an invaluable "asset" to me and my family.

During deployment nurses are faced with the decision about what to share with family and what to keep to themselves. The fear faced, the toll of taking care of the injured, and the exhaustion are sometimes kept secret from family members as a way to shield them from worry. Letters and Skype sessions are kept lighthearted and focused on the family. Editing on both sides is to be expected as distance and the reality of what the nurse and their significant other are dealing with are out of reach to be ameliorated. Nurses may also report moving into a necessary state of numbness during deployment; often it is not until they return home that they begin to deal with the many emotions they experienced while away. However, a patient or event may break through the barrier and allow the emotions to flood in.

There are some memories that are a blur and others that remain vivid. One such vivid memory was of a young woman who came into our ER in Baghdad. For me, looking at her was like looking in a mirror; her hair color, her body shape, a mole on her neck, and her profile corresponded to mine. The difference was she was pale from blood loss and was not breathing. My movements were robotic while the team cared for her; it was like I was watching it all unfold from a distance. In my head I was saying, "Come back ... Please ... Come back now." I did not want to watch her – watch myself – die. But, she did. That night I remember the distant noises of the conflict that I could always hear from my sleeping quarters seemed louder. I pulled my flack vest over the top of me and tried to sleep but I was unable. I realized that life, my life, was fragile and for the first time, I was really scared.

The common experience of deployment bonds people together in an inexplicable way. Deployed nurses share heartache and joy in life or death situations and come to rely on each other. However, the intensity of the situation and quantity of time spent together can also cause friction. During deployment so much time is spent together that, upon return, service members may report wanting some space away from those they deployed with. In time, most nurses would report a bond remains with those they served even if they do not stay in immediate close contact. The ability to reach out to others that have shared the deployment experience can be helpful, however for those who leave the service, as well as Reserve or Guard service members, this can be challenging because they may be geographically separated and may not have the same robust support structure that is readily available to active-duty service members.

You just go through things that you could never imagine are real and there is a special bond you form that allows for lifetime friendships. These bonds you create will also help you get through the immediate post-deployment and reintegration phases. There are some rough times during redeployment and having the ability to call those who you deployed with is a priceless commodity.

Professional Growth

Many nurses feel that the experience they have while deployed makes them better at their job. Deployed nurses often work in a fast-paced environment where they see rare illnesses and dramatic injuries. In this environment they are challenged professionally and learn new skills. This can also make returning to non-deployed nursing seem mundane, routine, and frustrating.

During deployment, there are often missions and tasks that can take you places you never thought possible. You are building full-functioning trauma hospitals out of airports or tents. Objects you would never thought you could use are being utilized to save a life. It is easy to get engulfed into the deployment lifestyle and volunteer for missions you would never dream of when you were in garrison back home. It is easy to overlook the request of family back home to stay safe for the opportunity to get out and do something you never thought possible. Because you don't have anything else that you are responsible for except for patient care, there is downtime where you may spend time up at the hospital learning new skills or researching new clinical pathways.

Returning Home

Nurses may experience post-traumatic stress symptoms upon returning from home and many find coming home more difficult than anticipated (Scannell-Desch & Doherty, 2013). Generally, the first few weeks are filled with celebration and feelings of relief at returning home. However, the reintegration into family and work comes with its own challenges.

> When I look back over my life, there are certain events that immediately stand out: my wedding day, the birth of my children, my son being baptized. But above all others, the moment at the homecoming celebration when the Commander said "dismissed" and my family ran out to find me and hug me was the best 90 seconds of my life. From the instant I landed in the Middle East, I dreamed of this moment. I had been a deployed Soldier 24/7 for the last ten months and now I was home but, I still could not unplug mentally from the Army and truly bond with my family.

"Not the Same"

> While deployed, there is an elevated sense of urgency and satisfaction that I had never felt before. Many of the strategic actions that took weeks to get accomplished back at a stateside hospital were completed within hours. Patients were happy to be alive, safe, and within reach of a working air-conditioner. The hospital staff was engulfed in their jobs every minute of every day. This became the new routine and nurses grew accustomed to this environment; I've never seen people work so hard.
>
> When reintegrating back into a stateside hospital, things feel much differently than before. Nurses bring back the deployed focus with them and expect a similar environment and response from patients and staff as they were accustomed to when deployed. My first day back as the head nurse of a unit, I remember very vividly the first 15 minutes of my tenure. A nurse called me to tell me she was sick and wouldn't be there today, another called me to tell me she was running late because her dog wouldn't get into his kennel, a night shift nurse was upset that she was scheduled to work two weekends in a row, and that I needed to visit a patient, an 18-year-old Private who was upset because the cafeteria sent up the wrong flavored Jello. I had to force a chuckle out and let everyone know that everything is going to be ok. I said a quick prayer and asked God to grant me patience with my patients, empathy for my staff, and sanity for my wife who will be hearing my aggravation for months to come!

Nurses may also struggle with transitions back into routine life. During deployment, many of the decisions and choices common in daily life are absent and come flooding upon return. Once the celebration of returning home is over, the struggles of the service member may begin.

> At first, even going to the grocery store felt exciting and a bit overwhelming. I'd forgotten how many choices there were; it seemed there were a hundred options of cereal. Quickly the joy of returning turned into something else. I had forgotten how frustrating people

(even those I loved) could be and perhaps my threshold for tolerance of others was lowered. At work and at home I felt like I'd lost patience. I felt like I had changed; I was focused on wanting to enjoy "normal" life yet those around me were more irritating than before. It felt like they were all focused on what I thought were silly, insignificant hang-ups.

Memories, Dreams, and Stories

Nurses may feel compelled to tell stories of their service and deployment or they may choose to keep them private. Some may aim to forget where others feel compelled to remember.

I feel like it's my responsibility to remember each and every person I cared for. I have dreams; sometimes they're of service members and sometimes of the civilians and injured and sick children. I get frustrated when I can't sleep, but I also don't want them to go away. I feel a sense of duty, an obligation, to remember.

Early on in my career, I took care of a very young 2Lt. who had blast injuries secondary to an explosion. He couldn't have been more than 23 years old. His mother and older brother stayed with him at his side the entire stay. Respiratory complications continued to affect his progress and a chest tube needed to be inserted at the bedside expeditiously. I'll never forget the look in his eyes; terrified, innocent, immature, and desperate. His mother looked around the room for reassurances from the hospital staff that her son was going to be ok. The older brother took his hand and let him know he was going to be ok and to suck it up. It was a welcomed improvement to the tension in the room. I took the 2Lt.'s other hand and asked if he wanted to pray. He took me up on the offer and we prayed together for 30 seconds. He said, "Sir, I am sorry this keeps happening and you have to stay late. I hate to keep bothering you with this." This interaction nearly brought me to my knees. *He* was worried about *me*? This event speaks to so many facets of military nursing, but the main thing that I realized was that I am here for a much greater purpose than myself, I am here to serve and care for America's sons and daughters. I easily replied with "Brother, I am here for you. You are the only reason I get out of bed in the morning, and the only reason I have a job in the Army. You spend up to 24 hours per day on the front lines to get the job done, I do the same thing here in this safe stateside hospital. I will be here with you until you are back on your feet and ready to go back to work. I promise."

Leaving Military Nursing

The active military is downsizing; the goal is to reduce the force by 80,000 service members by 2017 (US Department of Defense, 2013). For many service members, this means that their military service may end not by their choice, but due to mandatory force reduction. Service members who are selected to leave may be faced with a stigma by those inside and outside the military. Potential employers may wonder why they were not selected to stay and continue their service. Many people forget that as with any business, when a nurse joins the service, they are entering into a four-year contract with an employer. There is no guarantee that you will have a job after those four years even if they have done the job well. Especially when the military is downsizing, they may not have the option to stay simply because the military did not need to renew their contract. Many people use the military as a means for paying for higher education through a multitude of programs. Each program carries an obligation of service. Once this obligation expires, nurses may opt to stay in the service, providing there is a need, or leave the service and pursue civilian nursing. Many nurses with prior military experience are now working in local hospitals.

> I'm extremely proud of my military service. If I have to leave because of downsizing and someone asks me why I left I'm not sure what I'll say. The cutbacks also make me feel anxious about the security of my job; I've only ever been a nurse in the military and I don't know what civilian nursing is like. I also feel angry. I thought I'd get out on my terms and not someone else's. I've done everything the military asked me and now they're just going to push me out.

Transitioning Out

The transition out of the military, like any life transition, can be challenging. If an individual has experienced all they wanted to during their service, planned when they would terminate service, and has left voluntarily they may be excited about transition. An individual who has not made the choice voluntarily or who is leaving with unfulfilled expectations may have a different experience as they transition out of the military. No matter the length of service, those leaving may have anxiety about transitioning into civilian healthcare.

Those Who Do Not Deploy

After the September 11, 2001 terrorist attacks on the US, the military increased the number of service members on active duty. Those who joined after that time had a reasonable expectation that they would deploy overseas in support of the war effort. Many who joined during this time did deploy but there are those who, perhaps due only to timing, did not. Of course, not all military nurses deployed and some nurses may find themselves feeling unfulfilled. The training and responsibilities for a nurse who does not deploy are similar to those of a deploying nurse with regard to annual required training. For the nurse that does not deploy and who did not care directly care for young, wounded service members, those skills may not be used and they may be left feeling as if they have missed out on a part of what it means to be a military nurse. However, when viewing their career in a retrospective sense, the majority of military nurses feel clinically and professionally satisfied. They are able to utilize their skillset and training in a stateside hospital and care for critically injured service members, their families, and retirees on a daily basis; a major goal of a military nurse. When caring for a military nurse, remember that nurses who did not deploy may still have some of the same caregiver strain as those who did, especially if providing care to service members shortly after their return to permanent military hospital.

> I did not deploy but instead worked on an orthopedic unit caring primarily for service members with severe orthopedic trauma. Most were missing at least one limb. Just because I wasn't there immediately after the injury doesn't mean I'm not affected by the injuries I see day in and day out.

In addition, a nurse who did not deploy might also feel relief at having "avoided" that part of military service but may feel guilt or shame for admitting so. No matter the concerns of the military nurse, or their family members, the most important message in caring for military nurses is that you must take time to understand the meaning and value placed on military service by the individual as well as the effects one's service has on their family system.

> Whatever the reason nurses have for joining the military, whether it is an educational opportunity, a dedication to service, love for their country, or a calling from God, one thing remains constant in my mind: Military Nursing is one of the greatest professions around. This feeling is realized on a daily basis throughout the organization. The bonds and friendships formed are unceasing, and the privilege to take care of the most wonderful patients in the world is incredible.

In Conclusion

Nurses, by definition, are caregivers. Their mission is to heal, care for, and administer to those who are ill and ailing. In the military this mission takes on special meaning. Nurses are the front-line caregivers of the wounded, the amputee, those with head and limb injuries, the terrorized soldier who has been shot – all sustained in the act of war. Their dedication and hard work takes a toll which is often not realized until they return home and leave the hectic and dramatic arena of service. It is hoped that the information in this chapter will guide interventions as we help heal the healers.

References

Fry, S. T., Harvey, R. M., Hurley, A. C., & Foley, B. J. (2002). Development of a model of moral distress in military nursing. *Nursing Ethics*, 9(4), 373–387. doi: 10.1191/0969733002ne522oa

McManus, J., Mehta, S. G., McClinton, A. R., De Lorenzo, R. A., & Baskin, T. W. (2005). Informed consent and ethical issues in military medical research. *Academic Emergency Medicine*, 12(11), 1120–1126. doi: 10.1197/j.aem.2005.05.037

Raju, D., Su, X. & Patrician, P. A. (2014). Using item response theory models to evaluate the practice environment scale. *Journal of Nursing Measurement*, 22(2), 323–341. doi: 10.1891/1061-3749.22.2.323

Scannell-Desch, E., & Doherty, M. E. (2013). The lived experience of nurse-parents deployed to war. *American Journal of Maternal Child Nursing*, 38(1), 28–33. doi: 10.1097/NMC.0b013e31826187b7

Schwab, E. R. (Producer). (2013, June 26, 2015). *The History of the Army Nurse Corps*. Retrieved from www.youtube.com/watch?v=iDExHl_aVQ8&list=UUiPX96lTaNjB54dg8VZYxxw&index=1

Stanton-Bandiero, M. P. (1998). Shared meanings for military nurse Veterans: follow up survey of nurse Veterans from WWII, Korea, Vietnam, and Operation Desert Storm. *Journal of the New York State Nurses' Association*, 29(3–4), 4–8.

US Department of Defense. (2013). Army announces force structure and stationing decisions. (413–461). *Press Operations*. Retrieved from: www.defense.gov/releases/release.aspx?releaseid=16114

Zangaro, G. A. & Kelley, P. A. (2010). Job satisfaction and retention of military nurses: a review of the literature. *Annual Review of Nursing Research*, 28, 19–41.

14

TREATING CO-OCCURRING CONDITIONS IN THE RETURNING WARRIOR

COL Jeffrey S. Yarvis, LTC (ret.) Gabrielle N. Bryen and CPT Hannah Stryker-Thomas

Introduction

Anxiety disorders such as post-traumatic stress disorder (PTSD) and traumatic brain injury (TBI) in warriors co-occur frequently. The resultant prescribing of opiates or the warrior's need to self-medicate to "numb" the pain of these psychological and physical injuries often engenders substance use disorders (SUDs). As PTSD and TBI are often considered and managed separately, deciphering the medical and psychological boundaries between these comorbid conditions is important in their treatment. We propose a conceptualization that broadens the base — from diagnosing PTSD, TBI, or SUDs as separate entities – allowing practitioners to more effectively assess and treat those with co-occurring conditions. This chapter presents a case study representative of a patient being seen routinely in military behavioral health and goes on to explore theoretical explanations for co-occurring conditions as well as existing treatment options. Finally, the chapter presents an integrated treatment model that may be useful for guiding civilian and other behavioral health workers to employ intervention strategies for co-occurring conditions in the warrior population.

CASE STUDY

Specialist Y is a 20-year-old active-duty Army Service Member (SM) who was referred for counseling after surviving an improvised explosive device (IED) blast in Afghanistan. The IED was hidden inside a culvert under a bridge that the SM's convoy was passing over and was detonated by a remote control device. This SM was the driver of one of the convoy vehicles that was hit. The SM's squad leader, who was sitting next to him in the front seat, was killed in the explosion. SPC Y was medically evacuated from Afghanistan within hours of the blast and was treated in Landstuhl, Germany. He spent approximately 48 hours in Landstuhl, having two simultaneous orthopedic surgeries on his leg before being sent to Virginia for recuperation and treatment. Upon arrival in Virginia, SPC Y was assigned to the Warrior Transition Battalion (WTB).

The Army established a formal WTB in major military treatment facilities around the world in 2007. These Warrior Transition Units (WTUs) provide medical and social support to wounded soldiers who require at least six months of rehabilitative care and complex medical management (Warrior Transition Command, 2013). A WTU closely resembles a "line" Army unit, with processes that build on the Army's strength of unit cohesion and teamwork so that wounded warriors can focus on healing in order to transition back to the Army or to civilian status. These warriors have one mission: to heal. All soldiers develop a comprehensive treatment plan with personalized goals, which allows them, and their families to move forward toward life post-injury.

As the nature of SPC Y's orthopedic traumas would not have allowed continued active-duty service, he had two choices: (1) ask a medical board to reassign him to a less physically demanding position; or (2) leave the Army after undergoing a Medical Evaluation Board (MEB), which would determine if he would receive medical retirement or severance pay from the military and the Department of Veteran's Affairs (Warrior Transition Command, 2013). SPC Y determined he would choose the latter, opting for a plan to become a welder after leaving the Army. At this point in his treatment, SPC Y was still in the rehabilitative process so the MEB would not begin until he had a chance to recover from his surgeries and assess his fitness and progress. If a MEB had been warranted, he would be assessed both by the Army and the VA and they would jointly make a determination for either return to duty or separation with severance or disability. As his wounds occurred in a combat zone and he did not want to continue on active duty, it is likely that he would receive disability pay. Most SMs are also offered occupational training, which is funded by the VA. Initially, SPC Y declined therapy/counseling appointments, stating he did not need them. However, as part of the WTB screening process, he was required to meet with his assigned Social Worker (part of the WTB treatment team) biweekly for continued risk assessments. He admitted that he was experiencing insomnia and feelings of guilt over the death of his squad leader in Afghanistan. He was then referred to Behavioral Health for medication to treat the insomnia and for therapy to help him process grief. SPC Y presented in counseling reporting increased irrit-ability, hyper vigilance, grief and loss, difficulty falling asleep, feeling restless and "on edge," having angry outbursts, and feeling isolated.

SPC Y was born to an intact union but his parents divorced when he was 6-months old. The SM has in total five half-siblings and he is second in birth order. SPC Y described his childhood home as loving, comfortable, and supportive. He denied any childhood abuse or neglect. However, the SM acknowledged that he had a history of depression on the maternal side of his family; both his mother and older sister were taking medication for depression. Overall, SM stated that he had a good relationship with his family and iden-tified them as his support system. SPC Y denied any family, financial, legal, or substance abuse issues. He also denied any issues of domestic violence. The SM reported no educa-tional problems, graduating high school on time and joining the military after graduation. He stated he had always wanted to join the military; joining was "part of the plan."

Upon his return to the US after his injury, SPC Y was not sent to have treatment in his home state; rather, he was sent to a facility in another state, far from his home. Not only was he away from his family and friends but he was also a bit of an oddity as an infantry soldier at a post where there are no infantry units. He felt a bit misunderstood by his superiors and alone in his situation, believing the other soldiers did not understand his combat experiences. This may have contributed to his depression and general irritability.

SPC Y is married and, when he started therapy, he was in the process of getting a divorce. He stated that he and his wife met in high school and married before he deployed. According to SPC Y, while he was deployed, his wife cheated on him. The couple do not have any children. During the course of his therapy work, the SM admitted that he had reconnected with his wife and was open to continuing their relationship. He stated that she had been very supportive of him during his rehabilitation and he was willing to overlook her indiscretion, stating, "We are both immature."

One of the unique cultural patterns of young SMs is a tendency toward early marriages (Hall, 2008). This can be attributed to a variety of factors. A significant factor that influences early marriages is a lack of developmental understanding, i.e. a level of maturity about issues related to commitment and caring for another. It is not uncommon for soldiers with chaotic origins to marry young in order to establish a home that will be more stable and emotionally supportive than their family of origin. However, what happens frequently is that the soldiers with chaotic families find themselves ill equipped to be a partner, since it had never been appropriately modeled for them. This is what happened with SPC Y in his own marriage. He admitted that, although his parents were divorced, their subsequent marriages were rocky and created a life of emotional upheaval for himself and his siblings. In his marriage, he wanted to create a constant emotional environment. When this did not happen and communication fell apart during his deployment, he was hurt and angry. During therapy, SPC Y realized that he did not have skills initially to be a productive partner and became willing to work on developing those skills through education and counseling in the hope that he would be able to establish a more positive relationship with his estranged wife. After a lengthy intake assessment, SPC Y's treatment plan had the following goals: address his insomnia, his PTSD and depression. Medications were prescribed to address these issues.

Although it was not listed exactly in the treatment plan, one of the biggest barriers to reducing SPC Y's irritability was his persistent feeling of guilt regarding the death of his squad leader. When their attack occurred, SPC Y was driving their armored HMMWV. Unfortunately, SPC Y's vehicle took the brunt of the explosion with the impact killing his squad leader. It is interesting to note that SPC Y never once discussed how the attack affected him or caused him pain; he was much more focused on his friend's death. After the incident, the recovery team who went back to remove the damaged vehicles noted there was no way any of the soldiers could have spotted the IED, which was well concealed and placed physically below them. SPC Y repeatedly blamed himself for not seeing the IED (although impossible). He was eventually able to accept the situation after acting out the explosion several times using small models where he could actually visualize that there was no way any of the convoy participants would have known that there was a hidden IED.

In therapy, SPC Y identified some other factors that were influencing his irritability. He was particularly sensitive to driving and would often swerve to avoid objects in the road ("they might be IEDs"); and crowded traffic conditions made him agitated and jumpy. He also disliked crowds, especially when it was hard to get out of a location. The driving issues were self-treated by finding a friend who would accompany him on outings and reassure him; helping him to tolerate trash in the roads, crowds, and so on. After about a month of practicing with his friend and utilizing his cognitive therapy techniques to refocus during times of stress, he felt that he had "improved a lot."

One issue that had hampered some of SPC Y's progress in therapy was a mild–TBI (m–TBI) that occurred during the explosion. He believes that he hit the top of vehicle during the blast. Although he was wearing body armor and a Kevlar helmet, the injury manifested with headaches, periodic forgetfulness, and some impulsive behavior. He had one incident of poor judgment in which he brought a pistol into the barracks and did not think to register the weapon on post (in accordance with post policy). When the weapon was discovered during a room inspection, the entire WTB (400-plus personnel) was locked down for security reasons until the weapon was secured. SPC Y was disciplined for the violation of the policy and lost rank. He reported that he thought the incident was "a stupid overreaction" but later could see why such preventative measures were taken. The m-TBI may have far-reaching effects beyond SPC Y's military service. Some warriors report chronic short-term memory loss, difficulty concentrating, frequent headaches, slight speech disruptions (such as an inability to quickly recall words) and impulsivity. The chronic symptoms of m-TBI are not static and may change as his brain changes with age (Centers for Disease Control and Prevention, 2008). In sum, SPC Y is suffering from two presenting problems – PTSD and a m-TBI – with a potential for a third situation related to substance abuse issues.

Scientific attention devoted to understanding the relationship between PTSD and TBI is still burgeoning and knowledge about TBI develops nearly daily. The gap in knowledge in the literature is concerning, as warrior care is caught at the crossroads of this ever-changing landscape and there are high prevalence rates of PTSD, TBI, and SUDs among warriors (Hall, 2008). Clinically meaningful relationships between these conditions are important to their onset, maintenance, course, and prognosis. Using the case of SPC Y to illustrate critical concepts, the remainder of this chapter will examine key considerations with respect to the relationships between PTSD, TBI, and the complications associated with co-occurring SUDs.

Post-traumatic Stress Disorder

PTSD, as defined in the *Diagnostic and Statistical Manual of Mental Disorders*, 5th Edition (American Psychiatric Association, 2013) is the most common psychiatric problem associated with the stress experienced by soldiers in combat. Diagnosis of PTSD requires exposure to a traumatic event that involves experiencing, witnessing, or being confronted by death or serious injury to self or others; a response of intense fear, helplessness, or horror; and development of a set of symptoms that persist for at least a month and cause significant impairment of functioning (American Psychiatric Association, 2013). Studies have demonstrated four basic PTSD symptoms: re-experiencing (e.g. nightmares and flashbacks), avoidance (e.g. efforts to avoid thinking about the trauma), numbing of general responsiveness (e.g. restricted range of affect), and hyperarousal (e.g. exaggerated startle response) (Forbes et al., 2010; McWilliams, Cox, & Asmundson, 2005). Most individuals who develop chronic PTSD experience immediate distress that then persists over time (Buckley, Blanchard, & Hickling, 1996). However, a small but significant number of individuals report increases in PTSD symptoms over time, defined as delayed onset PTSD (Palm, Strong, & McPherson, 2009; Tanielian & Jaycox, 2008).

Current data suggests that approximately 5–20% of armed forces personnel deployed for combat, peacekeeping, or humanitarian disaster relief will develop PTSD following their tour of duty (Bramsen, Dirkzwager, & van der Ploeg, 2000; Dohrenwend et al., 2006; Mehlum & Weisaeth, 2002; Tanielian & Jaycox, 2008; Ward, 2002). Estimates for those serving in Iraq/Afghanistan run as high as 15%, and, while exposure to specific combat traumas are the single best predictor for the development of PTSD, SMs who have experienced more lengthy and more frequent deployments are at the greatest risk (Tanielian & Jaycox, 2008). In considering the problem of PTSD, it should be acknowledged that problematic reactions to trauma are not limited to full-blown PTSD; a considerable percentage (i.e. 10%–25%) of those not meeting diagnostic criteria for PTSD experience significant symptoms that may require treatment. Even for those who have partial PTSD, there are differing levels of impairment of social, occupational, and family functioning (Gellis, Mavandadi, & Oslin, 2010; Yarvis, Bordnick, Spivey, & Pedlar, 2005; Zlotnick, Franklin, & Zimmerman, 2002) often similar to those reported in individuals with full-blown PTSD. Those diagnosed with PTSD, full or partial, almost always experience concurrent additional mental health disorders, such as SUDs, other anxiety disorders, or major depressive disorder (Breslau, Davis, Peterson, & Schultz, 2000; Yarvis, 2008; McDevitt-Murphy, Williams, Bracken, Fields, Monahan, & Murphy, 2012; Schnurr, Lunney, Bovin, & Marx, 2009)

Risk factors for development of PTSD include characteristics of the traumatic event itself, pre-trauma factors, and post-trauma factors. Event characteristics that increase the risk for chronic PTSD include the type of trauma, greater amount of exposure, injury, involvement in atrocities, and perceived life threat (Schnurr et al., 2009). Degree of exposure to potentially traumatic combat events during deployment is strongly associated with development of PTSD (Hoge et al., 2004) as is military sexual trauma (Yaeger, Himmelfarb, Cammack, & Mintz, 2006). In a sample of female Veterans seeking treatment for stress disorders, sexual stress was found to be almost four times as influential in the development of PTSD as duty-related stress (Fontana & Rosenheck, 1998; Luxton, Skopp, & Maguen, 2010). In Veterans, predisposing factors have included non-Caucasian ethnicity, lower intelligence or education, younger age at exposure, lower socioeconomic status, family problems in childhood, pre-trauma psychopathology, and childhood behavioral problems (Engdahl, Dikel, Eberly, & Blank, 1997; King et al., 1995; McNally & Shin, 1995). Post-event factors that predict chronic PTSD in Veterans include low levels of social support, negative homecoming experiences, poor coping, and adverse life events post-trauma (Boscarino, 1995; Brewin, Andrews, & Valentine, 2000; Engdahl et al., 1997; King et al., 1998). While many risk factors exert a similar effect in military and civilian populations, trauma severity and post-trauma social support may be more important in military than in civilian samples.

Some of the evidenced-based treatment for PTSD is cognitive behavioral-based therapies such as cognitive behavioral therapy (CBT), cognitive processing therapy (CPT), eye-movement desensitization and reprocessing (EMDR), and acceptance and commitment therapy (ACT) to name a few. In vivo, imaginal or virtual-reality exposure therapies also are theoretically tied to CBT and been proven effective. Therapies commonly used to treat soldiers like SPC Y could include the following: (1) hypnotherapy. One of the complementary and alternative medicine (CAM) procedures proven most efficacious is hypnotherapy (Yarvis et al., 2005), which involves traditional hypnosis; (2) a CBT approach has the individual reconstruct the trauma memory, elaborate on the memory, and integrate the memory into the context of the individual's preceding and subsequent experience. Problematic appraisals that maintain a sense of threat needs to be modified; dysfunctional coping strategies that prevent emotional processing of the trauma event need to be reduced. Interpersonal skills training, anger management training, guided self-dialogue, and thought stopping are examples of skills taught to individuals. Variations of CBT in treatments for PTSD sometimes effectively supplement exposure therapy components with cognitive procedures intended to address issues of guilt, cognitive distortions, irrational beliefs, and dysfunctional values (Foa, Hembree, & Rothbaum, 2005).

Traumatic Brain Injury

TBI, an injury that can often create lasting impairments for one warrior but may not in another, has been recognized as a serious public health problem by the Centers for Disease Control (Langois, Rutland-Brown, & Thomas, 2006). Along with PTSD, TBI has become one of the "signature injuries" of this so-called Global War on Terror. Today's asymmetric battlefield is a fertile breeding ground for exposures to IEDs; and the detonation of these devices exposes warriors to multiple risks of TBI, including injury sustained from projectiles, shrapnel, and blast waves. Eye and ear injuries are often sustained along with concussive injuries; and of course, the psychological component is significant. It is estimated that a minimum of 30% of troops engaged in combat in Afghanistan or Iraq for four months or more had sustained a m-TBI as a result of IED blast waves alone (Hoge et al., 2008). The majority of mild and moderate TBI symptoms will abate and have an outstanding prognosis in general. Persistent problems do occur in some warriors, most often with severe TBI or moderate cases that involve some inter-cranial involvement. As with the case of SPC Y, correct identification and diagnosis is essential since soldiers who sustained even m-TBI under combat conditions can experience a complex recovery process. Those with severe TBI will likely require ongoing structure and treatment to optimize healing and maximal recovery.

Care for those with a moderate to severe TBI is interdisciplinary; there must be a medical component often suggesting teaming with VA specialists or civilian neurologists. Many Service Members (SMs) are treated away from the military Treatment Facility (MTF) in the civilian community. For the civilian provider, there are a few things to keep in mind when working with this population: the population that have incurred a traumatic brain injury and have associated PTSD.

For the civilian treatment provider active engagement and alliance building are key when treating military members, particularly military members with PTSD and a co-occurring m-TBI. However, many SMs are reluctant to seek mental health treatment with civilians (Maguen & Litz, 2006).

If the SM is a Warrior Transition soldier, it is recommended that the civilian treatment provider have the name and contact information of the SM's nurse case manager or primary care provider at their VA. The civilian therapist can have a release of information for these individuals so that everyone who is treating the SM is part of the continuum of care. If it is a retired or discharged SM in the VA system, a release should also be signed for the primary care provider.

Medication is an important treatment option that should be considered for soldiers presenting with significant PTSD-related symptoms. Initiating medication may occur at different phases of the SM's treatment depending on a number of co-occurring factors, but there are some things civilian practitioners should always be mindful of when considering medication consults.

If the civilian provider has arranged for a medication consult, the service member must be given multiple copies of their prescriptions and the civilian provider should fax a copy of the prescription to the nurse case manager at the VA. If an off post medication is controlled and not recorded, it can show up on a routine urinalysis and can result in disciplinary action against the SM for non-authorized drug use. Additionally, it a good idea to keep the MTF medical team apprised of all additional medications due to the potential for adverse drug reactions.

Despite the dearth of medication used for war-induced, combat-related PTSD, there is a relative lack of definitive evidence for their efficacy (Institute of Medicine, 2007). The most thoroughly investigated agents are serotonin reuptake inhibitors (SSRIs). Therefore, while some SSRIs indeed are indicated for PTSD, practitioners should follow the least restrictive approach to treatment and use evidence-based treatments first (Schuster-Wachen et al., 2016).

If using a prolonged treatment regime, it is a good idea to speak with the SM's VA nurse case manager to ensure there are no duty conflicts. For example, some forms of outpatient treatments such as long-term partial hospitalizations, will not mesh with the SM's schedule or expected duties while on active duty.

Military-related PTSD is also associated with a number of other treatment concerns such as impaired social functioning, impaired workplace functioning, physical pain and physical health problems, traumatic bereavement, substance use disorders, suicidality, depression and anxiety, anger/violence, impaired family functioning, and of course traumatic brain injury.

Substance Use Disorders

Definitions of SUDs have achieved a degree of consistent recognition within the scientific and clinical/medical communities. These perspectives recognize the consistent and common characteristics across the spectrum of different types of SUDs, including identification of symptom patterns and so-called classic signs of impairment. In general these signs or characteristics include the following: (1) impaired psychological functioning that focuses on, in the case of SUDs for example, craving for drugs or drug-related experiences; (2) frequent drug use behavior that occurs despite negative consequences for the warrior related to substance use; (3) the development of tolerance (biological adaptation to exposures to the substance); and (4) withdrawal symptoms beginning with discontinuation of substance use. Warriors with SUDs often lose control over their ability to manage their substance use behavior, particularly during periods of positive or negative escalated affect; for example feeling anxious or happy (Yarvis, Bordnick, Spivey, & Pedlar, 2009). The DSM-V (American Psychiatric Association, 2013) describes three separate categories of substance use severity: use, abuse, dependence. Substance use reflects non-problematic consumption of drugs or alcohol. Substance abuse describes use when there is evidence of negative consequences. Substance dependence refers to a more severe form of use whereby there is a pervasive pattern of loss of control or drug use behavior as well as clinical features of withdrawal and tolerance. When presented with these classic signs of impairment, it is clear to see that there is a high degree of overlap between symptoms of SUDs with TBI and PTSD. The bottom line is that the savvy clinician should recognize that rarely do these conditions occur alone. Research by Yarvis et al. (2005) suggests that warriors will underreport SUDs but report more substance-related symptoms with the more PTSD symptoms they report. In other words, warriors minimize substance use in proportion to their other physical and psychological symptom severity.

Further confounding the SUDs picture is the legitimate prescribing of pain control medications in the opiate family. Warriors often do not associate legally prescribed medications with misuse. However, these medications are often misused and secondary SUDs are created. Although warriors are required to report any civilian prescribed medications to their treatment team, many do not. This can lead to both accidental overdose and addictive behaviors that military medical providers are not following. One of the most pressing issues given co-occurrence of SUDs and the other two conditions is explicating the nature of the associations. It is important to consider an integrated orientation toward deciphering these associations.

An Integrated Orientation

Developmental contextualism posits that the association between substance use behavior and PTSD and TBI are reciprocal and dynamic. That is, these variables affect the etiology, maintenance, and course of not only each disorder, but the other. This model also predicts that moderators (variables that influence the association between PTSD-related psychopathology or TBI-induced behavior and substance use behavior) and mediators (variables that account for the relationships between substance use behavior and PTSD-related psychopathology and TBI-induced behaviors) qualify and explicate that nature and extent of co-occurrence. In general, a moderator alters the strength and direction of the relationship between a predictor and outcome. Yarvis and Schiess (2008) bear this out in their study of PTSD and its relationship to SUDs, depression and physical health, predicting the level of PTSD in a large sample of soldiers. A major theoretical consideration is explication of specificity between differential substance use behaviors, moderators, mediators, and psychopathology; and TBI physical complaints. That is, a specific type of drug and use pattern (e.g. dependence) is linked to a particular type of problem presentation (change in cognitive functioning) via a specified mediating process (for example, impaired control over cognitive process due to TBI) in the context of certain moderating variables (for example, high anxiety). The central idea being that the underlying mechanism between substance misuse and psychopathology and physical impairment may be distinctly different from that explaining other types of substance abuse.

Finally, another key element is that a third, common or shared, variable may predict the development of all of the morbidities discussed. Thus, assessment and conceptual tactics need to cover a relatively broad array of factors that could be linked to co-occurring problems; for example, familial–social contexts, genetic history, and military experiences. Understanding co-occurring disorders within a developmental context is critical in elucidating explanations and models linking issues facing returning soldiers from war.

Assessment and Treatment

The complex interplay between PTSD, m-TBI, and SUDs forces the question of how do we clinically address such problems in the most efficacious manner and create an optimal healing environment for warriors. Three approaches exist for the treatment for these co-occurring conditions: (1) sequential, in which clinical providers treat one problem before treating another; (2) parallel or multidisciplinary, in which two or more treatments are used simultaneously but not in an integrated manner; and (3) interdisciplinary, in which all treatments are integrated in a simultaneous manner. It is standard practice for licensed independent providers to use sequential methods in their own practice and refer out after their treatment is done or for parallel adjunct care. One of the fundamental flaws in sequential care and parallel care, however, is seen in the example of caring for substance abuse when actively using and then treating PTSD when not using, ignoring the factors associated with the anxiety around using behavior and cravings and the potential loss of impulse control associated with TBI.

For the civilian practitioner, the suggestion to partner with VA care providers is highlighted. If the practitioner suspects that there is indeed interplay between the PTSD, substance abuse, and possible m-TBI (as strongly supported in this chapter) integrated care becomes a necessity. The role for the civilian practitioner is assessment and offering direction to the service member and family.

Conclusion

Overall, empirically based literature suggests that clinically meaningful reciprocal interactions and associations between PTSD, SUDs, and m-TBI are evident. As a result, for warrior care, careful clinical conceptualization assessment, treatment, and prevention strategies grounded in theory are aimed at understanding and addressing these co-occurring conditions. An interdisciplinary delivery system of care is needed to enhance the delivery of evidenced-based therapies for America's returning warriors. Physical injuries are obvious and support perhaps is more obvious; when they are invisible wounds such as PTSD and coupled with stigmatizing (e.g. SUDs) and confusing co-occurring disorders (e.g. m-TBI), the warrior finds them difficult to describe and solicit support and the provider finds the diagnostic picture nebulous. Despite the range and severity of PTSD, m-TBI, and SUDs, the majority of those who sustain some or all of these injuries will notice immediate sequelae such as alterations in domains of functioning; including mood disturbance, sleep dysfunction, cognitive deficits, other psychological symptoms (such as anxiety and depression), and physical symptoms (to include chronic pain). Many of the symptoms can fully resolve with treatment and warriors will be able to function well within the family, community, military, and larger societal contexts. For those with more serious physical injuries and more chronic disorders, adapting to life with permanent deficits will present ongoing challenges; because much of warrior care occurs beyond military and Veterans Administration facilities, civilian clinical providers will play an important role in the returning warrior's care. For both military and civilian providers, an interdisciplinary and patient-centered approach mitigates some of the confounding problems associated with sequential and parallel multidisciplinary care that will likely result in poorer treatment outcomes and prognoses.

References

American Psychiatric Association (2013). *American Psychiatric Association Desk Reference to the DSM 5.* Arlington, VA: American Psychiatric Association.

Boscarino, J. A. (1995). Post-traumatic stress and associated disorders among Vietnam Veterans: The significance of combat exposure and social support. *Journal of Traumatic Stress*, 8, 317–336.

Bramsen, I., Dirkzwager, A. J. E., & van der Ploeg, H. M. (2000). Pre-deployment personality traits and exposure to trauma as predictors of posttraumatic stress symptoms: A prospective study of former peacekeepers. *American Journal of Psychiatry*, 157, 1115–1119.

Breslau, N., Davis, G. C., Peterson, E. L., & Schultz, L. R. (2000). A second look at co-morbidity in victims of trauma: The posttraumatic stress disorder – major depression connection. *Biological Psychiatry*, 48, 902–909.

Brewin, C. R., Andrews, B., Valentine, J. D. (2000) Meta-analysis of risk factors for posttraumatic stress disorder in trauma-exposed adults. *Journal of Consulting and Clinical Psychology*, 68, 748–766.

Buckley, T. C., Blanchard, E. B., & Hickling, E. J. (1996). A prospective examination of delayed onset PTSD secondary to motor vehicle accidents. *Journal of Abnormal Psychology*, 105, 617–625.

Centers for Disease Control and Prevention (2008). Traumatic brain injury: DoD/VA code proposal. www.cdc.gov/nchs/data/icd9/Sep08TBI.pdf (accessed October 29, 2013).

Dohrenwend, B. P., Turner, J. B., Turse, N. A., Adams, B. G., Koenen, K. C., & Marshal, L. R. (2006). The psychological risks of Vietnam for US Veterans: A revisit with new data and methods. *Science*, 313, 979–982.

Engdahl, B., Dikel, T. N., Eberly, R., Blank, A. (1997). Posttraumatic Stress Disorder in a community sample of former prisoners of war: A normative response to severe trauma. *American Journal of Psychiatry*, 154(11), 1576–1581.

Foa, E., Hembree, E., Rothbaum, B. (2005). *Prolonged exposure therapy for PTSD: Emotional processing of traumatic experiences*. Oxford: Oxford University Press.

Fontana, A. & Rosenheck, R. (1998). Duty-related and sexual stress in the etiology of PTSD among women Veterans who seek treatment. *Psychiatric Services*, 49, 658–662.

Forbes, D., Creaner, M., Bisson, J., Cohen, J., Crow, B., & Foa, E. et al. (2010). A guide to guidelines for treatment of PTSD and related conditions. *Journal of Traumatic Stress*, 61(5), 537–552.

Gellis, L., Mavandadi, S., & Oslin, D. (2010). Functional quality of life in full versus partial PTSD among Veterans returning from Iraq and Afghanistan. *Journal of Clinical Psychology*, 12(3), 1–6.

Hall, L. K. (2008). *Counseling military families: What mental health professionals need to know*. New York: Routledge.

Hoge, C. W., Castro, C. A., Messer, S. C., McGurk, D., Cotting, D. I., & Koffman, R. L. (2004). Combat duty in Iraq and Afghanistan, mental health problems, and barriers to care. *New England Journal of Medicine*, 351, 13–22.

Hoge, C. W., McGurk, D., Thomas, J. L., Cox, A. L., Engel, C. C., & Castro, C. A. (2008). Mild Traumatic Brain Injury in soldiers returning from Iraq. *NEJM*, 5, 453–463.

Institute of Medicine (2007). *Treatment of posttraumatic stress disorder: An assessment of evidence*. Washington, DC: National Academy of Sciences.

King, L. A., King, D. W., Fairbank, J. A., Keane, T. M., & Adams, G. A. (1998). Resilience/recovery factors in posttraumatic stress disorder among female and male Vietnam Veterans: Hardiness, postwar social support, and additional stressful life events. *Journal of Personality and Social Psychology*, 74, 420–434.

Langois, J. A., Rutland-Brown, W., & Thomas, K. E. (2006). *Traumatic brain injury in the United States: Emergency department visits, hospitalizations, and deaths*. Atlanta, GA: CDC.

Luxton, D. D., Skopp, N. A., & Maguen, S. (2010). Gender differences in depression and PTSD symptoms following combat exposure. *Depress. Anxiety*, 27(11), 1027–1033.

McDevitt-Murphy, M., Williams, J., Bracken, K., Fields, J., Monahan, C., & Murphy, J. (2012). PTSD symptoms, hazardous drinking, and health functioning among US OEF and OIF Veterans presenting to primary care. *Journal of Traumatic Stress*, 23(1), 108–111.

McNally, R. & Shin, L. (1995). Association of intelligence with severity of posttraumatic stress disorder symptoms in Vietnam combat Veterans. *American Journal of Psychiatry*, 152, 936–938.

McWilliams, L. A., Cox, B. J., & Asmundson, G. J. G. (2005). Symptom structure of posttraumatic stress disorder in a nationally representative sample. *Journal of Anxiety Disorders*, 19, 626–641.

Maguen, S. & Litz, B. T. (2006). Predictors of barriers to mental health treatment for Kosovo and Bosnia peacekeepers: A preliminary report. *Military Medicine*, 171, 454–458.

Mehlum, L. & Weisaeth, L. (2002). Predictors of posttraumatic stress reactions in Norwegian UN Peacekeepers 7 years after service. *Journal of Traumatic Stress*, 15(1), 17–26.

Palm, K., Strong, D., & MacPherson, L. (2009). Evaluating symptom expression as a function of posttraumatic stress disorder severity. *Journal of Anxiety Disorder*, 23(1), 27–37.

Schnurr, P., Lunney, C. A., Bovin, M., & Marx, B. (2009). Posttraumatic stress disorder and quality of life: Extension of findings to Veterans of the wars in Iraq and Afghanistan. *Clinical Psychology Review*, 29(8), 727–735.

Schuster-Wachen, J., Dondanville, K. A., Pruiksma, K. E., Molino, A., Carson, C., & Blankenship, A. E. et al. (2016). Implementing cognitive processing therapy for posttraumatic stress disorder with active duty US Military personnel: Special considerations and case examples. *Cognitive and Behavioral Practice*, (3), 133–147.

Tanielian, T. & Jaycox, L. H. (2008). *Invisible wounds of war: Psychological and cognitive injuries, their consequences, and services to assist recovery*. Santa Monica, CA: RAND.

Ward, J. (2002). Stress hits 1 in 5 Afghan war vets, ombudsman says: Stigma "is still very much alive," Marin warns of possible law suits. *Toronto Star*. A06.

Warrior Transition Command (2013). Medical evaluation boards and physical evaluation boards. www.wtc.army.mil/soldier/medical_boards.html (accessed November 5, 2013).

Wolfe, J., Erickson, D., Sharkansky, E., King, D., & King, L. (1999). Course and predictors of posttraumatic stress disorder among Gulf War Veterans: A prospective analysis. *Journal of Consulting and Clinical Psychology*, 67, 520–528.

Yaeger, D., Himmelfarb, N., Cammack, A., & Mintz, J. (2006). DSM-IV diagnosed posttraumatic stress disorder in women Veterans with and without military sexual trauma. *JGIM: Journal of General Internal Medicine*, 21(Suppl.), S65–S69.

Yarvis, J. (2008). *Subthreshold PTSD in Veterans with different levels of traumatic stress: Implications for prevention and treatment with populations with PTSD.* Saarbrucken, Germany: VDM Verlag Dr. Muller Publishers.

Yarvis, J., Bordnick, P., Spivey, C., & Pedlar, D. (2005). Subthreshold PTSD: A comparison of depression, alcohol and physical health problems in Canadian peacekeepers with different levels of traumatic stress. *Stress, Trauma, and Crisis: An International Journal*, 8(2–3), 195–213.

Yarvis, J., Bordnick, P., Spivey, C., & Pedlar, D. (2009). Subthreshold PTSD: A comparison of depression, alcohol and physical health problems in Canadian peacekeepers with different levels of traumatic stress. In B. E. Bride & S. A. MacMaster (Eds.), *Stress, trauma and substance use* (pp. 117–135). New York: Routledge.

Yarvis, J. & Schiess, L. (2008). Sub-threshold PTSD as a predictor of depression, alcohol use, and health problems in soldiers. *Journal of Workplace Behavioral Health*, 23(4): 395–424.

Zlotnick, C., Franklin, C. L., & Zimmerman, M. (2002). Does "Sub-threshold" posttraumatic stress disorder have any clinical relevance? *Comprehensive Psychiatry*, 43(6): 413–419.

15

OCCUPATIONAL THERAPY FOR OUR MILITARY

Challenges and Roles

Kristen Leigh Maisano and Joan Beder

CASE STUDY

Pete is a 29-year-old male referred for occupational therapy (OT) service by his Warrior Transition Battalion primary care physician. Pete was on his third deployment in Afghanistan when a Humvee he was driving rolled over an improvised explosive device (IED). Pete reports that he struck his head on the windshield and his right fibula and tibia were fractured. The fracture broke through the skin. He reports that he did not lose consciousness. After the explosion, Pete was evacuated from Afghanistan to Germany then transferred to the US. At the time of his first OT session, he had been back in the US for four weeks. He had multiple surgeries on his right leg and it was healing well. During the first OT with Pete, he became tearful and slightly agitated when he discussed the explosion. He attempted to regain his composure and continue with the session. Pete became tearful and agitated again when asked about his support system. He reported having "no support system" after losing his battle buddies in the explosion. He spoke about the guilt he carries for living while the three men he was closest to lost their lives because he hit an IED. He tells of the difficulty he has discussing the accident with his wife and the wives of his battle buddies. He reports difficulty being a passenger in the car, difficulty concentrating, decreased frustration tolerance, difficulty making decisions, inability to tolerate public places (such as his daughter's soccer games and ballet recitals), headaches, and nightmares. He sleeps about 90 minutes a night. OT was one area of care that was suggested to address some of the difficulties he was having with daily activities.

For Pete and the thousands who return from the wars in Iraq and Afghanistan with functional difficulties, OT has become a front-line treatment intervention. This chapter will explore the history of OT and describe the many ways that occupational therapists (OTs) work with our military. The goal of the chapter is to inform practitioners of the breadth of services that OTs can perform in the goal of supporting our military as they transition to civilian life. In light of the "drastic changes in daily living skills and habits needed to successfully navigate the civilian world after surviving several months in a war zone" (Cogan, 2014a, p. 478), the role of the OT has assumed even greater importance in recent years.

History of OT

The roots of OT with the military population date back to the early 1900s. James P. Monroe, Thomas R. Marshall, and other members of the Federal Board for Vocational Education penned an explanation of research that occurred dissecting the "problem of rehabilitation" that was occurring during the early 1900s. The report, *Training of Teachers for Occupational Therapy for the Rehabilitation of Disabled Soldiers and Sailors*, discussed utilizing OT for persons with diseases, injuries, and mental health disorders. The report focused on the psychological and physiological functions of OT to decrease performance deficits in soldiers and sailors (Federal Board for Vocational Education, 1918).

"Between the time when the disabled soldier or sailor enters the hospital and his final placement in industry, commerce, agriculture, or less frequently in the special workshop or home, there lies a long period of reeducation and adaptation" (Federal Board for Vocational Education, 1918). It was clear in 1918 that the Board valued the opportunity to rehabilitate service members through reeducation and adaptation of context, adaptation of task, and/or adjusting a person's ability to complete a task. The Board understood the importance of utilizing OTs and other healthcare providers to assist service members in returning to purpose and function after illness or injury.

Since these early beginnings, the profession has grown with greater involvement not only in Veteran care but also in the care of any person who has sustained a physical trauma and experiences difficult returning to pre-traumatization functioning in personal, work, and social areas that become compromised due to their injury. The *occupational* in OT refers broadly to everyday activates and roles that are meaningful and/or necessary to the individual (e.g., activities of daily living, work, parenting, educational activities). Perhaps unique to the OT orientation to care is the concentration on the relationship between daily activities and health as well as its emphasis on facilitating full participation in life in the presence of disability (Cogan, 2014b).

OT in the Military

A holistic interdisciplinary team is usually engaged to address the complex needs of Veterans and their families. OT practitioners are often members of a Veterans healthcare team who address a variety of issues that impact functioning that result from combat and service. OT practitioners utilize everyday activities – occupations – to help persons regain function after an illness or injury. The American Occupational Therapy Association (AOTA, 2011) defines the practice of OT as, "therapeutic use of occupations, including everyday life activities with individuals, groups, populations, or organizations to support participation, performance, and function in roles and situations in home, school, workplace, community, and other settings."

OT practitioners have completed one of three of accredited educational pathways and have successfully pasted a certification exam. Certified Occupational Therapy Assistants (COTAs) have earned a degree. Registered Occupational Therapists (OTRs) earned a master's degree and/or a doctoral degree in OT. OTRs who completed educational programs prior to 2007 may have a bachelor's degree in OT. In 2007, the entry-level degree for OT was moved to at least a master's.

The education of an OT includes a holistic understanding of the psychological, physical, and social aspects of a person. Coursework often includes human anatomy and physiology, neuroscience, psychology, human development, and research. In addition, OT practitioners are educated to uniquely analyze any activity. Practitioners utilize their knowledge of activity analysis to view a client's current level of function, analyze what aspects of the task the person is experiencing difficulty with, and develop a plan to address the deficit area. Typically, OT practitioners address deficits areas by adjusting the context, adjusting the task, and/or adjusting the abilities of the person.

What OTs Do

The role of OT in the military has expanded and grown since the Federal Board for Vocational Education first advocated the use of the therapy in 1918. OTs can be found working with service members and Veterans in a variety of settings. OTs work with service members and Veterans with deficits in functioning and also with service members to assist in preventing illness or injury.

The OT practitioner will ask questions about how the Veteran or service member is achieving his or her goals related to activities of daily living (ADLs) and instrumental activities of daily living (IADLs), rest and sleep, education, work, play, leisure, and social participation. ADLs are "activities oriented toward taking care of one's own body" and include dressing, bathing, functional mobility, toileting, feeding, and engaging in sexual activity (AOTA, 2014, p. S19). IADLs include "activities to support daily life within the home and community that often require more complex interactions than those used in ADLs" (AOTA, 2014, p. S19). OTs evaluate numerous areas to gain an understanding and holistic view of the service member's life. Evaluation may include interviews both with the service member and family member(s), standardized and non-standardized assessments. Once the OT has an understanding of the client's strengths and areas of challenge, an intervention plan is developed. Plach and Sells (2013) researched the occupational performance issues facing young Veterans of the Iraq and Afghanistan conflicts. Utilizing the Canadian Occupational Performance Measure, 30 Veterans were interviewed. In addition, the Veterans were screened for post-traumatic stress disorder (PTSD), traumatic brain injury, depression, and alcohol abuse or dependency. Multiple occupational challenges emerged from the interviews. The findings showed that:

- 77% reported challenges with relationships (managing social interactions, finding meaningful relationships, belonging, isolating, being desensitized emotionally, reconnecting);
- 70% reported challenges with school (transitioning to the student role, being older and having served overseas or conveying experiences, having to take basic courses, relating to classmates, concentrating);
- 50% reported challenges with physical health (physical injuries, limited activity, weight gain);
- 37% reported challenges with sleeping (poor sleep hygiene, inadequate rest, nightmares); and
- 33% report challenges with driving (reckless driving, discomfort, impatience, heightened alert).

OTs address all of the above areas through the use of occupation-based treatments and activities. Activities are selected as intervention for specific clients and designed to meet therapeutic goals and address underlying needs of the mind, body, and spirit of the client. To use occupations and activities therapeutically, the practitioner considers activity demands, client factors in relation to the client's therapeutic goals, contexts, and environments (AOTA, 2014, p. S29).

OT treatment may look different from other approaches to care because of the use of occupations and activities. For example, Plach and Sells (2013) state that 70% of Veterans have difficult transitioning to the role of a student. The authors discuss that this difficulty frequently presents as challenges related to social interaction and decreased concentration. An OT may use a client-centered task group to address socialization and concentration for this cohort. The task of the group may be occupation or activity based, such as designing and building a swing set for a local playground. The group members will need to work together, concentrate, and apply certain skills to complete the task over a number of weeks. The group allows the Veterans a safe place to practice skills learned in therapy. Once skills are learned and practiced, Veterans may feel more comfortable utilizing these skills in everyday life situations.

How Do I Know When Someone Needs OT?

If a Veteran is experiencing difficulty with the ADLs, IADLs, sleep, education, work, play, leisure, and social participation, he or she may benefit from skilled OT services. Treatment will vary based on the goal areas and areas of need. For example, a Veteran presents with a diagnosis of PTSD and depression. He complains of nightmares, difficulty communicating with his significant other, difficulty concentrating while at work, and a lack of interest in things that he used to do for fun. He has been enrolled in multiple intensive outpatient programs and can verbalize many strategies learned to cope with his signs and symptoms of PTSD and depression. It is clear that he is having difficulty utilizing the strategies during everyday life situations and a decision is reached to refer him to an OT to assist the client in implementing/integrating strategies learned into his everyday occupations. The OT evaluates the Veteran and develops an intervention plan. The Veteran and the therapist work together to analyze difficult activities and brainstorm to adjust the task or context of the occupation. As the interdisciplinary team works with the Veteran to address the underlying effects of PTSD and depression, the OT practitioner works with occupations, and everyday activities, to assist in recovery and return to their prior level of function.

OT treatments for Veterans with behavioral health concerns may look different based on the unique situation posed by each individual. With that said, all OT treatments will focus on analyzing difficult areas of a person's occupational profile and using occupation-based treatments to remediate or compensate for the areas of challenge. If you are treating a client that is struggling with implementing self-care strategies or has difficulty with ADLs, IADLS, work, sleep, education, etc., a referral to an OT would certainly be warranted.

OTs' Role with PTSD

PTSD is a result of experiencing a traumatic event that is life-threatening, is sudden, and threatens the integrity of the individual. The symptoms of PTSD cause significant distress that impacts social and occupational functioning and participation. The OT will conduct a comprehensive evaluation to identify strengths and barriers to occupations performance and their causes. OT interventions would include: individual and/or group sessions that address trauma triggers from the PTSD experience, specific training on control of emotional response, increasing participation in meaningful roles, making needed home modifications, and support for specific exercises and tasks to address losses in functionality (AOTA, 2014).

OTs' Role in Mild-Traumatic Brain Injury (m-TBI)

OTs are essential rehabilitation professionals in assisting individuals with traumatic brain injury to reintegrate back into the community. As OTs are trained at evaluation and analysis of an individual's performance, they are able to determine what intervention is needed in a specific case and include activities directed at self-care, home, and work management and they can help clients relearn certain skills lost due to the brain injury. These might include teaching memory compensation techniques (e.g., use of a daily planner), creating routines, assisting in relearning certain social skills, and providing training in skills of daily living (grooming, dressing, bathing). As with PTSD, those with an m-TBI must be educated toward what is realistic in terms of recovery and performance (Cogan, 2014b). In addition, the OT will assess whether the service member has sustained vision difficulties as a result of their m-TBI; the OT will assess difficulties with cognition, as those with an m-TBI often experience impairments in information processing (including attention and memory) for up to three months after their injury and the OT will work with the service members to compensate for m-TBI-related errors and inefficiencies (Radomski, Davidson, Voydetich, & Erickson, 2009).

What Do Civilian Practitioners Need to Know about OT?

Like many other populations, service members and Veterans respond well to honesty and transparency. Many service members and Veterans were trained, as part of their service, to quickly assess situations and read body language. This level of training and competence requires providers to be even more aware of the environment in which they treat clients and how their verbal and non-verbal communication can be interpreted.

Unique to the military population, command and battle buddies as a support system may be utilized as a therapeutic tool. With permission from the client, providers may find it helpful to incorporate friends, co-workers, and battle buddies to assist in the rehabilitation process. Educating friends and battle buddies about concepts being developed in therapeutic sessions, such as strategies to decrease anxiety, anger, or frustration may assist with carryover. Military support systems may look different from ones found in the civilian world, but these systems have often been faced with heavy challenges from which they have grown strong.

The family is often the first-line support system for many Veterans/service members who are in need of OT services. The service member experience impacts every member of a family. Multiple deployments and protracted separation take a toll on a family and contribute to the stress of the reintegration process. This can be especially complicated if the returning service member has been injured and/or returns with multiple functional impairments. As a civilian practitioner, it is important to assess functional limitations in a client, and assess whether these limitations are due to emotional disturbance, mental health issues, physiological issues, or a combination of all three.

Every service member has the same goal – to be as independent as possible. Because of the desire to return to their military tasks and jobs, many service members will set unrealistic goals for their recovery. It is important for the practitioner to understand that regardless of the cause of the impairment (physical issues or mental health issues), the goal of OT is to maximize independence and help return the individual to their highest level of functionality possible. This requires that the clinician be knowledgeable about the role of OT in the care of our service members, be realistic in terms of expectations of progress, and be able to educate the family and service member as to what to expect in their treatment and a realistic time frame toward recovery.

It is important for providers to be aware of their own opinions and feelings so that it does not interfere with the therapeutic relationship. Clients may have strong opinions about political issues (e.g., gun control, marriage equality), religion, child rearing philosophies, etc. Providers must be aware of their own opinions and biases to ensure those feelings do not impact the therapeutic relationship.

How Does a Healthcare Provider Motivate Someone to Get the OT Services They Need?

If a Veteran is experiencing difficulty with the ADLs, IADLs, sleep, education, work, play, leisure, and social participation, he or she may benefit from skilled OT services. If a provider feels a service member or Veteran would benefit from OT services, he or she may want to discuss the following points with the client.

Focus on Function and Client Goals

OTs focuses on function and assisting people in returning to maximum functional status. The goal of OT is to help clients get back to their prior level of function after an illness or injury. OTs focus on a client's goals and build intervention plans based on the current abilities of the client. The OT provider will then use therapeutic interventions to get a person to *their* goal.

OTs Cannot Diagnose or Prescribe Medicine

In the military healthcare system, OTs cannot diagnose or prescribe medicine. This allows for a safe environment to express needs, feelings, and goals.

Making Sense of It All

OTs can assist in translating concepts learned in psychology/social work into everyday life (e.g. grading prolonged exposure tasks to find a just right fit). OTs specialize in activity analysis and grading activities. OT providers can investigate roadblocks that may be preventing someone from implementing strategies learned in therapy. OTs can analyze a task, strategies, and/or a client's abilities and hypothesize and remediate reasons why a person may have difficulty implementing strategies learned into everyday life.

What Else Do We Need to Think About?

Behavioral health providers educate patients to balance work, play, leisure, and activities of daily living. All too often, behavioral health providers do not practice the same strategies discussed in therapy session for themselves. Lack of care for the professional can lead to compassion fatigue and/or burnout which compromises their ability to work effectively with this high stress, high impact population.

Back to Pete ...

Pete was referred to OT services to address difficulty with occupational performance. His OT utilized the Canadian Occupational Performance Measure and other standardized assessments along with an interview to assess Pete's situation. Pete determined that he would like to prioritize his areas of concern as follows:

a   sleep;
b   tolerating public places; and
c   frustration tolerance.

The OT and the behavioral health counselor met with Pete to discuss a plan to address Pete's concerns. The resulting plan was rooted in the concepts of cognitive behavior therapy (CBT). The counselor and the Veteran worked through imaginal components. The OT and the Veteran analyzed his current status and where he would like to be. Together, they developed and executed the in vivo component of care. The OT ensured that the Veteran and the in vivo work were a challenge, as it required that Pete break down and analyze tasks related to the experience. The OT utilized skills of activity analysis to match the current abilities of the client with a task and context that would advance the Veteran's abilities to complete desired occupations. The OT reinforced the techniques taught by the members of the interdisciplinary team during the in vivo work.

With the work of all interdisciplinary team members and the reinforcement of a united plan of care, Pete made progress toward his goals. At his nine-week team meeting, Pete reported that he was sleeping about four to five hours a night and credits cognitive behavioral therapy for insomnia (CBT-i) techniques of sleep hygiene education and stimulus control for the gains he made in this area. He felt that the imaginal work with his counselor and the in vivo work with OT had increased his ability to tolerate public places and decreased his level of frustration. He also reported that he was having an easier time at work and felt that his concentration was improving. His wife reported that Pete utilized the techniques learned in treatment during their daughter's soccer games and was now able to tolerate standing on the sidelines at games for half of the game with minimal anxiety. She stated that this was a huge improvement from the start of his OT treatment when he was not able to tolerate more than ten minutes on the sidelines. Pete stated that he realized that he had "a long road ahead of him," but he sees, for the first time, that things "can and will get better."

Conclusion

OT practitioners have been working with the military population for a century. OTs work with service members and Veterans with deficits in function as a result of a variety of illnesses or injuries. They also work with service members to assist in preventing illness or injury. Whether OTs are working with Veterans after an amputation, analyzing a service member's workstation to avoid repetitive use injuries, or working with a Veteran diagnosed with PTSD or a TBI, the focus will always be on functional occupational performance. As such, "OT practitioners are uniquely positioned to serve Veterans in all adult practice settings. The ultimate achievement is to offer the service member/Veteran hope and skills for occupational freedom" (Plach & Sells, 2013, p. 80).

References

American Occupational Therapy Association (2011). Definition of occupational therapy practice for the AOTA Model Practice Act. Retrieved October 16, 2015, from: www.aota.org/-/media/Corporate/Files/Advocacy/State/Resources/Practice Act/Model Definition of OT Practice Adopted 41411.ashx

American Occupational Therapy Association (2014). Occupational therapy practice framework: Domain and process (3rd ed.). *American Journal of Occupational Therapy*, 68(Suppl. 1), S1–S48.

Cogan, A. (2014a). Occupational needs and intervention strategies for military personnel with mild traumatic brain injury and persistent post-concussion symptoms. *Journal of Occupational Therapy*, 34(3), 150–159.

Cogan, A. (2014b). Supporting our military families: A case for a larger role for occupational therapy in prevention and mental health care. *American Journal of Occupational Therapy*, 68(4), 478–483.

Federal Board for Vocational Education (1918). *Training of teachers for occupational therapy for the rehabilitation of disabled soldiers and sailors*. Washington, DC: Government Printing Office.

Plach, H. L. & Sells, C. H. (2013). Occupational performance needs of young Veterans. *American Journal of Occupational Therapy*, 67, 73–81.

Radomski, M., Davidson, L., Voydetich, D., & Erickson, M. (2009). Occupational therapy for service members with mild traumatic brain injury. *American Journal for Occupational Therapy*, 63(5), 646–654.

16

MORAL INJURY

Joan Beder

War changes lives. War is the realm of the paradoxical: the morally repugnant is the morally permissible and even the morally necessary. Killing, even enemy combatants; destroying, even legitimate wartime targets … all involve taking away the most sacred and essential elements of a human being, his or her life … War justifies what in peacetime would be unjustifiable: the destruction and the lives of others. "What kind of person am I to have done this?" reconciling war's paradoxes … involves moral injury.

(Sherman, 2015, p. xiv)

He was a Veteran having served in Iraq. He ran more than 400 combat missions as a machine gunner in the turret of a Humvee. Daniel suffered greatly from PTSD (and moral injury) and had been diagnosed with TBI and other war-related conditions. He was haunted by his memories of battle, death and pain. He was 30 years old when he took his life: He wrote: "I am left with basically nothing. Too trapped in a war to be at peace, too damaged to be at war … Not only am I better off dead, but the world is better off without me. It is not suicide but a mercy killing."

(Somers, 2013)

In war we have to deal with heavy contradictions … You cannot be a Warrior and not be deeply involved with suffering and responsibility. You're causing a lot of it … Warriors must touch their souls because their job involves killing people, Warriors deal with eternity.

(Marlantes, 2011, p. 44)

The resistance to close range killing of one's own species is so great that it is often overlooked as a burden. If the soldier in combat is able to overcome this resistance to killing and kills an enemy soldier in close combat, he/she will be forever burdened with blood guilt, and if he elects not to kill, then the blood guilt of his fallen comrades and the shame of his profession, nation and cause lie upon him/her. He is damned if he does and damned if he doesn't.

(Grossman, 2009, p. 120)

Moral Injury Defined

As the quoted material above suggests, there is a component of morality in the engagements involved in war. Many of our service members may struggle with acts performed during their service, actions that they had to perform or witnessed. These actions and situations leave a lasting emotional impression with subsequent emotional challenges, defined as moral injury (MI).

Litz and colleagues (2009) state that "Moral injury requires an act of transgression that severely and abruptly contradicts an individual's personal or shared expectation about the rules of conduct, either during the event or sometime after" (p. 700). MI is a term used in the mental health community that describes the psychological damage service members face when their actions, especially in battle, contradict their moral beliefs. The distress that emerges from these episodes includes deep feelings of shame, guilt, and existential struggle. Nash and Litz (2013) expand the definition by noting that MI is a psychological trauma that develops through violation of what a person considers right or wrong.

In war, there are numerous potentially morally injurious experiences; experiences that hold a different set of moral values and rules that are inconsistent with civilian society. These include: participating or witnessing inhumane or cruel actions, being present when a fellow service member is killed, repeated exposure to dead bodies, failing to prevent the immoral acts of others, and acts of cowardice, killing a woman or child by mistake (Litz et al., 2009), giving or receiving orders that are perceived as gross moral violations (Drescher, Foy, Kelly, Leshner, Schultz, & Litz, 2011), and bearing witness to transgression of peers and leaders who betray expectations in egregious ways (Maguen & Litz, 2012). In time, these episodes accumulate and the service member is unable to accommodate or incorporate their actions or the actions of others into their worldview, their moral code. What occurs is a "corruption of the soul" and ensuing shame regarding the behaviors. In religious traditions, these feelings have been described as the "dark night of the soul" (Mahedy, 1986).

> It was the middle of the night. Farmers were out in their fields in Afghanistan, creating a dangerous situation that might result in the loss of our men through planted IEDs. As a Marine officer, I had the authority to order these men killed, I wanted confirmation from a higher authority (a commander) to do the abhorrent, something I'd spent my entire life believing was evil (taking a life). "Take the shot" I commanded of the Marine by my side. Shots rang out and a part of me wanted the round to miss their target but they struck flesh and the men fell dead. In war there are many ways to kill. I did so by giving orders.
>
> *(Kudo, 2015)*

Military personnel serving in war are confronted with ethical and moral challenges, most of which they navigate because of effective and learned rules of war backed by their leadership and the purposefulness that arises in units. We train our military to obey orders, respect leadership and function as warriors. In war, it is the unspeakable part of war that most people push far out of awareness, leaving those who suffer with MI alone in their memories. It's the stuff "we never talked about" or the stuff "I have never told anyone about, not even the guy who was with me." These acts of transgression lead to serious inner conflicts because they are at odds with core ethical and moral beliefs. This is at the core of MI.

In the current wars, and due to the nature of these wars – counterinsurgency actions, guerrilla, warfare, urban contexts, unmarked enemy, civilian threats, improvised explosive device (IEDs) – all create greater risk of MI. These are wars that are fought on the ground for the most part, in face-to-face situations and without a clearly defined enemy. There is no clear-cut line differentiating the enemy from the civilians and added to that are the multiple and lengthy deployments, the demands on families and service members and unexpressed anger and frustrations about losses, sacrifices, and adversities. These factors may cloud moral and ethical judgments that lead to acts that are morally questionable. Although killing may be a strong component of MI, it is important to note that not all killing in war results in MI; it is the element of perceived transgression that goes against an individual's moral code that is the major factor. Nevertheless, many state that the act of taking the life of another is the primary predictor of MI (Sherman, 2015).

Moral Injury vs. Post-Traumatic Stress Disorder

MI is different from post-traumatic stress disorder (PTSD) although it can be a factor in it. PTSD is a mental disorder that requires a diagnosis with specific indicators; MI is a dimensional problem, it occurs with no threshold or parameters. PTSD occurs when there is harm to self and others; MI occurs when one is the perpetrator or the witness. MI is not a diagnosable mental disorder as defined in the DSM V; instead, it functions as a contributor to a person's overall state of mind. Some of the behavioral symptoms of MI will overlap with those of PTSD but not all persons with MI will develop PTSD and not all people with PTSD experience MI. Interestingly, transgression is not a factor in PTSD nor does PTSD sufficiently capture the depth of feelings related to MI (Maguen & Litz, 2012). It is important for clinicians to understand that, according to recent research (Currier, Holland, & Malott, 2014), morally injurious experiences demonstrated a statistically significant relationship with mental health problems; not necessarily with PTSD.

Symptoms of MI

Building on the definition of MI as a consequence of transgressive acts, states of inner conflict and turmoil are to be expected. The internal conflict may include feelings of shame (as noted in the initial quote from Sherman, 2015), guilt, depression, emotional numbing, questioning the meaning of life, anxiety about consequences, and anger which may be based on betrayal-based incidents. Also there may be negative changes in ethical attitudes and behavior, changes in spirituality, negative views on God and alienation from others.

Behavioral manifestations include distrust in social and cultural contacts, aggressive behaviors, poor self-care or self-harm, social instability, withdrawal, self-harming, alcohol and/or drug abuse, failed relationships, employment difficulties, and even suicidal ideation (Maguen & Litz, 2012).

In an effort to understand some of the internal dynamic forces for the person struggling with MI, it is important to highlight the aspects of shame and guilt. While both feelings may be present, they touch different facets of the response to a transgressive episode(s).

Guilt is a painful and motivating cognitive experience tied to specific acts of transgression; guilt often makes the guilty person want to make amends. This can be transformative because the person wants to correct a vile behavior (e.g. if I volunteer at a soup kitchen, then some of the bad things I have done will be erased). This is different from shame. Shame involves global evaluations of the self along with tendencies to withdraw and avoid. It comes with toxic interpersonal tendencies such as anger or decreased empathy for others. Shame is more damaging to emotional and mental health than guilt. We do not readily discuss the hateful or shameful things we have done; they are buried and kept in secret. Those experiencing shame want to withdraw, to conceal their actions. There is the fear of being morally judged, thus self-forgiveness becomes very difficult. With shame, the more time passes, the more the service member will be convinced and confident that not only their actions but also they are unforgiveable. Sherman (2015) notes that the combination of guilt and shame, usually present in combination for those suffering with MI "can tear a self into pieces, to the point that one loses sound judgments about who one is and who one can be" (p. 161). This is the tragedy of MI.

Routes to Moral Repair

There are numerous routes to addressing MI in our service members. The therapeutic challenge, according to Marlantes (2011), is that the service member has to learn to integrate the war; the horror has to be absorbed, the psyche stretched to accommodate the trauma. Judith Herman (1992), a noted scholar in the field of trauma and trauma treatment, notes that trauma recovery unfolds in three stages: safety, remembrance and mourning, and reconnection with ordinary life. While not writing specifically about service members and the impact of service, these stages are applicable in working with the morally injured.

In applying this model to working with the morally injured service member, one of the primary goals of the first stage is developing a relationship of safety with the counselor. This feeling of safety and respect is essential for the later work of telling their story. Interestingly, the first stage does not require the service member to discuss or process their memories of the morally injurious event(s). Stage 2, referred to as remembrance and mourning, does include evoking memories and working through the grief about unwanted experiences and their negative impact on one's life. This stage can only be accomplished if stage 1 has been achieved. The explanation for this linearity is because shame and guilt are such prominent aspects of MI (i.e. the service member must feel safe before exposing his/her shame over incidents that provoked the MI). The unspoken fear is that the counselor may find what the service member is describing to be so heinous that the counselor will reject the service member. The success of the counseling rests on the service member being able to reveal their moral failure without retribution. In stage 3, the service member is supported and encouraged to reconnect with their current and former life and engage as fully as possible with others.

Other treatment modalities for those with MI include cognitive processing therapy (CPT), an adaptation of cognitive behavioral therapy. This approach has been helpful for those suffering with PTSD and has been shown to be effective for those struggling with MI. CPT usually consists of 12 sessions with the overriding goal of helping the service member gain an understanding of and modifying the meaning attributed to their traumatic event. Service members are encouraged to explore their traumatic event(s) and to try to increase awareness of responses to the episodes to enable management of negative behaviors and feelings (Payne, 2014).

Another treatment approach is adaptive disclosure. This approach consists of six 90-minute weekly sessions, shorter than traditional CPT and trauma therapy as described by Herman (1992). The first session is used to evaluate the current status of the service member, establish the event to be targeted (the most recent MI violation), and establish both rapport and realistic goals. The next four sessions include imaginal exposure exercises and are devoted to emotionally processing the war memory, describing various elements and associations as well as helping the service member describe the emotional uncensored beliefs about the event (e.g. shame, self-loathing, perceptions that are defined by the event). The last session is used to review experiences, underscore positive lessons learned and to plan for the long period toward ultimate healing. In a preliminary assessment of the approach, the treatment was well tolerated and promoted significant reductions in symptoms (Gray et al., 2012).

Sherman (2015) emphasizes that most of the work of MI repair is done at the individual level with a counselor and/or with other civilians. It is to be seen as long term – in contrast to adaptive disclosure – as trust is an essential ingredient that enables the work and it may take a long time for a therapeutic level of trust to be achieved. The work must ultimately focus on the facts of each case of moral violation. The goal is to help the service member to understand that they were functioning in a random, tragic situation (i.e. fighting in a war zone, and that they were called upon in their service to act in a prescribed way). There has to be the recognition that acts of war can be vile but that they are part of the experience. The ultimate goal is catharsis and self-forgiveness, for the morally injured to be able to acknowledge that there is sadness that people must behave this way in war. This sadness can be part of their grief and eventually overcome.

Elements on the part of the counselor

Irrespective of which treatment approach a counselor takes, there are certain common elements in working with the morally injured service member/Veteran. They include the following.

Developing a Strong Working Alliance and Trusting, Respectful and Caring Relationship

At the core of a strong working relationship is trust. According to Shay (2014), the development of the relationship is essential and demands that the counselor be able to listen to the unique story of the service member/Veteran. Once trust has been established, the counselor must be able to hear and not react negatively to the gory and sometimes dreadful admissions of the morally injured individual.

Educating Toward MI

It behooves all who counsel the morally injured to understand the dynamics of the condition: how it impacts each one who struggles with their MI, and to be able to chart a course with the service member toward regaining their footing in life. Education is essential to the person who is struggling, as it gives direction to their treatment and creates hope for redemption and self-forgiveness.

Being Able to Tolerate the Details and Encourage Greater Exploration of the MI Event

This is often difficult for those who counsel the military as those who are stateside may have limited understanding of the day-to-day experiences of active duty in a war zone. For many in the helping professions, there is the tendency and the desire to jump in and "fix the hurt." The best course in working with the morally injured is to be able to listen without judgment, and for the counselor to be able to process reactions with good supervision and caring colleagues (Lyons, 2007).

Moving Toward Subsequent Careful and Directive Examination of the Implications of the Experience for the Client's Self Schemas

In this area of practice, the counselor is expected to help the client see that their experience is only one facet of who they are; they may be father, mother, friend, daughter, etc., and that they can move beyond their self-definition as flawed, due to their moral violation, and redefine themselves in familiar but obscured roles.

Fostering Reconnection with Various Communities – Faith, Family

This final step in care may take a long time, as healing from shame and guilt is not easily overcome. In addition, the emotional numbing and withdrawal, which is common in those with MI, makes social situations difficult, relationships strained, and communication a challenge. Reconnection becomes a goal which is sometimes difficult to attain (Lyons, 2007). Some will find forgiveness and reconnection through their spiritual/religious life and others in their family and close relationships. Many have to be strongly supported to move on and take the risk of reconnecting. The hesitancy resides in the dynamic of shame and once shame has been relieved, most with MI will move on, albeit slowly.

Conclusion

Working with the military, with warriors who have experienced MI, is simultaneously deeply rewarding and challenging. Those who counsel must accept the reality that the pressures of war leave a lasting imprint on the warrior; much of it is positive but it can leave deep scars and long-lasting emotional pain (Lyons, 2007). Our goal in working with this population is to acknowledge the struggles inherent in the warrior's life and help them to regain their footing in their civilian life. Yes, many are haunted by memories of what they experienced and will suffer with symptoms of PTSD. Others will suffer with deeper feelings of self-loathing and despair provoked by morally injurious behaviors. No question, our work with these warriors is difficult but nowhere near as difficult as the struggles faced by those returning with MI. The work with these populations can be seen as life-sustaining, perhaps even life-giving, as it allows the service member/Veteran to redefine themselves as worthwhile persons who have a place in society and in the hearts of those who care for and love them.

References

Currier, J. M., Holland, J. M., & Malott, J. (2014). Moral injury, meaning making, and mental health in returning Veterans. *Journal of Clinical Psychology*, 71(3), 229–240.

Drescher, K. D., Foy, D. W., Kelly, C., Leshner, A. Schultz, K., & Litz, B. (2011). An exploration of the viability and usefulness of the construct of moral injury in war Veterans. *Traumatology*, 17(8), 8–13. doi: 10.1177/1534765610395615

Gray, M., Schorr, Y., Nash, W., Lebowitz, L., Amidon, A., & Lansing, A. et al. (2012). Adaptive disclosure: An open trial of a novel exposure-based intervention for service members with combat-related psychological stress injuries. *Behavior Therapy*, 43, 407–415.

Grossman, D. (2009). *On killing*. New York: Back Bay Books.

Herman, J. (1992). *Trauma and recovery: The aftermath of violence – from domestic abuse to political terror*. New York: Basic Books.

Kudo, T. (2015, Feb. 27). How we learned to kill. *NY Times, Opinion*.

Litz, B. T., Stein, N., Delaney, E., Leibowitz, L., Nash, W. P., Silva, C., & Maguen, S. (2009). Moral injury and moral repair in war Veterans: A preliminary model and intervention strategy. *Clinical Psychology Review*, 29, 695–706. doi: 10,1016/j.cpr.2009.07.003

Lyons, J. (2007). The returning warrior: Advice for families and friends. In C. R. Figley and W. Nash (Eds.), *Combat stress injury* (ch. 14). New York: Routledge.

Maguen, S. & Litz, B. (2012). Moral injury in Veterans of war. *PTSD Research Quarterly*, 23(1), 1–3.

Mahedy, W. P. (1986). *Out of the night: The spiritual journey of Vietnam Vets*. New York: Ballantine Books.

Marlantes, K. (2011). *What it is like to go to war*. New York: Atlantic Monthly Press.

Nash, W. P. & Litz, B. T. (2013) Moral injury: A mechanism for war-related psychological trauma in military family members. *Clinical Child and Family Psychology Reviews*, 16(4), 365–375. doi: 10,1007/s10567–10013–0146-y

Payne, M. (2014). *Modern social work theory* (4th ed.). New York: Palgrave.

Shay, J. (2014). Moral injury. *Psychoanalytic Psychology*, 31(2), 182–191.

Sherman, N. (2015). *Afterwar*. New York: Oxford University Press.

Somers, D. (2013). "I am sorry it has come to this": A soldier's last words. Retrieved November 24, 2015 from htpp://Gawker.com

17

TELE-BEHAVIORAL HEALTH

Julie M. Landry-Poole, Lynette Pujol and Bret A. Moore

> Mary C. served two combat deployments to Iraq during her active-duty career. She was recently diagnosed with combat-related post-traumatic stress disorder and additionally suffers from severe back pain, which began during her most recent deployment. Mary lives 125 miles from her home VA and has requested behavioral health services but, due to her back problems, is unable to be in a car for more than 15 minutes without serious discomfort. The behavioral health team has suggested that Mary access tele-behavioral health services, as she is computer literate and is unable to get to the VA for face-to-face treatment. She has now had her fifth session with a therapist and acknowledges she is "feeling better" already but has a "long way to go."

Tele-behavioral health (TBH) is the delivery of behavioral health services via technological means such as videoconferencing. TBH is arguably one of the fastest growing segments of clinical practice in mental healthcare today. This growth is evidenced by the development or adoption of practice guidelines and standards by various national professional organizations such as the American Psychological Association (2013), American Telemedicine Association (2009, 2013, 2014), and National Association of Social Workers (2005) as well as state entities (Ohio Psychological Association, 2010). The expansion of position papers on ethical, legal, and professional issues within the professional literature regarding the use of technology in the delivery of behavioral health services also highlights the growing interest and engagement in this area (Baker & Bufka, 2011; Mohr, 2009; Reed, McLaughlin, & Milholland, 2000).

If one were to delve into the TBH literature, one notes the varied terms used to describe the practice. Depending on the organization (e.g. Veterans Affairs, Department of Defense) and behavioral health specialty (e.g. psychology, psychiatry, social work), you will find terms such as "telemental health," "telepsychology," "telepsychiatry," and others. We have chosen to use the term "tele-behavioral health" in this chapter as it is a broader term, which encompasses all specialties that deliver behavioral healthcare services.

In keeping with the term TBH, a more expansive definition is in order. TBH is broadly defined as the delivery of behavioral health services via technological means. The most common means within larger organizations such as the Department of Defense, Indian Health Service, and Department of Veterans Affairs is videoconferencing. Videoconferencing is the synchronous (i.e. real-time) interactive process that involves provision of psychotherapy, psychoeducation, assessment, pharmacotherapy, and other related behavioral health services by a licensed behavioral health professional from an originating site to an identified client or patient at a receiving site. An example is the delivery of cognitive processing therapy (CPT) by a psychologist from San Antonio, Texas to a Soldier at Ft. Benning, Georgia who is dealing with post-traumatic stress disorder (PTSD). This interaction is completed securely via portable desktop video cameras, standalone monitors with integrated audio and video capabilities, or a combination of the two. Another example is described in the vignette above. Mary C. was able to connect with a behavioral health practitioner via TBH services through a Community Based Outpatient Center (CBOC) and receive treatment that would have been impossible otherwise.

Other technological means of behavioral health service delivery include telephone, email, chat, text and the Internet (e.g., social media, blogs) (American Psychological Association, 2013). These methods are used more often by private practitioners who may not be financially able to invest in videoconferencing equipment. However, as technology has advanced, the cost of equipment has lessened and the use of videoconferencing by private behavioral health practitioners has increased.

In addition to direct patient care, the military has leveraged videoconferencing capabilities for consultation between military behavioral health clinicians and unit commanders. Most often these consultations revolve around communicating fitness for duty, risk and safety concerns, and recommendations for managing complex behavioral health cases which cause disruption to unit cohesion and morale. Although not technically a behavioral health intervention as defined above, the use of videoconferencing in providing command consultations is a value-added service which enhances organizational functioning of the military unit. For example, a commander who is completing a 30-day field training exercise at Ft. Irwin, California becomes aware that one of his soldiers is having emotional difficulties related to a pending divorce. Concerned about the soldier's ability to complete the remainder of the exercise, the commander contacts the soldier's behavioral health provider at their home station at Ft. Hood, Texas. The provider assures the commander that even though the soldier is having difficulties, he has made significant progress in therapy and has the emotional resources and necessary social support within the unit to complete the training exercise. Consequently, the commander decides to keep the soldier in place. The soldier completes the training exercise, which further increases his confidence and belief that members of his unit are a strong and effective support system for him. Furthermore, the commander is able to maintain his required "troop strength" and successfully complete the training exercise.

In the following pages, we outline the core aspects of TBH practice within the military. Specifically, we focus on the use of TBH services within the US Army. Our focus is due to our familiarity with how this service works and the similarities it shares with other organizations such as the Department of Veterans Affairs and other branches of the military. That being said, it is important to consider that certain concepts, processes, and policies may not align with other branches, departments, or clinics that provide services to active-duty service members and Veterans.

Ethical and Legal Considerations

The use of TBH requires unique ethical and legal considerations beyond those routinely required to perform clinical care. All major professional behavioral health organizations provide TBH specific guidelines (Wells, Mitchell, Finkelhor, & Becker-Blease, 2007). Multiple federal agencies and sub-agencies have also developed TBH policies, including the Department of Defense, NASA, the Veterans Health Administration, the Commerce Department, the Department of Agriculture, the Federal Communications Commission, the General Accounting Office, the Department of Justice, the Office of Management and Budget, and the Department of Health and Human Services (Nickelson, 1996). The American Telemedicine Association (ATA) has similarly published practice guidelines in order to "advance the science and to assure the uniform quality of services to patients" (American Telemedicine Association, 2013). In general, providers must follow federal, state, and local regulatory and licensure requirements related to their scope of services; confidentiality must be assessed and environmental constraints determined to ensure privacy.

The American Psychological Association (APA) and the National Association of Social Workers (NASW) along with the Association of Social Work Boards provide several recommendations within their published guidelines specific to the complex issues related to TBH use. The following section briefly reviews the central concepts as outlined by the APA and NASW.

Clinicians using TBH should ensure that they are familiar enough with the technology to provide competent care. This may require training and/or consultation with a technology subject matter expert (SME) in order to develop the necessary knowledge and skills. Prior to beginning treatment, it is imperative to also ensure the patient is able to understand and use the technology. Informed consent should be obtained and documented prior to the initial session. Additionally, clinicians should consider how the patient's individual characteristics (e.g. physical/cognitive disability, cultural, personal preferences) may impact effective use of TBH. Since there are no generally accepted contraindications, the decision to provide behavioral health services via TBH must be based on sound clinical judgment. Research supports the use of TBH across a wide range of diagnoses (Dongier, Tempier, Lalince-Michaud, & Meunier, 1986), including PTSD (Porcari et al. 2009); obsessive–compulsive disorder (Baer, Cukor, Jenike, Leahy, O'Laughlen, & Coyle, 1995); traumatic brain injury (Ng et al., 2013); psychotic disorders (i.e. schizophrenia) (Folsom, 1995); as well as a wide range of populations, including American Indians, indigenous and non-indigenous, asylum seekers, refugees, migrants, veterans, and active-duty service members (Jones, Etherage, Harmon, & Okiishi, 2012; Mucic, 2010; Porcari et al., 2009; Sabesan et al., 2013; Stetz, Folen, Van Horn, Ruseborn, & Samuel, 2013). In addition, patient acuity, agitation, and imminent danger should be considered when making TBH feasibility decisions.

Clinicians must also consider technology-related vulnerabilities and safeguard against potential threats to confidentiality. Providers must ensure patient information is appropriately stored and transmitted and only accessible to authorized individuals. Commonly used precautions include encryption and use of a secure server. Within Department of Defense (DoD) settings, these technological issues are managed by information technology specialists with expertise in the area of TBH, specially trained staff at each military treatment facility (MTF), and use of the electronic medical record. Civilian behavioral health counselors must be cognizant of the multiple layers of confidentiality and provide adequate seclusion for sessions and record-keeping storage.

A proper TBH introduction to a potential client is essential. New patients may question the feasibility and efficacy of this form of treatment and may resist the TBH approach. It is important to explain the value and efficacy of TBH as a treatment tool and explore the levels of resistance proffered.

Sergeant (SGT) X is a 26-year-old Caucasian male. He has served as an infantryman during two combat deployments. He was identified as having "deployment related symptoms" on a recent periodic health assessment and was therefore referred for therapy. Prior to the initial therapy session, SGT X completed the clinic's required paperwork, including a consent form for psychotherapy via TBH. On the morning of his appointment, SGT X presents to the clinic with some mild anxiety related to seeking treatment. When the provider was ready, SGT X was brought into the treatment room, which is a small room with two monitors on a desk, a single chair, and acoustic padding on the walls. Upon entering the room, his anxiety immediately increased, and he becomes agitated. As the therapist introduced herself, SGT X interrupted, saying "I don't want to talk to someone over Skype." He additionally stated he felt "uncomfortable in this room." The provider explained the technology and its use along with the rationale for treatment via TBH.

The case of SGT X illustrates several aspects of the discussion above, including informed consent and patient preference. It is clear from SGT X's response he was not expecting to see a provider over a monitor rather than in person. The patient's negative reaction could have been avoided if the administrative staff at the remote location discussed TBH with the patient prior to the initial meeting with the provider. This discussion would have ideally occurred prior to scheduling the TBH appointment and prior to SGT X signing the consent form. It is possible SGT X would have declined TBH services during that dialogue and would have therefore been scheduled with an in-house provider. Or SGT X may have made an informed decision to participate in TBH treatment based on the information provided by the staff. It is important to note while SGT X signed the consent form, he was not providing informed consent.

Providers performing psychological testing and assessment are encouraged by the APA to ensure the integrity of the psychometric properties of the procedures and to preserve the conditions of administration indicated in the testing manual. Any adaptations should be considered during the interpretation of testing data and documented within the report. Testing norms derived from TBH administration should be used when available. If testing materials are located at the same site as the patient, the counselor will need to ensure local personnel maintain the security of the testing materials. Additionally, the atmosphere at the remote location must be conducive to psychological administration, including a quiet space free from distractions.

Emergency planning in clinical work is complex. When clinical services are performed via TBH, the planning becomes all the more intricate. Providers must be familiar with the local laws and regulations, specific duties, and resources for each state in which they treat patients. Within the military setting, these concerns are lessened due to MTF similarities; however, each MTF and behavioral health clinic functions under their own standard operating procedures (SOPs). Providers must be familiar with the SOPs at each MTF for which they provide services. For example, the procedures for referring a patient for medication management are different at the various locations.

SOPs for active psychosis, suicidal ideation, and homicidal ideation should be created and should include contingency plans for voluntary and involuntary hospitalization. These procedures will include logistical details such as transporting the patient to the emergency department and contacting someone in the Service Member's Chain of Command or a family member. Emergency planning should be discussed with patients to ensure they know what to do in case of an emergency. Contingency plans should also address possible technological difficulties such as interrupted transmission or poor audio/video quality.

The use of TBH often results in the crossing of jurisdictional lines. Traditionally, providers have been required to hold a full and unrestricted license in each state in which they practice (federal agencies such as the DoD and VA are exceptions – clinicians only need to be licensed in a single state regardless of where they practice). Recent changes, however, indicate licensure rules are gradually catching up to technology. In February 2015, the Association of State and Provincial Psychology Boards created a Psychology Interjurisdictional Compact (PSYPACT), which is designed to facilitate TBH and temporary face-to-face (FTF) treatment across jurisdictional boundaries. The PSYPACT is unique to psychologists, though, and several conditions apply. For example, states where patients receive TBH must have a procedure for receiving and investigating complaints about TBH providers. Also the psychologist may not have a criminal record that violates the Rules of the Commission and must hold a special authorization in order to practice under the PSYPACT.

Additional Considerations

Provider anxiety related to the use of TBH is likely to occur just as it would with the use of any other new delivery method or treatment modality. A qualitative study by May et al. (2000) cited loss of nonverbal cues and an inability to establish a therapeutic alliance as initial provider concerns related to TBH. However, several studies, in addition to those cited below, contradict these common assumptions and conclude apprehension related to TBH limitations is held more by providers than patients (Capner, 2000; Omodei & McClennan, 1998).

Beyond mastering the use of the technology, TBH work does not require a provider to learn new techniques. Omodei and McClennan (1998) found clinicians may use unnatural nonverbal behaviors (e.g. intensified head nods) to compensate for perceived limitations at the onset of TBH work, but patient feedback affirms preference for the use of ordinary skills and habits.

Clinical considerations such as determining the frequency of sessions or concerns related to rapport building are addressed with clinical judgment in the same way they would be in traditional FTF treatment. Similarly, most administrative issues in TBH work are dependent on organizational SOPs as they would be in a traditional setting. For example, if a TBH therapy patient misses an appointment, the clinician or an administrative staff member will likely follow up with the patient by telephone to rule out any safety concerns and reschedule just as they would with a FTF patient.

Other considerations may include more practical issues. Yellowlees, Shore, and Roberts (2010) offer suggestions related to the treatment room layout, lighting, backdrops, etc. A particularly important factor addressed by the authors relates to the angle between the users' cameras and where the users look on the screens. This "gaze angle" is imperative to emulate natural eye contact.

Patient Satisfaction

Many TBH operations follow the "hub-and-spoke" model, where providers are aggregated in one place and deliver services to outlying military installations. The development of TBH services in the Southern Regional Medical Command (SRMC) began with one installation and one type of evaluation and grew over a period of six years to eight installations and many different types of services (e.g. individual and group therapy, medication management, administrative evaluations).

A primary consideration in the development of the program was the acceptability of TBH by soldiers and other stakeholders (i.e. installations receiving TBH services and the regional command that funded the project). Provider satisfaction with clinical aspects of the encounter, as well as their opinions about the reliability of the technology, was especially important to determine provider acceptability.

During the pilot phase, TBH encounters were one-time mental health evaluations that are required for administrative separation or acceptance into a school for advanced training. Administrative separation is separation from military service for a variety of reasons (i.e. not meeting weight standards over a period of time, inappropriate or illegal behavior, such as drug or alcohol misuse, lack of appropriate childcare). Advanced schools are assignments or experiences that generally require a high degree of individual responsibility and trust (i.e. drill sergeant, recruiter, sniper). Only military or Department of the Army psychologists are able to perform these evaluations which consist of a clinical interview, review of screening instruments and completion of required paperwork. Evaluations conducted through TBH are the same as FTF except for the use of technology.

Soldiers were asked for their opinion about the video and audio quality during the encounter and whether they would choose TBH again. Questionnaires were completed following most encounters and were voluntary and anonymous. Results after the first year (2010; 1,327 encounters) revealed high overall satisfaction from soldiers (4.57) on a 1–5 scale (1 = poor, 5 = excellent), with 88% indicating they would choose TBH again. Surveys were collected over the next three fiscal years (FY11, FY12, FY13) as the type of encounters and number of installations expanded, with overall satisfaction levels of 4.5, 4.6, and 4.7 respectively over 4,140 clinical encounters. Soldiers continued to express the opinion they would use TBH again over the same three years, with acceptance rates of 84%, 85%, and 92% respectively. These results are inconsistent with those of Jones et al. (2012), who reported that in three large samples of soldiers undergoing redeployment screening evaluations (i.e. screening performed after returning from deployments to Iraq or Afghanistan), FTF screening was preferred by soldiers who had not experienced screening through TBH before. Additionally, soldiers who had experienced TBH before, still reported a preference for FTF, but had more ambivalence, i.e. selected the "unsure" option for the question "I prefer a face-to-face interview" (Jones et al., 2012). Differences between these samples could be related to a number of factors (e.g., length of session, type of evaluation) that future program evaluation or research may address.

Staff Sergeant (SSG) Y is a 46-year-old African-American Service Member (SM) with three combat deployments whose presenting problem was "nightmares from deployments" and "difficult memories." When asked early in the initial session whether he had questions about TBH, SGT Y said he "was a people person" and did not know how he would do with therapy through TBH. SM and therapist discussed the pros and cons and he decided to "try TBH," but was informed that he could decide to see a face-to-face therapist at any time. He was encouraged to be honest about his experiences. SM was subsequently diagnosed with PTSD and underwent a course of CPT. Several weeks into the therapy, SSG Y said, "I just want to tell you that I was dead set against this type of therapy, but now I think it is great." SM explained that he was surprised about the ability to have a good therapeutic relationship through TBH and how helpful the treatment was for him.

This situation illustrates that an initially reluctant patient, even one who describes himself as a "people person," may be open to trying TBH. Once a therapeutic relationship is formed, SM found himself engaged in therapy and in favor of TBH. One aspect of this encounter was that the therapist informed the patient that if he did not like TBH, he could opt for FTF therapy. Perhaps the option of having an out was a factor in allowing the SM to try TBH. Although TBH may not be for everyone, some individuals with initial difficulty become fans, after a trial alleviates fears.

Provider Satisfaction

Providers were surveyed following each encounter during the pilot phase of the rollout of TBH and periodically thereafter to assess their experience of audio and video quality, response of the medical treatment facility to their requests, efficiency of the medical treatment facility staff at distal locations, and their overall satisfaction with TBH encounters. Provider perceptions were critical in identifying technological and administrative difficulties. Overall, providers gave high ratings to audio and video quality, as well as to the ability to establish rapport during a TBH encounter. The efficiency of staff at distant sites was generally the most common concern, since clinical flow depends on timely connections. Collection of intake paperwork and outcome measures was inefficient at first, conducted through fax or e-mail. However, since the Army's adoption of a system that collects demographic and social information, as well as clinical screening measures, this problem has been resolved. There are few studies in the literature that focus on provider perceptions of providing TBH to military members. Stetz et al. (2013) note that providers in their study who easily conducted eight encounters per day became fatigued after four hours of TBH. The authors reasoned that TBH takes increased attention and concentration of the provider, thereby increasing fatigue. They hypothesized that the reduced perception of nonverbal cues was one reason for the need for increased attention (Stetz et al., 2013). In sum, our experience has been that the majority of soldiers and providers have responded positively to the use of TBH.

Efficacy

One natural question when considering TBH is whether it is as effective as FTF treatment. Comparisons of TBH and FTF treatment in the literature show that in the two available randomized trials (e.g. Nelson et al., 2003, Ruskin et al., 2004) and less rigorous studies (e.g. Frueh et al., 2007; Tuerk, Yoder, Ruggiero, Gros, & Acierno, 2010), there is no difference or there are better outcomes using TBH compared with FTF for most problems (see Backhaus et al., 2012, for a review). These studies were conducted with a variety of populations, none of which were active-duty military. The active-duty military culture is one in which there is a stigma toward behavioral health treatment, a situation that was of especially high importance to military leaders during the heavy deployment years (i.e. OIF, OEF). It was beyond our mission to compare TBH with FTF directly, but we conducted a proxy by asking soldiers whether they had experienced FTF treatment prior to a TBH evaluation. We found no difference in soldiers' perceptions of their willingness to disclose information in a TBH encounter (n = 1,477) whether they had prior FTF behavioral health treatment or not (Crow, Brady, Baker, Pujol, & LaVoy, 2012). There was also no difference in overall satisfaction with a TBH encounter between soldiers who had prior FTF treatment (4.5/5.0) and those who had not (4.6/5.0). In spite of high rates of acceptance and satisfaction, some soldiers expressed negative views; 8.1% with no prior treatment and 7.9% with prior behavioral health treatment (7.9%) indicated an unwillingness to use TBH again (Crow et al., 2012). It is possible that the type of evaluation or demographic factors (e.g. age, experience with technology) may have differentiated those who were more inclined to have a positive perception from those who did not, but systematic study would be needed. Practically, it is our experience that many soldiers who are initially skeptical of TBH become supporters after an encounter with a caring clinician.

Conclusion

TBH is no longer considered "advanced technology" or "cutting edge"; it is here to stay and is a vital tool for military and civilian clinicians in helping Veterans and military personnel access behavioral health services. TBH offers those who live in remote areas, or those who have difficulty traveling to treatment facilities, the ability to access behavioral health services as needed and allows clinicians to expand the base of service to all those in need.

References

American Psychological Association (2013). Guidelines for the practice of telepsychology. *American Psychologist*, 68(9), 791–800.

American Telemedicine Association (2009). Practice guidelines for videoconferencing-based telemental health.

American Telemedicine Association (2013). Core operational guidelines for telehealth services involving provider-patient interactions.

American Telemedicine Association (2014). Practice guidelines for video-based online mental health services.

Backhaus, A., Agha, Z., Maglione, M. L., Repp, A., Ross, B., & Zuest, D. et al. (2012). Videoconferencing psychotherapy: A systematic review. *Psychological Services*, 9, 111–131.

Baer, L., Cukor, P., Jenike, M. A., Leahy, L., O'Laughlen, J., & Coyle, J. T. (1995). Pilot studies of telemedicine for patients with obsessive–compulsive disorder. *American Journal of Psychiatry*, 152, 1383–1385.

Baker, D. C. & Bufka, L. F. (2011). Preparing for the telehealth world: Navigating legal, regulatory, reimbursement and ethical issues in an electronic age. *Professional Psychology: Research and Practice*, 42(6), 405–411.

Capner, M. (2000). Videoconferencing in the provision of psychological services at a distance. *Journal of Telemedicine and Telecare*, 6, 311–319.

Crow, B. C., Brady, P., Baker, F., Pujol, L., & LaVoy, M. (2012). Practical strategies for overcoming challenges during tele-behavioral health implementation. Presented at the American Psychological Association, Orlando FL.

Dongier, M., Tempier, R., Lalinec-Michaud, M., & Meunier, D. (1986). Telepsychiatry. Psychiatric consultation through two-way television: A controlled study. *Canadian Journal of Psychiatry*, 31, 32–34.

Folsom, J. P. (1995). Clinical efficacy of telepsychiatry. *Telemedicine Journal*, 3, 187–188.

Frueh, B. C., Monnier, J., Yim, E., Grubaugh, A. L., Hammer, M. B., & Knapp, R. G. (2007). A randomized trial of telepsychiatry for post-traumatic stress disorder. *Journal of Telemedicine and Telecare*, 13, 142–147.

Jones, M. D., Etherage, J. R., Harmon, S. C., & Okiishi, J. C. (2012). Acceptability and cost-effectiveness of military telehealth mental health screening. *Psychological Services*, 9, 132–143.

May, C. et al. (2000). Telepsychiatry evaluation in the north-west of England: Preliminary results of a qualitative study. *Journal of Telemedicine and Telecare*, 3, 100–102.

Mohr, D. C. (2009). Telemental health: Reflections on how to move the field forward. *Clinical Psychology: Science and Practice*, 16, 343–347.

Mucic, D. (2010). Transcultural telepsychiatry and its impact on patient satisfaction. *Journal of Telemedicine and Telecare*, 16, 237–242.

National Association of Social Workers Association of Social Work Boards (2005). NASW & ASWB standards of technology and social work practice.

Nelson, E., Barnard, M., Cain, S., & Bui, T. (2003). Treating childhood depression over videoconferencing. *Telemedicine Journal and e-Health*, 9, 49–55.

Ng, E. M. et al. (2013). Telerehabilitation for addressing executive dysfunction after traumatic brain injury. *Brain Injury*, 27(5), 548–564.

Nickelson, D. W. (1996). Behavioral telehealth: Emerging practice, research, and policy opportunities. *Behavioral Sciences and the Law*, 14, 443–457.

Ohio Psychological Association (2010). Telepsychology guidelines. Retrieved from www.ohpsych. org/psychologists/files/2011/06/OPATelepsychologyGuidelines41710.pdf

Omodei, M. & McClennan, J. (1998). "The more I see you"? Face-to-face, video and telephone counselling compared. A programme of research investigating the emerging technology of videophone for counselling. *Australian Journal of Psychology*, 50, 109.

Porcari, C. E. et al. (2009). Assessment of post-traumatic stress disorder in veterans by videoconferencing and by face-to-face methods. *Journal of Telemedicine and Telecare*, 15, 89–94.

Reed, G. M., McLaughlin, C. J., & Millholland, K. (2000). Ten interdisciplinary principles for professional practice in telehealth: Implications for psychology. *Professional Psychology: Research and Practice*, 31(2), 170–178.

Ruskin, P. E., Silver-Aylaian, M., Kling, M. A., Reed, S. A., Bradham, D. D., Hebel, J. R., Barrett, D., Knowles, F., & Hauser, P. (2004). Treatment outcomes in depression: Comparison of remote treatment through telepsychiatry to in-person treatment. *American Journal of Psychiatry*, 161, 1471–1476.

Sabesan, S. et al. (2013). Practical aspects of telehealth: Are my patients suited to telehealth? *Internal Medicine Journal*, 43, 581–584.

Stetz, M. C., Folen, R. A., Van Horn, S., Ruseborn, D., & Samuel, K. M. (2013). Technology complementing military psychology programs and services in the Pacific Regional Medical Command. *Psychological Services*, 10, 283–288.

Tuerk, P. W., Yoder, M., Ruggiero, K. J., Gros, D. F., & Acierno, R. (2010). A pilot study for prolonged exposure therapy for posttraumatic stress disorder delivered via telehealth technology. *Journal of Traumatic Stress*, 23, 116–123.

Wells, M., Mitchell, K., Finkelhor, D., & Becker-Blease, K. (2007). Online mental health treatment: Concerns and considerations. *Cyber Psychology & Behavior*, 10(3), 453–459.

Yellowlees, P., Shore, J., & Roberts, L. (2010). Practice guidelines for videoconferencing-based telemental health. *Telemedicine Journal and e-Health*, 10, 1074–1089.

Zarate, C. A., Weinstock, L., Cukor, P., & Morabito, C. (1997). Applicability of telemedicine for assessing patients with schizophrenia: Reliability and acceptance. *Journal of Clinical Psychiatry*, 58, 22–25.

18

TRADITIONAL AND WHOLE HEALTH AND PATIENT-CENTERED CARE AT THE VETERANS HEALTH ADMINISTRATION

An Overview

Grace W. Yan

Introduction

Veterans Health Administration Overview

The Veterans Health Administration (VHA) is one of the largest healthcare organizations in the US, with over 100 major hospitals, 800 community-based outpatient clinics, 300 Vet Centers, as well as a number of community living centers, to over 1,700 sites of care (National Center for Veterans Analysis and Statistics, 2012). In 2013, the VHA had 8.9 million Veterans enrolled in its health care system, and saw 86.4 million outpatient visits and 694.7 million inpatient admissions (National Center for Veterans Analysis and Statistics, 2014). In most major VHA hospitals, specialty and emergency care are available in addition to primary care services. Some major hospitals also provide surgical care to Veterans in their home states but also in surrounding geographical locations.

As the largest health system in the US, the VHA historically performs better than private sector and Medicaid programs in terms of patient satisfaction and some measures of quality care (Bloomberg News, 2009; Keating et al., 2011; Ryoo & Malin, 2011). Recent media scrutiny on the VHA's budget woes and reports of corruption, however, have significantly affected public perception, leading to distrust of the "VA system" by Veterans and the general public alike. Despite the current challenges, the VHA remains one of the most accessible venues of care for Veterans. This is especially noted in specialty areas such as mental health, where, despite the Affordable Care Act, access in the private sector is still fraught with challenges (Barry & Huskamp, 2011). Veterans separated from the military under any condition other than dishonorable discharge qualify for enrollment for VHA healthcare services. Eligible Veterans can initiate their VHA care by completing the VA Form 10–10EZ, after which they will obtain a VA Veterans Health Identification Card (VHIC; US Department of Veterans Affairs, 2015a). The VHA employs "eligibility priority groups" to categorize Veterans for priority enrollment, as a response to limited yearly budgets. Priority group criteria include service-connected disabilities, POWs, award recipients, period of service, income level, among others.

Once enrolled into the VHA, Veterans may access a variety of benefits. Some benefits are considered "standard" benefits available to the majority of Veterans. These benefits include access to primary care, preventative care services, mental health (including substance abuse), prescription drugs, and respite care. Other benefits are of limited availability and may only be accessed by Veterans meeting specific criteria. These services include hearing aids, home health aide, caregiver support, dental care, and nursing home care.

Patient-aligned Care Teams

The Patient Aligned Care Teams (PACT) is the VHA's primary care service. Using a patient-centered medical home model, the VHA structures its primary care clinics into teams that ideally include a primary care provider (physician or nurse practitioner), RN care manager, LPN/health tech, and a medical support assistant. These individuals work as one PACT team around the needs of patients assigned to the team's panel. Their work is further supported by social workers, primary care mental health, and clinical pharmacists.

VA Transition and Care Case Management Team

In response to the health needs of the newest cohorts of post-9/11 Veterans, the VHA instituted the VA Transition and Care Case Management Team at its major facilities. This team provides care coordination for Veterans who served in the Operation Enduring Freedom/Operation Iraqi Freedom/Operation New Dawn (OEF/OIF/OND) conflicts, and assists Veterans with navigating the VA's benefits system. Of note, OEF/OIF/OND combat Veterans are eligible for five years of free medical care (no co-pay) at the VA. Therefore, to optimize the length of coverage, eligible Veterans are advised to enroll in the VHA as soon as possible (US Department of Veterans Affairs, 2015d).

Current Challenges

The VHA has recently received public attention for, most notably, problems in access to care. Partly in response to the scandal at the Phoenix, AZ facility in 2014, the Veterans Choice Program was created to assist Veterans in obtaining more timely care (NBC News, 2015; US Department of Veterans Affairs, 2015e). Veterans are eligible for the program if they face a wait time of more than 30 days for VA medical care, or if they live more than 40 miles away from a medical care facility or encounter "excessive travel burden." Veterans can find out if they are eligible by calling the VA Choice Program hotline (1-866-606-8198). The program allows eligible Veterans to use a "Choice Card" to access community (non-VA) healthcare providers who are enrolled in the Choice Program. The use of this program is optional and eligible Veterans can opt to use VA Choice for some services and continue to access other healthcare services at VA facilities. Community providers in the VA Choice Program are clinicians who must undergo the same credentialing process as VHA providers, and they are compensated through the Choice Program.

In addition to concerns over access to care, anecdotal statements from Veterans also illustrate concerns over their experience once they are *within* a VA facility. As with many hospitals in the US, care is often geographically and administratively divided into different categories, creating a "silo" effect in which interdisciplinary collaboration and proactive communication between clinicians become difficult. Indeed, this effect is not unique to the VHA and has been a problem for Western healthcare models for some time. As a result, patients' experiences at a hospital can often feel confusing, frustrating, and overwhelming, rather than straightforward, safe, and health-promoting.

VA Office of Patient-centered Care and Cultural Transformation

In 2011, the VA Office of Patient-Centered Care and Cultural Transformation (OPCC&CT) was established with the mission to "work with VA leadership and healthcare providers to transform VA's health system from the traditional medical model, which focuses on treating specific issues, to a personalized, proactive, patient-driven model that promotes whole health for Veterans and their families" (VA Patient Centered Care, 2015).

Patient-centered care encompasses "providing care that is respectful of and responsive to individual patient preferences, needs, and values, and ensuring that patient values guide all clinical decisions" (Institute of Medicine, 2011). Up until today, however, it is still a matter of debate whether this country's healthcare system has fully embraced patient-centered care.

The VA is making a concerted effort to educate and train its healthcare providers in patient-centered care, and specifically, a "Whole Health" approach to Veterans' health. The primary foundation of "Whole Health" is the use of a goal-oriented rather than a disease-oriented approach to providing healthcare. In addition to emphasizing patient-centered care as "personalized, proactive and patient-driven," the Whole Health approach also focuses on healing environments, healing relationships, use of personalized health approaches, and incorporation of components of proactive health and well-being. Proponents of whole health approach point to evidence in the last decade showing that despite the US's high rate of healthcare utilization and healthcare costs, the US ranks as one of the lowest in the developed world in terms of overall health and mortality, a consistent finding since 2004 (Davis, Stremikis, Schoen, & Squires, 2014). It is apparent that the current healthcare approach in the US is in desperate need of new innovations that will change the current traditional approach to healthcare.

This chapter will provide an overview of some of the VA projects currently underway that exemplifies the Whole Health approach, including resources available to non-VA clinicians and social workers and other behavioral health providers. Examples of how patient-centered care and Whole Health is being implemented in the VA will use the Center for Health and Wellness, a "living laboratory" at the New Jersey VA Health Care System, as an example of an integrated patient-centered care approach at a primary clinic at the East Orange, NJ campus.

VA Whole Health Programs and Resources

Components of Proactive Health and Well-Being

To introduce the concept of Whole Health and providers and patients, the OPCC&CT published the "Components of Proactive Health & Well-Being" (VA Patient Centered Care, 2013), a circular graphic that clinicians can use to introduce Whole Health to patients and engage them in conversations about all components of well-being. This "wheel of health" encompasses the following eight areas of health.

Working the Body

This component emphasizes movement and exercise as part of an overall wellness plan for individuals. In addition to exercise, recreational therapy and games are also included as part of this component.

Surroundings

This component addresses the physical and emotional environment of each person, focusing on topics such as safety, noise, and living quality. The Housing and Urban Development Veterans Affairs Supportive Housing (HUD/VASH) department is a valuable resource for working with Veterans who are homeless or do not have a permanent and safe residence (US Department of Veterans Affairs, 2015b).

Personal Development

This portion of the wheel emphasizes the need for personal enrichment and professional growth that exists in every individual. This includes career counseling, education and training, as well as engagement in the arts (music and art therapy).

Food and Drink

Maintaining a healthy diet is an important component of the wheel of health. This pertains not only to eating healthily, but to also abstain from harmful substances, such as sugar and tobacco. Within the VHA, nutritionists are on hand to provide one-on-one consultation and cooking classes in demonstration kitchens. The VA MOVE! Weight Management Program and Tobacco Cessation Program also support Veterans in their pursuit of food and drink goals.

Recharge

Sleep and relaxation has its own component within this wheel. Clinicians are encouraged to discuss with patients their sleeping habits, and to teach and to encourage patients to use relaxation techniques, such as mindfulness meditation, progressive muscle relaxation, and guided imagery.

Family, Friends, and Co-workers

This component addresses the interpersonal aspect of health, recognizing that one's relationship to others significantly affects overall physical and mental well-being. The VHA, in addition to offering marriage and family therapy, also has a Caregiver Support Program with at least one caregiver support coordinator located at each VHA main facility. In some specialties, such as mental health, peer counselors are available to provide support to Veterans recovering from stressful life events, mental health issues, and addictions.

Spirit and Soul

This area focuses on individuals' search for personal identity and meaning. Coping, resilience, and spiritual guidance are also topics of interest under this spoke of the wheel. The VA Chaplain Center offers a useful online search engine where individuals can search for a chaplain by last name or by geographical location (National Chaplain Center, 2015). Services for major religious holidays are also held at VA facilities. Of note, VHA offers the Mental Health Integration for Chaplain Services (MHICS) Certification (one-year training) for VHA chaplains to better equip them to provide care to Veterans with mental health diagnoses. Mental health practitioners working with Veterans with strong religious convictions may choose to contact chaplains in there geographic area who are certified through this course. In addition to chaplains, Veterans are also encouraged to participate in activities that provide their lives with joy and meaning, including the Living History Project, VA greenhouses/gardening programs, drum circles (art and music therapy), and labyrinths.

Power of the Mind

Techniques such as mindfulness-based stress reduction, biofeedback, guided imagery, and tai chi are emphasized in this module. Caring for one's mental health by decreasing detrimental effects of stress is a priority. The National Center For Telehealth & Technology has developed a number of free mobile applications that help Veterans manage stress effectively, such as Breathe2relax and the Virtual Hope Box, both accessible on iPhone and Android platforms to the public (National Center for Telehealth & Technology, 2015).

Other Factors Associated with Personal Well-Being

Professional care refers to the need to seek treatment for illness and the need to focus on preventative efforts. Screenings, routine check-ups, and proper use of specialty care are just parts of this component. Engagement in complementary medicine (or integrative medicine (IM)) is also encouraged at the VA, and some VA facilities offer yoga or tai chi lessons, meditation classes, and acupuncture for patients with a variety of physical and mental health issues. The Star Well Kit is a free resource produced by OPCC&CT that introduces Veterans and their providers to Integrative Medicine (War-Related Illness and Injury Study Center, 2014). Users can stream videos that provide an overview of IM, testimonials from Veterans who have used IM techniques, and demonstrations of some of these techniques.

Lastly, the wheel of health stresses the importance of community – the interconnection between individuals and where he/she "live, work, and worship." This includes relationships with children, spouses/partners, family members, friends, and co-workers.

Linking Values to Health Goals: Personalized Health Inventory

MyStory: Personal Health Inventory (PHI) is a free product created by OPCC&CT for healthcare providers to use in assessing a patient's needs in a Whole Health manner (Health For Life, 2013a). The PHI is a self-report assessment that poses questions about a person's physical, emotional, and global well-being, using open-ended inquiries and Likert scales. The first three questions invite patients to answer the following:

1. What *really* matters to you in your life?
2. What brings you a sense of joy or happiness?
3. On the following scales from 1–5, with 1 being miserable and 5 being great, circle where you feel you are on the scale. (Three scales on physical well-being, emotional well-being, and daily functioning then follow.)

These questions may allow healthcare providers to gain a better understanding on the context surrounding patients' medical problems, as well as patients' responses to such problems and patterns of adherence to treatment recommendations.

The second half of the PHI includes questions on eight areas of proactive health and well-being, colloquially referred to as the "wheel of health." Areas of health include sleep quality, exercise, interpersonal relationships, spirituality, nutrition, and others. The PHI provides opportunities for patients to reflect on how they currently fare in each area, followed by their preferred level of wellness in that area. Using a Likert scale of 1–5 in both questions, the PHI mirrors a motivational interviewing format in which Veterans are encouraged to consider committing to positive health behaviors.

The PHI is an open resource available on VA OPCC&CT's public website and is available for public use.

Whole Health Coaching

A new program now being piloted at some VHA facilities, whole health coaching is a new initiative developed to provide Veterans with clinicians who can set health goals with Veterans and assist them in the execution of these goals. Health coaches are "facilitators of mindset and behavior change that generates sustainable healthy lifestyles, which prevent or treat disease, and foster well-being and thriving" (Wellcoaches, 2015). These clinicians have been trained in specific communication and coaching skills through a six-day intensive course at VAs throughout the country. So far, over 556 VHA employees have completed this training (Health For Life, 2013b). At some facilities, such as the New Jersey VA Health Care System, health coaches are available to meet with Veterans for one-on-one appointments to help them reach their health goals. These goals are developed collaboratively with the Veterans using the PHI and the wheel of health. Veterans in health coaching programs identify an area of their life they may want to improve, then work with health coaches to develop SMART goals (*s*pecific, *m*easurable, *a*chievable, *r*ealistic, and *t*imely). The health coaches, using motivational language and problem-solving approaches, work with Veterans to proactively address obstacles, to implement goal-focused plans, and to provide account-ability so individuals are reinforced when their goals are met. Health coaches at the VHA are supported in their work through collaboration with each Veteran's primary care team of doctors and nurses as well as primary care mental health clinicians.

Currently, health coaching is a pilot program at the VA and only available at two facilities designated as centers of innovation (New Jersey VA Health Care System and VA Greater Los Angeles Healthcare System). Within this new program, efforts are also in place to further enrich the experiences of health coaching patients, which includes the implementation of the Patient Activation Measure (PAM; Hibbard, Stockard, Mahoney, & Tusler, 2004) and the Coaching For Activation resource from Insignia Health (Insignia Health, 2015a). The PAM is a 13-item self-report measure in which patients are provided with a Likert scale to rate how much control and efficacy they feel over their own health and management of health problems. A PAM score (levels 1–4) is then generated to provide clinicians a snapshot of how activated their patients are in managing their health (level 1 can be described as an "unengaged" individual while level 4 is "fully activated"). Patient activation has been shown to significantly correlate with health outcomes, hospital readmission rates, and overall cost of care (Insignia Health, 2015b). The Coaching For Activation (CFA) tool allows health coaches at the VA to provide coaching and education in a format and language that is appropriate for each patient's activation level in order to maximize the benefits of health coaching. Both the PAM and CFA are products which require licenses to use.

Health Promotion and Disease Prevention

In addition to providing medical intervention, the VHA is committed to promoting healthy living through its National Center for Health Promotion and Disease Prevention (NCP).

NCP's mission is to "advocate for health promotion, disease prevention, and health education; advise VHA leadership on evidence-based health promotion and disease prevention policy; and provide programs, education, resources, coordination, guidance, and oversight for the field to enhance health, well-being, and quality of life for Veterans" (US Department of Veterans Affairs, 2015b). As part of its mission, the NCP provides each local VA facility at least one Health Promotion and Disease Prevention coordinator who organizes the local NCP programs of each facility.

NCP's programs are varied and wide-reaching, ranging from clinical preventative services (e.g. flu shots, immunizations) to weight loss (MOVE! Program). In addition, NCP targets specific key areas of prevention which they have titled as "Healthy Living Messages." The areas covered in these Healthy Living Messages are:

- be physically active;
- eat wisely;
- strive for a healthy weight;
- get recommended screening tests and immunizations;
- be involved in your healthcare;
- be tobacco free;
- limit alcohol;
- manage stress; and
- be safe.

As it is evident in these Healthy Living Messages, NCP's mission supports the patient-centered and Whole Health approach through emphasis on proactive management of preventable health problems. The NCP provides free publications and resources to clinicians and offers many of their programs (such as smoking cessation support groups) free of charge to patients.

The Center for Health and Wellness – VA Innovation in Action

As part of OPCC&CT's initiative to transition traditional medical care to a patient-centered model, the CHW was established at the VANJHCS. The CHW is a living laboratory for healthcare culture transformation, primarily in the area of primary care. As a primary care clinic, the CHW's primary goal is to integrate current VHA programs and initiatives into a patient care setting that shows what patient-centered care might look like within the VHA in the future. Currently, the focus is on the development of best practices for dissemination within the VHA system, and implementation of new innovations outside of the CHW is still in a nascent stage.

In the CHW's developmental stages, the vision for this center focused on improvements to the physical space and structure, and patient care and operations of a primary care clinic.

Physical Space and Structure – The Old Way

In most traditional primary care settings at the VHA, physicians, nurses, and administrative assistants use separate offices for administrative work. Patients who check in for an appointment are directed to a waiting room. The administrative staff calls the primary care team to let clinicians know of a patient's arrival. At times, some patients may be shuffled from one exam room to another as they complete triage with nurses and move toward their full examination with physicians. Aside from the waiting area, no other rooms are provided for patients. The waiting area has minimal stimulation – perhaps a couple of magazines or flyers for patients to peruse.

Physical Space and Structure – CHW

The CHW piloted the use of co-located teaming rooms in VANJHCS. No one on the core primary care team has his/her own office space on clinical days. The lead physician, nurses, and an administrative assistant are all co-located in the same room, leading to increased efficiency in patient care and improved communication between team members in order to take care of Veterans' needs.

At the lobby, administrative assistants are available to check in patients. Check-in kiosks are also offered as an alternative. Providers can be alerted via a website when a patient checks in through the kiosks instead of waiting for a phone call from front desk personnel. Instead of directing patients to a waiting room, patients are escorted by front desk personnel to an exam room immediately upon completion of the check-in process.

During a patient's appointment, all providers come to the room to provide services. At the CHW, patients are never asked to relocate to another room to meet a specialty provider (e.g. primary care mental health, social work). All initial contacts or "warm hand-offs" are completed by providers coming to the location of the patient instead of the patient wandering around the clinic to meet with various clinicians for initial contacts.

The CHW's waiting room was thoughtfully renovated to exemplify a healing environment. Computer terminals are located in the waiting area for Veterans to peruse health resources on the VA's websites or watch an internal TV network that airs health programs. Chess, board games, and reading materials are provided for mental stimulation. The waiting room's layout is more akin to a hotel lounge than a traditional hospital waiting area, as it was designed to be a social space where patients can feel comfortable conversing with other Veterans.

In addition to the lounge, CHW Veterans have access to the yoga room, located within the clinic. A small area in the yoga room is partitioned to provide meditation space. Lastly, the CHW has a central courtyard that is maintained by the VA's greenhouse team, providing a relaxing view and allowing for increased natural light to illuminate the clinic.

Patient Care – The Old Way

The traditional primary care approach does not optimize collaboration with specialty care, such as mental health and IM. Primary Care Mental Health Integration (PCMH-I) was established by the VA to provide a "model for mental health disorders that elevates mental health care to the same level of urgency/intervention as medical health care" (Veterans Health Administration, 2015). Providing mental health within primary care is often complicated by mental health stigma, "siloing" of specialties, and lack of appropriate training for primary care staff on the management of psychiatric disorders other than depression (Unützer, Schoenbaum, Druss, & Katon, 2014). Furthermore, the initial appointment wait time a patient experiences between the initial primary care referral to actual mental health appointment can result in a higher no-show rate for those mental health appointments (Gallucci, Swartz, & Hackerman, 2005).

In addition to the mental health gap, traditional primary care also struggle with meeting the Whole Health needs of their patients. Integrative medicine (formerly called complementary or alternative medicine) includes the use of acupuncture, tai chi, yoga, mindfulness meditation, and herbal supplements, among others. In 2007, at least 40% of all US adults surveyed had tried IM treatments (Barnes, Bloom, & Nahin, 2008). The actual integration of IM with primary care has not matched consumer interest in this collaboration. Many traditional primary care settings continue to follow the notion that the physician, not the patient, is the expert on the patient's health.

Patient Care – CHW

VHA has invested in placing mental health professionals in primary care settings in order to facilitate mental health access and referral to mental health specialty clinics (e.g. PTSD, substance abuse). The PCMH-I team at the CHW are not only co-located and available as mental health specialists within the CHW, but they also proactively provide consultation and training to primary care staff on topics such as motivational interviewing, health coaching, and interpersonal effectiveness with "difficult" patients. As a result, the CHW PCMH-I is able to make contact with 13–15% of all primary care patients seen at the CHW, consistently meeting the national VA benchmark of 6% for PCMH-I penetration. A similar approach is used for integrating Health Promotion and Disease Prevention into CHW primary care. Instead of simply referring patients to HPDP programs, the CHW benefits from the regular presence of HPDP coordinators at their case conferences and staff meetings. This encourages CHW primary care teams to take an increasingly active role in promoting health and prevention strategies with their patients, rather than seeing those programs as solely under the purview of the HPDP team.

In terms of Whole Health, the CHW spearheaded the VANJHCS health coaching program and a health coach champion clinical training for other primary care teams in the state. CHW health coaches use the PHI to complete a thorough assessment of an individual's Whole Health needs, and then work with him/her to achieve goals that will increase the patient's mastery and self-efficacy in health promoting behaviors. The PAM is used both as a baseline and outcome measure to track the anticipated change in activation levels for patients who undergo health coaching.

Meanwhile, the CHW also offers yoga classes within its clinic. Yoga classes are often tailored for a specific condition (e.g. PTSD, chronic pain). Acupuncture is also available to VANJHCS patients at the CHW. CHW psychologists and social workers lead group courses on mindfulness and mindfulness-based relaxation. Twice a year, a ten-session spiritual fitness course is offered for Veterans interested in integrating their spiritual beliefs and practices in service of physical and mental health.

To ensure CHW's services are meeting the needs of its Veterans, the CHW hosts a Veterans Voice Committee meeting on a quarterly basis. These meetings are attended by eight to ten volunteer Veterans who receive their care at the CHW. During the meetings, the committee members are able to provide feedback, suggestions, and constructive criticisms on the programs and operations of the CHW. This honors the clinical philosophy of shared decision-making and emphasizes performance improvement in every aspect of the center's operations. CHW staff members are encouraged to participate in performance improvement projects at the center, using PDSA (plan, do, study, act) cycles and LEAN concepts to better the center's clinical and operational performance. As a result, CHW Veterans endorse a high level of satisfaction with obtaining their care at the center, illustrated by the center's performance on VHA patient satisfaction measures.

Moving Forward

Now in its third year, the CHW's future goals in many ways mirror the direction of patient-centered care at the VHA as a whole. Current focus at the CHW is on sustainability of new programs piloted at the clinic, increasing buy-in and engagement of staff that may be resistant to change by finding common ground, and balancing innovation with resource management. Long-term evaluation efforts include monitoring of both quantitative and qualitative patient outcomes. The CHW is an example of how the VHA strives to incorporate its various patient-centered programs into a primary care setting through continuous innovation and performance improvement.

Implications for Civilian Practitioners

Many resources provided in this chapter are public and freely accessible to non-VA providers and Veterans who are not currently seeking care in the VA system. By being aware of VHA's patient-centered care initiative, non-VA practitioners may be the best champion of VA care for Veterans who may have concerns about engaging in the care at the VA because of previous personal experiences, anecdotal horror stories or the current media scrutiny on the VA's handling of various budget and personnel matters. While some concerns are valid and merit attention, the fact remains that many Veterans – OEF, OIF, and OND Veterans, and women Veterans in particular – underutilize VA services and benefits to which they are entitled (VHA Office of Public Health, 2015; Washington, Bean-Mayberry, Riopelle, & Yano, 2011). Therefore, practitioners outside the VA are in unique positions to introduce VA resources to their Veteran clients.

Summary

The VHA has made significant effort in the implementation of patient-centered care through OPCC&CT. Within this patient-centered care initiative, the concept of Whole Health is of particular interest to both providers and patients. The VHA has a bevy of resources available for Veterans and outside practitioners to use, although they may not be well publicized or well known. Clinicians working with Veterans in the civilian sector can adapt these resources to promote health and well-being among their clients, as well as encourage them to use other VA care and benefits in the pursuit of Whole Health. The CHW is an ongoing example of how the VHA is moving toward a patient-centered practice of whole health through its innovative approaches and dissemination of best practices.

Note

The views expressed in this chapter are those of the author and do not necessarily reflect the position or policy of the Department of Veterans Affairs or the US government.

References

Barnes, P. M., Bloom, B., & Nahin, R. L. (2008). Complementary and alternative medicine use among adults and children: United States, 2007. *Natl Health Stat Report, 12*, 1–23. Retrieved from: www. methodesurrender.org/docs/art_nhsr_2007.pdf

Barry, C. L. & Huskamp, H. A. (2011). Moving beyond parity – mental health and addiction care under the ACA. *New England Journal of Medicine, 365*, 973–975.

Bloomberg News (2009, October 2). Vets loving socialized medicine show government offers savings. Retrieved from: www.bloomberg.com/apps/news?pid=newsarchive&sid=aLIc5ABThjBk

Davis, K., Stremikis, K., Schoen, C., & Squires, D. (2014). Mirror, mirror on the wall, 2014 Update: How the US health care system compares internationally. Commonwealth Fund. Online: www.comm onwealthfund.org/publications/fund-reports/2014/jun/mirror-mirror (date of access: April 2016).

Gallucci, G., Swartz, W., & Hackerman, F. (2005). Brief reports: Impact of the wait for an initial appointment on the rate of kept appointments at a mental health center. *Psychiatric Services*, 56(3), 344–346.

Health For Life (2013a). MyStory: Personal health inventory. Retrieved from: www.va.gov/PATIENTCENTEREDCARE/docs/VA-OPCC-Personal-Health-Inventory-final-508.pdf

Health For Life (2013b). Whole health coaching course. Retrieved from: http://healthforlife.vacloud.us/index.php?option=com_content&view=article&id=90

Hibbard, J. H., Stockard, J., Mahoney, E. R., & Tusler, M. (2004). Development of the Patient Activation Measure (PAM): Conceptualizing and measuring activation in patients and consumers. *Health Services Research*, 39(4p1), 1005–1026.

Insignia Health (2015a). Coaching for activation. Retrieved from: www.insigniahealth.com/products/cfa

Insignia Health (2015b). PAM research archive. Retrieved from: https://insignia-health.herokuapp.com/research/archive

Institute of Medicine (2011). Crossing the quality chasm: A new health system for the 21st century. Retrieved from: http://iom.edu/Reports/2001/Crossing-the-Quality-Chasm-A-New-Health-System-for-the-21st-Century.aspx

Keating, N. L., Landrum, M. B., Lamont, E. B., Bozeman, S. R., Krasnow, S. H., & Shulman, L. N. et al. (2011). Quality of care for older patients with cancer in the Veterans Health Administration versus the private sector: A cohort study. *Annals of Internal Medicine*, 154, 727–736

National Center for Telehealth & Technology (2015). Breathe2relax. Retrieved from: http://t2health.dcoe.mil/apps/breathe2relax

National Center for Veterans Analysis and Statistics (2012). Statistics at a glance. Retrieved from: www.va.gov/vetdata/docs/quickfacts/homepage-slideshow.pdf

National Center for Veterans Analysis and Statistics (2014). Selected Veterans Health Administration characteristics: FY2002 to FY2013. Retrieved from: www.va.gov/vetdata/Utilization.asp

National Chaplain Center (2015). Index of VA Chaplains. Retrieved from: www.va.gov/chaplain

NBC News (2015). VA hospital scandal. Retrieved from: www.nbcnews.com/storyline/va-hospital-scandal

Ryoo, J. J. & Malin, J. L. (2011). Reconsidering the Veterans Health Administration: A model and a moment for publicly funded health care delivery. *Annals of Internal Medicine*, 772–773.

Unützer, J., Schoenbaum, M., Druss, B. G., & Katon, W. J. (2014). Transforming mental health care at the interface with general medicine: Report for the president's commission. *Psychiatric Services*, 57(1), 37–47.

US Department of Veterans Affairs (2015a). Health benefits. Retrieved from: www.va.gov/health benefits

US Department of Veterans Affairs (2015b). Housing and Urban Development Veterans Affairs Supportive Housing (2015). Retrieved from: www.va.gov/homeless/hud-vash.asp

US Department of Veterans Affairs (2015c). National Center for Health Promotion and Disease Prevention. www.prevention.va.gov

US Department of Veterans Affairs (2015d). Returning service members (OEF/OIF/OND). Retrieved from: www.oefoif.va.gov/index.asp

US Department of Veterans Affairs (2015e). Veterans Choice Program. Retrieved from www.va.gov/opa/choiceact

VA Patient Centered Care (2013). Components of proactive health and well-being. Retrieved from: www.va.gov/PATIENTCENTEREDCARE/components-health-well-being.asp

VA Patient Centered Care (2015). Office of Patient Centered Care and Cultural Transformation: Promoting Whole Health. Retrieved from: www.va.gov/PATIENTCENTEREDCARE/about.asp

Veterans Health Administration (2015). Mental health and physical health – A critical connection. Retrieved from: www.va.gov/health/NewsFeatures/20120430a.asp

VHA Office of Public Health (2015). Analysis of VA health care utilization among Operation Enduring Freedom (OEF), Operation Iraqi Freedom (OIF), and Operation New Dawn (OND) Veterans: Cumulative from 1st Qtr FY 2002 through 1st Qtr FY 2015 (October 1, 2001–December 31, 2014). Retrieved from: www.publichealth.va.gov/docs/epidemiology/healthcare-utilization-report-fy2015-qtr1.pdf

War-Related Illness and Injury Study Center (2014). STAR Well-Kit. Retrieved from: www.warrelate dillness.va.gov/education/STAR

Washington, D. L., Bean-Mayberry, B., Riopelle, D., & Yano, E. M. (2011). Access to care for women veterans: Delayed healthcare and unmet need. *Journal of General Internal Medicine*, 26(2), 655–661.

Wellcoaches (2015). Wellcoaches: School of coaching. Retrieved from: http://wellcoachesschool.com

19

THE COST OF CARING

Charles R. Figley and Joan Beder

The Veteran's Health Administration's long-standing motto is quoted from the post-Civil War commitment to its Veterans (as stated by Abraham Lincoln to a grateful nation): "To care for him who shall have borne the battle and for his Widow, and his orphan." It is a sacred covenant to Veterans and has become the mandate for those who serve and care for them.

However, there is a cost to caring, especially when working with our military. In general, professionals who listen to clients' stories of fear, pain, and suffering will often struggle with parallel emotions, leaving them prone to compassion fatigue aka, secondary traumatization. These feelings can extract a high cost to the caring professional.

This chapter is about the costs that result from being part of any caring human service organization; these emotional and sometimes physical costs come with the territory of being a helper in a helping profession. The cost of caring is greater when serving Veterans, because as a group there is a deep sense of patriotism and a unique set of stressors to which the helper is exposed. Waging war can extract a high price for the service member; he/she may have experienced face-to-face combat, seen situations in which they were exposed to death and dying, and may have experienced moral injury (see Chapter 16 in this volume). These are not situations that are easy for the service member/Veteran to readily discuss and may be very difficult for the helper to hear. Our professionalism in managing our reactions can often be put to a test. This internal struggle faced by the helpers is the cost of caring.

In professions like social work, nursing, and psychology, training most often focuses on patient/client care and not care of the provider. Those of us who are in the helping professions struggle, at times, with the high price it extracts from us, as we bear witness to and are introduced to the many dire and dreadful acts that impact lives, especially in the articulation of engaging in war. As we listen to our clients who have experienced trauma, pain and anguish, we often begin to feel anguished as we empathize with and embrace their pain in the process of helping.

This chapter was placed last in this book for a purpose. Primed by the stressful stories and problems throughout the book, this chapter is a reminder to the reader that delivering critical services requires healthy and rested professionals who take care of those who have served in the military and their families.

In this chapter we will review numerous studies that document the positive and negative impact of working with the traumatized. It will be noted that there are certain capabilities needed for professionals to maintain their resilience in working with the traumatized, especially those working with traumatized service members/Veterans and their families. If providers are impaired or unable to manage their emotions to the extent that it affects their capabilities as a professional, they must be excused from duty and/or serving the service member/Veteran population. This chapter provides a strategy for addressing compassion fatigue – the fatigue that comes from helping others – and encourages resilience in providers to assure the highest standard of care for the traumatized and also enabling the professionals to live and thrive as human beings in their personal as well as work life.

Helping Professionals Who Care for Returning Service Members

Behavioral health workers within a large agency and system are expected to work with the civilian sector, often charged with caring for the military. The US is now gradually emerging from an extended set of engagements in Iraq and Afghanistan. The costs to the US in lost lives are immeasurable. These sacrifices are demonstrated daily for those professionals responsible for the behavioral health of our Veterans.

At present we are engaged in Operation Enduring Freedom (Afghanistan), Operation Iraqi Freedom, and Operation New Dawn (Modified Iraq force as of 9/2010). Since October 2001 approximately 2.5 million US troops have been deployed to Operation Enduring Freedom and Operation Iraqi Freedom. As of September 2015, the total number of troops who have returned to the US for medical care exceeds 250,000. This includes those who have post-traumatic stress disorder (PTSD), traumatic brain injury (TBI), serious wounding and amputations (Fischer, 2015). Each of these service members is being treated in the Department of Defense and/or the VA medical system and by civilian behavioral health and mental health providers across the US.

Rehabilitation of the injured service members is geared to restoring those who have served to their highest level of functionality. Behavioral health workers as part of the multi-disciplinary medical teams in the VA/DoD system and civilian providers as well, are involved in managing caseloads of patients with complex psychosocial, mental, and physical needs. In the course of their work, behavioral health workers are encountering war casualties on a daily basis in most inpatient and outpatient units.

Contact with the service member is frequently focused on case management and counseling, with involvement of both the patient and his/her family. However, most behavioral health workers bear witness to the lives of their clients, their struggles, and their anguish; they are involved in their progress and setbacks; they hear their pain and accomplishments; they see the tears and frustrations; they applaud the accomplishments and bemoan the setbacks. As we do our work, as we invest in our clients, as we devote ourselves to their care, it takes a toll on us … This is the cost of caring!

How Do We Understand What Happens to Helpers?

Three major constructs explain the potential for the high cost of caring: compassion fatigue (secondary traumatic stress), compassion satisfaction, and burnout.

Those professionals who work with the traumatized – those who may have been the victim of rape, domestic violence, disaster, or war – are most prone to developing secondary traumatic stress (STS). STS occurs when one is exposed to traumatic and extreme events by another; in the act of listening to the content of the traumatic event(s), and wanting to help or ease the suffering of the traumatized individual, stress is created for the helper (Figley,

1995; Figley & Ludick, in press; Kintzle, Yarvis, & Bride, 2013). The helper may develop a range of responses, similar to those of PTSD that include numbing, startle response, intrusive thoughts, nightmares, insomnia and anxiety, and avoidance of situations. STS is manifested as compassion fatigue (CF). CF refers to how and why we as helpers, even though we are not directly traumatized, can become traumatized ourselves and possibly become secondary victims of the trauma we are listening to and absorbing (Figley, 1995). CF is a direct result of exposure to client suffering. Rather than a pathological condition for the caring professional, it is a natural consequence of working with and listening to people who have related their experiences of extremely stressful events. Professionals who listen to those who have been traumatized may themselves come to need assistance to cope with the effects of listening to others' traumatic experiences (Figley, 1995, 2002; Figley & Ludick, in press).

The double bind for the empathic professional is the higher tendency to develop CF as the professional immerses him/herself in the life and drama of the traumatized. In contrast, compassion satisfaction is experienced as the pleasure derived from being a helper, from being able to do their work well. Those who experience compassion satisfaction feel positively about their colleagues and feel secure in their ability to contribute to the work and the work setting (Stamm, 2010). Compassion satisfaction is an antidote to CF.

Effective work with those who have experienced trauma often involves assisting the client in working through their traumatic event(s) through discussion and description, often in graphic detail. The process of recall and description helps to bring closure to the event for the client; in the process, however, the clinician is exposed to the traumatic event through vivid imagery and the act of listening (Bride, Radey, & Figley, 2007).

An additional factor in the development of CF may be the day-to-day bureaucratic struggles inherent in working in settings (agencies, hospitals, etc.) where counseling takes place. A combination of forces – content, empathic engagement, setting – creates the potential for the clinician to experience secondary trauma and the development of CF. The experience of CF tends to develop cumulatively over time (Newell & MacNeil, 2010). Some helpers are at greater risk of CF; it is more common in those workers with a personal history of trauma or negative life events, and in those who have limited social supports (Adams, Boscarino, & Figley, 2006).

Burnout and CF

Burnout is a set of symptoms associated with feelings of hopelessness and difficulties in dealing with work or doing one's job effectively (Phelps, Lloyd, Creamer, & Forbes, 2009; Stamm, 2010). Often, burnout reflects bureaucratic and environmental difficulties that might include too much paperwork, office space, long hours, low pay, and limited opportunities for advancement. The relationship between burnout and CF has been documented (Adams et al., 2006; Figley, 1995; Shoji, Lesnierowska, Smoktunowicz, et al., 2015) with burnout noted as a contributing factor to CF.

CF is defined as a syndrome consisting of symptoms of secondary traumatic stress and burnout (Adams et al., 2006; Bride et al., 2007). Burnout tends to develop over time and is cumulative. It is realistic to expect that most helping professionals will at some point in their work life experience secondary traumatic stress and feelings of burnout leading to CF. However, the likelihood of developing CF is significantly heightened for those who bear witness to the traumatized (i.e. those who work with the military population).

Figley (1995) sees the development of CF as normative rather than pathological and as an occupational hazard for those working with trauma survivors. "The professional work centered on the relief of the emotional suffering of clients automatically includes absorbing information that is about suffering. Often it includes absorbing that suffering as well" (Figley, 1995, p. 2). As with any condition, the degree and intensity of the CF may be borne and easily relieved or may become chronic and debilitating to the helper and have an impact on the clinician's work.

Helpers experiencing CF may be at higher risk of making poor professional judgments, creating poor treatment plans, and taking out some of their anguish on clients who are not experiencing trauma (Stamm, 2010). In addition, these helpers may start missing work, may decide that they cannot accept any more clients, may become "unreliable" in the work environment. Some who struggle with CF report feeling numb, cut-off; they question their effectiveness as helpers and their ability to make decisions that are in the best interests of the client. They may lose their sense of hopefulness and optimism (Hesse, 2002). Among nurses, a study (Yoder, 2010) of 106 nurses found that as high as 15% were at risk of CF. The participants were asked to describe a situation during which they experienced either CF or burnout and what strategies they used to deal with the situation, or how they got through the experience. The burnout and CF/secondary trauma scales correlated, suggesting that they are overlapping phenomena. CF/secondary trauma was significantly higher in nurses who worked eight-hour shifts compared with nurses who worked 12-hour shifts. Yoder (2014) found that nurses with the least experience reported significantly higher rates of compassion satisfaction than the more experienced nurses. Compassion satisfaction was strongly negatively correlated with numerous items on the CF/secondary trauma and burnout subscales. Thus, like other human service providers caring for Veterans, nurses who had higher compassion satisfaction scores were more interpersonally "fulfilled," as defined by scores on "being happy," "being me," and "being connected to others." These nurses did not feel as trapped and did not experience difficulty separating personal life and work. They were less likely to feel exhausted, bogged down, or "on the edge." Beder (2009) surveyed 161 social workers who worked in the Department of Defense hospitals using the Professional Quality of Life Scale. Fifty-nine percent of the subjects scored above the threshold (were prone toward) for CF; those workers who worked in outpatient clinic settings, not hospital based, had higher levels of CF than those who were hospital based. Interestingly, those workers who were in the system longer than five years had lower levels of CF than the newer workers. Both studies – Beder and Yoder – highlight the propensity for helpers to develop CF in the process of doing the work.

CF Resilience – Prevention of CF

Preventing the unwanted signs of CF requires efforts by both the employer organization and the behavioral healthcare providers. The provider should be reassured that their symptoms are not an indication of some pathological weakness or disease or personal failing. Rather, the symptoms are a natural consequence of providing care for traumatized individuals.

Recently, Figley (2014) noted that CF resilience is the current estimate of one's ability to spring back in five capability domains:

1. Physically capable, meaning that the provider is in good physical and medical conditional.
2. Psychologically capable, meaning the worker has a clear sense of presence, mindful of responsibilities at work and at home, able to make good decisions, can connect with others and apply effective empathic response to clients.

3.   Interpersonally capable, meaning that the worker has good social support and is able to connect with others at a personal and human level at work and at home.
4.   Technically capable, meaning that the worker is an effective employee, knowledgeable of her or his scope of work, including meeting all work expectations represented by client and supervisor feedback.
5.   Self-(care) regulation capable, meaning that the worker is mindful of her or his own markers of health and human development and knows both their limitations and is capable of devising their own self-care plan accordingly.

Using this framework enables caregivers, caregiver colleagues, and employers to be more proactive in preventing burnout and CF.

The first step in preventing and treating secondary traumatic stress/CF is to recognize the signs and symptoms of CF in the context of the worker's capabilities toward building resilience. As CF manifests at a symptoms level, workers need to be continually self-monitoring for the presence of numbing, startle response, intrusive thoughts, nightmares, insomnia and anxiety, and avoidance of situations. Conscientious monitoring of both the worker's work environment and personal life needs to be implemented to address the build-up and continuation of CF (Bride & Figley, 2009).

Work Stress and Colleagues

Another factor that addresses burnout and accompanying CF is interactions with colleagues, clients, and personal supporters and the general workplace environment. Each of these groups of people can affect the overall emotional climate of the behavioral health professional. In the context of work, factors that enable compassion are functions of the general morale and supportiveness of fellow workers, especially one's supervisor and the administration. Feeling valued goes a long way to addressing the feelings and symptoms of CF.

A positive work environment includes workers who care about each other and show it. They genuinely like one another, and they may joke around and/or pitch in when needed and often without being asked to do so. They pick up on even the most subtle mood changes of fellow workers and ask about them in a caring and supportive manner. A negative work environment, on the other hand, can be emotionally toxic. In a supportive organizational culture, caregivers are able to validate their feelings through ongoing supervision in a safe and supportive environment (Bride & Figley, 2009). This allows for ventilation and needed affirmation.

When relationships among workers, and especially with supervisory staff, are strained, staff morale tends to be negative. What is lacking in a toxic work environment is a sense of trust, optimism, and mutual support among and between staff members. As with other social psychological components, the vital resources of supportive colleagues, friends, and family enable the behavioral health provider to rebound from emotionally upsetting events, a key factor in the avoidance and minimization of CF.

The general workplace environment – with expectations for productivity, paperwork requirements, physical space, and creature comforts – can contribute to burnout, a factor in CF. This is another area to be mindful of when making efforts to address CF. Caseload/workload management strategies to help avoid CF include balancing a clinical caseload with other professional activities, having traumatized clients as well as non-traumatized, engaging in advocacy activities on behalf of clients and taking time off for respite. CF can be addressed by helping the worker build their resilience through increased self-support, self-care, better management of work stress, addressing past trauma, and increasing compassion satisfaction.

The final factor that contributes to CF is the "other" category: other life demands. Often these demands have little to do with the job and everything to do with being stressful. Even positive activities such as getting a new car or falling in love demand time and attention and therefore restrict the resources needed to cope with work. More often, however, other life demands are negative, caused by personal issues, such as family obligations, which can distract and deplete the worker.

Collectively these factors serve as either protective factors that increase CF resilience or risk factors that diminish it. There are alternative roads leading to alternative destinations, however. They address ways of transforming CF into opportunities for change that enable workers to be far more productive, useful, and happy at work and at home.

On a Personal Level

In their personal lives, providers should strive to maintain a balance between their professional and personal lives. This balance includes stress management, meditation, and exercise, spending time with loved ones and engaging in personal psychotherapy if needed.

Self-care is the ability to refill and refuel oneself in healthy ways. Healthy practices would include sharing with colleagues, exercise, meditation, nutrition, and spirituality. Conversely, many caregivers redouble their efforts, feeling that if they did more, they would reap more benefits from the work (i.e. they work harder to feel better). This is an unfortunate adaptation to the symptoms and feeling associated with CF and potentially can worsen the condition rather than helping.

Another facet of self-care is that caregivers "need to soften their critical and coercive self-talk and shift their motivational styles toward more self-accepting and affirming language and tone if they wish to resolve their compassion fatigue symptoms" (Gentry, 2002, p. 52).

A major factor that reduces CF is compassion satisfaction, a sense of fulfillment or gratification from the work. Sodeke-Gregson, Holttum, and Billings (2013) found that compassion satisfaction among psychotherapists was associated with age, time spent engaging in research and development activities, a higher perceived supportiveness of management, and supervision. The opposite was found for burnout and low compassion satisfaction.

For many helpers it is the joy of easing the burden of clients who are suffering and need support and care. It is inspiring to witness the resilience and strength of many. Sometimes counselors need to remember these very real satisfactions when feeling the weight of compassion stress and CF from the work. Caregivers must remember that they cannot fix everything and everyone, that there are situations that go beyond immediate repair, and that the best we can do for a traumatized client is listen to them and acknowledge their pain and anguish. We must be content that allowing the verbalization of trauma gives the traumatized person a venue and permission to speak of their worst fears and stories. We must be satisfied that this makes a significant contribution to the healing of the client. This acknowledgement contributes to compassion satisfaction.

Final Thoughts

Trauma work can be extremely stressful and draining. Working with war Veterans is especially challenging because war often provokes behaviors that are extremely difficult to retell and repeat and to hear. This is counterbalanced by the rewards of being trusted enough to witness the struggles of our service members to overcome war-related distress and its consequences. Feeling good about facilitating the traumatized to regain their strength and reintegrate into their lives having been helped through our efforts is energizing. The connections we make with those who have experienced trauma are often the strongest that people make, involving an intimacy and a trust that our service member clients may have lost as a result of their trauma (Hesse, 2002). We become the agents who help those traumatized in war to be able to regain trust in others and themselves. Because of our work, we risk CF. If we are vigilant about our self-care and can monitor our reactions, we will be able to continue to touch our clients and gain needed compassion satisfaction in the process and "soldier on."

This book and this chapter are about helping our military members. For us to do the best work possible for this cohort, we have to take care of ourselves. We, and those we serve, have earned the care!

References

Adams, R. E., Boscarino, J., & Figley, C. (2006). Compassion fatigue and psychological distress among social workers. *American Journal of Orthopsychiatry*, 76, 103–118.

Beder, J. (2009). Social work in the Department of Defense hospital. *Military Medicine*, 174(5), 486–490.

Bride, B. & Figley, C. (2009). Secondary trauma and military veteran caregivers. *Smith College Studies in Social Work*, 79(3–4), 4314–4329.

Bride, B. E., Radey, M., & Figley, C. (2007). Measuring compassion fatigue. *Clinical Social Work Journal*, 35, 155–163.

Figley, C. (Ed.) (1995). *Compassion fatigue: Coping with secondary traumatic stress disorder in those who treat the traumatized*. New York: Bruner/Mazel.

Figley, C. (2002). Compassion fatigue: Psychotherapists' chronic lack of self-care. *Journal of Clinical Psychology*, 58(11), 1433–1441.

Figley, C. R. (2014). *Stress Disorders Among Vietnam Veterans: Theory, Research* (No. 1). Routledge.

Fischer, H. (2015). A guide to US Military casualty statistics: Operation Freedom's Sentinel, Operation Inherent Resolve, Operation New Dawn, Operation Iraqi Freedom and Operation Enduring Freedom. *Congressional Research Service*, 7-5700.

Gentry, J. (2002). Compassion fatigue: A crucible of transformation. *Journal of Trauma Practice*, 1(3–4), 37–61.

Hesse, A. (2002). Secondary trauma: How working with trauma survivors affects therapists. *Clinical Social Work Journal*, 30(3), 293–309.

Kintzle, S., Yarvis, J., & Bride, B. (2013). Secondary traumatic stress in military primary and mental health care providers. *Military Medicine*, 178(12), 1310–1315.

Newell, J. & MacNeil, G. (2010). Professional burnout, vicarious trauma, secondary traumatic stress, and compassion fatigue: A review of theoretical terms, risk factors, and preventive methods for clinicians and researchers. *Best Practices in Mental Health*, 6(2), 57–68.

Phelps, A., Lloyd, D., Creamer, M., & Forbes, D. (2009). Caring for carers in the aftermath of trauma. *Journal of Aggression, Maltreatment & Trauma*, 18(3), 313–330.

Shoji, K., Lesnierowska, M., Smoktunowicz, E., Bock, J., & Luszczynska, A., et al. (2015) What comes first, job burnout or secondary traumatic stress? *PLoS ONE*, 10(8), e0136730. doi: 10.1371/journal.pone.0136730

Sodeke-Gregson, E., Holttum, S., & Billings, J. (2013). Compassion satisfaction, burnout, and secondary traumatic stress in UK therapists who work with adult trauma clients. *European Journal of Psychotraumatology*, 4. doi: 10.3402/ejpt.v4i0.21869

Stamm, B. (2010). *The concise ProQoL Manual*. Pocatello, ID.

Yoder, E. A. (2010). Compassion fatigue in nurses. *Appl. Nurs. Res.*, 23, 191–197.

Yoder, E. A. (2014). *Leading and managing in nursing*. Missouri: Elsevier.

INDEX

References to figures are shown in *italics*. References to tables are shown in **bold**.